A DYNAMIC READING OF
THE HOLY SPIRIT IN LUKE–ACTS

A DYNAMIC READING OF THE HOLY SPIRIT IN LUKE–ACTS

JU HUR

T & T CLARK INTERNATIONAL
A Continuum imprint
LONDON • NEW YORK

To In-Hyang and Hyuck, with love and gratitude

Published by T&T Clark International
A Continuum imprint
The Tower Building, 11 York Road, London SE1 7NX
15 East 26th Street, Suite 1703, New York, NY 10010

www.tandtclark.com

Copyright © 2001 Sheffield Academic Press
First published as JSNTS 211 by Sheffield Academic Press
This edition published 2004

British Library Cataloguing-in-Publication Data
A catalogue record for this book is available from the British Library

ISBN 0567041808 (paperback)

Typeset by Sheffield Academic Press
Printed on acid-free paper in Great Britain by The Bath Press, Bath

CONTENTS

PREFACE

Forasmuch as many have undertaken to examine the subject of the Holy Spirit in Luke–Acts, and the Holy Spirit has been interpreted for us by biblical/theological scholars in various ways, it seemed good to me also to set out my reading in order with a new perspective for you, most gentle reader(s), so that you may check the reliability of that of which you have been informed.

This book is a little-revised version of my dissertation submitted for the degree of PhD at the University of Sheffield in 1998. Several changes allowed in this present form, however, are concerned only with its stylistic format, that is, not with its content at all.

Without the support and encouragement of many people, the completion of the doctoral work and this final form as a book would not have been possible. It is thus a pleasant duty and privilege to express my gratitude. First and foremost, I am deeply grateful to Dr Margaret Davies, my supervisor who patiently and thoroughly read every draft of each chapter and gave incisive comments along with great interest and guidance throughout my research from October 1993 to March 1998. She helped me to avoid many errors and inconsistencies that would otherwise have entered the work.

My sincere thanks are also due to: Professor Richard B. Gaffin, Jr who first inspired me to look closely at the Lukan Holy Spirit and encouraged my study in England and Professor Tremper Longman, III by whom I was first exposed to a literary approach to biblical interpretation (both were my mentors when I was engaged in the Master of Divinity [1990–93] at Westminster Theological Seminary, Philadelphia, USA); Dr Mark W.G. Stibbe, the former Honorary Lecturer at Sheffield who was interested in my subject and approach, and gave me some useful academic information in encouragement; Dr Max M.B. Turner of London Bible College who kindly allowed me to have a copy of the entire manuscript of his great work, *Power from on High* before its publication; my two doctoral examiners, Dr Andrew Chester of the University of Cambridge and Dr Loveday Alexander of Sheffield, who offered helpful criticisms and encouragement to seek publication.

I would like to express my special appreciation to three families for their earnest love and prayers for my study and family: Mr and Mrs Jin-Ho and Pat Na; Dr and Mrs John and Gill Taylor; Dr and Mrs David and Pat Brentnall. I have treasured the Sheffield days that I shared not only with them through Bible study, but also with other Korean and English families and friends in the love of Christ.

I have incalculable debts to my parents and parents-in law that I can never pay back: Won Hur and Yi-Don Kwon, and Revd Moo-Young Lee and Myung-Ja Hahn. Without such constant financial and spiritual support along with unfailing love and prayers during my study abroad (1990–98), my present work would never have been imagined, not to mention accomplished. Revd Dr Won-Tae Suk, President of Korea Theological Seminary at Munsan, generously provided me with a scholarship since September 1995 which lightened my family's financial load. Since 1999 back in my home country, my wife, son and I also owe a debt of love not only to my elder brother's and sister's families, but also to all the congregation at Eun-Hae (Grace) Church at Noryangjin, Seoul. Most of all, her spiritual atmosphere has rekindled real *dynamics* of the Spirit in my heart.

I wish to acknowledge my gratitude to both Professor S.E. Porter, Executive Editor and one anonymous examiner, a member of the Editorial Board who accepted this work for publication into the JSNT Supplement Series. My appreciation is also to be extended to the staff of Sheffield Academic Press, especially to Ms Ailsa Parkin, Production Controller and Mr Steve Barganski, Managing Editor, who have sent me not a few e-mails during the process of publication.

Finally, my greatest thanks and love are reserved for my *reliable* wife, In-Hyang (Rachel) and lovely son, Hyuck (Ben), who have shared and suffered good *and* bad times, yet have never stopped trusting me, inspiring me and providing me with countless refreshing diversions from this somewhat stony academic work. They have been the constant source of my happiness and joy, helping me keep my priorities in order throughout the whole period of research. To them I dedicate this book as a small token of my heartfelt gratitude.

Soli Deo Gloria.
Ilsan, Kyonggi-do
South Korea
30 November 2000

ABBREVIATIONS

AB	Anchor Bible
ABD	David Noel Freedman (ed.), *The Anchor Bible Dictionary* (New York: Doubleday, 1992)
AnGreg	Analecta Gregoriana
ANTC	Abingdon New Testament Commentaries
ASTI	*Annual of the Swedish Theological Institute*
BAGD	Walter Bauer, William F. Arndt, F. William Gingrich and Frederick W. Danker, *A Greek–English Lexicon of the New Testament and Other Early Christian Literature* (Chicago: University of Chicago Press, 2nd edn, 1958)
BARev	*Biblical Archaeology Review*
BDB	Francis Brown, S.R. Driver and Charles A. Briggs, *A Hebrew and English Lexicon of the Old Testament* (Oxford: Clarendon Press, 1907)
BECNT	Baker Exegetical Commentary on the New Testament
Bib	*Biblica*
BibInt	*Biblical Interpretation: A Journal of Contemporary Approaches*
BR	*Bible Review*
BTB	*Biblical Theology Bulletin*
CBQ	*Catholic Biblical Quarterly*
CD	Cairo Damascus
CI	*Critical Inquiry*
CIS	Copenhagen International Seminar
CTR	*Criswell Theological Review*
DL	*Doctrine and Life*
EC	Epworth Commentaries
ESEC	Emory Studies in Early Christianity
FCI	Foundations of Contemporary Interpretation
FRLANT	Forschungen zur Religion und Literatur des Alten und Neuen Testaments
HM	Heythrop Monographs
HTKNT	Herders theologischer Kommentar zum Neuen Testament
HTR	*Harvard Theological Review*
IBS	*Irish Biblical Studies*
ICC	International Critical Commentary

Int	*Interpretation*
JBL	*Journal of Biblical Literature*
JLS	*Journal of Literary Semantics*
JPT	*Journal of Pentecostal Theology*
JPTSup	*Journal of Pentecostal Theology*, Supplement Series
JR	*Journal of Religion*
JSNT	*Journal for the Study of the New Testament*
JSNTSup	*Journal for the Study of the New Testament*, Supplement Series
JSOTSup	*Journal for the Study of the Old Testament*, Supplement Series
JSPSup	*Journal for the Study of the Pseudepigrapha*, Supplement Series
JSS	*Journal of Semitic Studies*
KTJ	*Korea Theological Journal*
LCBI	Literary Currents in Biblical Interpretation
LD	Lectio divina
MLT	Mowbrays Library of Theology
NAC	New American Commentary
NCB	New Century Bible
NICNT	New International Commentary on the New Testament
NIGTC	The New International Greek Testament Commentary
NLH	*New Literary History*
NovT	*Novum Testamentum*
NovTSup	*Novum Testamentum*, Supplements
NTC	New Testament Commentary
NTG	New Testament Guides
NTS	*New Testament Studies*
OBT	Overtures to Biblical Theology
OBS	The Oxford Bible Series
ÖTKNT	Ökumenischer Taschenbuchkommentar zum Neuen Testament
OTL	Old Testament Library
PT	*Poetics Today*
PTMS	Pittsburgh Theological Monograph Series
RevExp	*Review and Expositor*
RevQ	*Revue de Qumran*
RevRel	*Review for Religions*
SBLDS	Society of Biblical Literature Dissertation Series
SBLMS	Society of Biblical Monograph Series
SBLSP	Society of Biblical Seminar Papers
SBT	Studies in Biblical Theology
SJT	*Scottish Journal of Theology*
SNT	Studien zum Neuen Testament
SNTSMS	Society for New Testament Studies Monograph Series
SPS	Sacra Pagina Series

SSEJC	Studies in Scripture in Early Judaism and Christianity
ST	*Studia theologica*
StBt	*Studia Biblica et Theologica*
SWJT	*South Western Journal of Theology*
TBS	The Biblical Seminar
TDNT	Gerhard Kittel and Gerhard Friedrich (eds.), *Theological Dictionary of the New Testament* (trans. Geoffrey W. Bromiley; 10 vols.; Grand Rapids: Eerdmans, 1964–)
TJ	*Trinity Journal*
TNTC	Tyndale New Testament Commentaries
TynBul	*Tyndale Bulletin*
UBS	United Bible Societies
USQR	*Union Seminary Quarterly Review*
VE	*Vox Evangelica*
WBC	Word Biblical Commentary
WTJ	*Westminster Theological Journal*
WUNT	Wissenschaftliche Untersuchungen zum Neuen Testament
YR	*The Yale Review*
ZNW	*Zeitschrift für die neutestamentliche Wissenschaft*

Chapter 1

INTRODUCTION

Lukan writings have received considerable attention in New Testament scholarship since a series of seminal works by Henry J. Cadbury, called the 'doyen of Anglo-Saxon research on Acts' (Haenchen 1971: 43), was published in the 1920s.[1] In the following decades, Luke–Acts has been recognized as a 'storm center in contemporary scholarship' (van Unnik 1966), as 'shifting sands' (Talbert 1981) and as a 'fruitful field' (Gasque 1989a).

Among many issues concerning Luke and/or Acts, the Holy Spirit has been one of the most constantly debated subjects since 1920 (see below). One of the reasons why scholars have often visited this subject is the frequent references to the divine πνεῦμα in Luke–Acts: 74 occurrences in 52 chapters (17 in the Gospel; 57 in Acts).[2] It is thus no wonder that Luke is designated as the 'enthusiast in/for the Spirit' (Dunn 1990: 180-84) or that the Acts of the Apostles is called 'the Acts of the Holy Spirit' (Bruce 1990b: 18-19).[3]

This study will re-visit the topic of the Holy Spirit in Luke–Acts through a new perspective. In what follows, I shall first briefly review

---

1. There are 32 articles and 3 books published or presented in the 1920s. Cadbury's first article, 'A Possible Case of Lukan Authorship (John 7.53–8.11)', appeared in 1917. For his writings (1917–72) on biblical studies, see Gaventa (1992: 45-51); for his contributions to Lukan studies, see Parsons and Tyson (1992: 7-44). It has been held that Cadbury's most pioneering contribution is the elucidation of Luke's literary qualities along with designating the two Lukan writings Luke–Acts. For my view on the unity of Luke and Acts, see p. 87 n. 2.

2. Cf. 6 in Mark; 12 in Matthew; 15 in John. For the expressions that refer to the divine Spirit in Luke–Acts in comparison with the other synoptic Gospels and the Jewish Bible, see p. 131 §5.1.1.1 and Appendices I, II and IV.

3. Ehrhardt (1958: 67) and Hanson (1967: 42) called the book of Acts 'the Gospel of the Holy Spirit'.

three contemporary scholars' understandings of Lukan pneumatology:[4] (1) J.D.G. Dunn, (2) R.P. Menzies and (3) M.M.B. Turner, which are representative of three different positions in regard to this subject, particularly on the meaning of 'receiving the Holy Spirit'. Then, I shall set out my methodology and procedure for 'A Dynamic Reading[5] of the Holy Spirit in Luke–Acts'. In so doing, I hope, not only to provide some new significant issues which have not previously been undertaken or ignored, but also to bring clarity to contentious issues in relation to the Lukan Holy Spirit by using insights from 'dynamic biblical narrative criticism'.

1. Retrospect: Previous Studies of the Holy Spirit in Luke and Acts

1.1. *J.D.G. Dunn*[6]

James Dunn's initial work, *Baptism in the Holy Spirit* (1970), which was accepted as 'classic' along with its sequel *Jesus and the Spirit* (1975), attempts to criticize both Pentecostal and sacramental interpretations of the gift of the Holy Spirit in the New Testament (1970a: 1-7).[7] His main argument here is that for all New Testament writers 'the baptism in or gift of the Spirit was part of the event (or process) of becoming a Christian' (1970a: 4; 1975: 6). More explicitly, he insists, 'The high point in conversion-initiation is the gift of the Spirit, and the beginning of the Christian life is to be reckoned from the experience of Spirit-baptism' (1970a: 4). In other words, baptism in the Spirit or the gift of the Spirit, according to Dunn, is neither a second blessing given to people who are 'already' Christians and distinct from their conversion-initiation, nor is it equated with water-baptism.

In regard to Lukan writings, Dunn focuses on both the events of Jesus' baptism at Jordan and the outpouring of the Spirit at Pentecost in the light of the scheme of salvation-history, that is, the period of Israel

---

4. For comprehensive surveys, see Bovon (1987: 202-238); Turner (1981b: 131-58; 1996b: 20-79); Menzies (1991a: 18-47). In the following section, I am only summarizing their essential arguments; some detailed issues relevant to my study will be offered in Chapter 5.

5. As for my book's title, I prefer the word 'reading' to 'interpretation' in an attempt to 'signal a paradigm-shift' in which the subject matter of the Holy Spirit in Luke–Acts is to be assessed. For this use of 'reading', see Thiselton 1992: 2, 28.

6. See my bibliography.

7. Menzies (1994b: 115) says, 'Dunn quickly became a champion of the non-Pentecostal Evangelical community'.

before Jesus' baptism, the period of Jesus from his Jordan baptism and the period of the Church from Pentecost to Jesus' *parousia* (1970a: 24, 40-43).[8] He argues here that Jesus' experience of the Spirit at Jordan marks his sense of sonship (1970a: 29; 1975: 62-67)[9] and thus signals his initiation into 'the beginning of a new epoch in salvation-history—the beginning...of the End-time, the messianic age, the new covenant' (1970a: 24).[10] Likewise, in Acts, Pentecost is presented as the beginning of the new covenant for the disciples in fulfilling the Abrahamic covenant-promise in Gen. 17.7-10 and fulfilling the promises in Ezek. 36.27 and Jer. 31.33 (1970a: 47-49). In this sense, Jesus' experience of the Spirit at Jordan is construed as archetypal for both his disciples' and every Christian's conversion-initiation (1970a: 32, 37, 40).[11] In the remaining chapters of part two of his work, Dunn continues to demonstrate how receiving the Spirit is inseparable from the genuine faith of the recipient, i.e. Samaritans, Paul, Cornelius and the disciples at Ephesus, in the four incidents of Acts 8, 9, 15 and 19 (1970a: 55-89). Thus, Dunn concludes that the gift of the Spirit is the essence and embodiment of the new covenant in Luke–Acts, as in other New Testament writings, especially Paul's and John's as 'the most important element in Christian conversion-initiation' (1970a: 92, 96, 229).

8.   The scheme of 'salvation-history' in Luke–Acts is noticed by Baer (1926: 45-50) in terms of the different effects of the Holy Spirit: (1) the first epoch: before Jesus' birth; (2) the second epoch: beginning from Jesus' birth to Pentecost; (3) the third epoch: beginning with Pentecost; cf. Conzelmann's scheme (1960: 16-17, 150), which is based on the 'delay of parousia': (1) the period of Israel until John the Baptist's ministry; (2) the period of Jesus' ministry until the Ascension; (3) the period of the Church and the Spirit since the Ascension (Conzelmann's debt to Baer's work can be indicated in his quotation of it; see 1960: 31, 45, 103, 179, esp. 150, 184, 209).

9.   Jesus' experience of the Spirit as sonship was already emphasized by Büchsel: 'Jesu Geistbesitz ist Gottessohnschaft' (1926: 165, 168).

10.   'At each new phase of salvation-history Jesus enters upon a new and fuller phase of his messiahship and sonship' (1970a: 29); 'Jesus' birth belongs entirely to the old covenant, the epoch of Israel' (31). Thus according to Dunn, '"the empowering for service" should not however be taken as the primary purpose of the anointing—it is only a corollary to it' (32; see also 54).

11.   At the same time, he mentions Jesus' unique anointing as the Messiah and the Son of God: 'It is this unique anointing of this unique person which brings in the End' (1970a: 26; see also 27). This distinctiveness of Jesus is further described (1975: 21-26; 1980: 137-43).

Recently, Dunn has replied to Pentecostal scholars[12] who criticized his views in different ways and accepted at least two criticisms: (1) 'The Spirit for Luke is indeed pre-eminently the "Spirit of prophecy", the Spirit that inspires speech and witness' (1993: 8).[13] (2) The import of Luke 1-2 suggests that it is dangerous to make sharp divisions among the three epochs in salvation-history in Luke–Acts (1993: 16-17). Nevertheless, through this article, he has attempted to clarify his former views in critical dialogue with the Pentecostal scholars and has reaffirmed the original assertion argued in the 1970a work:

> [A]ccording to *Lukan* theology, the gift of the Spirit is the most funda-
> mental *sine qua non* in the making of a Christian... Should we not con-
> clude, then, that the pneumatology of Luke is essentially one with the
> pneumatology of Paul at this point, precisely because they reflect the
> dynamic character of earliest Christian experience of conversion-initia-
> tion? (1993: 25, 27).

In a word, receiving the Holy Spirit in Luke–Acts is, according to Dunn, the matrix of Christian life, in a manner similar to that found in John and Paul.

1.2. *R.P. Menzies*[14]

Robert Menzies's 1989 Aberdeen PhD dissertation, 'The Development of Early Christian Pneumatology with Special Reference to Luke–Acts', was published in 1991.[15] In this thesis, he attempts to reconstruct the development of the concept of the Spirit from Judaism (mainly based on Jewish intertestamental literature) to early Christianity (with reference to Luke–Acts along with several Pauline passages). In so doing, he intends to compare Luke's *own* understanding of the Holy

---

12. For instance, Ervin (1984); Stronstad (1984); Shelton (1991); Menzies (1991a: 115-38). The often indicated criticism of Dunn's approach is that he under-stands the Lukan Spirit from a Pauline point of view and thus fails to recognize Luke's *own* distinct voice as an independent theologian: see Ervin (1984: 27); Stronstad (1984: 9-12); Shelton (1991: 2-6); Menzies (1991b: 19-22).

13. Namely, he (see also 26) admits more than before that Luke closely asso-ciates the Spirit with inspired speech and witness (i.e. not as a corollary to Jesus' sonship).

14. See my bibliography.

15. This book was re-published in 1994 in a slightly revised version, entitled *Empowered for Witness: The Spirit in Luke–Acts*, more accessible to a (non-academic) wider audience.

Spirit with both Paul's pneumatology and that of the non-Pauline primitive Church reflected in Matthew, Mark and Q (1991a: 17). At the end of the introductory chapter, he makes clear what he tries to demonstrate:

> I shall seek to establish that Paul was the first Christian to attribute soteriological functions to the Spirit and that this original element of Paul's pneumatology did not influence wider (non-Pauline) sectors of the early church until after the writing of Luke–Acts... The important corollary is that neither Luke nor the primitive church attributes soteriological significance to the pneumatic gift in a manner analogous to Paul. Thus I shall distinguish Luke's 'prophetic' pneumatology from the 'charismatic' perspective of the primitive church on the one hand, and Paul's 'soteriological' understanding of the Spirit on the other (1991a: 48).[16]

For his argument, Menzies first examines the references to the Spirit in Jewish intertestamental (diaspora, Palestinian, Qumran and rabbinic) literature and claims that the Jewish concept of the Spirit, except in the sapiential tradition, e.g. *Wisdom of Solomon* and 1QH, is foreign to a soteriological (and ethical) function; it is *exclusively* associated with 'inspired speech' including 'revelation' and 'wisdom', *but* dissociated from 'miracle' (1991a: 112; 1993b: 12-15). He thus characterizes the typical Jewish understanding of the Spirit as the 'Spirit of prophecy' (1991a: 97).

Then, he proceeds to examine the references to the Spirit in Luke–Acts and other parallel Synoptic passages and insists,

> Whereas the primitive church, following in the footsteps of Jesus, broadened the functions traditionally ascribed to the Spirit in first-century Judaism and thus presented the Spirit as the source of miracle-working power, Luke retained the traditional Jewish understanding of the Spirit as the source of special insight and inspired speech. Luke, in accordance with the primitive church, does not present reception of the Spirit as necessary for one to enter into and remain with the community of salvation (1991a: 279).

Therefore, for Luke, according to Menzies, Jesus and his disciples receive the Spirit *not* as the Spirit of sonship or of new age or covenant, *but* as a prophetic *donum superadditum* which enables them to

---

16. Menzies's basic frame of argument can be traced back to Gunkel (1979 [orig. 1888]). According to Gunkel (1979: 75-97, 89, 91, 96), Paul distances himself from 'the popular view of the Apostolic age' by first recognizing 'ethical significance' in the gift of the Spirit.

accomplish successfully their appointed tasks. In other words, the Spirit in Luke–Acts can be understood as the (typical) Jewish 'Spirit of prophecy'. Thus, he distinguishes three developments of the concept of the Spirit in the early Church: (1) Pauline 'soteriological' pneumatology possibly influenced by 1QH and Wisdom literature, (2) that of the primitive community represented by Mark, Matthew and Q, which takes up the Jewish concept of the 'Spirit of prophecy', yet also includes miracles of healing and exorcism—'charismatic' pneumatology and (3) the *Urgemeinde* of the non-Pauline early Church inclusive of Luke–Acts, as the typical Jewish concept of the 'Spirit of prophecy'—'prophetic' pneumatology irrespective of miracle function (1991a: 282-84, 317-18).[17]

In many respects, Menzies's basic thesis reminds us of Schweizer's interpretations.[18] On the other hand, as a Pentecostal scholar, he (1994b: 115-38) criticizes Dunn's essential view of the Lukan Spirit (i.e. the Spirit as the essence of conversion-initiation for Christians) at a number of points in the process of his main argument (i.e. the Spirit as a prophetic *donum superadditum* for people who are already Christians).[19] Menzies's main contribution, however, is his thorough examination of the Jewish concept of the Spirit delineated in the intertestamental

---

17. So Menzies (1994b: 127) insists elsewhere, 'like most Jewish writers of the intertestamental period, Luke was reluctant to attribute miracles (as opposed to prophetic inspiration) directly or exclusively (for Luke, without the qualifying term δύναμις) to the Spirit'.

18. Schweizer (1968: 404-15) raised three important issues in relation to Lukan pneumatology: (1) the Lukan concept of the Spirit is that of Jewish understanding, i.e., the 'Spirit of prophecy'. (2) In Luke, unlike in Mark and Matthew, the Holy Spirit understood as the 'Spirit of prophecy' is not portrayed as the source of miracle. (3) The Lukan Spirit, unlike Paul's soteriological Spirit, is the Spirit of empowering for mission. Schweizer (1968: 405) further claims that Jesus' baptism is quite different from that of his disciples, namely Jesus is the 'Lord of the *pneuma*', whereas the disciples are pneumatic Christians; contra Menzies (1991a: 156-57). See also Schweizer 1952: 259-78.

19. 'The crucial point of disagreement with Dunn was my insistence that Luke never attributes soteriological functions to the Spirit and that his narrative presupposes a pneumatology which excludes this dimension (for example Lk. 11.13; Acts 8.4-17; 19.1-7). Or, to put it positively, Luke describes the gift of the Spirit *exclusively* in charismatic terms as the source of power for effective witness' (1994b: 117; emphasis original). Cf. Shelton's review (1994: 139-43) of Dunn's 1993 article; for his critique of Menzies, see 140, 141.

literature[20] and his attempt to identify it with the concept of the Holy Spirit in Luke–Acts. Nevertheless, Menzies's understanding or reconstruction of the *typical* Jewish concept of the Spirit and its development in early Christianity have recently been questioned by Turner.

1.3. *M.M.B. Turner*[21]

Max Turner's first contribution to Lukan pneumatology appeared in the 1980 Cambridge PhD dissertation, 'Luke and the Spirit: Studies in the Significance of Receiving the Spirit in Luke–Acts'. And his ongoing interest in this subject was published both in several articles in the 1980s and 90s and in two books in 1996.[22]

Turner's major concern was presented in the 1980 dissertation as follows: 'What activity (or nexus of activities) of the divine Spirit is being thought to be communicated to the disciple (or initiated in him) when he "receives the Spirit"?' (1980: 35, 39). In order to answer this question in relation to Luke–Acts, Turner examines both (1) Jesus' baptismal experience in Lk. 3.21-22 and his reception of the Spirit through resurrection-exaltation in Acts 2.33, and (2) Jesus' disciples' relationship to the Spirit in the ministry of Jesus in Lk. 9.1-6, 10.1-20 and their reception of the Spirit at Pentecost in Acts 2.1-4. His major assertions are as follows:

(1) There are some points of contact between Jesus' reception of the Spirit at Jordan and that of the disciples at Pentecost: the Spirit that both parties receive, according to Turner, is the Jewish Spirit of prophecy, which functions not *primarily* as 'an existential grace of moral and religious renewal', but as 'the organ of revelation' (1980: 181-82).[23] He disagrees with Dunn's view of the Spirit in terms of sonship

---

20. Cf. Schweizer's study (1981: 29-45) of the Spirit in intertestamental Judaism.

21. See my bibliography.

22. Turner's study of Lukan pneumatology can be divided into two periods: (1) a series of articles published between 1980 and 1985, which introduces his argument as delineated in his PhD dissertation, in criticizing mainly the views of Dunn and Schweizer and (2) a series of articles and books between 1991 and 1996, which defend and elaborate his former assertions by further investigating the Jewish concept of the Spirit in intertestamental literature. At the second stage of his research, Turner's main critical dialogue partner is Menzies. See Turner 1996b: 11-12, 82-85.

23. We can notice Turner's somewhat shifted view of the disciples' reception at Pentecost in the later writings (see below).

in relation to Jesus' experience and claims, 'The Spirit received at Jordan is not depicted as a force controlling or moulding Jesus' inner existential life before God, but rather as the charismatic power in his words and acts making them effective against Satan or towards his hearers' (1980: 95, 53; 1996b: 199, 211-12, 266).

(2) In spite of some common elements, there are also some fundamental differences between Jesus' reception of the Spirit and that of the disciples. In this light, Turner again criticizes Dunn who argues for Jesus' archetypal experience of the Spirit in entering into the new age or new covenant which is parallel not only to his disciples' experience, but also to that of contemporary Christians. Thus he (1980: 95) claims,

> Contrary to Dunn's view that the Spirit received at Jordan is mainly to be understood as an archetypal experience of the christian Spirit and, only as a corollary to this, as an 'empowering for service', our evidence suggests that Luke identifies the Spirit received there primarily, if not exclusively, as a power enabling Jesus to effect the unique task of the prophet-like-Moses.[24]

Turner continues to argue that Jesus, after his resurrection and exaltation, receives the Spirit in a different way from the way he received the Spirit at his baptism and then he, functioning as the Spirit of the Lord,[25] pours out the gift of the Spirit upon his disciples, which alters their Christian existence. So he contends, 'The Pentecost event involves a new sphere of activity of the Spirit in the lives of the apostles; but it is by no means their first encounter with the Spirit of the new age: the Pentecostal gift of the Spirit is not the matrix of new covenant life, but an important element within it' (1980: 155, 182-83).[26] In other words, Jesus as the messianic prophet received the Spirit (of God) for releasing

---

24. Turner (1996b: 243, 266, 206) further develops his view of the Lukan portrait of Jesus not only as the Davidic king and the Mosaic prophet, but also as the Isaianic soteriological prophet by highlighting the 'New Exodus' theme in Lk. 4.16-30.

25. This idea is further elaborated: 1982: 168-90; 1994b: 413-36; 1996b: 303-306.

26. Accordingly, Turner (1980: 86-88, 96-116; 1981c: 60 n. 11; 1981a: 33-34; 1996b: 333-41), following the view of Jeremias (1971: 80), suggests that the disciples might experience the Spirit *before* Pentecost in terms of their participating in the kingdom enterprise through Jesus' power and proclamation.

others, whereas the disciples received the Spirit (of Jesus) for themselves (1980: 183-85).[27]

(3) Turner, on the one hand, like Schweizer, understands the Lukan
Spirit in terms of the Jewish 'Spirit of prophecy' mostly as the source
of prophetic inspiration and/or the revelation; on the other hand, however, he, unlike Schweizer, maintains that this Jewish 'Spirit of prophecy' is also associated with miracles, yet is not related to the power
of 'preaching', a perception later developed in Hellenistic-Jewish
Christian circles. Thus, Luke, according to Turner, not only adopted the
Jewish Spirit of prophecy, but also modified it.[28] In this way, the Spirit
for Luke is depicted as the 'organ of revelation' or the 'organ of communication' between both God and Jesus, and the risen Jesus and his
disciples (1980: 185; 1985: 40). Later, Turner elaborates his study of
the Spirit of prophecy in Judaism (contra Menzies as well as Schweizer)
and regards it as the source of 'charismatic revelation', 'wisdom',
'invasive prophetic speech', 'charismatic praise', 'miracle' and 'ethical
and religious renewal', which is also further extended in Luke–Acts as
embracing the power of 'authoritative preaching' (1992b: 86-88; 1994c:
186-90; 1996b: 138, 348-52). Thus, he argues that 'it is the Spirit as a
Christianized version of the Jewish "Spirit of prophecy" which is
central to Christian "life" and transformation' (1994c: 190; 1996b:
351).

In short, for Luke, according to Turner, receiving the gift of the Spirit
(particularly at Pentecost) is not a *donum superadditum* in Christian
life. Rather it is the *sine qua non* of Christian existence (1985: 41).[29]

---

27. 'What it *means* to receive the Spirit for the respective parties is so
differently nuanced by Luke that it would be hollow to assert that they receive the
"same" Spirit' (1980: 185; emphasis original).

28. For Turner's criticism of Schweizer's view of Spirit of prophecy, see Turner
1980: 62-67.

29. We may see that Turner's argument here (1985) is getting closer to Dunn's
than is his previous position in 1980: cf. 'he [Luke] did not identify receiving the
Spirit as the gift of messianic salvation itself, but as one particular nexus within it:
the christian version of judaism's hope for the Spirit of prophecy' (1980: 170; see
also 178-79); 'I think all this means that for Luke the Spirit is not merely a *donum
superadditum*, but necessary for salvation' (1994c: 187); 'Luke sees the Spirit as
the principal means of God's saving/transforming presence for Israel (and through
her to the nations), and that receiving the gift of the Spirit enables participation in
this' (1996b: 402; see also 356, 186). For Turner's definition of 'salvation' in
Luke–Acts, see 1996b: 346, 145.

1.4. *'Conventional Criticism' and Main Issues Debated*
As indicated above, these three scholars express different interpretations of the Holy Spirit in Luke–Acts. Nevertheless, it should be noticed
that each of them examined the text by employing the same academic
methodology:

> The method...is to take each author and book separately and to (attempt
> to) outline his or its particular theological emphasis; only when he has
> set a text in the context of its author's thought and intention (as expres-
> sed in his writing), only then can the biblical-theologian feel free to let
> that text interact with other texts from other books (Dunn 1970a: 39).[30]

My goal in the following section is to uncover Luke's distinctive
pneumatology. The method of analysis employed is redaction-critical. I
shall examine relevant passages in Luke–Acts in an effort to detect
Luke's 'creative contribution in all its aspects' to the tradition concerning the work of the Spirit which he transmits. I shall not assume
Luke's theological perspective is revealed only in his modification of
received sources; thus my concern will include Luke's selection, as well
as his arrangement and modification of received material (Menzies
1991a: 114).

The perspective within which this study is undertaken may be termed
'redaction-critical': we are seeking to explore an aspect of the Lukan
pneumatology. We shall not, however, limit our conclusions to what may
be deduced from a study of the changes introduced by Luke to his
sources. This is only one of the tools available for discovering editorial
interest and activity; at times material Luke has included without significant alteration is equally important for an understanding of his theology,
especially when such material occurs in programmatic positions within
the structure of his work, when the material is emphasized by repetition,
or when an account has a high percentage of favoured Lukan expressions
(Turner 1980: 40-41; see also 1996b: 13).

In other words, the study of the Holy Spirit in Luke and/or Acts has
mostly been undertaken through 'historical-criticism', particularly
'redaction criticism' based on the two-document hypothesis, i.e. Mark
and Q, in comparison with Mark and Matthew. Other leading scholars,
who investigated the same subject, used the same hermeneutical tool:

---

30. These words are quoted from the context where Dunn begins to explain the
Lukan understanding of Pentecost in Acts 2, while having in mind Jn 20.22. Otherwise, he does not explicitly mention his method in the work; yet it goes without
saying that he uses 'historical criticism', especially when he deals with the Gospels
(1970a: 8-37).

Table 1. *Methodology Used for the Study of Lukan Pneumatology*

(Representative) Scholars	Methodology
Baer (1926: 5-13)[31]	'embryonic' Redaction Criticism
Barrett (1947)	Tradition/Source Criticism
Schweizer (1968: 404-415)	Redaction Criticism
Lampe (1957)	Redaction Criticism
Hill (1967: 253-65)	Redaction Criticism
Dunn (1970a: 75)	Tradition and Redaction Criticism
Haya-Prats (1975: 13-14; 73-82)	Tradition and Redaction Criticism
Turner (1980: 40-41; 1996b: 13)	Tradition and Redaction Criticism
Stronstad (1984: 1-12)	Redaction Criticism
Menzies (1991a: 114-15)	Tradition and Redaction Criticism
Shelton (1991: 1)	Redaction Criticism

In what follows, I shall highlight the four main issues concerning Lukan pneumatology by identifying some notable scholars' positions in each table (including Dunn, Menzies and Turner).

(1) Granted that the major issues related to the Lukan Spirit were historically and/or theologically oriented, one of the most controversial issues is how to understand the expression 'receiving the Holy Spirit' or 'baptism in the Holy Spirit' in Luke and Acts: Does it mean (as in Paul's letters) that the recipient enters into the new age and covenant as the matrix for Christian life? Or does it indicate that he or she, who is already regenerated, is additionally endowed with the gift of the Holy Spirit as a *donum superadditum*, that is, the gift received subsequent to conversion-initiation? In accordance with their different answers to this question, some sharply distinguish the Lukan concept of the Spirit from that of Paul (including the pre-Pauline community) or even from those of the other Synoptic evangelists; others say that we cannot do so:

31. The title of the first part of his book is 'Der Heilige Geist als eines der Leit-motive im Aufbau des lukanischen Doppelwerkes' (1926: 43-112). Turner (1981a: 138) regards him as 'a remarkable and surefooted forerunner of modern redaction criticism'.

Table 2. *On the Meaning of 'Receiving the Spirit' in Luke and Acts*

A Donum Superadditum as Christian's Second Blessing (i.e. the Power for Service)	Mediating Position	A Gift as New Covenant Life and Sonship (i.e. the Sign of Conversion-Initiation)
Gunkel (1888: [1979: 43]) Lampe (1951: 65; 1957: 193) Schweizer (1968: 407-413) Hill (1967: 264) Ervin (1984: vii-viii) Stronstad (1984: 12) Menzies (1991a: 47-49)	Baer (1926: 103; 186-92) cf. Hull (1967: 98, 143) ← Haya-Prats (1975: 93-116) cf. Lampe (1977: 69-70) Turner (1980: 185; 1996a) → . ← cf. Shelton (1991: 135)[32]	Büchsel (1926: 165) Dunn (1970a: 4, 23-37) Bruner (1970: 155-224) Gaffin (1979: 13-39) cf. Isaacs (1976: 124, 142)

(2) Another issue frequently debated concerns the nature of the Holy Spirit: Is the Holy Spirit understood as personal being (who) or impersonal force (what)? Those who are of the former view emphasize the personal expressions in relation to the Holy Spirit, e.g. 'the Holy Spirit says' in Acts 8.29 or 'the Spirit sends' in Acts 10.20, whereas those who are of the latter note the impersonal expressions, e.g. 'Jesus is full of the Holy Spirit' in Lk. 4.1 or 'the Spirit is poured out' in Acts 10.45, namely like water or oil:

Table 3. *The Nature of the Holy Spirit*[33]

Personal Being (Who)	Mediating Position	Impersonal Force (What)
Swete (1921: 291)	Cadbury (1927: 270)	Gunkel (1888 [1979: 6-7])
Hull (1967: 172)	Bultmann (1951: I, 155-57)	Leisegang (1922: 22)
Bruner (1970)		Scott (1923: 87)
Bruce (1973: 173)	Haya-Prats (1975: 82)	Lampe (1957: 160-63)
Bovon (1987: 218-19)	Isaacs (1976: 89)	Schweizer (1968: 406)
cf. Turner (1980: 36-38)[34]	Fitzmyer (1981: I, 228)	

32. Shelton (1991: 135) perceives, 'Luke does not clearly delineate between the Spirit's role in conversion and empowerment for mission... Why is Luke not clear? It is primarily because the role of the Holy Spirit in conversion is not his major interest. His fundamental concern is to show how the witness concerning Jesus spread. Luke is not averse to associating the Holy Spirit with conversion but, unlike Paul, he does not ardently press ontological issues onto his pneumatology. Luke's major emphasis concerning the role of the Holy Spirit is much simpler: inspiring and empowering witness'; see also 1994: 143.

33. See Turner 1981c: 45-63; Powell 1991: 51-53; Shepherd 1994: 3-11.

(3) Scholars, however, have by and large agreed that Lukan pneumatology is strongly indebted to the Jewish tradition or understanding of the Spirit:[35] the 'Spirit of prophecy'.[36] In spite of this consensus, there is also disagreement concerning the scope of the (typical) 'Spirit of prophecy' in Judaism especially between Schweizer and Menzies, and Turner (as indicated),[37] which influences their own views in regard to both the Lukan Holy Spirit and the development of early Christian pneumatology:

34. Turner suggests the distinction 'saying that we receive the Spirit whose actions in us are "personal"' from 'saying that we receive the Spirit as a person: the Spirit *himself*' (1980: 37; emphasis original). And he proposes that the former description is more applicable to the New Testament than the latter and further comments, 'It cannot be said that Luke stresses the personality of the Spirit much beyond what can be found in the OT and in the literature of Judaism; and neither of these was strictly binitarian' (37; see also 196-98).

35. It is rather strange, however, that scholars interested in the Lukan Spirit have not given as much attention to the Jewish Bible as to Jewish intertestamental literature, and tend to understand the Lukan Spirit in terms of the (intertestamental or targumic) 'Spirit of prophecy' (cf. Aune 1983: 200); this expression, never found in the Jewish Bible, is often used later in Jewish targums along with the term 'Holy Spirit'. See p. 231 n. 154. For this reason, I prefer to employ the term 'Spirit of the Lord/God' as representing the Jewish traditional concept of the Spirit in general. For this, see Chapter 2. Cf. Turner (1996b: 86), who explains the Lukan Spirit in terms of Jewish 'Spirit of prophecy', admits a certain problem in using this term as referring to God's Spirit in the Jewish Bible: 'So when we apply the term "Spirit of prophecy" to pre-Christian Jewish views we are in some danger of anachronism'. More problematic, however, is that this term is never used in Luke–Acts (and other books in the New Testament, only except in Rev. 19.10: 'For the testimony of Jesus is the spirit of prophecy' [τὸ πνεῦμα τῆς προφητείας]).

36. For instance, Baer (1926: 112), Büchsel (1926: 253), Lampe (1957: 159-64, 193-94) and Hill (1967: 254, 264-65) emphasize this Jewish background of Lukan pneumatology in general.

37. Menzies (1991a: 112, 278-80), like Schweizer, after examining the Jewish concept of the Spirit in intertestamental writings, insists that for Luke the Holy Spirit is understood as the *typical* Jewish 'Spirit of prophecy', which is mainly identified with prophetic inspiration along with revelation and wisdom, yet not associated with miracles and ethics; contra Turner (1992b: 86-88; 1996a: 351).

Table 4. *On the Concept of the 'Spirit of Prophecy' in Luke–Acts*

'Narrow' Concept: inspired speech/prophecy, revelation, wisdom, yet excluding miracle and ethics	*'Broad' Concept: inspired speech/prophecy, revelation, wisdom, including miracle and ethics*
Schweizer (1968: 409)[38] Haya-Prats (1975: 37-44) Menzies (1991a: 122-30)	Turner (1992b: 86-88; 1994c: 174, 188; 1996b: 105-37) cf. Shelton (1991: 78-83); Dunn (1993: 7-11)

(4) Baer claimed that Luke designs the theological scheme of 'salvation-history' in terms of the different effects of the Holy Spirit and divides it into three distinct epochs: (1) the period of Israel (Lk. 1–3.20), (2) the period of Jesus (Lk. 3.21–Acts 1) and (3) the period of Church (Acts 2–28). At the same time, however, he noticed that the Holy Spirit is constantly seen as the driving force throughout this scheme. Scholars who disagree with this scheme suggest the pattern of 'promise-fulfilment', and aver that the new age or covenant already begins with the announcement of Jesus' birth in Luke 1 where the same pneumatological expressions, that is, 'to be full/filled of/with the Holy Spirit', are used in Luke 1–2 as in Acts:

Table 5. *The Lukan Spirit and 'Salvation-History' Scheme*

Pro-Salvation-History Scheme	*Anti-Salvation-History Scheme*
Baer (1926: 45-49, 92-93)	Stronstad (1984: 3-4)
Conzelmann (1953: [1960 = 26, 150])	Menzies (1991a: 130-34)
Dunn (1970a: 31, 43; cf. 1993: 16-17)	Shelton (1991: 16, 24-26)
Haya-Prats (1975: 192-93)	Johnson (1991: 17-21)
cf. Turner (1980: 96; 1996b: 63-64)	

2. Prospect: Towards a More Holistic Reading of the Holy Spirit in Luke–Acts

Different methodological approaches to exegetical study may be likened to a set of keys on a ring. The various keys open different doors and grant access to different types of insight. Narrative criticism has been

---

38. The English version, as Turner (1981b: 148 n. 121) indicated, was mistranslated by making the sentence negative: 'This does *not* prevent him from directly attributing to the πνεῦμα both the χαρίσματα ἰαμάτων on the one side and strongly ethical effects like the common life of the primitive community on the other' (Schweizer 1968: 409; emphasis added; see *TWNT*, VI, 407).

able to open some doors that had previously been closed to scholars...
But it will not open all the doors... [T]he wise interpreter of the Bible
will want to have as full a set of keys as possible (Powell 1993: 101).

From Baer (1926) to Turner (1996b), my subject has almost always
been analysed by historical-critical methods. In particular, since Conzelmann's thesis, *Die Mitte der Zeit*, was published in 1953, Luke has
been confirmed as a 'theologian' and Luke's own theological understanding of the Spirit in comparison with those of other Gospel writers
has been variously tackled through 'redaction criticism' on the basis of
the two-document *hypothesis*.

It should be noted, however, that this two-document hypothesis in
Gospel studies has now been critically challenged in several ways.[39]
Hence Tyson (1983: 303) claims,

> Reliance on the two-document hypothesis has surely facilitated the task
> of redaction criticism, but confidence in that hypothesis as the correct
> solution to the synoptic source problem seems to be eroding. If one takes
> seriously the various challenges to the two-document hypothesis and the
> proposed alternatives to it, it then becomes necessary to raise questions
> about the relationship between redaction criticism and any particular
> solution to the synoptic problem, as well as questions about the useful-
> ness of results that depend upon source theories.

At any event, New Testament scholars for a long time have attempted
to trace the *historical* development of the concept of the Spirit in the
early Church, or to decipher Luke's own *theological* or redactional concept of the Spirit by distinguishing it from either that of Mark, Matthew
and Q or that of John and Paul. Even so, in the Acts of Apostles it has
been acknowledged that it is difficult to identify whether a certain intention or concept related to the passages referring to the Holy Spirit is
Lukan or traditional (cf. Haenchen 1966). In other words, although these
historical-critical debates on the Holy Spirit in Luke and/or Acts have
unquestionably provided considerable insights into Lukan pneumatology

---

39. For instance, Talbert (1981: 209-11) attacks the method of 'redaction criticism' in at least three aspects and raises an appropriate question about Luke–Acts in
general: 'The issue before us today is, How can one study the distinctive perspective of the third evangelist without assuming any source theories?' (211). See also
Farmer (1988: 49-57; 1994); Goulder (1994: I, 3-71). We should also notice that
several scholars attempted to reconstruct the Gospel of Luke on the basis of the
two-Gospel hypothesis, i.e., regardless of the two-document hypothesis: Cope *et al.*
(1992, 1993, 1994, 1995).

in its various aspects, it is hard to deny that efforts to grasp Luke's original concept of the Holy Spirit have usually been preoccupied with scholars' own dogmatic or theological preunderstanding of the Spirit. In addition, it is quite doubtful whether Luke, who can be considered a 'historian' and 'theologian' *in his own times*,[40] attempted to provide primarily and consciously his audience with comprehensive dogmatic instruction about the Holy Spirit.[41]

Put differently, it would be inappropriate to look at Luke–Acts as a theological treatise about the doctrine of the Holy Spirit.[42] Rather, it is proper and fair to see Luke–Acts *as narrative* (διήγησις in Lk. 1.2),[43] in which the how and why of the Holy Spirit is presented in close association with both Jesus in Luke and his disciples or witnesses in Acts.

If the latter statement can be regarded as convincing, first of all, we need to look at the narrative *of* Luke–Acts as a final literary form[44] in

---

40. Haenchen (1971: 91) comments, 'Luke is no systematic theologian... Nevertheless he has a theology of his own; he sets out from definite theological premises and treats the immediate theological questions of his age'. Cf. Barrett (1961); Marshall (1970); Fitzmyer (1989).

41. In this sense, Gunkel's statement in the 1888 work is still of value: 'Our most important observation, one which is decisive for grasping what was understood by "Holy Spirit" in the apostolic period, is that the primitive community was not at all concerned with a doctrine of the Holy Spirit and his activities' (1979: 13). See also Baer (1926: 4); Gaventa (1988: 150).

42. Culpepper (1984: 474) rightly pinpoints the inadequacy of doctrine-oriented study of the Gospels: 'The gospel was not given to us as a statement of doctrinal principles, and it can never be captured in doctrinal codes. The narratives remain the indispensable source of life and vitality for faith. Both historical reconstruction and doctrinal abstraction reify the biblical narratives; that is, they objectify the meaning of the stories, tear the message from its narrative context, and attempt to force it into categories of thought which cannot contain the distinctiveness of the biblical narratives.' Cf. Fee (1994: 2).

43. Gaventa (1988: 149-50) avers, 'What is missing from all of these methods [i.e. 'historical criticism'] is some attempt to deal seriously with the character of Acts as a narrative. Each of them treats Acts as if it were a theological argument somehow encased—or even imprisoned—in a narrative. The assumption seems to be that Luke has a thesis or main point to demonstrate, and he creates his story in order to bear the thesis.' For the term διήγησις, see p. 193 n. 38.

44. Redaction criticism and narrative criticism of the Gospels in some ways overlap; nevertheless there are considerable discrepancies between the two methods when applied: see Petersen (1978: 17-20). Recently Moore (1989a: 56-68) mentions the difference between composition criticism and narrative criticism, 'Whereas composition criticism extends the tradition of redaction criticism by reason of an

order to understand its presentation or function of the Holy Spirit, rather than to reconstruct the historical and theological concepts of the Spirit that lie *behind* it. This means that my present project inevitably requires a different methodology or hermeneutical perspective, that of 'narrative criticism'.[45] This fresh perspective has already been recognized as an academic paradigm shift in general for biblical studies, especially for the studies of the Gospels and Acts in the New Testament.[46] In other words, this paradigm shift of biblical interpretation from 'historical' and 'theological' to 'literary' means that the author of Luke–Acts can be conceived not only as a 'historian' and 'theologian', but also as a (biblical literary) 'artist'.[47]

Quite recently, W.H. Shepherd, *The Narrative Function of the Holy Spirit as a Character in Luke–Acts* (1994), challenges previous traditional approaches to the understanding of the Holy Spirit in Luke–Acts by means of narrative criticism.[48] Through this new perspective,[49]

---

overriding interest in the evangelists' theologies, narrative criticism represents a break with that tradition in the sense that the focus is no longer *primarily* on theology' (7; emphasis added).

45. It is helpful to quote Tiede's prediction for the future of Lukan studies, 'Promising avenues of interpretation, therefore, have been staked out by methods and discoveries in non-theological fields of academic inquiry' (1992: 256); 'A very productive future is, therefore, emerging in studies of Luke–Acts. No longer preoccupied with theological modifications of Mark or "Q" or even contrasts with Paul or the Paulinists, this scholarship will focus upon *Luke–Acts as a literary narrative*, an artful rendition of Hellenistic rhetoric through which the author builds a case, enters into Israel's argument about how to "read" the Scriptures and how to discern the work of God's Spirit in "the present time" (see Luke 12.56).' (263; emphasis added).

46. To illustrate just some seminal books, on *the Gospel of Matthew*: Kingsbury 1989b; Bauer 1988; Weaver 1990; Howell 1990; M. Davies 1993; on *the Gospel of Mark*: Rhoads and Michie 1982; Malbon 1986; Kingsbury 1989a; Tolbert 1989; on *the Gospel of Luke and Acts*: Tannehill 1986; 1990; Parsons 1987; Gooding 1987; 1990; Pervo 1987; Brawley 1990; Kingsbury 1991; Gowler 1990; Sheeley 1992; Darr 1992; Spencer 1992, 1993, 1997; Kurz 1993; Denova 1997; Roth 1997; on *the Gospel of John*: Culpepper 1983; Staley 1988; M. Davies 1992; Stibbe 1992, 1993a, 1994.

47. For instance, see Richard (1983); Karris (1985); Powell (1989: 5-15); Marshall (1992: 13-26). Cf. Renan, who in 1877 called the Third Gospel 'the most beautiful book in the world', and Harnack designated that Luke 'was a master of language'; quoted in Stonehouse (1979: 9).

48. It was his 1993 PhD dissertation at Emory University. In the second

Shepherd makes two main points in regard to the portrait of the Holy Spirit in Luke–Acts:[50] (1) the Holy Spirit is characterized as God's onstage representative and (2) the crucial function of the Holy Spirit is thus to provide 'narrative-reliability' for the reader (which are tentatively indicated by Brawley and Darr). Thus he suggests and asserts,

> My goal in making use of these literary theorists is to determine how the character of the Holy Spirit functions in the narrative—how it works, what it represents, and why. I will finally be asking, in light of the close correlation between characters and people, what Luke's characterization of the Holy Spirit implies for the God of Luke's proclamation. My thesis is that in Luke–Acts, the character of the Holy Spirit signals narrative reliability, and that ultimately the Spirit's presence and action is that of God (1994: 101).

academic year (1994–95) of my research, I received the book (published in 1994) in January 1995 by air-mail order. Although he and I alike criticize the traditional approaches to the Lukan Spirit by using the same narrative criticism, its application along with its implications is differently undertaken. See below.

49. There are two forerunners, as Shepherd (1994: 37-40) recognizes, who mention in passing the portrait or function of the Holy Spirit in Luke–Acts *in terms of literary-critical point of view*: Brawley (1990) and Darr (1992). Brawley indirectly describes the Holy Spirit when he deals with the characterization of God in his Chapter 5 by applying the literary critic Roland Barthes's 'code of semes' (see §2.1 in Chapter 4): 'Although the divine appellation "Holy Spirit" may serve as nothing more than a convenient designation of God, it frequently occurs in situations where God is particularly related to human beings... In brief, the title Holy Spirit clarifies relationships positive and negative between God and human beings' (115-16). On the other hand, Darr more directly addresses the role of the Holy Spirit in discussing the 'rhetoric of character in Luke–Acts', when he categorizes the Holy Spirit in the 'divine frame of reference' (see §3.3.1 in Chapter 3), saying, 'The divine frame of reference (e.g. the Holy Spirit) provides the audience with a consistent and highly authoritative guide for constructing and/or evaluating characters and their roles in the action' (53; see §3.3 in Chapter 3).

50. The table of contents of his work consists of the following: Chapter 1, 'Introduction' (1-41), which briefly surveys traditional views on the Holy Spirit as to 'What (or Who) is the Holy Spirit?' and 'What does the Holy Spirit do?' and proposes a literary approach to the Spirit as a character; Chapter 2, 'Characterization in Narrative Theory' (43-98); Chapter 3, 'The Characterization of the Holy Spirit in Luke–Acts (I): The Gospel of Luke' (99-151); Chapter 4, 'The Characterization of the Holy Spirit in Luke–Acts (II): The Acts of the Apostles' (153-243); Chapter 5, 'Conclusion' (245-57), which summarizes his previous argument and elucidates the potential relationship of the character of the Holy Spirit in Luke–Acts to the hypostatic entity of later trinitarian theology in early Christianity.

Above all, his major contribution to scholarship is to examine the Holy Spirit of Luke–Acts as a *literary character* by using literary-critical theories and categories and to offer a significant alternative in appreciating the *narrative function* of the Holy Spirit to most historically and theologically driven concerns. Thus, he concludes as follows,

> It has been the contention of this study that the Holy Spirit is best understood as a character in the narrative of Luke–Acts, and that the function of that character is to signal narrative reliability... The characterization of the Holy Spirit in Luke–Acts is an indirect characterization of God (1994: 247, 255).

His study of the Holy Spirit as a character through narrative criticism[51] makes an undeniably important contribution to the understanding of the narrative function of the Holy Spirit, suggesting some valuable insights on passages about the Spirit in Luke–Acts.[52] Nevertheless, his thesis's method and its application to the Holy Spirit need to be supplemented or reinforced in at least four ways.

First of all, Shepherd does not explore *the overall and specific plot of Luke–Acts*, which is, I believe, fundamental in analysing *the narrative function* of the Holy Spirit.[53] Accordingly, he fails to elucidate *the Lukan narrative function of the Holy Spirit in terms of the plot*, and he does not discern the nuanced function of the Spirit when the narrative advances from the Gospel to Acts. So in my opinion, the narrative function of the Spirit undertaken by Shepherd would be better understood *as the immediate narrative effect of the Spirit in relation to the reader* in Luke–Acts: 'narrative reliability'.

Secondly, in his two main Chapters 3 and 4, when he applies the literary theories of characterization to the Holy Spirit, he more or less prefers Hochman's eight categories of characters' aspect and mode to

---

51. Shepherd's theoretical way of characterizing the Holy Spirit is built on (1) Hochman's character-classification scheme, (2) Gowler's scheme of the presentation of character and (3) reader-response criticism (1994: 97-100).

52. See Karris's review (1996: 744-45) of Shepherd's work.

53. Shepherd (1994: 98) acknowledges the inseparable relationship between the function of characters and the plot of the narrative and assumes that the plot of Luke–Acts is 'conflict' without defining the term plot: 'Character goes with plot, and plot implies conflict' (94). I can simply find the term plot here and there in his work (e.g. 100, 101, 126, 130, 137, 140, 147, 149, 150, 187 n. 111 etc.). For my discussion on plot, see §3 in Chapter 5.

Rimmon-Kenan's model of character-presentation.[54] By doing so, he misses substantial definitions along with their implications which directly highlight the traits of the Holy Spirit; for instance, he does not draw any or much attention to the words *Holy* Spirit, *God's* Spirit/the Spirit *of the Lord* and the Spirit *of Jesus*,[55] which can be seen as the most explicit direct definitions of the Spirit *as a character*. In addition, he does not seem to deal adequately with the Holy Spirit as a literary character: Shepherd does not properly discuss the trait of 'person-unlikeness' of the Holy Spirit as a character; he rather emphasizes the Spirit as an ('person-like') actor (90-93, 120 n. 60).[56]

Thirdly, although he perceives the significance of the LXX for examining the Lukan portrait of the Spirit as an actor (14-15, 89, 93), especially when considering Hochman's category of stylization/ naturalism (73, 134), he does not separately investigate the roles or presentation of the divine Spirit in the Jewish Bible nor deal with the similarities and differences in the portrait of the Spirit in Luke–Acts and the Jewish Bible (especially the LXX).[57]

Finally, although he is much indebted to Darr (for instance, see Shepherd 1994: 38-40), he is not concerned with Darr's significant coinage 'divine frame of reference', which includes the Holy Spirit

---

54. The inadequacy of Hochman's model (particularly to ancient biblical characters; for Hochman's model developed out of debates on characterization in modern novels, see §3 in Chapter 4) is already pointed out by Gowler (1990: 321): 'Baruch Hochman's model for classifying characters is an approach that helps to elucidate conceptualized images of various characters. This model, however, was not the primary model utilized in this work, because it does not adequately evaluate the process and means by which characterization is achieved in narratives.' See also §3.1 in Chapter 4.

55. Shepherd indicates in passing (1994: 223, 251) the significance of the unusual expression, the 'Spirit of Jesus' (Acts 16.7); yet he fails to discern the dynamic interaction among the Holy Spirit, God and the exalted Jesus in Luke–Acts by simply focusing on the characterization of the Spirit as an indirect presentation of God. Cf. my view in §5.1.1 in Chapter 4 and §5 in Chapter 5.

56. Cf. §§4 and 5.1.2.3 in Chapter 4.

57. In regard to the historical concept of the Lukan Spirit, Shepherd accepts the term 'Spirit of prophecy' in saying, 'In summary, there is wide consensus that Luke stands in continuity with the Old Testament in portraying the Holy Spirit as the Spirit of prophecy, responsible for inspired human speech. This is the major contribution of scholarship to date, and I will base much of my subsequent argument on this foundation' (1994: 22-23).

along with the narrator's point of view and Scripture (i.e. the LXX).[58] This means that he does not take into consideration two important factors which shed light on appreciating the Holy Spirit as rhetorically presented in Luke–Acts: the relationship (1) between the Lukan narrator or implied author and the Holy Spirit, and (2) between the Holy Spirit and other components of the divine frame of reference, especially in association with human reliable characters in Luke–Acts.[59] Hence he fails to grasp (the narrative function of) the Holy Spirit adequately *within the religio-biblical ideology*[60] *of the Lukan narrator or implied author.*

From this critical point of view, Shepherd, in spite of his remarkable contribution in seeing the Holy Spirit as a character through his use of literary critical theories, does not seem to offer a *holistic reading of the Holy Spirit* in Luke–Acts. My reading seeks to appreciate Luke–Acts not simply as narrative, but as *dynamic biblical narrative.*[61]

2.1. *Methodology: 'Dynamic Biblical Narrative Criticism'*

In regard to the methodology of my present project, I basically share with Shepherd the attempt to examine the Holy Spirit in Luke–Acts by means of narrative criticism. However, in order to pursue a more persuasive and holistic reading, I shall explore (1) *the literary traits* of the Holy Spirit in terms of the following three aspects: the Lukan (a) narrator's point of view, (b) character-presentation and (c) plot-function. Prior to doing so, I shall provide (2) *the literary repertoire*[62] for the

---

58. Darr (1992: 50-53) briefly discusses the three components listed above as the "divine frame of reference" and just mentions, in his footnote (182 n. 20), "angelic appearances", "voices from heaven" and "visions" that are sometimes presented to express or authenticate the 'divine point of view' in Luke–Acts. See also §3.3.1 in Chapter 3.

59. See my whole Chapter 3.

60. For the term 'religious/biblical ideology', see p. 95 n. 24, p. 98 n. 33.

61. For potential dangers or pitfalls when applying literary/narrative criticism to (ancient) *biblical* text, see Powell (1993: 91-98); cf. Longman (1987: 47-58).

62. The text of Luke–Acts is unquestionably written in Hellenistic Greek in the first century CE for early (Jewish or Gentile or both) Christians in both a Jewish and a Graeco-Roman milieu. By literary repertoire, I mean the references to God's Spirit in the Jewish Bible that are often explicitly cited and/or implicitly embedded in Luke–Acts. For Lukan citation from the Jewish Bible (esp. the LXX), see §3.3.1.4 in Chapter 3. For the term 'literary repertoire', see also p. 34 n. 68 in this chapter.

Lukan references to the Holy Spirit in an attempt to produce (3) *the theological significance*[63] of the Spirit in Luke–Acts.[64] In addition, (4) the implications of the Lukan Spirit will be noted *through the interaction between (implied) author/narrator, text and (implied) reader* in the reading process.[65] This is why I call my methodology *dynamic biblical* narrative criticism.

My method thus combines to some extent both a diachronic analysis as 'a methodological approach characterized by its treatment of a phenomenon in terms of the temporal process or historical development', viz. the Jewish Bible as the literary repertoire of Luke–Acts as a 'window' on the Holy Spirit, *and* a synchronic analysis as a method which is 'primarily concerned with enabling the text itself to yield the depth and richness of its meaning', viz. Luke–Acts as a 'mirror'.[66]

Thus, in Chapter 2, while noting that the narrative of Luke–Acts is not a modern narrative, but a biblical, i.e. *ancient* and *canonical*, narrative, I shall focus on the Jewish Bible[67] as the most influential extratext,[68] that is, the literary repertoire for the Holy Spirit in Luke–Acts.

---

63. Here I am not attempting to distinguish Luke's own theological presentation of the Holy Spirit from the other Synoptic evangelists' understanding of it (though, in Chapter 4, I note any differences in the Synoptic parallel contexts referring to the Holy Spirit). I do not regard Luke–Acts as a systematic-theological thesis on the Holy Spirit. Instead, the 'theological significance' of the Holy Spirit in Luke–Acts recognizes a certain development or discontinuity in comparison with God's Spirit in the Jewish Bible. We may also say that Luke–Acts is a *theo*logical narrative in that it not only narrates about God or his purpose, but also seeks to represent God's point of view. Cf. §3.3 in Chapter 3.

64. Cf. Morgan and Barton (1988: 171); Tolbert's five criteria (1989: 8-13) for adjudicating interpretation.

65. Cf. W. Tate's 'integrated approach' to the biblical interpretation: (1) 'the world *behind* the text', (2) 'the world *within* the text' and (3) 'the world *in front of* the text' (1991: xv-xxi; 173-205).

66. See Keegan (1985: 167, 30). For a holistic approach, see Kelber (1987: 112-16); Parsons (1987: 13-25); Tolbert (1989: 10-13); M. Davies (1992: 7, 20); Stibbe (1992: 13).

67. Leisegang (1922), preoccupied with *religionsgeschichte*, claimed that the Synoptic material referring to the Holy Spirit stems from Greek mysticism, rather than from Jewish traditions. But his argument has been rightly criticized (e.g. by Baer [1926: 112-13, 131, 138, 161]; Barrett [1947: 2-5, 35-45]; Isaacs [1976: 141-42]; Keener [1997: 7-8]; cf. Hill [1967: 264-65]; Aune [1983: 34]). See also nn. 35-36.

68. The term 'extratext' is used as equivalent to literary repertoire or inter-

This chapter will show how the presentation or role of the Holy Spirit in Luke–Acts is characterized in continuity with that of God's Spirit in the Jewish Bible. I shall also provide one excursus, which deals with the use of *rûaḥ* in the Qumran Literature with special reference to 1QS, 1QM, CD and 1QH as an indication of developments from the Hebrew Bible in Jewish literature roughly contemporary with Luke–Acts.[69]

The literary characteristics of the Holy Spirit will then be explored in the next three chapters. Before examining the Holy Spirit as a character, in Chapter 3, I shall discuss the Lukan narrator's point of view with special reference to the Holy Spirit and how the Spirit is *rhetorically* presented in connection with the narrative reliability of the narrator and other human characters in terms of the 'divine frame of reference'. Then, in Chapter 4, I shall focus on the Holy Spirit as a literary *divine character* that can be analysed not only in terms of the Lukan present-ation, so, *character-centred characterization* of the Spirit, but also, in Chapter 5, in the light of the overall plot of Luke–Acts, so, *plot-centred characterization* of the Spirit. In the process of this character-building, I shall emphasize that the portrait of the Holy Spirit is generated and actualized *through the text by the reader*, especially the reader's acti-vities of anticipation and retrospection and consistency-building. At the same time, I shall draw out the similarities and differences of the roles

textuality, and Julia Kristeva conceives every discourse or text as intertextual. Abrams explains (1993: 285; emphasis original): 'The term intertextuality...is used to signify the multiple ways in which any one literary text is inseparably inter-involved with other texts, whether by its open or covert citations and *allusions*, or by its assimilation of the formal and substantive features of an earlier text or texts, or simply by its unavoidable participation in the common stock of linguistic and literary conventions and procedures that are 'always already' in place and constitute the discourses into which we are born'. See also Culler (1975: 139) and Iser (1978: 53-85). Beal (1992: 21-24) briefly introduces intertextuality with other related terms such as allusion, echo, inner-biblical exegesis, intertext, intratextuality, poetic influence and trace. Darr's comments (1992: 22) on the 'extratext' focus on the reader, rather than the text itself: 'The extratext is made up of all the skills and knowledge that readers of a particular culture are expected to possess in order to read competently: (1) language; (2) social norms and cultural scripts; (3) classical or canonical literature; (4) literary conventions (e.g. genres, type scenes, standard plots, stock characters) and reading rules (e.g. how to categorize, rank and process various kinds of textual data); (5) commonly-known historical and geographical facts'.

69. For the comparative study of parallels found in both the DSS and Luke and/or Acts, see Fitzmyer (1966: 233-57); Brooke (1995: 72-90, esp. 78-79).

and presentations of the Lukan Spirit with those of God's Spirit in the Jewish Bible (esp. the LXX) in Chapter 4 (and partially in Chapter 5; cf. two appendices at the end of this book). At the beginning of each chapter, I shall present narrative theories and literary definitions for each related subject, e.g. narrator and point of view, character and characterization, plot and so forth.

Chapter 6 will summarize the results of the earlier chapters and briefly exhibit two implications: (1) the theological significance of the Holy Spirit in Luke–Acts; (2) the relationship of the Holy Spirit to (a) the narrator or implied author, (b) the text and (c) the implied reader of Luke–Acts, with final remarks about the legitimacy of Lukan ideology, the power of modern readers and my reading.

To sum up, my dynamic and holistic reading of the Holy Spirit will be attentive to the narrator's rhetoric in employing the Holy Spirit for his point of view (Chapter 3), will be contextual and analytic in examining the narrator's character-presentation of the Spirit within each immediate narrative context (Chapter 4), and relational and comprehensive in exploring the narrative function of the Spirit within the overall plot (Chapter 5). It will also recognize the import of the Jewish Bible as the extratext of Luke–Acts (Chapter 2), inferring the theological significance of the Lukan Holy Spirit in comparison with the earlier Jewish understanding of the Spirit of the Lord/God, based on Chapters 2 and 4, and will recognize relations among author/narrator, text and reader in relation to the Holy Spirit, based on Chapters 3 and 5 (Chapter 6).

Chapter 2

THE USAGE OF *RÛAḤ/PNEUMA* IN THE
EXTRATEXT OF LUKE–ACTS AS LITERARY REPERTOIRE

1. *Introduction*

In this chapter, I shall explore the usage of *rûaḥ* in the Hebrew Bible[1]
and that of *pneuma* in the Septuagint in order to sketch a possible fore-
ground for the word *pneuma*, especially the divine Spirit, in Luke–Acts.
For this purpose, after first examining all the references to *rûaḥ* used in
the MT under the following section, I shall then note briefly additions
and omissions of the term *pneuma* in the Greek version under section 3,
which will be followed by the study of the usage of *pneuma* in the other
books contained in the LXX under section 4.

For my reading of the Holy Spirit in Luke–Acts, the Jewish Bible
(i.e. the LXX) is thus to be traversed as one of the most essential extra-
texts[2] in the literary repertoire of Luke–Acts.[3] For this aim, I shall
classify every reference to *rûaḥ* in the Hebrew Bible and *pneuma* in the
Jewish Bible synchronically rather than diachronically. In the last

---

1.   I do not presuppose that the author of Luke–Acts knew the MT or any
Hebrew; for Septuagintal expressions or influence in Luke, see Fitzmyer (1981:
114-16: 'Septuagintism in Lukan Greek'; 116-27: 'Supposed Aramaisms, Heb-
raisms, and Semitisms') along with the bibliography cited. There are at least two
reasons, however, that I want to consider the MT: (1) the LXX is the Greek version
of the Hebrew Bible, with some additional Jewish works in Greek; it is, thus,
natural to examine, first of all, the references to *rûaḥ* in the MT for the Septuagintal
understanding of *pneuma* in terms of its usage and (2) it is worth observing how
much the authors of the LXX follow the usage of *rûaḥ* when they translated it into
pneuma while noting any additions and omissions in the LXX. For discussion concerning the inter-relationship between the MT and the LXX in New Testament times,
see Müller (1996: 19-45, esp. 23-24).

2.   For the term extratext, see p. 34 n. 68 in Chapter 1.

3.   For example, Luke–Acts often quotes from and alludes to the Jewish Bible.
See §3.3.1.4 in Chapter 3.

section of this chapter, I shall also provide four tables that unfold relevant features of God's Spirit delineated in the extratext for reading the Holy Spirit in Luke–Acts.

2. The Hebrew Bible

The MT has 389 references[4] to *rûaḥ*, which have generally been arranged and classified in the following way:[5] 125 referring to wind;[6] 48 to breath;[7] 97 to anthropological spirit;[8] 21 to an evil spirit; 98 to the

4.   Out of 389, 378 references are found in Hebrew narratives and 11 in Aramaic texts. I have used the computer program *Bible Windows 2.1* (Texas: Silver Mount Software, 1993) to establish the occurrences of *rûaḥ* in the MT.

5.   In not a few cases, however, categories overlap with one another; because of this, scholars have had a different numbering for God's Spirit (cf. according to BDB [925], *rûaḥ* denotes God's Spirit 94 times); meanwhile, partly because of this ambiguity, the LXX translators, instead of *pneuma*, sometimes employ other terms like ἄνεμος, ψυχή, θύμος and so forth. See §2.3 below. For a useful survey of the Spirit in the Jewish Bible, see Briggs (1900: 132-45); Schoemaker (1904: 13-35); Eichrodt (1967: 46-68); Horn (1992: 260-80); Hill (1967: 202-17); Kamlah (1975: 689-93); Baumgärtel (1968: 359-67); Krodel (1978: 10-46); Schweizer (1981: 10-28); Montague (1994: 3-98).

6.   About one-third of the occurrences of *rûaḥ* denote wind (e.g. Gen. 3.8; 2 Kgs 3.17; Prov. 25.14, 23; Eccl. 8.8; Isa. 7.2; Jer. 2.24; Ezek. 1.4; Hos. 8.7; Ps. 1.4; Job 4.9; Amos 4.13) which is usually seen as under Yahweh's control (e.g. Exod. 15.10; Ps. 147.18; Isa. 17.13; Hos. 13.15) and used as his powerful tool to demonstrate his sovereign task before the Gentiles as well as the Israelites (e.g. 1 Kgs 19.11; Isa. 41.16; Hos. 4.19; Jon. 1.4; Ps. 107.25; Job 1.19; Eccl. 11.5). The wind as an invisible and mysterious power protects the people of God (e.g. Exod. 10.13; 14.21; Num. 11.31) and also judges them or their enemy (e.g. Isa. 17.13; Jer. 4.11; Ezek. 13.11; Hab. 1.11; Ps. 11.6; Job 21.18; Dan. 2.35) in the process of salvation history. Sometimes by metonymy, *rûaḥ* is used for the four directions from which the wind blows (e.g. Jer. 49.32, 36; Ezek. 5.10, 12; Zech. 2.6; Dan. 7.12; 1 Chron. 9.24), sometimes as a symbol of vanity or nothingness (e.g. Job 6.26; 7.7; Ps. 78.39; Prov. 11.29; 25.14; Eccl. 1.6, 14, 17).

7.   Like wind, *rûaḥ* as breath is another divine agent under the direct control of God (e.g. Job 27.3; 34.14; Isa. 30.28; 40.7; Ps. 104.30). Here it is mainly used as the principle of living existence in both human beings and animals (e.g. Num. 16.22; 27.16; Ezek. 1.20, 21; Zech. 12.1; Ps. 31.5; Job 9.18; Eccl. 3.19; Lam. 4.20). Along with this, a few uses refer to God's miraculous force and judgment (e.g. Isa. 4.4; 11.4; 30.28; 40.7). Other terms such as חיים (Gen. 6.17; 7.15), נשמה (Gen. 7.22; Isa. 42.5; Job 32.8; 34.14), אף (Job 4.9; 27.3) and פי (Isa. 11.4) are from time to time found with *rûaḥ* in the contexts above. In several cases, however, *rûaḥ* in

Spirit of the Lord/God. In what follows, I shall focus on the last two cases.

2.1. *Divine Spirit*

2.1.1. Evil Spirit. Generally speaking, an evil spirit or an evil spirit from the Lord/God in the MT[9] is not understood to be in opposition to or independent of God and his power. Rather an 'evil spirit' is another agent who or which carries out the will/plan of God, ultimately for his name's sake.

2.1.1.1. An Evil Spirit. There are only two occasions in which an evil spirit (רוח רעה) appears: 'God (אלהים) sent an evil spirit (רוח רעה) between Abimelech and the lords of Shechem; and the lords of Shechem dealt treacherously with Abimelech' in Judg. 9.23 and 'Saul would be relieved and feel better, and the evil spirit (רוח הרעה) would depart from him' in 1 Sam. 16.23b. However, this latter case, in its own context, should be considered an 'evil spirit from God' or even

this category might also be understood as 'spirit' rather than as 'breath'; it is very difficult to distinguish them: e.g. Ps. 104.30; Job 34.14; Ezek. 1.20, 21; 10.17; 37.14.

8.   When *rûaḥ* denotes spirit in human beings (e.g. Gen. 41.8; Exod. 35.21; Deut. 2.30; Judg. 15.19; 1 Kgs 21.5; 2 Chron. 9.4; Isa. 38.16), it is variously used with other emotional and psychological adjectives, pronouns and verbs in each context ('anger': Judg. 8.3; Isa. 25.4; 33.11; Ezek. 3.14; Job 6.4; 21.4; Eccl. 10.4; 'hasty temper': Prov. 14.29; 16.32; 25.28; 29.11; 'pride': Exod. 6.9; Prov. 16.18; Eccl. 7.8b; 'jealousy': Num. 5.14a, 14b, 30; 'grief': Gen. 26.35; Isa. 54.6; 61.3; 'confusion': Isa. 19.14; 'humility': Isa. 57.15; Prov. 16.19; 29.23; Eccl. 7.8; 'broken spirit': Isa. 65.14; 66.2; Ps. 34.18; 51.19; Prov. 15.13; 17.22; 18.14b; 'oppressed spirit': 1 Sam. 1.15; 'distressed spirit': Dan. 2.1, 3; 7.15; 'fainting spirit': Ps. 77.3; 124.3, 4, 7). In some contexts, *rûaḥ* is used of various emotional conditions and of one's will or mind (e.g. Ps. 76.12; 77.6; Job 15.13; 20.3; Prov. 11.13; 16.2; 17.27; Ezra 1.1; 2 Chron. 36.22). There is, however, no clear boundary among these segments; and various English translators try to grasp nuances in different ways. It is clear, however, that *rûaḥ* is used as an anthropological term, apart from wind, breath and the divine Spirit. Nevertheless, we should also note that the Lord/God, as the first cause, is frequently represented manipulating the human *rûaḥ*, just as in the case of wind or breath: the human *rûaḥ* is also providentially controlled by the Lord (e.g. Hag. 1.14; Isa. 29.24; Jer. 51.11; Ezek. 11.5b, 19; 13.3; 18.31; 20.32; 36.26; 1 Chron. 28.12; 2 Chron. 21.16).

9.   21 references to an evil spirit or the like are as follows: Judg. 9.23; 1 Sam. 16.14b, 15, 16, 23a, 23b; 18.10; 19.9; 1 Kgs 22.21, 22, 23; 2 Kgs 19.7; Isa. 19.14; 29.10; 37.7; Hos. 4.12; 5.4; Zech. 13.2; 2 Chron. 18.20, 21, 22. See also Appendix I.

as the 'spirit of God'. In the former case, we should also note that it is God who sends an evil spirit to accomplish God's will/purpose. Thus, we could infer that an 'evil spirit' in the MT is not the evil spirit, as an independent being apart from the control of God.

2.1.1.2. An Evil Spirit from the Lord/God. In the context of 1 Samuel 16, we may observe that the 'spirit of the Lord' and an 'evil spirit from the Lord' cannot be identical: 'Now the spirit of the Lord departed from Saul, and an evil spirit from the Lord tormented him' (1 Sam. 16.14). There is, however, no clear evidence that an evil spirit itself is a separate personality alongside of God.[10] Rather, even in this context, it is said that the origin is the Lord who endows both a 'good spirit' and a 'bad spirit'. It is interesting that there are five alterations with reference to an evil spirit in this Hebrew text: רוח־רעה מאת יהוה (1 Sam. 16.14: an 'evil spirit from the Lord'), רוח־אלהים רעה (16.15,16; 18.10: an 'evil spirit from/of God' or the 'spirit of God [for] evil'), רוח־אלהים (16.23a: the '[evil] spirit of God'), רוח הרעה (16.23b: the 'evil spirit') and רוח יהוה רעה (19.9: an 'evil spirit from/of the Lord' or the 'spirit of the Lord [for] evil'). These are all interchangeable or identical, referring to the evil spirit, and in 1 Sam. 16.23a this evil spirit is just presented as the 'spirit of God' (רוח־אלהים). Thus, the function of an evil spirit in the Hebrew Bible is regarded as directly under the control of God.[11]

2.1.1.3. Other References Related to an Evil Spirit. These references denote *rûaḥ* as a lying spirit, a spirit of confusion and a spirit of whoredom: 'a [the] spirit (הרוח)[12] came forward and stood before the Lord, saying, "I will entice him [Ahab]"… "I will go out and be a lying spirit (רוח שקר) in the mouth of all his prophets"… [T]he Lord (יהוה) has put a lying spirit (רוח שקר) in the mouth of all these your prophets; the Lord has decreed disaster for you [Ahab]' (1 Kgs 22.21-23//2 Chron. 18.20-22); 'I [the Lord] myself will put a spirit (רוח) in him [the king of Assyria], so that he shall hear a rumour and return to his own land; I will cause him to fall by the sword in his own land' (2 Kgs 19.7//Isa. 37.7); 'The Lord (יהוה) has poured into them a spirit of confusion

---

10. Cf. Klein (1983: 165), who also observes that the Hebrew Bible often attributes evil or temptation to the 'hand of the Lord' (e.g. Deut. 13.2-4; Amos 3.6; 2 Sam. 24.1//1 Chron. 21.1).

11. See Brueggemann (1990: 125).

12. NRSV and NIV translate הרוח into a 'spirit' without considering the article.

(רוח עועים); and they have made Egypt stagger in all its doings as a drunkard staggers around in vomit' (Isa. 19.14); 'For the Lord (יהוה) has poured out upon you a spirit of deep sleep (רוח תרדמה); he has closed your eyes, you prophets, and covered your heads, you seers' (Isa. 29.10); 'For a spirit of whoredom (רוח זנונים) has led them astray, and they have played the whore, forsaking their God' (Hos. 4.12); 'For the spirit of whoredom (רוח זנונים) is within them, and they do not know the Lord' (Hos. 5.4). I may also observe here that the spirit itself is not an independent being apart from the control of God; it is the Lord/God who allows the spirit to do evil, so that the spirit entices and misleads a certain individual or a group. In other words, the spirit itself is not an evil spirit in (cosmic) conflict with God. Rather the effect or the result upon the objects is evil or harm. Particularly see the immediate context in 1 Kgs 22.21-23//2 Chron. 18.20-22.

2.1.1.4. Summary. In the Hebrew Bible, therefore, I may say that an 'evil spirit' or an 'evil spirit from the Lord' in some contexts, even including an 'evil spirit' found in Judg. 9.23, is not a spirit against or beyond the power of God, but another agent for fulfilling his sovereign plan. In fact, there is essentially no difference between a 'good spirit' and a 'bad spirit' in respect of their origin; there is(are), so to speak, the spirit(s) from God (רוח־אלהים; see 1 Kgs 22.21 and 1 Sam. 16.23).

2.1.2. The Spirit of the Lord/God
2.1.2.1. General Divine Agent. The Spirit of the Lord/God in the Hebrew Bible[13] is generally an extended expression for God's power or

---

13. 98 references to God's Spirit are found in that following: Gen. 1.2; 6.3; 41.38; Exod. 28.3; 31.3; 35.31; Num. 11.17; 11.25a, b, 26, 29; 24.2; 27.18; Deut. 34.9; Judg. 3.10; 6.34; 11.29; 13.25; 14.6, 19; 15.14; 1 Sam. 10.6, 10; 11.6; 16.13, 14a; 19.20, 23; 2 Sam. 23.2; 1 Kgs 18.12; 22.24; 2 Kgs 2.9, 15, 16; Isa. 11.2a, b, c, d; 28.6; 30.1; 31.3; 32.15; 34.16; 40.13; 42.1; 44.3; 48.16; 59.21; 61.1; 63.10, 11, 14; Ezek. 1.12, 20a, b; 2.2; 3.12, 14, 24; 8.3; 11.1, 5a, 24a, b; 36.27; 37.1, 14; 39.29; 43.5; Hos. 9.7; Joel 3.1 (ET: 2.28); 3.2 (ET: 2.29); Mic. 2.7; 3.8; Hag. 2.5; Zech. 4.6; 6.8; 7.12; 12.10; Mal. 2.15a; Ps. 51.13 (ET: 51.11); 106.33; 139.7; 143.10; Job 34.4; Prov. 1.23; Dan 4.5, 6, 15 (ET: 4.8, 9, 18); 5.11, 14; Neh. 9.20, 30; 1 Chron. 12.19 (ET: 12.18); 2 Chron. 15.1; 18.23; 20.14; 24.20. It can be noted that the following books in the Hebrew Bible do not have any reference to God's Spirit: Leviticus; Joshua; Jeremiah; Amos; Obadiah; Jonah; Nahum; Habakkuk; Zephaniah; Ruth; Song of Solomon; Ecclesiastes; Lamentations; Esther; Ezra. It may be further noticed that in the contexts of revelation in Isa. 6, Amos 7 and Jer. 1 God's Spirit is not mentioned; on the other hand, the authors employ the phrases

presence by which he accomplishes his divine/mighty deeds (e.g. in the context of creation: Gen. 1.2; cf. Ps. 104.30; Job 26.13; 33.4 and in the contexts of miracles: 1 Kgs 18.12; 2 Kgs 2.16; Isa. 34.16; Ezek. 2.2; 3.12; 3.14, 24; 8.3; 11.1, 24; 37.1; Hag. 2.5; Mal. 2.15).[14]

2.1.2.2. God's Spirit, his Will and Dispositions. God is sometimes described as the divine Spirit in contrast to human/animal mortal flesh (Gen. 6.3: 'Then the Lord said, "My Spirit shall not abide in mortals forever, for they are flesh"'; Isa. 31.3: 'The Egyptians are human, and not God; their horses are flesh, and not spirit'). More basically, by *rûaḥ* the texts profess not only God's omnipresence (Ps. 139.7: 'Where can I go from your spirit? Or where can I flee from your presence?'), but also his absolute sovereignty (Isa. 40.13: 'Who has directed the spirit of the Lord, or as his counsellor has instructed him?'). On the other hand, on a few occasions, God's Spirit expresses his will or his personal disposition: the rebellious Israelites do not follow his Spirit/will (Isa. 30.1: 'Oh, rebellious children, says the Lord, who carry out a plan, but not mine; who make an alliance, but against my will [רוּחִי], adding sin to sin'; see also Ps. 106.33; Zech. 6.8); his disposition, unlike that of human beings, is not impatient (Mic. 2.7: 'Is the Lord's patience [רוּחַ יהוה] exhausted?').

2.1.2.3. God's Spirit, Charismatic Power and/or Guidance. In the Hebrew Bible there are some leaders such as judges, kings and prophets, who receive the charismatic endowments of God's Spirit. Even among

---

'hand of the Lord' and/or 'word of God' (e.g. Isa. 8.11; Jer. 15.17; Ezek. 1.3; 33.22; 40.1; cf. this expression 'hand of the Lord' is used in parallel with the Spirit of the Lord in Ezek. 3.14, 22-24; 8.1-3; 37.1; for the close relationship between God's Spirit and word, see 2 Sam. 23.2; Isa. 59.21; Ps. 33.6; 147.18). In this sense, the 'great reforming prophets' like Isaiah and Jeremiah appear to avoid referring their calling or divine inspiration to the Spirit of God (presumably to distinguish themselves from other popular [or false] prophets who used this appeal; cf. Zedekiah's appeal to God's Spirit in 2 Kgs 22.24//2 Chron. 18.23). In relation to this issue, Eichrodt (who regards Mic. 3.8 as a later interpolation), following Mowinckel's argument (1934: 199), seems to overemphasize this phenomenon in saying '...in the line of divine messengers from Amos onwards there is *absolutely* no mention of the *rûaḥ* as the power that equips and legitimates the prophet' (1967: 56: emphasis added); cf. Krodel (1978: 14).

14. Sometimes, however, God's divine activity is described by other terms such as the 'wisdom of God' (Exod. 28.3; 1 Kgs 3.28; Job 32.8), the 'hand of God' (Ps. 19.1; 102.25) and the 'word of God' (Ps. 33.6; 147.15, 18).

judges, kings and prophets, however, the Hebrew Bible does not specifically state that every individual who held these offices received this special endowment of the Spirit.[15] In addition, this charismatic endowment appears to be very special and unexpected since God sovereignly bestows his Spirit on several individuals, and he also takes the Spirit back from them (e.g. 1 Sam. 16.14).

There are four individuals endowed unexpectedly and extraordinarily with the Spirit, who thus become the judges for Israel: Othniel: 'The spirit of the Lord (רוח יהוה) came upon him (ותהי עליו)' (Judg. 3.10); Gideon: 'But the spirit of the Lord took possession of (לבשׁה) Gideon' (6.34); Jephthah: 'Then the spirit of the Lord came upon (על־ ותהי יפתח) Jephthah' (11.29); Samson: 'The spirit of the Lord began to stir (ותחל) him in Mahaneh-dan, between Zorah and Eshtaol' (13.25); 'The spirit of the Lord rushed on him (ותצלח עליו)' (14.6, 19; 15.14).

Because of this endowment, each of them possesses an extraordinary valour/boldness and leads the rest of the Israelites who are in fear and at last they obtain victory against their enemies. In other words, for his people, God is depicted selecting several individuals and raising them up as warriors/leaders on whom he bestows the miraculous power of leadership through his Spirit. This endowment, however, does not seem to be permanent, but temporary. Thus, Samson needs repeated endowment to carry out his tasks.[16] We should also notice that this endowment with the Spirit of the Lord is not connected with the private business of individuals, but rather with the national crises caused by Israelite infidelity, and it is only when they cry to the Lord for help that the Israelites have peace and rest during the period ruled by their judges due to God's mercy towards them.

---

15. For instance, only 4 out of 12 judges are endowed with the charismatic gift of the Spirit. It is clear, however, that the other judges, not endowed with the Spirit, are also raised as religious/military leaders by God. In this regard, we can only assume that the author of Judges privileges the narratives about the major judges empowered by the Spirit: e.g. Othniel (3.9-11), Gideon (6.7–8.35), Jephthah (10.10–12.7) and Samson (13.2–16.31); the other judges: Ehud (3.15-30), Shamgar (3.31), Deborah (4.4–5.31, but note that she is described as a prophetess), Tola (10.1-2), Jair (10.3-6), Ibzan (12.8-10), Elon (12.11-12) and Abdon (12.13-15). For the major judges' structure in Judges, see Soggin (1981: 1-13; esp. 3).

16. Cf. Samson's hair being mentioned twice in association with his power (Judg. 16.17, 19; cf. 16.22), which yet appears to originate from the Lord (Judg. 16.20). See Soggin (1981: 257).

In the first book of Samuel, Saul and David, like judges, are endowed with the Spirit of the Lord/God as not only warriors, but also political leaders and legitimate kings. In comparison with the judges above, their endowments are not immediately related to fighting enemies. In particular, Saul's possessing the divine Spirit is expressed by his prophesying (1 Sam. 10.6, 10; 19.23—three out of four occurrences, except 1 Sam. 11.6; cf. 2 Sam. 23.2 in David's case). In spite of this, we cannot argue that the endowments of Saul and David[17] as kings are quite different from those of the judges,[18] since both Saul and David are also depicted as successful military leaders.[19] Meanwhile, the narratives tend to relate that Saul and David as kings ruled the whole of Israel with God's authorized permission through their endowment with God's Spirit, which was recognized by others as well as themselves. Interestingly, when God has determined to forsake Saul and to choose David, 1 Sam. 16.13b-14a says, 'the spirit of the Lord came mightily upon David from that day forward... Now the spirit of the Lord departed from Saul'.

Moses as the exodus leader is portrayed as the man of the Spirit in Num. 11.17a, 25a. Moses is also seen as a prophet (cf. Deut. 18.18) who speaks God's oracles/inspired words and performs God's miracles. The Spirit is thus presented as God's empowering, which enables Moses to lead the Israelites in the wilderness, that is, to accomplish God's will (cf. Exod. 3.9-14). The narrative in Numbers, however, explains Moses' possession of the Spirit indirectly: 'I [God] will come

17. Nevertheless, it should also be noted that the manner of David's possession of God's Spirit (1 Sam. 16.13) is somewhat distinguished from that of Saul and other judges: (1) direct connection between Spirit-possession and anointing and (2) presumably permanent nature of Spirit-endowment (cf. 1 Sam. 30.25; 2 Sam. 23.2: 'The spirit of the Lord speaks through me, his word is upon my tongue'). Thus, Klein (1983: 162) comments, 'While historical and chronological reasons may lie behind these distinctions, a comparison of the present accounts of Saul's and David's anointing demonstrates the superiority of David's spirit endowment, both in its close connection with anointing and in its permanence'; cf. Brueggemann (1990: 123).

18. There is the same verb (צלח) used, which is found both in Judges and in 1 Sam. 10.6, 10; 11.6, 13. See also Table 4 in this chapter.

19. 1 Sam. 11.6: 'And the spirit of God came upon Saul in power when he heard these words, and his anger was greatly kindled'; 1 Sam. 16.13: 'Then Samuel took the horn of oil, and anointed him in the presence of his brothers, and the spirit of the Lord came mightily upon David from that day forward'.

down and talk with you [Moses] there; and I will take some of the spirit that is on you and put it on them' (Num. 11.17a); 'Then the Lord came down in the cloud and spoke to him, and took some of the spirit that was on him [Moses], and put it on the seventy elders' (Num. 11.25a). The Spirit is, thus, also said to rest upon the seventy elders according to God's promise/will including two elders still in the camp. They are then said to prophesy (Num. 11.25b, 26b; see also the next subsection) and to be regarded as 'prophets' (Num. 11.29) who support Moses in carrying out his mission (Num. 11.17b).[20]

The stories of Elijah and Elisha also present these men as prophets whose endowment with God's Spirit allowed them to speak God's oracles/inspired words and to perform miracles. 2 Kgs 2.9 and 15, however, both read 'your [Elijah's] spirit', namely, the 'spirit of Elijah', but throughout the immediate context, the 'spirit of Elijah' can be regarded as the Spirit of the Lord that has been working in Elijah. Similarly, the 'Lord, the God of Elijah' (2.14) refers to the Lord who had inspired Elijah. Therefore, Elisha's asking for a double portion of Elijah's spirit is nothing but a request for a double portion of the Spirit of the Lord through whom or which Elijah had carried out his miracles during his ministry. At last, Elisha performs a miracle as Elijah did (2 Kgs 2.14), which proves that Elisha with the Spirit of the Lord had succeeded to the office of prophet and is recognized as another outstanding leader among the group of prophets (2.15). And later on, like the judges, Elisha is also represented carrying out miraculous signs (2 Kgs 2.22, 24). Interestingly, Elisha, who had the double portion of the Spirit, seems to be represented as performing twice as many miracles as Elijah did (cf. Sir. 48.12).

2.1.2.4. God's Spirit, Prophetic Oracles and/or Revelation. God's Spirit is prominently presented in contexts of prophetic oracles/inspired words and/or revelation in the Hebrew Bible. The effect is represented in two ways: non-revelatory ecstasy and revelatory message.

Examples of the former case are Saul (1 Sam. 10.6, 10; 19.23) and his messengers (1 Sam. 19.20); they prophesied in a state of ecstasy

---

20. This endowment on the seventy elders can also be understood in the context of the prophetic Spirit as another special charismatic gift. E. Davies (1995: 109) suggests that the elders' possession of the Spirit which is upon Moses indicates their subordination to Moses. For the effects of Spirit-endowment in the MT, see §5 in this chapter and Appendix I.

without delivering any revelatory message after having been endowed
with the Spirit of the Lord. Perhaps the seventy elders in the wilderness
(Num. 11.25, 26) are seen as another instance. In fact, in Genesis and
Exodus, God is frequently represented as delivering his messages to his
people by means of other methods, namely by direct communication
(e.g. Gen. 21.12; 22.1; Exod. 3.6) or by a messenger or an angel (e.g.
Gen. 16.7-11; 21.17; 22.11; 24.7; 31.11; 32.1; Exod. 3.2)[21] or in a
dream (e.g. Gen. 20.3, 6; 31.11, 24; 37.5-20). Even in these cases, however, the recipients are called 'prophets': 'Would that all the Lord's
people were prophets, and that the Lord would put his spirit on them!'
(Num. 11.29); 'Is Saul also among the prophets?' (1 Sam. 10.12;
19.24).[22] And this coming of the Spirit of the Lord, as in the case of the
judges of Israel, proves to be an unexpected and temporary endowment.
One noted account is that Balaam the son of Beor (Num. 22.5), who is
described as a pagan diviner (Josh. 13.22; Deut. 23.4), is also presented
as God's prophetic agent (Num. 22.9, 12, 20, 31; 23.4, 5, 16, 26), and
he is said to be endowed with the Spirit of God and given an inspired
oracle to proclaim Yahweh's blessing for His people, Israel (Num.
24.2-24; cf. the LXX Num. 23.7).

In the case of the later prophetic books, *rûaḥ* functions to give
prophetic revelation to the people of the Lord.[23] In Isa. 61.1-2, when the

21. Like God's Spirit, the divine angel is presented as an angel *of God* (e.g.
Gen. 21.17; 31.11; Exod. 14.19; Judg. 6.20; 13.6) and/or an angel *of the Lord* (e.g.
Gen. 16.7, 9-11; 22.11, 15; Exod. 3.2). In addition, an angel of the Lord/God, like
God's Spirit, is sometimes portrayed as God's presence or God himself (e.g. Gen.
16.13; 31.11, 13; see the use of the 'divine I' in Gen. 21.18; 22.11) and also as
God's emissary particularly during the exodus journey (Exod. 14.19; 23.20, 23;
32.34; 33.2; Num. 20.16; cf. Isa. 63.10-14; Neh. 9.20, 30). For the angel of Yahweh
in general, see Eichrodt (1967: 23-29); von Rad (1964: 76-80).

22. Not every man is called a 'prophet' when he is endowed with the Spirit. For
example, the chief of the thirty warriors, Amasai prophesied for David after the
endowment of the Spirit, but he is not called a 'prophet' (1 Chron. 12.18).

23. See the occurrences of God's Spirit in pre-exilic texts: 'But as for me, I am
filled with power, with *the spirit of the Lord*, and with justice and might, to declare
to Jacob his transgression and to Israel his sin' in Mic. 3.8 (if not considered a later
interpolation); 'The days of punishment have come, the days of recompense have
come; Israel cries, "The prophet is a fool, the man of the spirit is mad!"' in Hos. 9.7
(by the mouth of an Israelite); 'Woe to the rebellious children, declares the Lord,
who execute a plan, but not Mine, And make an alliance, but not of My Spirit' in
Isa. 30.1 (NASB). In most cases, prophets in the pre-exilic period tend to claim their
inspiration in terms of the formula of 'Thus says the Lord'. Cf. Ezekiel's appeal to

speaker, probably the prophet himself, was anointed by the Lord, he claimed that the Spirit of the Lord came upon him.[24] Thus, as the leader of God's people, he proclaimed God's revelatory and salvific message towards his people to accomplish his prophetic mission sanctioned by God. Looking back on the earlier period of prophecy, post-exilic texts bemoan Israel's refusal to heed prophetic warnings, inspired by God's Spirit: 'Many years you were patient with them, and warned them by your spirit through your prophets; yet they would not listen' (Neh. 9.30); 'They made their hearts adamant in order not to hear the law and the words that the Lord of hosts had sent by his spirit through the former prophets' (Zech. 7.12; cf. Isa. 63.10, 11, 14).

The prophet, Azariah the son of Oded, is said to have prophesied and instructed Asa in the righteous way of God, when the Spirit of the Lord had come on him (2 Chron. 15.1 and see 15.2-19). Similarly, the Spirit of the Lord is also said to have come upon Jahaziel, a Levite, and compelled him to proclaim and predict a future for Jehoshaphat and his people (2 Chron. 20.14-17). Again, Zechariah, the son of the priest Jehoiada, after being possessed by the Spirit of God, is said to have pointed out the people's transgressions boldly by means of God's authority, 'Thus says God' (2 Chron. 24.20). Even the false prophet, Zedekiah, the son of Chenaanah, is also represented as acknowledging prophecy as through the Spirit of the Lord (1 Kgs 22.24//2 Chron. 18.23).

God's Spirit as an exilic prophet: 1.12, 20; 2.2; 3.12, 14, 24; 8.3; 11.1, 5, 24; 37.1; 43.5.

24. This passage possibly reminds a reader both of the servant who is *endowed with the Spirit* (Isa. 42.1-2) but is not anointed, and of *anointed* Cyrus (Isa. 45.1-2), who is, however, neither called a servant nor is endowed with the Spirit. On the other hand, the prophet's picture of his possession of God's Spirit through the divine anointing (cf. 1 Kgs 19.16) also recalls the occasion of David (1 Sam. 16.13; cf. 16.3; 2 Sam. 2.4, 7; 5.3, 17; 12.7; Ps. 89.20; 1 Chron. 11.3; 14.8), who received God's Spirit while being anointed (cf. Saul's case in 1 Sam. 10.1-13). This shows that the relationship between reception of God's Spirit and anointing (מָשַׁח) is not commonly found in the Hebrew Bible (while the verb מָשַׁח occurs 69 times), but occurs only three times in contexts referring to the establishment of God's chosen individuals who are authorized to function as a king or a prophet for a specific mission assigned by Yahweh (cf. the Persian king Cyrus in Isa. 45.1-2). For the general concept and usage of מָשַׁח in the Hebrew Bible, see Hesse (1974: 496-509). For 'Spirit-reception' verbs used in the Jewish Bible, see Tables 4 and 5 in this chapter.

These observations imply that receiving the prophetic Spirit from the Lord is not always limited to a 'prophet', but open to any individuals chosen by God. But those endowed with the prophetic Spirit are to become the human messengers or agents of God in order to remind the hearers of their transgressions (past and present) and/or to predict their destiny (future) in the whole counsel of God.

2.1.2.5. God's Spirit and Other Charismatic Gifts. In the book of Exodus, some skilful persons with whom God endows the Spirit of wisdom (רוח חכמה) are said to be able to make Aaron's vestments (Exod. 28.3). In particular, Bezalel (maybe Oholiab too; yet this is not clearly delineated in Exod. 31.6) is called and is filled with the Spirit of God (ואמלא אתו רוח אלהים) in order to devise artistic designs for God's tabernacle (Exod. 31.3; 35.31). Joshua, as a new leader for the next generation in Israel, is said to be filled with the Spirit of wisdom (רוח חכמה מלא) in Deut. 34.9; cf. Num. 27.18: 'Joshua the son of Nun, a man in whom is the spirit') in order that he should lead and encourage Israel without fear to cross over the Jordan river.[25]

In a similar vein, Joseph is portrayed as the man of wisdom who is able to interpret strange dreams and is called 'one in whom is the spirit of God (איש אשר רוח אלהים בו)' in Gen. 41.38 by the foreign king, Pharaoh. Likewise, Daniel, who is said to be inspired by the Spirit (Dan. 4. 8, 9, 18; 5.11, 14), is capable of interpreting visions.[26]

---

25. Joshua's reception of God's Spirit is connected with Moses' laying on his hands: 'Joshua son of Nun was full of the spirit of wisdom, because Moses had laid his hands on him' (Deut. 34.9). Elsewhere, however, Moses' laying hands upon Joshua (symbolically) implies a rite of transfer of authority or power, apart from endowment of the Spirit: 'So the Lord said to Moses, "Take Joshua son of Nun, a man in whom is the spirit, and lay your hand upon him; ... You shall give him some of your authority, so that all the congregation of the Israelites may obey"' in Num. 27.18-20. For this, see E. Davies (1995: 304); Lohse (1974: 428-29). On the other hand, the pattern of this successive endowment-inheritance from Moses to Joshua is also found in the relationship between Elijah and Elisha. See also the Spirit from Moses to the elders and the Spirit from Saul to David. These four references suggest a succession pattern for responsible leadership. Cf. Stronstad (1980: 35): 'The most striking motif or theme for the charismatic activity of the Spirit of God is the transfer of the Spirit as part of the transfer of leadership responsibilities'.

26. Dan. 4.9: 'O Belteshazzar, chief of the magicians, I know that you are endowed with a spirit of the holy gods (רוח אלהין קדישין בך) and that no mystery is too difficult for you'. Here, a 'spirit of the holy gods' does not seem to denote the 'spirit of the God of Israel', but Nebuchadnezzar in Dan. 4 and Belshazzar in

In these cases, *rûaḥ* of the Lord/God is considered the source and origin of extraordinary capacities, i.e. wisdom, leadership, craftsmanship and the interpretation of visions-dreams. And it is God who endows his selected individuals (Joseph, Bezalel, Joshua and Daniel) with his Spirit for his own purpose.

2.1.2.6. God's Spirit as 'Holy' Spirit and 'Good' Spirit. In the MT, the term 'holy Spirit' appears only in two contexts in Ps. 51.11 (MT: 51.13) and Isa. 63.10, 11 (cf. Wis. 1.5; 9.17; Sus. 1.45), where it refers to the divine Spirit of God himself: the phrase 'your holy spirit' (רוח קדשך) is employed in parallel that of 'your presence' in both immediate contexts.[27] Thus it cannot be assumed that the holy Spirit has a separate or independent identity apart from God himself.[28] God himself (Exod. 22.32; 29.43; Lev. 10.3; 19.2; Num. 39.27; 1 Sam. 6.20; Isa. 5.16; 6.3; 11.9; Ezek. 20.41; 28.22, 25; 36.23; 38.16; 39.27; Dan. 4.8, 9, 15; 5.11, 14; Hos. 11.9; cf. 2 Macc. 14.36; *3 Macc.* 2.2; Sir. 23.9; Tob. 12.12, 15; esp. note the expression קדוש ישראל in Isa. 12.6; 17.7; 29.19; 40.25; 41.14, 20; 43.3; 45.11, 15, 18; 47.4) and his name (Lev. 20.3; 22.2; 1 Chron. 16.10, 35; Pss. 33.21; 103.1; Ezek. 36.20, 21, 22; cf. Tob. 3.11; 8.5-6) are holy, so his Spirit and his word (e.g. Isa. 5.24) are holy, too.[29]

We should notice in what narrative contexts both the prophetic book and the psalmist employ the term 'holy' Spirit (cf. Zech. 7.12; Ps. 106.33; Neh. 9.20, 30 referring to past incidents; Isa. 59.21; 61.1; Hag. 2.5; Ps. 139.7; 143.10 referring to present situations). According to Isa. 63.9-10, God put his Spirit into leaders like Moses to lead and guide the Israelites in the wilderness, but they did not obey God or Moses. Thus, the passage implies that they rebelled and grieved God's holy Spirit, because they behaved immorally/evilly before God on their journey toward the promised land, Canaan. In a similar vein, the psalmist is eager to renew his heart and spirit as a 'clean heart, a new and right spirit' (Ps. 51.10) and asks God not to 'take your holy spirit' (51.11) from him, but to take away 'his sins and all his iniquities' (51.9). This

Dan. 5 regard Daniel as the one who has extraordinary spirit (5.12, 20) originating from the divine power. Cf. the LXX Dan. 4.8, 9, 18; 5.11; see Table 3 in this chapter.

27. Thus, Tate comments (1990: 24; emphasis added), 'Thus God's holy Spirit is *his* awe-inspiring, empowering, and joy-provoking *presence*'.

28. See Tate (1990: 23-24); Anderson (1972: I, 399).

29. See Procksch (1964: 91-95).

is the reason why the divine *rûaḥ*, in these contexts, is not described simply as the Spirit, but as the Spirit of holiness.[30] Elsewhere God's Spirit is sometimes called 'your [God's] good Spirit' (רוחך טובה) which God gives to instruct people in the way of righteousness: 'Teach me to do your will, for you are my God. Let your good spirit lead me on a level path' (Ps. 143.10); 'You gave your good spirit to instruct them, and did not withhold your manna from their mouths, and gave them water for their thirst' (Neh. 9.20; cf. 9.30).

Therefore, in the life of the individual and the community, it is God's holy Spirit or God's good Spirit which empowers and encourages them to conduct their holy or righteous lives according to God's demand. In this sense, God's Spirit as holy or good Spirit is considered to be the divine source or power to sustain his people's religio-ethical lives. Once again, we should remember that the 'holy' Spirit or the 'good' Spirit is another expression for the Spirit of the Lord/God, and the holy/good Spirit is not considered to be distinct from God himself.

2.1.2.7. God's Spirit and Future Expectations for Individuals and Community. There are also future expectations for the coming/out-pouring of the Spirit of the Lord both upon the Messiah as an individual and upon the community as God's covenant people. This is the day that Moses looked forward to seeing and prayed that God would accomplish for his people of Israel (Num. 11.29).

In Isa. 11.1-2, it is said that the Spirit of the Lord shall rest on the future king, the 'shoot from the stump of Jesse', a descendent of David, Jesse's son, who would also be endowed with the 'spirit of wisdom and understanding, the spirit of counsel and might, the spirit of knowledge and the fear of the Lord' (cf. *1 En.* 49.3; 62.2; *Pss. Sol.* 17.37; 18.7). This text shows that the future king born in the covenantal line of David (cf. 2 Sam. 23.2) will be a figure who is endowed with God's Spirit *par excellence* (note the word 'Spirit' appears in v. 2 four times along with five different qualities). And he will be characterized not only as the man of wisdom/understanding/counsel/knowledge and might in word and deed, but also one who fears God. In another instance, it is the servant who is endowed with the Spirit, and the endowment is depicted

---

30. It is really difficult to separate the dimension of ethics from that of religion in these texts (cf. the Yahweh-centred life principle of the Israelites in Leviticus and Deuteronomy). See Hill (1967: 210, 212).

in the past tense; yet his mission is described in the future tense:[31] 'Here
is my servant, whom I uphold, my chosen, in whom my soul delights; I
have put (נתתי) my spirit upon him; he will bring forth justice to the
nations' (Isa. 42.1). Like the future Davidic king described in Isa. 11.1-
2, the servant endowed with the Spirit is concerned with justice or
righteousness (cf. the nature of the prophet's task in Isa. 61.1-3).

On the other hand, some prophetic oracles promise a future outpouring of the Spirit of the Lord upon God's covenantal people or
community in the contexts of future national restoration/salvation: 'For
the palace will be forsaken, the populous city deserted; the hill and the
watchtower will become dens forever, the joy of wild asses, a pasture
for flocks; until a spirit from on high is poured out on us [the restored
people of Israel], and the wilderness becomes a fruitful field, and the
fruitful field is deemed a forest' (Isa. 32.14-15); 'I will pour my spirit
upon your descendants, and my blessing on your offspring' (Isa. 44.3b);
'And as for me, this is my covenant with them, says the Lord: my spirit
that is upon you, and my words that I have put in your mouth, shall not
depart out of your mouth, or out of the mouths of your children, or out
of the mouths of your children's children, says the Lord, from now on
and forever' (Isa. 59.21). Likewise elsewhere, the future outpouring of
the Spirit upon God's restored people would bring forth religious obedience and moral/ethical renewal in the hearts of the people (especially
in Ezek. 36.25-32; cf. Prov. 1.23): 'I will put my spirit within you, and
make you follow my statutes and be careful to observe my ordinances'
(Ezek. 36.27); 'I will put my spirit within you, and you shall live'
(Ezek. 37.14a); 'and I will never again hide my face from them, when I
pour out my spirit upon the house of Israel, says the Lord God' (Ezek.
39.29). The 'spirit of grace and supplication' will work on the 'house of
David' to remind it of its sins and bring forth repentance (Zech. 12.10).

---

31. The word servant occurs 33 times in the book of Isaiah (20 times in chs. 40–
53; 11 times with all the plural forms in chs. 54–66). And the servant songs are
found in Isa. 42.1-4 (the speaker is God); 49.1-6 (the speaker is the servant); 50.4-
11 (the speaker is the servant) and 52.13–53.12 (the speaker is unidentified), in
which the servant is sometimes called 'Israel' (49.3), 'Jacob' (48.20), 'Jacob Israel'
(41.8, 9; 44.1, 2, 21; 45.4). In most cases, however, it is difficult to designate who
the servant is in each of the four passages. Thus, there is no consensus among
scholars about the identity of the servant. Cf. Mckenzies (1968: xxxviii-lv) who
introduces both 'collective interpretation' and 'individual interpretations', and then
criticizes both of them respectively. In so doing, he suggests the 'mythological
interpretation' of an ideal figure, who is not historical.

Finally, Joel's prophetic message about the outpouring of God's Spirit recalls the prayer of Moses (Num. 11.29) that all the people of Israel would be prophets in the future and thus indicates God's Spirit as the Spirit of prophecy: 'Then afterward I will pour out my spirit on all flesh; your sons and your daughters shall prophesy, your old men shall dream dreams, and your young men shall see visions. Even on the male and female slaves, in those days, I will pour out my spirit' (Joel 3.1-2; ET: 2.28-29).[32]

2.1.2.8. Summary. From my examination, it can be seen that the divine Spirit in the MT is presented as God's Spirit active in the world,[33] indicating God's power and/or presence (esp. see Gen. 6.3; Isa. 3; 30.1; 40.13; Pss. 103.33; 139.7; Zech. 6.8; Mic. 2.7) especially in relation to charismatic leaders, i.e. judges, kings, prophets and other individuals, who perform miracles, give prophetic/revelatory words or wisdom, become craftsmen or live righteous/holy lives in past and present situations. In the future expectations, the MT suggests that God promises to pour out his Spirit not only upon the Davidic Messiah *par excellence*, but also upon his restored people. The (past, present and future) intervention of God through his Spirit in the narratives of the MT is thus often closely connected with salvation history within covenant contexts: 'I will be their God, and they shall be my people' (Ezek. 37.27; cf. Jer. 32.31-34).

2.2. Section Conclusion

The term *rûah* in the MT is used to denote (1) wind, (2) breath, (3) anthropological spirit, (4) evil spirit and (5) the divine Spirit including the divine disposition. In almost all cases, these references link the Spirit to the direct (sometimes indirect) control of God himself. For instance, even an 'evil spirit' is described as directly controlled by God and this is often expressed as an 'evil spirit from the Lord/God' (1 Sam. 16.14, 15, 16; 18.10; 19.9). As God's Spirit, the MT presents the 'holy Spirit' or the 'good Spirit' as inspiring the Israelites' religio-ethical life

---

32. McQueen (1995: 21-43) recently proposes that the nature of the promise of the Spirit of Yahweh in Joel is to be appreciated in the light of the overall three-fold thematic structure of the book, i.e. lamentation (1.1–2.17), salvation (2.18–3.5) and judgment (4.1-21). Thus, he highlights that the outpouring of the Spirit of Yahweh can be seen as a future sign of salvation and judgment.

33. For possessive expressions in relation to God's Spirit, see Table 3 in this chapter.

before the God of holiness. Once again, we should notice that these five references to the 'holy Spirit' and the 'good Spirit' do not prove the Spirit to be an independent personality *apart from* God, but rather to be the divine presence or activity.[34]

We should note the following two aspects: (1) the Spirit is consistently presented as Yahweh's Spirit fulfilling God's will/purpose through his human agents, i.e. God's Spirit representing God's power, activity and presence[35] and (2) the divine Spirit is only given to some particular figures chosen by God. In so doing, the following features are closely concerned with the will/plan of God (often mediated through his chosen individuals) towards his people: (a) charismatic endowment of special leaders (judges, kings, prophets and other individuals), which is expressed in miracles, prophetic/revelatory speeches (both including non-revelatory ecstasy and revelatory message, which is more prominent after the post-exilic period),[36] wisdom, craftsmanship and the interpretation of visions-dreams; (b) inspiring the religio-ethical life particularly as delineated in Ezek. 36.25-32; Ps. 51.11; Isa. 63.10 (cf. Zech. 12.10); (c) future expectations of God's endowment with his Spirit both of the coming Davidic figure in Isa. 11.1-2 and of the covenant community in Isa. 44.3; 59.21; Ezek. 39.29; Joel 3.1-2 (ET: 2.28, 29).

3. *The Septuagint*

In general, the LXX translators have a strong tendency to render *rûaḥ* by *pneuma*; the term *pneuma*, thus, covers all the following concepts: 'wind', 'breath', 'anthropological spirit', 'evil spirit' and the 'divine Spirit'.[37]

---

34. We may say that in the MT the activity or function of the divine Spirit receives more emphasis than the 'being' of the Spirit.

35. See Lampe (1977: 208, 219); Dunn (1980: 133) claims, 'Clearly then for these writers [Old Testament writers] "Spirit of God" is simply a way of speaking of God accomplishing his purpose in his world and through men; "Spirit of God" means God in effective relationship with (and within) his creation. To experience the Spirit of God is to experience God as Spirit'.

36. Prophetic speeches and miracles are often regarded as a sign to authenticate God's presence in his chosen leaders. In particular, see Num. 11.24-25; 1 Sam. 10.2-6; 10.9-11.

37. Cf. Schoemaker (1904: 36); Hill (1967: 217-18); Bieder (1967: 367-75).

Out of the 286 occurrences of *pneuma* in the Greek parallel texts to the MT, so, apart from the references to it in the Old Testament Apocrypha, there are approximately 59 referring to wind,[38] 44 to breath,[39] 66 to anthropological spirit,[40] 20 to evil spirit, 2 to supernatural spirits and 95 to the divine Spirit.[41] On the other hand, there are also other

38. There are 59 occurrences (2 additions and 20 omissions) found in the LXX. Additions: Ps. 148.8; Isa. 27.8; omissions: Gen. 3.8; Exod. (10.13, 19); (14.21); 2 Sam. (22.11); 1 Chron. (9.24); Job 6.26; (21.18); (28.25); 30.22; 37.21; (Ps. 1.4); (18.10, 42); (35.5); 55.8; (83.13); (104.3); (135.7); 147.18; Prov. (11.29); (25.14, 23); (27.16); (30.4); Eccl. (5.15); (11.4); Isa. (17.13); 32.2; (41.16), 29; (57.13); (59.19); (64.5); Jer. 2.24; (5.13); 10.13; (13.24); (14.6); (18.17); (22.22); (49.36a, b); 51.1; 52.23; Ezek. (5.10, 12); (12.14); [13.13: πνοή instead of *pneuma*]; (17.10, 21); (19.12); (37.9); 42.16, 17, 18, 19, 20; Dan. (2.35); (7.2); (8.8); (11.4); Hos. 8.7; (13.15); Zech. (2.1); (6.5), 8; *rûaḥ* in the bracketed verses is translated by ἄνεμος.

39. There are 44 occurrences (4 additions and 8 omissions; 2 cases [Num. 16.22; 27.16] seem to be transferred as supernatural spirits, see below) found in the LXX. Additions: 1 Kgs 17.17; Job 7.15; Ps. 119.131; Isa. 38.12; omissions: Gen. 7.22; Job 9.18; 15.30; 19.17; 26.13; Isa. 40.7; Jer. 51.17; Ezek. 1.21. The word נשמה is occasionally translated by *pneuma* (1 Kgs 17.17; cf. Job 34.14; Dan. 5.23; 10.17). There are also a few cases in which it is rendered by πνοή (Gen. 7.22; cf. Isa. 38.16; Prov. 1.23).

40. There are 66 occurrences (3 additions and 34 omissions). Additions: 2 Sam. 13.21; 2 Sam. 13.39; 1 Kgs 21.4; omissions: Gen. 26.35; Exod. 6.9; 35.21; Josh. 5.1; 1 Sam. 1.15; 1 Kgs 10.5; 2 Chron. 9.4; 21.16; Job 6.4; 7.11; 15.13; 21.4; Ps. 32.2; Prov. 11.13; 14.29; 15.13; 16.2; 16.18, 19, 32; 17.22, 27; 18.14; 25.28; 29.11, 23; Eccl. 7.8, 8; Isa. 38.16; 54.6; 57.15 [×2]; 66.2; Ezek. 13.3. We can see here that only about half of the passages of *rûaḥ* in this sense are translated by *pneuma*; the LXX translators more often translate *rûaḥ* with Greek words other than *pneuma*. Thus, they employ other terms or phrases to denote human disposition which was consistently expressed by the word *rûaḥ* in the MT: ψυχή (Gen. 41.8; Exod. 35.21), θυμός (Prov. 16.19,32; 17.27; 29.11; Eccl. 7.8, 9; Zech. 6.8; Ezek. 39.29), νοῦς (Isa. 40.13), ὀλιγόψυχος (Exod. 6.9; Isa. 54.6; 57.15; Prov. 14.29; 18.14), ἡσύχιος (Isa. 66.2), καρδία (Ezek. 13.3), ταπεινόφρων (Prov. 29.23), κακοφροσύνη (Prov. 16.18), φρόνησις (Josh. 5.1; Prov. 14.29), καὶ ἦσαν ἐρίζουσαι (Gen. 26.35), γυνή, ᾗ σκληρὰ ἡμέρα, ἐγὼ εἰμι (1 Sam. 1.15—Hanaah's spirit), καὶ ἐξ ἑαυτῆς ἐγένετο (1 Kgs 10.5—the queen of Sheba's spirit), ἀνὴρ φρόνιμος (Prov. 17.27) and so forth. Nevertheless, we should also note that on several occasions, the LXX translators retain *pneuma* to denote human emotion and thought (Num. 5.14; Deut. 2.30; Judg. 8.3). Furthermore, in three instances, they also add *pneuma* in an anthropological sense to the passages where there is no reference to *rûaḥ* in the MT (3 Kgs 20.4 [1 Kgs 21.4]—Ahab; 2 Kgs [2 Sam.] 13.21—Amnon; 13.39—David).

41. I have used the computer program, *Bible Windows 2.1* (1993), to establish the occurrences of *pneuma* in the LXX.

Greek terms employed with reference to the first three meanings. In the following subsections, I shall proceed by noting the additions and omissions of divine *pneuma* in the LXX in comparison with the MT.

3.1. *Divine Spirit*

3.1.1. *Evil Spirit.*[42] With respect to the references to an evil spirit, the LXX without any changes translates *rûaḥ* into *pneuma*. However, it may be questioned whether the LXX translators fully retain the theological concept of an evil spirit delineated in the Hebrew text as it stands.[43] On the one hand, it is rendered, like in the MT, by πνεῦμα κυρίου πονηρὸν (1 Sam. 16.15), πνεῦμα πονηρὸν παρὰ κυρίου (1 Sam. 16.14) and πνεῦμα θεοῦ πονηρὸν (1 Sam. 19.9). On the other hand, it is translated just by πνεῦμα πονηρὸν (1 Sam. 16.16, 23), which is not an exact translation of the original reference. Furthermore, in 1 Kgs 22.21, the LXX translates the (deceiving) spirit (הרוח) into just 'spirit' (πνεῦμα) without the article.[44]

When we reconsider their contexts, however, we cannot claim that the LXX denies or departs from the Hebrew conception of an 'evil spirit'. In particular, the translators also think of an evil spirit, not as an independent being, but as another agent under the direct control of God, as if it were one among many spirits from God.[45]

---

42. There are 20 occurrences referring to an evil spirit or the like in the LXX (cf. 21 in the MT; the LXX 1 Sam. 18.10 omits the reference).

43. See §4.1.1 in this chapter.

44. Cf. the LXX Num. 16.22 and 27.16: 'God of the breath/spirits of all flesh' in the MT is replaced by 'God of the spirits *and* of all flesh' in the LXX. Maybe the LXX translators think of supernatural spirits of God in the heavenly court. Cf. Schoemaker (1904: 37-38).

45. Schoemaker (1904: 37-38) has argued that a new concept of 'disembodied spirit' begins to be introduced in the LXX in attempting not to ascribe an 'evil spirit' to God; Hill (1967: 218-19) has inferred that there is a tendency for the 'disembodied spirit' to become separate from God (Ps. 50.11; Isa. 63.10-11), but he has also acknowledged that these tentative terms do not guarantee a new concept of spirit; Isaacs (1976: 14), reminding us of two Hebrew passages (1 Sam. 16; 1 Kgs 22.21-23), has, however, noticed, 'it would be extremely dangerous to postulate a separate hypostasis, based on foundations which may well be no more than poetic imagery. That the LXX introduces the idea of a separation between God and His spirit remains unproven'.

3.1.2. *The Spirit of the Lord/God.*[46] In almost all renderings in the LXX, the divine πνεῦμα retains the same sense as the divine *rûaḥ* in the MT ascribed to God himself or indicating his power, presence and activity, although there are some minor differences from the MT: the 'spirit of your holiness' (רוח קדשך) is changed to 'your holy spirit'(τὸ πνεῦμα τὸ ἅγιον σου) in Ps. 51.13 and Isa. 63.10; 'God of the spirits/breath of all flesh' (אלהי הרוחת לכל־בשר) to 'God of the spirits and all flesh' (θεὸς τῶν πνευμάτων καὶ πάσης σαρκός) in Num. 16.22 and 27.16 (cf. 1 Sam. 16.14; 1 Kgs 22.21-23). In a word, the divine *pneuma* in the LXX is consistently used for God's Spirit as presented in the MT in connection with the following features: (a) as divine agent, (b) as God's divine Spirit, (c) as charismatic power and/or guidance, (d) as the source of prophetic oracles and/or revelation, (e) as the source of other charismatic gifts like wisdom, craftsmanship and the interpretation of dreams, (f) as the source or power for God's people's religio-ethical life and (g) as promised for the future messianic appearance and the restoration of God's people.

As in the case of human dispositions, however, the LXX alters some references to the divine *pneuma* into other relevant Greek expressions: ἰδοὺ προήσομαι ὑμῖν ἐμῆς πνοῆς ῥῆσιν (Prov. 1.23); βοήθεια (Isa. 31.3); νοῦν κυρίου (Isa. 40.13); ἐξέχεα τὸν θυμόν μου (Ezek. 39.29); ὁ πνευματοφόρος (Hos. 9.7); θύμος μου (Zech. 6.8).

On the other hand, the LXX translators add πνεῦμα on three occasions: (1) in Num. 23.7, the phrase καὶ ἐγενήθη πνεῦμα θεοῦ ἐπ᾽ αὐτῷ is inserted, just before Balaam utters his prophecy; (2) in Zech. 1.6, when the word of the Lord came to the prophet Zechariah, the phrase 'by my [God's] Spirit', which was absent from the Hebrew text, is added in what follows: πλὴν τοὺς λόγους μου καὶ τὰ νόμιμά μου δέχεσθε, ὅσα ἐγὼ ἐντέλλομαι ἐν πνεύματί μου τοῖς δούλοις μου τοῖς προφήταις,... (cf. Zech. 7.12; Neh. 9.30); (3) in Isa. 11.2, the LXX describes six qualities of the future Davidic king in relation to God's Spirit (πνεῦμα σοφίας καὶ συνέσεως πνεῦμα βουλῆς καὶ ἰσχύος πνεῦμα γνώσεως καὶ εὐσεβείας; cf. the MT Isa. 11.2); yet adds in v. 3 one more reference to the Spirit, highlighting his faithful relationship to God: ἐμπλήσει αὐτὸν πνεῦμα φόβου θεοῦ (cf. *1 En.* 49.3; 62.2; *Pss. Sol.* 17.37; 18.7).

---

46. There are 95 occurrences (3 additions and 6 omissions) found in the LXX. Additions: Num. 23.7 (LXX); Isa. 11.3; Zech. 1.6; omissions: Prov. 1.23; Isa. 31.3; 40.13; Ezek. 39.29; Hos. 9.7; Zech. 6.8.

3.2. *Section Conclusion*

The Greek parallel texts to the MT have a strong tendency to translate *rûaḥ* by the Greek term *pneuma* with a wide range of references to wind, breath, anthropological spirit, evil spirit and the divine Spirit. The LXX translators, however, also use ἄνεμος or πνοή, not in a few cases, to denote 'wind' or 'breath', instead of employing *pneuma*. Likewise other appropriate Greek terms are often used in referring to human and divine dispositions. The LXX not only retains almost all characteristics found in the MT, but also enhances the close association between (1) the Spirit and prophetic inspiration,[47] and (2) the Spirit and the coming Davidic figure by inserting the term *pneuma* three times into the MT.

4. *The Old Testament Apocrypha*

The Old Testament Apocrypha[48] comprises the books not paralleled with the MT yet contained in the LXX.[49] Some books were originally written in the Hebrew language[50] and later translated into Greek. In the Old Testament Apocrypha, *pneuma* occurs 58 times.[51] These occurrences refer to wind,[52] breath,[53] anthropological spirit,[54] supernatural

47. Cf. Menzies (1991a: 54) who tends to overemphasize this Septuagintal feature in ignoring those passages which parallel the MT (esp. the Spirit as the source of miracles) found in the LXX. In addition, he does not mention the Septuagintal addition of *pneuma* in Isa. 11.3.

48. The major references that I have examined are: Charles (1913); Gilbert (1984: 283-324); Hill (1967: 220-23); Isaacs (1976: 147-52); Schoemaker (1904: 38-41); Scroggs (1967: 35-55); van Roon (1974: 207-39); J. Davis (1984: 9-26); Montague (1994: 91-110); Dunn (1980: 163-76); Menzies (1991a: 53-63).

49. The books are as follows: 1 Esdras; Tobit; Judith; (Additions to) Esther; Wisdom of Solomon; Sirach (Ecclesiasticus); Baruch; Epistle of Jeremiah; (Additions to) Daniel (Susanna, Bel and the Dragon, Prayer of Azariah and the Song of the Three Jews); Prayer of Manasseh; 1 Maccabees; 2 Maccabees; *3 Maccabees*; *4 Maccabees*. I omit the book of 2 Esdras (Ezra and Nehemiah) for it has been examined in the preceding sections

50. These are Sirach, Judith, Tobit, 1 Maccabees, 1 Esdras and Baruch.

51. See Hatch and Redpath (1954: II, 1151-53). All texts of the LXX cited are from Rahlfs 1979.

52. 11 occurrences are found in Sir. 39.28; 43.17; Wis. 5.11, 23; 11.20 [×2]; 13.2; 17.17 (18); Ep. Jer. 1.60 (61); Song 3 Childr. 3.50 (27), 65 (43). *Pneuma* simply denotes natural wind in Wis. 5.11; 17.17 (18); Let. Jer. 1.60 (61); Song of Thr. 1.27, 43. This is also employed in judgment context under God's control in Sir. 39.28; 43.17; Wis. 5.23; 11.20 [×2]. For the foolish, wind is regarded as one of

beings and God's Spirit in general. This is in accordance with its own literary context, and follows the use of *rûaḥ* employed in the MT. In the Wisdom of Solomon and Sirach, however, some developments of the concept of divine *pneuma* are discerned.

4.1. *Divine Spirit*

4.1.1. *Supernatural Beings*.[55] There are three references which denote supernatural being(s) in the Old Testament Apocrypha: one as a singular form referring to an evil spirit; the other two as a plural form referring to supernatural spirits (see also the LXX Num. 16.22; 27.16). Unlike in the MT, however, an evil spirit described in Tob. 6.8 is identified with a demon.[56] This is a very unusual expression when we recall

their gods (Wis. 13.2). Unlike the MT, *pneuma* as wind in the Old Testament Apocrypha is not used as a metonymy for the four directions, nor as a symbol of vanity which is often found in wisdom literature like Proverbs and Ecclesiastes.

53. 15 occurrences are found in Jdt. 10.13; Tob. 3.6; 2 Macc. 7.22, 23; 24.46; *3 Macc.* 6.24; *4 Macc.* 11.11; Sir. 38.23; Wis. 2.3; 5.11, 16; 16.14; Bar. 2.17; Ep. Jer. 1.24 (25); Add. Esth. 8.13 (16.12).

54. 15 occurrences are found in Jdt. 7.19; 14.6; Tob. 4.3; 1 Macc. 13.7; *4 Macc.* 7.14; Sir. 9.9; 34.13 [34.14]; Wis. 5.3; 7.23; Bar. 3.1; Song 3 Childr. 1.16, 64; Add. Esth. 5.1; 1 Esd. 2.1 (2), 5 (8). The use of anthropological spirit in the Old Testament Apocrypha is primarily found in the books originally composed in Hebrew. Several cases of this usage, however, are also found in the original Greek portions of the Apocrypha (contra Schoemaker [1904: 41]: 'This use of πνεῦμα is not found in any book of the Apocrypha which was composed in the Greek'; I have already found that in the LXX texts parallel to the MT, there are some additional instances of anthropological spirit, such as 3 Kgs 20.4 [1 Kgs 21.4], 2 Kgs [2 Sam.] 13.21 and 13.39), like *4 Macc.* 7.14; Wis. 5.3; 7.23 (cf. Wis. 2.3; 15.11; 16.14). As a human spirit, it is mainly employed in a singular form. But it occurs as a plural noun in one case (Add. Dan. [Song 3 Childr.] 3.86 [1.64]). In some cases this human spirit is seen to be emotionally threatened by certain circumstances or impressed by someone's persuasive speech (Jdt. 7.19; Tob. 4.3; 1 Macc. 13.7; cf. Jdt. 14.6). In particular it also refers to some emotional dispositions: 'wearied spirit' (πνεῦμα ἀκηδιῶν in Bar. 3.1), 'anguish of spirit' (στενοχωρίαν πνεύματος in Wis. 5.3; cf. 7.23) and 'humble spirit' (πνεύματι ταπεινώσεως in Song 3 Childr. 1.16). On four occasions (Sir. 9.9; Bar. 3.1; Song 3 Childr. 1.16, 64), πνεῦμα goes along with ψυχή (cf. Josephus, *Ant.* 1.34; 3.260; 11.240). This helps to confirm the correct interpretation of *pneuma*.

55. 3 occurrences are found in Tob. 6.8; Wis. 7.20; 2 Macc. 3.24.

56. Tob. 6.8: 'He replied, 'As for the fish's heart and liver, you must burn them to make a smoke in the presence of a man or woman afflicted by a demon or evil spirit (ἐνώπιον ἀνθρώπου ἢ γυναικός ᾧ ἀπάντημα δαιμονίου ἢ πνεύματος

the use of an evil spirit in the MT and in the other books of the LXX (cf. 1 Sam. 16.14, 15; 19.9).[57] Similarly, supernatural beings as spirits, not found in the MT, are introduced in a plural form as God's agents under his direct power (2 Macc. 3.24; Wis. 7.20).[58]

4.1.2. *The Spirit of the Lord/God*[59]

4.1.2.1. *God's Spirit in General.* The phrase 'Spirit of the Lord' (πνεῦμα κυρίου) is found only in Wis. 1.7: 'Because the spirit of the Lord has filled the world, and that which holds all things together knows what is said'. Along with a divine possessive pronoun, there are only three instances that denote God's Spirit or God's holy spirit: 'your spirit', 'your holy spirit' and 'your immortal spirit'.[60] God's Spirit relates to creation (Jdt. 16.14), sustaining people (Wis. 1.7; 12.1) and revelation (Wis. 9.17; see also Sir. 48.24). On some occasions, God's Spirit is probably the source of a miracle and/or bold speech; however, none of these three references (Sir. 48.12; Bel 1.36; Sus. 1.45) directly denotes God's Spirit, but rather implies the divine Spirit working through an angel of the Lord or men of God such as Elijah and Daniel

---

πονηροῦ), and every affliction will flee away and never remain with that person any longer"'

57. It is likely that there is a progressive development of the idea of an 'evil spirit' in the LXX, when compared with the MT: see Num. 16.22; 27.16; 1 Kgs 22.21. Cf. Josephus who equates an 'evil spirit' with δαιμόνια and does not associate it with (the Jewish) God (see *Ant.* 6.166, 168, 211, 214).

58. 2 Macc. 3.24: 'But when he [Heliodorus] arrived at the treasury with his bodyguard, then and there the Sovereign of spirits and of all authority caused so great a manifestation that all who had been so bold as to accompany him were astounded by the power of God, and became faint with terror'; Wis. 7.20: 'the natures of animals and the tempers of wild animals, the powers of spirits and the thoughts of human beings, the varieties of plants and the virtues of roots', see also 7.17 for God's sovereign power to control the structure of the world and the activity of the elements. This plural form of spirits referring to supernatural beings/angels is prominently developed in the DSS. See my excursus.

59. 14 occurrences are found in Jdt. 16.14; Sir. 39.6; 48.12, 24; Wis. 1.5, 6, 7; 7.7, 22; 9.17; 12.1; Sus. 1.45 (46), [62 (64): Dan. LXX Sus.]; Bel 1.36.

60. Jdt. 16.14: 'Let all your [God's] creatures serve you, for you spoke, and they were made. You sent forth your spirit, and it formed them; there is none that can resist your voice'; Wis. 9.17: 'Who has learned your counsel, unless you have given wisdom and sent your holy spirit form on high?'; 11.26–12.1: 'You spare all things, for they are yours, O Lord, you who love the living. For your immortal spirit is in all things'.

(see 2 Kgs 2.9, 15).⁶¹ With regard to God's Spirit in the Old Testament Apocrypha, it is, above all, its connection with wisdom that is more prominent than any other aspect, particularly in the wisdom literature like the Wisdom of Solomon and Sirach. There are by and large three features in connection with wisdom and God's Spirit: (1) identification between God's Spirit and wisdom, (2) the Spirit as the core/source of wisdom⁶² and (3) the Spirit/wisdom as the source of revelation and

61. Sir. 48.12: 'When Elijah was enveloped in the whirlwind, Elisha was filled with *his spirit*. He performed twice as many signs, and marvels with every utterances of his mouth'; Bel 1.36: 'Then the angel of the Lord took him [Habakkuk] by the crown of his head and carried him by his hair; with the speed of the wind [or by the power of *his spirit*: ἐν τῷ ῥοίζῳ τοῦ πνεύματος αὐτοῦ] he set him down in Babylon, right over the den'; Sus. 1.44-46: 'The Lord heard her [Susanna's] cry. Just as she was being led off to execution, God stirred up *the holy spirit of a young lad named Daniel* [ἐξήγειρεν ὁ θεὸς τὸ πνεῦμα τὸ ἅγιον παιδαρίου νεωτέρου ᾧ ὄνομα Δανιηλ, Dan. Theod. Sus.], and he shouted with a loud voice, 'I want no part in shedding this woman's blood!'''; but in Dan. LXX. Sus. 1.42, the translator attributes Daniel's wisdom to an angel who offered a 'spirit of understanding' (πνεῦμα συνέσεως). In other words, Theodotion alters the LXX so as to attribute Daniel's wisdom directly to the 'holy spirit'. Cf. Menzies (1991a: 55) who points out this fact, and then claims, 'the Spirit as the source of prophetic inspiration', due to the later revised version of Theodotion.

62. In the wisdom literature of the Old Testament Apocrypha, in particular in Sirach, wisdom is also inextricably associated with the Law and is sometimes attained through the study of the Law: 'Reflect on the statutes of the Lord, and meditate at all times on his commandments. It is he who will give insight to your mind, and your desire for wisdom will be granted' (6.37); 'Whoever fears the Lord will do this, and whoever holds to the law will obtain wisdom' (15.1); 'Whoever keeps the law controls his thoughts, and the fulfilment of the fear of the Lord is wisdom' (21.11). This close linkage between law and wisdom is found in *4 Macc.* as well: 'Reason I take to be the mind preferring with clear deliberation the life of wisdom. Wisdom I take to be the knowledge of things, divine and human, and of their causes. *This* [wisdom] I take to be the culture acquired under the Law, through which we learn with due reverence the things of God and for our worldly profit the things of man' (1.15-17). Additionally, along with this aspect, Ben Sira seems to link 'law and wisdom' to God's Spirit as the 'spirit of understanding' (πνεύματι συνέσεως) in 38.34b–39.8: 'How different the one who devotes himself to *the study of the law* of the Most High! He seeks out the *wisdom* of all the ancients, and is concerned with prophecies;... If the great Lord is willing, he will be filled with *the spirit of understanding*; he will pour forth words of *wisdom* of his own and give thanks to the Lord in prayer... He will show the *wisdom* of what he has learned, and will glory in the *law* of the Lord's covenant'. Cf. J. Davis (1984: 16-21) who persuasively argues not only for a 'complex of inter-relationships between wisdom,

preservation. These concepts are, however, interwoven. Furthermore, we can not exclude a religio-ethical aspect in God's Spirit as wisdom by which people are warned, corrected and freed from any wickedness (Wis. 1.5-6; 9.17; 11.26–12.2).[63]

4.1.2.2. *God's Spirit as Wisdom*

> For perverse thoughts separate people from God, and when his power is tested, it exposes the foolish; because wisdom will not enter a deceitful soul, or dwell in a body enslaved to sin. For a holy and disciplined spirit [ἅγιον πνεῦμα παιδείας] will flee from deceit, and will leave foolish thoughts behind, and will be ashamed at the approach of unrighteousness. For wisdom is a kindly spirit [φιλάνθρωπον γὰρ πνεῦμα σοφία], but will not free blasphemers from the guilt of their words; because God is witness of their inmost feelings, and a true observer of their hearts, and a hearer of their tongues (Wis. 1.3-6).
>
> Therefore I prayed, and understanding was given me; I called on God, and the spirit of wisdom came to me [καὶ ἦλθέν μοι πνεῦμα σοφίας] (Wis. 7.7).

Based on the above descriptions, we may infer that wisdom is more than one of the gifts of God's Spirit. For the author of the Wisdom of Solomon, wisdom is the gift of God, nothing but God's Spirit. Accordingly, it is not surprising that when the author prayed to God, God provided him with the Spirit of wisdom. We also need to pay attention to the attributive adjectives of God's Spirit; 'holy', 'disciplined' and 'kindly' Spirit could possibly be read as God's dispositions (cf. 7.22-

law and spirit', but also for the view that there are three levels or stages of sapiential acquisition in Sir. 38.24–39.11, and then considers the 'spirit of understanding' as wisdom of the highest level which comes from God's Spirit, whereas the wisdom achieved by studying the law is the second level (20-22); see also Montague (1994: 99-100).

63. In regard to the function of Spirit/wisdom in the Wisdom of Solomon, Menzies (1991a), following J.S. Vos's argument in *Traditionsgeschichtliche Untersuchungen zur paulinischen Pneumatologie*, asserts that the Spirit is not only the substantial source of moral and religious life, but also the necessary element of salvation, 'Thus the author of Wisdom views the gift of the Spirit as the essential source of moral and religious life. As such, it is necessary to possess the gift of the Spirit in order to attain salvation' (62; see also 63). However, the word σῴζω in Wis. 9.18 is better considered to connote 'physical preservation', especially when we have the immediate context in mind: 'When the earth was flooded because of him, wisdom again saved it, steering the righteous man by a paltry piece of wood' (10.4; see also the use of σῴζω in 14.4-5; 16.7).

23).[64] Another observation is that the author is granted the Spirit of wisdom by God in response to his prayer (7.7; cf. 8.20-21; 9.4).

4.1.2.3. *God's Spirit as the Core/Source of Wisdom*

> I learned both what is secret and what is manifest, for wisdom, the fashioner of all things, taught me. There is in her a spirit [ἐστίν γὰρ ἐν αὐτῇ πνεῦμα] that is intelligent, holy, unique, manifold, subtle, mobile, clear, unpolluted, distinct, invulnerable, loving the good, keen, irresistible, beneficent, humane, steadfast, sure, free from anxiety, all-powerful, overseeing all, and penetrating through all spirits that are intelligent, pure, and altogether subtle (Wis. 7.21-23).
>
> If the great Lord is willing, he will be filled with the spirit of understanding [πνεύματι συνέσεως]; he will pour forth words of wisdom [ῥήματα σοφίας] of his own and give thanks to the Lord in prayer. The Lord will direct his counsel and knowledge, as he meditates on his mysteries (Sir. 39.6-7).

The author of the Wisdom of Solomon not only identifies the Spirit of God with the wisdom of God, but also envisages God's Spirit as the core/source of wisdom. In Sirach, if a person is full of the Spirit of understanding (cf. Dan. LXX Sus. 1.45), he or she can not but speak words of wisdom and be grateful to the Lord in their prayer. It is noted that only the sovereign God is the giver of his Spirit to a person, while one's prayer is essential to obtain his Spirit of wisdom/understanding.

4.1.2.4. *God's Spirit/Wisdom as the Source of Revelation and Preservation*

> With you is wisdom, she who knows your works and was present when you made the world; she understands what is pleasing in your sight and what is right according to your commandments. Send her forth from the holy heavens, and from the throne of your glory send her (Wis. 9.9-10a)... For who can learn the counsel of God? Or who can discern what the Lord wills? (9.13)... Who has learned your counsel, unless you have given wisdom and sent your holy spirit from on high? And thus the paths of those on earth were set right, and people were taught what pleases you, and were saved by wisdom (9.17-18).

Without wisdom or God's holy Spirit, nobody can learn God's counsel (βουλήν σου) and thus please him. Accordingly, the author of the Wisdom of Solomon, like the psalmist of 1QH (see excursus), views

---

64. Montague (1994: 104) claims, 'Clearly the holy spirit of wisdom or discipline is related to the ethical life, without which it cannot dwell in man'.

God's Spirit/wisdom as the source of his revelation and preservation, maintaining their religio-ethical life.[65] This wisdom, however, is not a prerequisite gift before one is saved by God. In the literary context, the phrase 'and [people] were saved by wisdom' (καὶ τῇ σοφίᾳ ἐσώθησαν) does not connote the salvific feature of wisdom/Spirit of God. Rather, the term σώζω refers to physical preservation throughout the text (10.4; 14.4-5; 16.7, 11; 18.5).[66] As I have mentioned earlier, this acquisition of wisdom is intimately linked to the study of the law as well (Sir. 6.37; 15.1; 21.11; *4 Macc.* 1.15-17). Moreover, both wisdom and law are co-related to God's Spirit: therefore, he or she who attains the gift or gifts will be remembered through all generations due to their wisdom and knowledge (Sir. 38.34–39.11). In contrast to wisdom, however, law itself, in the wisdom literature, is by no means identified with God's Spirit; in almost all of the cases, the law or the study of the law is portrayed as the means of obtaining wisdom. This frequently parallels references to God's Spirit in other contexts. Thus, it is understandable why J. Davis (1984: 16-21) attempts to argue for three levels of sapiential achievement based on Sir. 38.25-34 (day-wisdom in life), Sir. 39.1-5 (law-wisdom by study) and Sir. 39.6 (God's Spirit-wisdom according to God's will?).[67] Or I might put the relationship between law, wisdom and God's Spirit as follows.[68]

---

65. For the revelatory function, Scroggs (1967: 48) claims, 'Jewish wisdom theology in the late- and post-Old Testament period moved towards a position which made wisdom a revelatory gift from God rather than an empirically obtainable knowledge... The establishment of a close relation between wisdom and the spirit as revelatory agent was almost inevitable'.

66. Scroggs (1967: 50) supports this view, 'If, as seems to me probable, chapter x is a continuation of chapter ix, then wisdom guides the history of Israel and teaches the Israelites what is God's will. In that case the primary meaning of ἐσώθησαν in ix. 18 must be the O.T. concept of rescue from danger and distress'.

67. Cf. H. Stadelmann's division of 'der reguläre Schriftgelehrte' (Sir. 38.34c–39.5) and 'der inspirierte Schriftgelehrte' (Sir. 39.6-8), quoted in Menzies (1991a: 69 n. 4).

68. Cf. Scroggs (1967: 50) attempts to distinguish to some extent between wisdom and spirit: 'The parallelism of the verse would suggest an identity of the terms [wisdom and spirit]. It is better, however, to allow for the distinction that is probably implied in i. 4-7 and vii. 22f. Σοφία is more the content of revelation, while πνεῦμα is the means by which this content is revealed'.

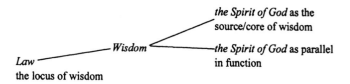

Wisdom, as found in the wisdom literature, especially in Sir. 24; Wis. 6.12–11.1; Bar. 3.9–4.4 (cf. Job 28; Prov. 8.22-31; *1 En.* 42), should be understood in the light of Jewish monotheistic speculation. The language of wisdom personification does not support the argument that wisdom is an independent deity apart from God, in spite of the fact that the authors were probably influenced by other ancient Near Eastern concepts or Stoicism. Dunn persuasively disputes the view of wisdom hypostasis and contends rigorously,

> It would appear then as although the Jewish wisdom writers do indeed take up some of the more widespread language of Near Eastern religious speculation, and do so in conscious awareness of its use elsewhere; but they do not draw the same conclusions for worship and practice as the polytheistic religions do. On the contrary they adapt this wider speculation to their own faith and make it serve to commend their own faith; to Wisdom understood (and worshipped) as a divine being (one of Isis' many names), they pose the alternative of Wisdom identified as the law given to Israel by (the one) God (1980: 171; emphasis original).[69]

4.2. Section Conclusion

The use of *pneuma* in the Old Testament Apocrypha corresponds almost exactly to that employed in the other books of the LXX;[70] it denotes

---

69. Thus Dunn concludes, 'Wisdom, like the name, the glory, the Spirit of Yahweh, was a way of asserting God's nearness, his involvement with his world, his concern for his people. All these words provided expressions of God's *immanence*, his active concern in creation, revelation and redemption, while at the same time protecting his holy transcendence and wholly otherness' (1980: 176; emphasis original).

70. Aside from God's Spirit, the frequency of *pneuma* referring to an evil spirit in the Apocrypha decreases. However, the one reference found in Tob. 6.8, which is identified with a demon, is an unusual expression when compared with the phrases, such as πνεῦμα κυρίου πονηρὸν, πνεῦμα πονηρόν παρὰ κυρίου and πνεῦμα θεοῦ πονηρὸν in the (other) books of the Septuagint; in regard to an anthropological spirit, most of the references (12) are found in the books originally composed in Hebrew, while three cases, found in Wis. 5.3; 7.23; *4 Macc.* 7.14 written in Greek, are not to be ignored. Contra Schoemaker (1904: 41); cf. Hill (1967), who, based on

'wind', 'breath', 'anthropological spirit', 'supernatural beings' and 'God's Spirit'. As seen in the following Table, I have compared the frequency of each category in the Old Testament Apocrypha with the other literature in the LXX and the MT.

Table 1. *Comparative Reference to Rûaḥ/Pneuma in the LXX and the MT*

Reference	Wind	Breath	Human Spirit	Supernatural Being(s)	God's Spirit	Total
the Old Testament Apocrypha	11	15	15	evil spirit 1 spirits 2 evil spirit 20	14	58
the other in the LXX	59	44	66	spirits 2	95	286
the MT	125	48	97	evil spirit 21	98	389

When *pneuma* refers to God's Spirit, it is recognized that God's Spirit is employed in creation or in sustaining contexts as seen in the MT. Similarly, God's Spirit, in a few cases, seems to be the source of a miracle or bold speech, particularly in the contexts of stories about figures or events in the MT. In contrast, God's Spirit as wisdom is a prominent feature in wisdom literature like the Wisdom of Solomon and Sirach. Accordingly, God's Spirit is, on some occasions, almost identical with wisdom in its function or is sometimes the source/core of wisdom. Accordingly, no one can learn God's counsel (ἡ βουλὴ τοῦ θεοῦ) and please him without God's Spirit/wisdom. In other words, the function of revelation and preservation is provided by the Spirit of God or wisdom for his people who pray earnestly or study the law diligently. It goes without saying that the one who receives the spiritual gift of wisdom as God's Spirit is also able to maintain a religio-ethical life more faithfully than before.

In sum, the use of *pneuma* in the Old Testament Apocrypha is, in general, the same as that found in the other books of the Septuagint, along with one unusual aspect: *pneuma* referring to an 'evil spirit' is identified with a demon in Tob. 6.8. In the wisdom literature, God's Spirit is almost always identical with 'wisdom' or as the source/core of

Schoemaker's argument, says 'πνεῦμα as "physical sense", denoting the seat of affections and emotion is almost non-existent in this period' (223). However, Hill did not even mention the three references described above, whereas Schoemaker only dealt with *4 Macc.* and put it in the category of God's spirit; cf. Isaacs (1976: 151), who views Wis. 5.3; 15.16; *4 Macc.* 7.14 as the spirit of man.

wisdom,[71] providing revelation and preservation, along with a religio-ethical life. Nevertheless, this development of the 'divine wisdom' concept, which is in part influenced by other ancient Near Eastern polytheistic notions, does not destroy belief in the Jewish monotheistic God.

5. God's Spirit and Other Observations about the Jewish Bible

In this section, I shall provide some other pertinent observations about God's Spirit in the Jewish Bible in order to add germane points of contact with understanding the Holy Spirit in Luke–Acts.[72] They are concerned with the following two questions: (1) which persons/characters in the Jewish Bible receive or engage with God's Spirit? and (2) which qualifying expressions are used to refer to possession by God's Spirit? I shall now answer both questions along with their resulting implications by showing the following four tables in order.

Table 2. *God's Spirit and its Inspired Characters in the Jewish Bible*[73]

Character	Text	Character	Text
Joseph	Gen. 41.38	Bezalel (cf. Oholiab)	Exod. 31.3; 35.31
Moses	Num. 11.17	Eldad and Medad	Num. 11.26
Balaam	Num. 24.2; LXX Num. 23.7	Joshua	Num. 27.18; Deut. 34.9
Othniel	Judg. 3.10	Gideon	Judg. 6.34
Jephthah	Judg. 11.29	Samson	Judg. 13.25; 14.6, 19; 15.14
Saul	1 Sam. 10.6, 10; 11.6; 19.23	David	1 Sam. 16.13; 2 Sam. 23.2
Elijah	1 Kgs 18.12; 2 Kgs 2.16; Sir. 48.12	Elisha	2 Kgs 2.15; cf. Sir. 48.12

71. As indicated, intimate relationships between God's Spirit and wisdom can also be discerned in the MT: Joseph (Gen. 41.38) and Daniel (Dan. 5.11, 14); Joshua who is filled with the spirit of wisdom (Deut. 34.9; cf. πνεύματος συνέσεως in the LXX); Bezalel and other skilful persons who are endowed with the spirit of wisdom (Exod. 28.3; cf. Exod. 31.3; 35.31); a descendent of David, Jesse's son who shall be endowed with the spirit of wisdom and understanding as the spirit of the Lord (Isa. 11.1-3); Prov. 1.23: 'Behold, I [wisdom] will pour out my spirit on you; I will make my words known to you'.

72. See also Appendix I in which I have offered the authors' presentation of God's Spirit in the Jewish Bible in terms of Rimmon-Kenan's characterizaion model. For Rimmon-Kenan's model, see Chapter 4.

73. Cf. Appendix III.

Character	Text	Character	Text
Isaiah	Isa. 61.1; Sir. 48.12	Ezekiel	Ezek. 2.2; 3.12, 14, 24; 8.3; 11.1, 5, 24; 37.1; 43.5
Micah	Mic. 3.8	Daniel	Dan. 4.5, 6, 15; 5.11, 14; Sus. 1.45; Bel 3.16
Amasai	1 Chron. 12.19	Azariah	2 Chron. 15.1
Jahaziel	2 Chron. 20.14	Zechariah	2 Chron. 24.20
Solomon	LXX Wis. 7.7	All the skilful persons	Exod. 28.3
the seventy elders	Num. 11.25	The messengers of Saul	1 Sam. 19.20
a shoot of Jesse as the coming Davidic Messiah (future)	Isa. 11.2; cf. 42.1 ('servant')	The restoring people of Israel (future)	Isa. 32.15; 44.33; 59.21; Ezek. 36.27; 37.14; 39.29; Joel 3.1-2; Zech. 12.10
psalmist (present/ future)	Pss. 51.13; 139.7; 143.10	God's prophets (past)	Neh. 9.30; cf. 9.20; Isa. 63.11; Hag. 2.5

According to Table 2, we can perceive that some Old Testament characters who are inspired by God's Spirit play an important role as the 'men of God',[74] in spite of different narrative-historical contexts. In other words, they are portrayed as obeying or accomplishing God's will or plan through being empowered, inspired and guided by God's Spirit. Thus, those who oppose such Spirit-inspired characters are regarded as opposing God himself (e.g. Num. 12; 16; 1 Sam. 17. 32-54; 1 Kgs 18.16-46).

It is interesting to note that Saul is the only character who is not only endowed with God's Spirit (1 Sam. 10.6, 10; 11.6), but also possessed by an evil spirit (1 Sam. 16.14b, 15, 16, 23a; 18.10; 19.9).[75] Most interesting is that Saul is later once more presented as being possessed by God's Spirit (1 Sam. 19.23). However, if this is considered in its

74. It is noted that there is no female Spirit-endowed character depicted in the Jewish Bible (cf. Deborah in Judg. 4.4–5.31).

75. Other people who are inspired by an evil spirit or the like are found as follows: Abimelech and the lords of Shechem (Judg. 9.23); Ahab (1 Kgs 22.21// 2 Chron. 18.20); Ahab's prophets (1 Kgs 22.22, 23/2 Chron. 18.21, 22); king Sennacherib of Assyria (2 Kgs 19.7//Isa. 37.7); the princes of Zoan and Memphis, i.e. Egypt (Isa. 19.14); the disobedient people of Israel (Isa. 29.10; Hos. 4.12; 5.4)

own context, the effect resulting from his (and his messengers') possession by God's Spirit is somewhat differently understood from the previous effect (compare 1 Sam. 10.10-13 with 19.23-24): the former endowment and prophecy are positively described as a sign indicating Saul is God's man, whereas the latter are negatively depicted as preventing Saul (and his messengers) from killing David.[76] In this sense, the phenomenon of prophecy itself does not guarantee that it always accompanies a positive effect in spite of being caused by God's Spirit. This view is supported by the reference to the same phenomenon of prophecy attributed to an evil spirit from God (1 Sam. 18.10).[77]

In the light of the above, the Old Testament named and unnamed figures (possibly including Saul and his messengers in 1 Sam. 19) who are endowed with God's Spirit are delineated as the human agents of God and are represented as reliable characters, fulfilling his purpose/will. And the Jewish Bible looks forward to a 'man of God' who will be the Davidic Messiah (Isa. 11.2) and to God's restored people (Isa. 32.15; 44.33; 59.21; Ezek. 36.27; 37.14; 39.29; Joel 3.1-2; Zech. 12.10) in the future, both of whom will be sanctioned by God's own Spirit.

Table 3. *God's Spirit and its Expressions in the Jewish Bible*

Expressions	Text
the Spirit of God [רוח אלהים; πνεῦμα θεοῦ] (13 times)	Gen. 1.2; 41.38; Exod. 31.3; 35.31; Num. 24.2; 1 Sam. 10.10; 11.6; 19.20, 23; Ezek. 11.24; Job 33.4; 1 Chron. 15.1; 24.20; cf. 1 Sam. 16.15, 16, 23; 18.10
the Spirit of the Lord [רוח-יהוה; πνεῦμα κυρίου] (24 + 1 [Old Testament Apocrypha])	Judg. 3.10; 6.34; 11.29; 13.25; 14.6, 19; 15.14; 1 Sam. 10.6; 16.13, 14a; 2 Sam. 23.2; 1 Kgs 18.12; 22.24; 2 Kgs 2.16; Isa. 11.2; 40.13; 61.1; 63.14; Ezek. 11.5; 37.1; Mic. 2.7; 3.8; 1 Chron. 18.23; 20.14; Wis. 1.7

76. Both Klein (1983: 188) and Brueggemman (1990: 145) interpret Saul's prophecy in 1 Sam. 19 negatively.

77. NRSV translates 1 Sam. 18.10a as follows: 'The next day an evil spirit from God rushed upon Saul, and he *raved* within his house'. But the MT employs the same verb נבא in Hithpael form as seen in 1 Sam. 10.6, 10; 19.20, 23 (see also Ahab's false prophets' prophecy in 1 Kgs 22. 10, 12). The verb צלח (to rush on) used in this verse is also employed as referring to God's Spirit reception, see Table 4 in this chapter.

Expressions	Text
My (God's) Spirit [רוחי; τὸ πνεῦμα μου] (14)	Gen. 6.3; Isa. 30.1; 42.1; 44.3; 59.21; Ezek. 36.27; 37.14; 39.29; Joel 3.1, 2; Hag. 2.5; Zech. 4.6; 6.8; Prov. 1.23
His (God's) Spirit [רוחו; τὸ πνεῦμα αὐτοῦ] (5 + 1)	Num. 11.29; Isa. 34.16; 48.16; Zech. 7.12; Ps. 106.33; Bel 1.36
Your (God's) Spirit [רוחך; τὸ πνεῦμα σου] (2 + 1)	Ps. 139.7; Neh. 9.30; Jdt. 16.14
His (God's) holy Spirit [רוח קדשו; τὸ πνεῦμα τὸ ἅγιον αὐτοῦ] (2)	Isa. 63.10, 11
Your (God's) holy Spirit [רוח קדשך; τὸ πνεῦμα τὸ ἅγιον σου] (1 + 1)	Ps. 51.13; Wis. 9.17
Your (God's) good Spirit [רוחך טובה; τὸ πνεῦμα σου τὸ ἀγαθον] (2)	Ps. 143.10; Neh. 9.20
Your (God's) immortal Spirit [τὸ ἄφθαρτόν σου πνεῦμα] (1)	Wis. 12.1
a Spirit of the holy gods/God [רוח-אלהין קדישין; πνεῦμα θεοῦ ἅγιον] (4)	Dan. 4.5, 6, 15; 5.11 (LXX 4.8, 9, 18)
a Spirit of gods/God [רוח אלהין; πνεῦμα θεοῦ] (1)	Dan. 5.14 (LXX 5.11)
the holy Spirit [τὸ πνεῦμα τὸ ἅγιον] (1)	Sus. 1.45
a holy and disciplined Spirit [ἅγιον πνεῦμα παιδείας] (1)	Wis. 1.5
the Spirit of wisdom [רוח חכמה; πνεῦμα σοφίας] (2 + 1)	Exod. 28.3; Deut. 34.9 (cf. LXX); Wis. 7.7
the Spirit of wisdom, understanding, counsel, might, knowledge, and the fear of the Lord (1 + 1)	Isa. 11.2;[78] Sir. 39.6;[79] cf. Dan. 5.14;[80] Wis. 7.22-23[81]

78. Isa. 11.2: רוח חכמה ובינה רוח עצה וגבורה רוח דעת ויראת יהוה; πνεῦμα σοφίας καὶ συνέσεως πνεῦμα βουλῆς καὶ ἰσχύος πνεῦμα γνώσεως καὶ εὐσεβείας; the LXX Isa. 11.3: πνεῦμα φόβου θεοῦ.

79. Sir. 39.6: 'If the great Lord is willing, he [the psalmist] will be filled with the spirit of understanding [πνεύματι συνέσεως]; he will pour forth words of wisdom of his own and give thanks to the Lord in prayer'.

80. Dan. 5.14: 'I [Belshazzar] have heard of you [Daniel] that a spirit of the gods is in you, and that enlightenment, understanding, and excellent wisdom are found in you'.

81. Wis. 7.22-23: 'There is in her [wisdom] a spirit that is intelligent, holy,

Expressions	Text
a Spirit of justice [רוּחַ מִשְׁפָּט; πνεῦμα κρίσεως] (1)	Isa. 28.6
a Spirit of compassion and supplication [רוּחַ חֵן וְתַחֲנוּנִים; πνεῦμα χάριτος καὶ οἰκτιρμοῦ] (1)	Zech. 12.10
a kindly Spirit [φιλάνθρωπον πνεῦμα] (1)	Wis. 1.6

In a few cases, God's Spirit is defined by qualifying adjectives (cf. Wis. 7.22-23): holy (6 times: Isa. 63.10, 11; Ps. 51.13; Wis. 1.5; 9.17; Sus. 1.45),[82] good (twice), immortal, disciplined and kindly. On some occasions, the Spirit is explained by qualifying nouns: wisdom; understanding; counsel; might; knowledge; the fear of the Lord/fidelity; justice; compassion/grace; supplication/pity. But in most cases, Table 3 shows clearly that the divine Spirit in the Jewish Bible is presented as God's own Spirit (68 times out of 80 cases) through possessive pronouns and/ or adjectives. Hence, the Spirit represents God's power, activity and presence in each related context.

Table 4. *Spirit Possession and its Related Verbs in the MT*

Spirit-Reception Verbs	Text
צלח [Qal: to fall/be powerful] (7 times)	Judg. 14.6, 19; 15.14; 1 Sam. 10.6, 10; 11.6; 16.13
מלא [Qal: to be full of] (6)	Deut. 34.9; Exod. 28.3; 31.3; 35.31; Mic. 3.8
נתן [Qal: to give/offer] (4)	Num. 11.29; Neh. 9.20; Isa. 42.1; Ezek. 37.14
שפך [Qal: to pour out] (4)	Joel 3.1, 2 (ET: 2.28, 29); Zech. 12.10; Ezek. 39.29
לבש [Qal: to clothe] (3)	Judg. 6.34; 1 Chron. 12.19 (ET: 12.18); 2 Chron. 24.20
נוח [Qal: to rest] (3)	Num. 11.25b, 26; Isa. 11.2
בוא [Qal: to go in] (2)	Ezek. 2.2a; 3.24
ערה [Niphal: to be poured out] (1)	Isa. 32.15

unique, manifold, subtle, mobile, clear, unpolluted, distinct, invulnerable, loving the good, keen, irresistible, beneficent, humane, steadfast, sure, free from anxiety, all-powerful, overseeing all, and penetrating through all spirits that are intelligent, pure, and altogether subtle'.

82. Cf. Dan. 4.5, 6, 15; 5.11. It is noted here that the LXX Daniel changed the original phrase (narrated by the pagan king Nebuchadnezzar) of the MT by replacing plural אֱלָהִין (see also 2.47; 4.31; cf. Gen. 31.48) with singular θεοῦ. This implies that the translator of the LXX Daniel attempts to alter a 'Spirit of the holy gods' into the Jewish monotheistic God's Spirit. Cf. Goldingay (1989: 80, 87).

Spirit-Reception Verbs	Text
שִׂים [Qal: to put] (1)	Num. 11.17
יָצַק [Qal: to pour out] (1)	Isa. 44.3
נָפַל [Qal: to fall upon] (1)	Ezek. 11.5
עַל הָיָה [to remain on] (11)	Num. 24.2; Judg. 3.10; 11.25a, 29; 1 Sam. 19.20, 23; 2 Kgs 2.15; Isa. 59.21; 61.1; 2 Chron. 15.1
בְ הָיָה [to remain in] (4)	Gen. 41.38; Num. 27.18; 2 Kgs 2.9; Dan. 4.5

Table 5. *Spirit Possession and its Related Verbs in the LXX*[83]

Spirit-Reception Verbs	Text
γίνομαι [to come upon] (9 times)	Num. 23.7 (LXX addition; ET: 23.6); 24.2; Judg. 3.10; 11.29; 1 Sam. 19.20, 23; 2 Kgs 2.9; 2 Chron. 15.1; 20.14
(ἐμ/ἐν)πίμπλημι [to fill/be filled with] (8)	Deut. 34.9; Exod. 28.3; 31.3; 35.31; LXX Isa. 11.3; Mic. 3.8; Sir. 39.6; 48.12
(ἐφ)ἅλλομαι [to rush on] (7)	Judg. 14.6, 19; 15.14; 1 Sam. 10.6, 10; 11.6; 16.13
δίδωμι [to put/give] (4)	Num. 11.29; Neh. 9.20; Isa. 42.1; Ezek. 37.14
ἐπαναπαύω [to rest on] (4)	Num. 11.25b, 26; 2 Kgs 2.15; Isa. 11.2
ἐνδύω [to clothe/take possession of] (3)	Judg. 6.34; 1 Chron. 12.19; 2 Chron. 24.20
(ἐπ)ἔρχομαι [to enter into] (3)	Isa. 32.15; Ezek. 2.2a; 3.24
ἐπιτίθημι [to put] (3)	Num. 11.17, 25a; Isa. 44.3
ἐκχέω [to pour out] (3)	Joel 3.1, 2; Zech. 12.10
ἔχω [to have] (3)	Gen. 41.38; Num. 27.18; Dan. 4.8 (MT: 4.5)
(ἐπὶ) πίπτω [to fall upon] (1)	Ezek. 11.5
(εἰμί) ἐπί [to be upon] (2)	Isa. 59.21; 61.1
(εἰμί) ἐν [to be in/on] (5)	Dan. 4.8, 9, 18; 5.11, 14

It can be seen that the authors of the MT and the LXX use 'Spirit-reception' verbs in a metaphorical way.[84] And the authors of the LXX

83. Cf. Atkinson's table (1995: 130-31); Stronstad (1984: 18). See also my Appendix I.

84. Some verbs (צלח; לבש; נוח; בוא; נפל; γίνομαι; [ἐφ]ἅλλομαι; ἐπαναπαύω; ἐνδύω; [ἐπ]ἔρχομαι; [ἐπι]πίπτω) are used in reference to the Spirit's action, whereas others to the Spirit acted upon by God (מלא; נתן; שפך; ערה; שים; יצק; [ἐμ/ἐν]πιμπλημι; δίδωμι; ἐπιτίθημι; ἐκχέω).

consistently translate five Hebrew verbs into equivalent Greek verbs respectively, i.e. צלח into (ἐφ)άλλομαι; מלא into (ἐμ/ἐν)πίμπλημι; לבש into ἐνδύω; שפך into ἐκχέω; נפל into (ἐπι)πίπτω; at other times they do not do so.

The most discernible effects due to the Spirit-reception (which do not always occur promptly) are the following four phenomena: (1) prophecy (Num. 11.25, 26; 1 Sam. 10.6, 10; cf. 19.20, 23) and/or propheticrevelatory oracles (Num. 24.2; 1 Chron. 12.19; 2 Chron. 15.1; 20.14; 24.20; Sus. 1.45; cf. Joel 3.1-2), (2) miraculous/extraordinary powers (Judg. 14.6, 19; 15.14; 2 Kgs 2.9-16; Isa. 61.1-3; Mic. 3.8; Sir. 48.12), (3) esoteric wisdom (Gen. 41.38; Exod. 28.3; 31.3; 35.31; Dan. 4.5, 6, 15; 5.11, 14; Sir. 39.6; Wis. 7.7, 22-23; 9.17) and (4) religio-ethical sustaining power (Isa. 11.2-5; 28.6; 32.15; 42.1; Ezek. 36.27; Zech. 12.10; Pss. 51.13; 139.7; 143.10; Wis. 1.5). As seen earlier, Spirit-reception, on a few occasions, is described in association with laying on of hands (Deut. 34.9; cf. Num. 27.18) and (a rite of) anointing (1 Sam. 16.13; 10.1-13; Isa. 61.1-2; cf. Isa. 45.1f.); yet it mostly occurs without those in the Jewish Bible.

6. Conclusion

In this chapter, I have explored the use of *rûaḥ* and *pneuma* in the MT and the LXX as the literary repertoire for *pneuma* in Luke–Acts. I have seen that the references to *rûaḥ* and *pneuma* are used as referring to (1) wind, (2) breath, (3) anthropological spirit, (4) an evil spirit or supernatural beings/spirits and (5) God's Spirit. It should be noted that an 'evil spirit' in the MT is presented as another divine Spirit *from* the Lord/God, functioning as his emissary controlled and delegated by Yahweh. On the other hand, if we do not count the MT parallel references to it in the Greek translation parts in the LXX, there is only one case found in the other parts of the LXX mentioning an 'evil spirit', which is then immediately identified with a demon. Also, unlike the MT, the LXX begins to introduce supernatural beings/spirits (as angels?) by employing a plural form of *pneuma* (LXX Num. 16.22; 27.16; Wis. 7.20; 2 Macc. 3.24).

With respect to the significance of the divine Spirit in the MT and the LXX, three factors can be summarized. (1) The Spirit is, from the beginning to the end, portrayed as Yahweh's own Spirit who thus reveals God's will/purpose or represents his power, activity and presence through his human agents. (2) God gives his Spirit to *particular charismatic leaders* (who are thus considered reliable and responsible) in relation to his counsel for the people of Israel. In relation to the second point, the Spirit is highlighted as *engendering prophecy or revelatory speeches, miracles, wisdom, craftsmanship and the interpretation of visions-dreams.* In addition, God's Spirit is depicted as *the source or sustaining power for the Israelites' religio-ethical life.* Finally (3) God's Spirit is promised in *the future in relation both to the coming Davidic figure* (individual; cf. *Pss. Sol.* 17.32; 18.7) and to the restored people of God (community).

These observations about God's Spirit in this chapter will serve as points of contact for my reading of the Holy Spirit in Luke–Acts. Particularly in Chapter 4 (and partly Chapter 5), we will see how far the portrait and roles of the Lukan Holy Spirit are presented in a manner similar to that of God's Spirit in the Jewish Bible.

EXCURSUS

THE USAGE OF *RÛAḤ* IN THE QUMRAN LITERATURE WITH SPECIAL REFERENCE TO 1QS, 1QM, CD AND 1QH

This excursus is intended to scrutinize the occurrences of *rûaḥ* and to explore its possible meanings and functions in 1QS, 1QM, CD and 1QH, which give us the sectarians' general[1] thoughts on *rûaḥ*.[2] To facilitate this examination, I shall classify the meanings of *rûaḥ* in five categories as I have done in relation to the Jewish Bible, namely wind, breath, anthropological spirit, supernatural spirits and God's Spirit. In this way, I shall compare the roles of *rûaḥ* in the Qumran literature[3] with those in the Jewish Bible, in order to see how the use of *rûaḥ* is developed in the DSS, while noting the roles of the 'Spirit of holiness'.

1. *Wind*[4]

1.1. *Wind*

The references to natural wind seem to be found only in CD 8.13; 19.25; 1QH 1.10; 6.23; 7.5, 23, but half of them seem to be employed metaphorically. In CD 8.13, the context concerns the punishment of disloyal sectarians who would rather listen to a 'man who raises the wind and preaches lies' (שוקל רוח ומטיף כזב; cf. הולך רוח ושקל סופות in CD 19.25; Mic. 2.11). The phrase רוח צוצײם ('whirlwind' by Vermes; a 'wind of confusion' by Dupont-Sommer) is used in stormy sea contexts both in 1QH 6.23 and in 1QH 7.5. It is unquestionable that 1QH 7.23—'my enemies are like chaff before the wind'—strongly reminds us of Isa. 17.13 and Ps. 1.4. There is a debate about the meaning (רוחות עוז) of 1QH 1.10, whether *rûaḥ* (the feminine plural form) denotes winds (Hill 1967; Vermes 1990; Dupont-

---

1. Sekki (1989: 1), describes the difficulties of interpreting *rûaḥ* in the Qumran literature as follows: 'A basic problem from the beginning of the study of the DSS and continuing to the present has been in determining when *ruah* in the sectarian literature refers to God's Spirit, man's spirit, angel/demon, wind or breath. The kinds of determinations scholars make in this regard will influence not only their views of sectarian pneumatology in general but also their views on the beliefs of the Qumran community in other areas'.

2. Kuhn (1960) lists almost 150 occurrences of *rûaḥ* and out of them 122 references are found in 1QS (39), 1QM (13), CD (9) and 1QH (61).

3. The texts that I consult are Lohse 1971; the versions are of Vermes (1990) and Dupont-Sommer (1961).

4. Eight references occur in 1QM (1), CD (2) and 1QH (5).

Sommer 1961; Schweizer 1968; Sekki 1989) or angels (Licht 1958; May 1963; Pryke 1965). It is, in fact, not easy to decide between the two, but we should note its creation context in which 'the mighty winds' might be formed through the counsel of God (cf. Ps. 104.4).[5]

1.2. Others

Rûaḥ also refers to directions or sides in 1QM 9.13 (הפנים רוחות לשלושת): the 'tower shall be surrounded on three sides by three hundred shields') and to the concept of vanity in 1QH 7.29 (רוח צבי כול): '...All majesty is but wind and none can brave Thy fury').[6] Both meanings are employed once only in 1QM and 1QH, whereas the former use for directions is found nine times in the Temple Scroll (6.6; 30.10; 31.10; 36.5 [×2]; 38.13; 38.14; 40.18 [×2]).

1.3. Summary

As in the Jewish Bible, *rûaḥ*, in the DSS, denotes not only wind but also its metaphorical meanings, directions and vanity. The occurrences are, however, much fewer in the Qumran Literature (8 out of 122) than in the Hebrew Bible (125 out of 389). So the concepts related to wind are still retained in the Qumran Literature presumably under the influence of the Jewish Bible, although the frequency of *rûaḥ* referring to wind notably diminishes.

2. Breath[7]

There is a disagreement among scholars on the meaning of *rûaḥ* in 1QM 6.12 (רוח אורכי). Some consider it to be breath,[8] whereas others understand it as horse's disposition referring to patience or gentleness.[9] The context, however, as Sekki demonstrates correctly, is more concerned with the physical power or energy related to the horse's breath. The other three references all occur in the creation context of 1QH 1.28, 29a, 29b as follows:

> It is Thou who hast created breath for the tongue
> and Thou knowest its words;
> Thou didst establish the fruit of the lips
> before ever they were.

---

5.   Anderson (1962: 302) points out the possibility of both meanings: 'A possible reference is 1QH i.10 where *Ruaḥ* can refer either to 'strong winds' or to "mighty spirits"'. While Sekki (1989: 177) puts it in the 'wind' category, he also assumes that the author probably uses this phrase with deliberate ambiguity.

6.   Vermes (1990) translates 1QH 7.29 as follows: 'For no spirit can reply to Thy rebuke, nor can any withstand Thy wrath'. This is due to the ambiguous term [צבי], but the context before and after 7.29 (as reminiscent of Isa. 23.9) makes it 'majesty' (Dupont-Sommer) or 'glory' (Sekki). Thus it probably refers to vanity; see also Sekki (1989: 175) and Hill (1967: 234).

7.   Four references occur in 1QM (1) and 1QH (3).

8.   Hill (1967: 234); Sekki (1989: 179-80); cf. 'sound of wind' (Vermes's) and 'long-winded' (Dupont-Sommer's).

9.   Anderson (1962: 296) describes it as 'long-winded' or 'patient'; Burrows (1955: 394) translates it as 'gentle'.

> Thou dost set words to measure
> and the flow of breath from the lips to metre.
> Thou bringest forth sounds
> according to their mysteries,
> and the flow of breath from the lips
> according to its reckoning (1QH 1.28-29).

Some scholars conceive רוח בלשון (1.28), מבעמב רוח שפתים (1.29a) and מבצי
רוחות (1.29b) as 'human disposition' or 'spiritual quality',[10] whereas most regard
them as 'breath'.[11] From the literary context, however, we can assume that the
breath here appears to depict the 'utterances of human breath', which are brought
forth by the Creator, God.[12] Thus the psalmist may acknowledge that God creates
and governs their speech and even knows its contents before the words are uttered.
In the DSS we cannot see 'breath' (*rûaḥ*) as the source of life which is employed as
a dominant notion in the Jewish Bible. *Rûaḥ*, referring to breath, is rather employed
to denote human breath in terms of utterances, and, on one occasion, to animal's
breathing.

3. *Anthropological Spirit*[13]

3.1. *Human Spirit in General*
In general, the use of *rûaḥ* which refers to human spirit (33 cases) as a whole is
possibly separate from human dispositions (18) or human spirituality (9). Let me
deal with each example concerning human spirit in the three documents respectively. In 1QS 7.23, it is said that the spirit of any man has been examined whether,
after being in the community for ten years, he has betrayed the rule in the council of
the community.[14] The God of Israel causes such a member to be condemned like a
'flaming torch in the straw' so that his spirit is broken (1QM 11.10).[15] In 1QH 1.32,
the psalmist exalts God's mercy and his goodness since God has strengthened the
spirit of man.[16]

Man's 'holy spirit' is also represented once each in a negative and in a positive
context: 'they defile *their* holy spirit and open their mouth with a blaspheming
tongue against the law of the Covenant of God saying, "They are not sure"' (CD
5.11); 'They shall keep apart from every uncleanness according to the statutes
relating to each one, and no man shall defile *his* holy spirit since God has set them
apart' (CD 7.4; emphasis added). The latter seems to be an echo of Ezek. 36.25-27,

10.   Johnston 1960: 36; Pryke 1965: 345.
11.   Vermes 1990: 168; Dupont-Sommer 1961: 204; Anderson 1962: 303; Schweizer 1968:
390; Sekki 1989: 180.
12.   Sekki (1989: 180) also indicates that there is some allusion here to the sense of *1 En.* 84.1,
i.e. 'God has put "breath" in the mouth of all men'.
13.   Sixty references occur in 1QS (25), 1QM (3), CD (5) and 1QH (27).
14.   Other cases are in 2.14; 7.18, 23; 8.12; 11.1a.
15.   Another is in 14.7.
16.   Others are in 1.15, 22; 3.21; 4.36; 5.36; 7.11; 8.29, 36; 9.12a, 12b, 16a, 16b; 13.13; 14.3;
15.13, 22; 16.10, 14; 17.25; 18.15.

now fulfilled. On the other hand, the former is probably used to denote human spirit which has been created from the beginning by the Holy God (cf. 1QH 4.31, here the 'spirit' is portrayed as God's created one).

In 1QH 17.17, however, the psalmist gives thanks to God 'because of the spirits (plural form) which Thou hast given to me!' (אשר נתתה בי). As we perceive the context before and after this saying, the 'spirits' seem not to be harmful, but those which are very wholesome, according to the psalmist. Thus it is likely that the spirits in this context may refer to various good human dispositions or qualities that God has given. These spirits are set apart both from the spirit that God has created from the beginning (1QH 4.31 as singular form) on the one hand, and from the spirits of good and evil in accordance with their lot (1QH 14.11 as good and evil spirits) on the other hand, because the spirits in 1QH 17.17, as good spirits in plural form, are also spiritual gifts which the psalmist has possessed after he entered the council of the community.[17]

3.2. Human Dispositions

It is also very common in the sectarian literature that *rûaḥ* denotes human dispositions with various adjectives and nouns. In 1QS 5.26, any member of the Qumran community should not 'address his companion with anger, or ill-temper, or obduracy, or with envy prompted by the spirit of wickedness'.[18] Abraham is depicted in CD 3.3 as a covenant-keeper who 'kept the commandments of God and did not choose his own will (*rûaḥ*)'. In spite of the obedience of Abraham, his offspring, the first members of the covenant, disobeyed God's commandments and 'chose their own will (*rûaḥ*) and walked in the stubbornness of their hearts each of them doing his own will' (CD 3.7). On some occasions in 1QH, *rûaḥ* connotes a 'spirit of jealousy' (2.15) and the 'perverse spirit' (11.12; 13.15), which are connected with the sinful nature of human beings (cf. the 'spirit of disaster' in 7.11 or 'my spirit is imprisoned with the dead' in 8.29).

3.3. Human Spirituality

A usage of peculiar interest and significance is that in several cases of 1QS *rûaḥ* refers to one's spirituality or spiritual quality, which describes the sectarian's religio-ethical life in the community. Interestingly, the members of the community are actually ranked according to their spiritual degree and religious order (1QS

17. Unless the examination concerning 1QH 17.17 is wrong, this text seems to be better categorized in 'human spirituality' in terms of spiritual gifts.

18. 1QS 3.8: the 'spirit of uprightness and humility'; 3.14: לכול מיני רוחותם—'according to the kind of spirit which they possess' (Vermes) or 'all the spirits which they possess, with their distinctive characters' (Dupont-Sommer)—Pryke (1965: 345), Treves (1962: 450), Wernberg-Møller (1961: 419) and Sekki (1989: 194-95) understand it as human spirits, whereas Johnston (1960: 30) and May (1963: 2) see it as two cosmic spirits; 4.3: a 'spirit of humility'; 4.4: a 'spirit of discernment'; 4.10: a 'spirit of lust'; 4.20: 'all spirit of falsehood'; 4.26: 'according to the spirit within [them at the time] of the visitation'; 5.26: 'by the spirit of wickedness'; 8.3: 'contrite spirit'; 9.22: a 'spirit of secrecy'; 10.18: a 'spirit of wickedness'; 11.1b: the 'proud of spirit'; 11.1c: a 'contrite spirit'.

6.22). Thus, when they convene the community meeting, 'the priests shall enter first, ranked one after another according to the perfection of their spirit' (1QS 2.20). Furthermore, after being accepted as the community member under the authority of the Master (*maskîl*), 'they (the holy congregation under the authority of the sons of Aaron) shall examine his spirit in the community with respect to his understanding and practice of the Law' (1QS 5.21). On the basis of this annual spiritual examination ('they shall examine their spirit and deeds yearly'), 'each man may be advanced in accordance with his understanding and perfection of way, or moved down in accordance with the offences committed by him' (1QS 5.24).[19] The Master as the instructor of the community also teaches and guides the congregation in accordance with their spiritual degree:[20]

> He shall separate and weigh the sons of righteousness according to their spirit (1QS 9.14)... He shall judge every man according to his spirit. He shall admit him in accordance with the cleanness of his hands and advance him in accordance with his understanding. And he shall love and hate likewise (1QS 9.15, 16)... He shall guide them all in knowledge according to the spirit of each and according to the rule of the age... (1QS 9.18).

3.4. *Summary*

Consistent with the Jewish Bible, the DSS employ the term *rûaḥ* in reference to anthropological spirit: (1) as created human spirit, (2) as a whole man, not only having a spirit but also as being a spirit and (3) as various human dispositions.

On the other hand, among these occurrences the human spirit is often portrayed as having a sinful or wicked nature.[21] In addition, *rûaḥ*, particularly in 1QS, also connotes one's spiritual quality or spirituality by which one's religio-ethical life is influenced. Spirituality is also, according to the sectarian literature, associated with the outside intervention of the supernatural beings, that is, the spirits of Light and Darkness (1QS 3.25).

---

19.   Any member shall not have any share of the property of the congregation unless he has been examined concerning his spirit and deeds (1QS 6.17); cf. 'They shall all be freely enlisted for war, perfect in spirit and body and prepared for the Day of Vengeance' (1QM 7.5).

20.   Cf. in the Jewish Bible, the Israelites are generally guided and ordered according to the 'law' or the 'word of Moses' commanded by God (Exod. 31.11; 32.28; 39.32, 42; Num. 2.34; 4.49; 8.20; 9.5; Josh. 11.23; 2 Chron. 35.6). Thus, they are rewarded or judged by their own 'ways' (Jer. 17.10; 32.19; Ezek. 7.3, 8, 9; 18.30; 24.14; 32.20) or 'doings' (Jer. 21.14; 32.19) on the basis of God's commandments. However, the psalmist appeals to God to judge him according to his own 'righteousness' (Pss. 7.8; 18.20, 24) or the 'cleanness of his hands' (Ps. 18.20, 24). On the other hand, the psalmist also humbly acknowledges his imperfect or unfaithful living before God. Thus he cannot but request God's mercy or promise in order to sustain his religious life (Pss. 103.10; 119.124—according to thy steadfast love; 119.41, 58, 116, 133, 154—according to thy promise; 119.156—according to thy justice). Among the passages above, the idea in Ezek. 18.30-31 is probably developed in the Qumran sect: 'Therefore I will judge you, O house of Israel, all of you according to your ways, says the Lord God. Repent and turn from all your transgressions; otherwise iniquity will be your ruin. Cast away from you all the transgressions that you have committed against me, and get yourselves a new heart and a new spirit! Why will you die, O house of Israel?'

21.   For instance, see 1QH 3.21; 7.11; 8.29; 9.16; 11.12; 13.15.

4. *Supernatural Beings*[22]

It is now recognized that, in the DSS, *rûaḥ* prominently denotes supernatural beings whereas, in the Jewish Bible, we cannot see *rûaḥ* as referring to any angelic being as a created separate being.[23] Thus, in the Jewish Bible even an 'evil spirit' is employed in terms of the evil spirit from the Lord/God. Every supernatural being or spirit, in the DSS, falls into one of two conflict groups: under the power of either the spirit of Truth/Light (i.e. the Prince of Light) or the spirit of Falsehood/Darkness (i.e. the Angel of Darkness), particularly in the context of 1QS 3.13–4.26. I shall first deal with angels as good spirits and demons as bad spirits in general and then take the two cosmic spirits into account.

4.1. *Angels*[24]

4.1.1. *God's Agents.* The use of *rûaḥ* referring to angels is basically concerned with the agents of God or the company of the Prince of Light in the context of helping the sons of righteousness (1QM 13.10). In 1QM 12.9, 'the Hero of war is with our congregation; the host of His spirits is with our foot-soldiers and horsemen' (see also 1QM 19.1). They are also named 'spirits of holiness' (1QH 8.12; 11.13) with whom the psalmist may stand before God in future. The psalmist, living in this world, is able to praise God's great design and his accomplishment since God has provided him or her with the 'spirits of knowledge' (1QH 3.22).

4.1.2. *In Creation Contexts.* In creation contexts, the angels as God's agents are also presented: '[Thou, O God, hast created] the expanse of the heavens and the host of heavenly lights, the tasks of the spirits and the dominion of the Holy Ones' (1QM 10.12; cf. 'eternal spirits' in 1QH 1.11); 'Thou hast created all the spirits [and hast established a statute] and law for all their works' (1QH 1.9); 'Lord of all spirits, and Ruler of all creatures; nothing is done without Thee, and nothing is known without Thy will' (1QH 10.8; cf. the 'host of Thy spirits' in 1QH 13.8).[25]

4.2. *Demons*[26]

4.2.1. *Satan's Agents.* In contrast with the angels as God's agents, the other supernatural beings are called demons in the company of Satan or Belial (cf. Tob. 6.8). In most instances, their identity as evil spirits is validated by the immediate contexts, while in some, their identity is validated by modified nouns like falsehood. 'All

---

22.   Twenty six references are found in 1QS (8), 1QM (8), CD (1) and 1QH (9).

23.   In the LXX, however, this tendency appears twice in Num. 16.22; 27.16: 'God of the spirits *and* all flesh', cf. 'God of the spirits of all flesh' in the MT.

24.   Eleven references are found to be in plural forms in 1QM (4: but 19.1 is too fragmentary) and 1 QH (7).

25.   In 1QM 10.12 and 1QH 10.8, theoretically speaking, the spirits seem to include the evil spirits like demons on the basis of 1QS 3.25, but it is likely that the evil spirits are to be excluded in the former immediate contexts.

26.   Nine references are found in plural forms in 1QS (1), 1QM (5), CD (1) and 1QH (2).

his—the Angel of Darkness—allotted spirits seek the overthrow of the sons of light' (1QS 3.24) so as to mislead the children of righteousness. In nature, 'all the spirits of his company, the Angel of Destruction, walk according to the precepts of Darkness' (1QM 13.11). Therefore, they cannot escape from the eternal wrath of God.

4.2.2. In Judgment Contexts. Judgment against Belial and his spirits is occasionally understood as already accomplished,[27] but in most cases it is understood as completely accomplished on the future day of judgment: 'Cursed be Satan for his sinful purpose and may he be execrated for his wicked rule! Cursed be all the spirits of his company for their ungodly purpose' (1QM 13.4-5); 'And the gates [of Hell] shall open [on all] the works of Vanity; and the doors of the Pit shall close on the conceivers of wickedness; and the everlasting bars shall be bolted on all the spirits of Naught' (1QH 3.17, 18). Not only Satan and his company, but also a man who 'preaches apostasy under the dominion of the spirits of Satan shall be judged according to the law relating to those possessed by a ghost or familiar spirit' (CD 12.2).

4.3. *Two Cosmic Beings*[28]

The identity of the two spirits in 1QS 3.13–4.26 is one of the most controversial subjects within the Qumran Literature.[29] Without any question, most of the references that come from this unique two spirits context are primarily concerned with various human dispositions (1QS 4.3-4 and 4.9-10); nevertheless, it is apparent that these psychological impulses are affected by the two cosmic spirits, i.e. the Prince of Light and the Angel of Darkness (1QS 3.19). Because of this cosmic trait, some scholars detect the influence of Persian dualistic thought or pre-Christian Jewish

---

27.   'During all the mysteries of his—Satan—Malevolence he has not made [us] stray from Thy Covenant; Thou—God—hast driven his spirits [of destruction] far from [us]' (1QM 14.10; see also 15.14; cf. 1QH 17.23).

28.   Six references are found in 1QS 3.18; 3.18/19; 3.25; 4.6; 4.9; 4.23.

29.   Wernberg-Møller (1961: 413-15) and Treves (1962: 449-52) argue that the two spirits in the *Rule* of the Community (1QS 3.13–4.26) are nothing but the spirits of human dispositions which are implanted in every man's heart. Their views are supported in the recent thesis of Menzies (1991a: 78-80), who also views the two spirits as human psychological impulses. In contrast, Burrow (1955: 279-80), Dupont-Sommer (1961), Vermes (1990), Licht (1958: 88-89), W. Davies (1958: 171-75) and May (1963: 1-14) emphasize the cosmological meaning of the two spirits. In a mediating position, there are Pryke (1965: 345-48), who regards them as a moral dualism without a metaphysical sense; Hill (1967) and Anderson (1962: 299) who both acknowledge the cosmic elements but emphasize various human characters in their literary contexts: Hill suggests, 'The 'two spirits' may have cosmic functions, but the emphasis in the passage under discussion is not on their transcendent character, but on their persistent involvement with the life and behaviour of men' (236-37); Sekki (1989), in the most recent and comprehensive thesis concerning this matter doesn't deny this cosmic feature of the two spirits in 1QS 3.13–4.26: 'In this way the author indicates that a man's good or evil spiritual disposition cannot be regarded as simply a personal or individual matter between himself and others (or even God) but is deeply involved in a cosmic Good or cosmic Evil' (198-99).

Gnosticism. It must be noted, however, that these two cosmic spirits of Light and Darkness are said to be created by God (1QS 3.25). This statement, thus, shows that the DSS develop, not the two universal opposites in the conflict dualism of Zoroastrianism, but simply the dualistic monotheism of traditional Judaism (cf. 1 Sam. 16.15; 19.9; 1 Kgs 19.21-23; Isa. 51.9-11).[30] In a similar vein, these dualistic spirits have also been represented in *The Testaments of the Twelve Patriarchs*:[31] 'Know, therefore, my children, that two spirits wait upon man—the spirit of truth and the spirit of deceit' (*T. Jud.* 20.1: Charles's translation [1913]; see also *T. Benj.* 6.1; *T. Reub.* 4.9; *T. Naph.* 2.5; *T. Jos.* 2.6; 7.4; *T. Jud.* 11.1; 13.8; 18.3; 25.3).

In his mysterious design (the author of 1QS emphasizes the 'mystery of God' through which God permits the influence of the two cosmic spirits on human hearts or will: see 1QS 3.16, 23; 4.18), God, from the beginning, has not only created man but also 'appointed for him two spirits in which to walk until the time of his visitation: the spirits of truth[32] and falsehood'[33] (1QS 3.18, 19; 4.6, 9, 23). Therefore, if we are asked to set forth some spiritual order in the heavenly realm on the basis of the sectarian's understanding, the following pattern may be conceived (cf. W. Davies 1958: 171-72):

The God of Israel
(The Spirit of Holiness)

The Spirit of Truth ⟵⟶ The Spirit of Error
as Prince of Light   as Angel of Darkness

The spirits of God as angels ⟵⟶ The spirits of Belial as demons

The sons of righteousness: ⟵⟶ The sons of wickedness:
humility; patience; etc.   greed; deceit; etc.

4.4. *Summary*

In the Qumran Literature the use of *rûaḥ*, unlike in the MT, denotes two kinds of supernatural beings: (1) angels as God's agents, particularly in creation contexts and (2) demons as Satan's agents, which are closely connected with judgment

---

30. Hill 1967: 236; Johnston 1960: 30; May 1963: 7.

31. The exact dating of *The Testaments of the Twelve Patriarchs* is, however, still in dispute; cf. de Jonge (1960: 182-235).

32. This spirit is also called the Prince of Light (1QS 3.20), which causes the following human dispositions: humility, patience, abundant charity, unending goodness, understanding, intelligence, mighty wisdom, discernment, zeal for laws, holy intent, great charity, admirable purity, humble conduct and faithful concealment of the mysteries of truth (1QS 4.3-6).

33. This spirit is also called the Angel of Darkness (1QS 3.20-21), which causes the following human dispositions: greed, slackness in search for righteousness, wickedness, lies, haughtiness, pride, falseness, deceit, cruelty, abundant evil, ill-temper and brazen insolence, abominable deeds of lust, ways of lewdness in the service of uncleanness, a blaspheming tongue, blindness of eye and dullness of ear, stiffness of neck and heaviness of heart (1QS 4.9-11).

contexts. Furthermore, *rûaḥ* also refers to the two cosmic spirits, which may be put in another category when we compare their identity with other angelic beings and human dispositions. Noticeable is that the supernatural *rûaḥ* is expressed almost always by masculine plural forms with some feminine plurals. As I have noted, however, it is more likely that the notion of these dualistic spirits in 1QS 3.13–4.26 is still understood within Jewish thought adhering to monotheism than from Persian cosmological dualism. It can be seen, therefore, that Qumran Literature's concept of *rûaḥ*, as referring to supernatural beings, has been developed more than it has been in the LXX.

5. *The Spirit of the Lord*[34]

In this section, I shall notice the use of *rûaḥ* with reference to God's Spirit, which is normally presented in terms of the 'spirit of holiness'[35] and occasionally with a possessive pronoun. The frequency of this usage is obviously distinct from other Jewish sources[36] (except the targums and other rabbinic literature; cf. *4 Ezra* 14.22; *Asc. Isa.* 5.14).[37] Let me then explore this feature of the Scrolls.

5.1. *God's 'Holy Spirit' and the 'Spirit of Holiness'*
5.1.1. *Cleansing Role*

> He shall be cleansed from all his sins by the spirit of holiness uniting him to His truth, and his iniquity shall be expiated by the spirit of uprightness and humility (1QS 3.7b-8a).
>
> He will cleanse him of all wicked deeds with the spirit of holiness: like purifying waters He will shed upon him the spirit of truth (1QS 4.21a).
>
> I implore Thee by the spirit which Thou hast given [me] to perfect Thy [favours] to Thy servant [for ever] purifying me by Thy Holy Spirit, and drawing me near to Thee by Thy grace according to the abundance of Thy mercies (1QH 16.12).

As one of the marked features of God's Spirit, 1QS recounts the cleansing role of the Spirit of holiness by which all sins and wicked deeds shall be expiated ('future tense'). In 1QH, on the other hand, God's Spirit has already effected this cleansing, at least in the Qumran community ('present tense'). In fact, it is often noted that, in the Scrolls, the members of the community consider themselves the 'true Israel'.[38]

---

34. Twenty references are found in 1QS (4), CD (1) and 1QH (15).

35. Thirteen out of twenty are translated by the phrase 'spirit of holiness'; within them ten (1QS 8.16; CD 2.12; 1QH 7.6; 9.32; 12.12; 14.13; 16.3, 7, 12; 17.26) are attributive forms with the divine possessive pronoun (e.g. His Holy Spirit or Thy Holy Spirit).

36. See Pinnock (1963: 51-52).

37. See n. 154 in Chapter 5.

38. The community is also portrayed as a House of Holiness, a House of Perfection and Truth (1QS 8.5, 9); a sure House, the members of the New Covenant in the land of Damascus (CD 3.19; 4.19). In view of this spiritual reality, the psalmist of 1QH exalts and gives thanks to God for his or her present salvation.

Thus, this evidence implies that entering into the community means nothing but participating in the eschatological reality through the gift of the holy Spirit.[39]

5.1.2. *Revelatory* Role

> This (path) is the study of the Law which He commanded by the hand of Moses, that they may do according to all that has been revealed from age to age, and as the Prophets have revealed by His Holy Spirit (1QS 8.15-16).
> And He makes known His Holy Spirit to them by the hand of His anointed ones, and He proclaimed the truth (to them) (CD 2.12-13a).
> I, the Master, know Thee O my God, by the spirit which Thou hast given to me and by Thy Holy Spirit I have faithfully hearkened to Thy marvellous counsel. In the mystery of Thy wisdom Thou has opened knowledge to me and in Thy mercies (1QH 12.11-12).
> And I, Thy servant, know by the spirit which Thou hast given to me [that Thy words are truth], and that all Thy works are righteous, and that Thou wilt not take back Thy word (1QH 13.18b-19).
> And I know through the understanding which comes from Thee that in Thy good will towards [ashes Thou hast shed] Thy Holy Spirit [upon me] and thus drawn me near to understanding of Thee (1QH 14.12b-13).

In 1QS and CD it is to the 'old Israel' that God has revealed his word of truth through his prophets, whereas in 1QH, the psalmist as a representative of the 'new Israel' realizes by the Spirit which God has given to him that his words are true and his works are righteous.

Menzies (1991a: 87-88) insists on the close connection between the Spirit and prophetic inspiration by citing 1QS 8.16, CD 2.12 and 1Q34[bis] 2.6-7.[40] This provides possible evidence that the Qumran Literature sees the Spirit as the source of prophetic inspiration. Nevertheless, we should note that this role is not so prominent in the Scrolls as other roles.[41] Furthermore, it is more likely that this prophetic role, if there is any, should be understood within the revelatory contexts, which are essentially concerned with wisdom and truth. Thus, the revelatory 'Spirit which God has given to the psalmist'[42] is necessary to understand God's truth.

---

39. Menzies (1991a: 86-87) claims that the pneumatology of 1QH, decidedly different from that of 1QS where the two spirits represent human impulses placed within every individual, attributes soteriological significance to the gift of the Spirit in the same way as in the Wisdom of Solomon (concerning the Wisdom of Solomon, see also 61-63). However, we should have in mind that the two spirits in 1QS 3.13–4.26 cannot be regarded as the whole concept of *rûaḥ* in 1QS (e.g. 1QS 3.7; 4.21; 8.16; 9.3), and moreover, the cleansing and the revelatory functions are found both in 1QS and 1QH. Therefore, I infer that the essential understanding of God's Spirit is attained from documents as a whole, in spite of some differences or developments.

40. 1Q34[bis] 2.6-7: 'And Thou didst renew for them Thy covenant [founded] on a glorious vision and on the words of Thy Holy [Spirit], on the works of Thy hands and the writing of Thy right hand, that they might know the foundation of glory and the steps towards eternity'; Menzies here also mentions the association between the Spirit and divine revelation (1991a: 88).

41. Cf. Ringgren (1963: 90), who contends, 'It should be pointed out that in Qumran there is also no reference to the spirit as the driving force in prophecy'.

42. Menzies (1991a: 85), agreeing with H. Kuhn, points out the formula נתתה [בי] ברוח אשר

5.1.3. *Sustaining Role*

When these become members of the Community in Israel according to all these rules, they shall establish the spirit of holiness according to everlasting truth (1QS 9.3-4a). I thank Thee, O Lord, for Thou hast upheld me by Thy strength. Thou hast shed Thy Holy Spirit upon me that I may not stumble (1QH 7.6-7).

Thou hast upheld me with certain truth; Thou hast delighted me with Thy Holy Spirit and [hast opened my heart] till this day (1QH 9.32).

Because I know all these things, my tongue shall utter a reply. Bowing down and [confessing all] my transgressions, I will seek [Thy] spirit [of knowledge]; cleaving to Thy spirit of [holiness] I will hold fast to the truth of Thy Covenant (1QH 16.6-7).

And I know that man is not righteous except through Thee, and therefore I implore Thee by the spirit which Thou hast given [me] to perfect Thy [favours] to Thy servant [for ever] (1QH 16.11b-12a).

It is by the spirit of holiness that the sectarian is not only liberated from all sins and discerns the truth of God, but also sustains his religio-ethical life. The psalmist thanks God, who does not allow him to stumble by providing his Holy Spirit. Besides, the Spirit delights the psalmist with God's truth and makes him perfect before God. It is apparent that without God's Holy Spirit, the psalmist cannot pursue the truth of God, nor carry on his holy life.[43]

5.1.4. *Others*.

The two references to *rûaḥ* in 1QH 16.2, 3 are too fragmentary to substantiate its exact meaning.[44] Based on the rest of 1QH 16, however, I may infer that these two references to the divine Spirit possibly denote a revelatory role. The other two references, a 'spirit of knowledge' and 'Thy spirit of mercy', may recall Isa. 11.2 (the 'spirit of wisdom and understanding; of counsel and might; of knowledge and the fear of the Lord'). Above all, their immediate contexts may help corroborate their identity as the divine Spirit, which allows the psalmist to enjoy their religio-ethical life toward God: 'Thou hast favoured me Thy servant, with a spirit of knowledge, [that I may choose] truth [and goodness] and loathe all the ways of iniquity' (1QH 14.25); 'Behold, Thou art pleased to favour [Thy servant], and hast graced me with Thy spirit of mercy and [with the radiance] of Thy glory' (1QH 16.9).

('by the Spirit which thou hast given me') as a technical term, referring to the Spirit as a gift given upon entrance into the community.

43. Turner (1994c: 179) has thus explained this ethical function of the Spirit in 1QH as follows: 'What is envisaged is not primarily esoteric knowledge, but *the sort of understanding of God and of his word that elicits righteous living*' (emphasis original).

44. There is no translation of 1QH 16.1-5 in Vermes's version; '(1) [...] And I, [I know] (2) because of the ho[ly] Spirit [which Thou hast pu]t in m[e] that [...] and that m[an] cannot [...] (3) [Thy] ho[ly] Spirit. [Thy glory] fills h[eave]n [and] earth [...] Thy [glo]ry fills [...]' in Dupont-Sommer's (1961: 274).

5.2. *Relationship between God's Spirit and Truth*[45]

> For it is through the spirit of true *counsel* concerning the ways of man that all his sins shall be expiated that he may contemplate the light of life (1QS 3.6).

> He will cleanse him of all wicked deeds with the spirit of holiness; like purifying waters He will shed upon him the spirit of truth (to cleanse him) of all abomination and falsehood (1QS 4.21).

There is much debate among scholars[46] about the spirit of true counsel (רוח עצת אמת) and the spirit of truth (רוח אמת ממה) respectively in 1QS 3.6; 4.21. As Sekki notices, in 1QS 3.6, the difficulty in identifying the meaning of *rûaḥ* lies in the term אל, which can be understood either as אֵל or אֶל. Even although most scholars regard אל as אֶל, according to Sekki, the construct phrase רוח עצת אמת-אל should be translated as the spirit of God's true counsel. Thus he (1989: 107-108) grasps its meaning as a proper religious disposition within the sectarian.

We should appreciate, however, the function of what the spirit of true counsel does for the sectarian. In other words, the spirit here, like God's holy Spirit, expiates all sins of a sectarian so that he may taste the light of life (cf. 1QS 3.7; 4.21; 1QH 16.12). In the same vein, the spirit of truth in 1QS 4.21 seems to be understood as another term referring to the spirit of holiness in the context, whereas some scholars think of the spirit of truth as the good cosmic spirit, that is, the angel of the Light.[47] We may, thus, assume that there is an intimate affinity between the spirit of holiness as God's Spirit and the spirit of truth, even although we cannot completely identify the spirit of holiness with the spirit of truth.

5.3. *Summary*

I should first note that it is the Spirit of holiness or the holy Spirit which is frequently used to denote God's Spirit in the DSS. Its dominant roles in the immediate contexts are delineated as follows: (1) cleansing, (2) revelatory and (3) sustaining, which are all connected with the sectarian's religio-ethical life in the community. In other words, the concept of God's holy Spirit in the Jewish Bible (Ps. 51.11 and Isa. 63.10, 11; cf. Ezek. 36.20-28) has been focused and then developed in the era of the Qumran community. In contrast, the usage of God's charismatic Spirit referring to miraculous power never occurs in the DSS, while God's prophetic Spirit is found at most two or three times.

I also discern divergent interests or contents represented in 1QS, 1QM, CD and

---

45. Please note the underlined word <u>truth</u> identified in the previous section.

46. Different scholars' positions are well introduced in Sekki (1989: 106-107, 208).

47. However, Menzies (1991a: 78-81) argues that the terms 'spirit of true counsel', 'spirit of holiness' and 'spirit of uprightness and humility' in 1QS 3.6-7 are no other than the human dispositions controlled by the non-cosmic two spirits; Turner (1994c: 180), disagreeing with Menzies, claims that "the spirit of truth" is not to be conceived exclusively in anthropological terms, but includes the influence of the Prince of Lights (1QS 3.20), God and the Angel of Truth (1QS 3.24) and so on'. Thus he also acknowledges the close connection between the holy spirit and the spirit of truth, 'The "holy spirit" and "spirit of truth" of 1QS 4.21, with which God will sprinkle his people and so purify them (again echoing Ezek. 36?), appears to include the divine Spirit' (180). Hill (1967: 238) has also suggested that in 1QS 'the spirit of truth and "holy spirit" seem to be identical'.

1QH. Nevertheless, it is impossible to make sharp distinctions in regard to the concept of God's Spirit among them, even between 1QS and 1QH. It is better to see that the psalmist in 1QH, as a member of the community, rather highlights the significance of the essential factor of God's holy Spirit, which causes their religio-ethical life in the holy eschatological community. This feature, as Menzies asserts, may attribute soteriological significance to the gift of the Spirit.[48]

The last, but not the least, point is that God's Spirit or the Spirit of holiness in the DSS is closely associated with the spirit of truth or truth itself. Thus, without possessing God's holy Spirit, no one can beseech God's will/purpose and thus live according to God's everlasting true counsel (1QS 3.7, 8; 9.3; CD 2.12; 1QH 14.25; 16.6, 7).

6. Conclusion

The study of *rûaḥ* in the DSS encounters difficulty in deciding the exact meanings of each instance, especially in the fragmentary texts. Hence, there is no unanimous agreement about the meaning of each example of *rûaḥ* in the Scrolls. Nevertheless in this excursus I have found some characteristics of *rûaḥ* in these non-biblical documents, which delineate by and large the sectarian's understanding of *rûaḥ*. Much usage of *rûaḥ* in the DSS follows the pattern set by the Jewish Bible, which denotes (1) wind, (2) breath, (3) anthropological spirit, (4) supernatural beings (including two cosmic beings) and (5) God's Spirit, although the first two usages are much fewer, whereas the last two are much more frequent. In regard to 'anthropological spirit', the Qumran Literature often uses *rûaḥ* to refer to one's spiritual quality (cf. Ezek. 18.30-31). The most prominent feature, however, is the reference to the 'Spirit of holiness' in terms of its frequency and roles. The 'Spirit of holiness' (cf. the 'Spirit of truth') is thus presented in relation to God's faithful people in contrast with the Spirit of Error. This is why God's holy Spirit is depicted as (1) cleansing all sins and all past wicked deeds of the sectarian, (2) revealing to him God's words and truth and (3) sustaining him earnestly in accordance with the way of righteousness. God's holy Spirit is also presented as the essential factor which (4) leads and guides the religio-ethical life of the sectarian even after he enters the Qumran community. Thus, rarely in the DSS, is God's Spirit described as the extraordinary power which inspires charismatic leaders (e.g. Moses, some judges, David and Elijah and so on) as in the Jewish Bible, but the DSS regard the Spirit as the essential (soteriological?) gift in every member of the community. This fact implies that the sectarian's understanding of God's Spirit is basically concerned with, or much influenced by, the references to the future expectation of the Spirit found in Isa. 44.3; Ezek. 36.27; 37.14 (cf. Joel 2.28-29). This could be the possible reason why the sectarians designate themselves as a 'House of Holiness' (1QS 8.5) or a 'House of Perfection and Truth' (1QS 8.9), that is, God's eschatological community.

---

48.   But we also notice that the primary purpose of the documents is not to explain their theological doctrine of salvation, i.e. soteriology. This means we cannot entirely grasp their 'doctrine' of salvation.

Chapter 3

NARRATOR, POINT OF VIEW AND THE HOLY SPIRIT

1. *Introduction*

In the last chapter, I explored the use of *rûaḥ/pneuma* in the Jewish Bible as literary repertoire for the Lukan divine Spirit. Now in the following three chapters, I shall elucidate the literary presentation of the Holy Spirit in Luke–Acts as dynamic biblical narrative. Prior to examining the characterization of the Holy Spirit, I shall, in this chapter,[1] first of all discuss the Lukan narrator's point of view, focusing on the Holy Spirit within the 'divine frame of reference'.[2] I shall define who

1. An earlier version of this chapter was given at the Synoptic Evangelists seminar of the 1997 British New Testament Conference in Leeds under the title 'The Literary Traits of the Lukan Narrator with Special Reference to the "Divine Frame of Reference" in Luke–Acts'; thanks are due to participants of the seminar for their comments.

2. As preliminary issues in regard to the narrative of Luke–Acts, I need to mention at least two issues: the unity and genre of Luke–Acts. For this in detail, see Hur (2000: 227-58). (1) On the unity: while I am inclined to the assumption that the Gospel and Acts are to be conceived as a two-volume work, titled Luke–Acts (originally coined by Cadbury [1927: 8-9]; confirmed by Gasque [1989b: 309]; cf. Powell [1994: 343]), this cannot be regarded as an absolute presupposition. In other words, either Luke–Acts or Luke and Acts may be studied in our academic context by means of different criticisms (e.g. source, form, redaction, narrative, reader-response and so forth) or various interests or topics (e.g. Jesus' parables, the apostles' speeches, Jesus' journey to Jerusalem, Paul's journey to Rome). In a sense, the answer to the question of unity in Lukan writings is affected by one's *pre-understanding* of the Gospel and Acts as Luke–Acts or Luke and Acts. In a practical sense, either opinion can thus be validated or legitimated in terms of one's methodology or subject matter. For my study, it is better to read Luke and Acts as a unified narrative, i.e. Luke–Acts. Both my methodology 'dynamic biblical narrative criticism' and my chief concern 'the character-building of the Holy Spirit in Lukan writings' make it appropriate for me to tackle them as Luke–Acts. Nevertheless, to read Luke–Acts as one story does not imply the assumption that they express no

the narrator is in connection with other related terms, implied author and real author, and then explain the three literary facets of the Lukan narrator's point of view in relation to the Holy Spirit, which is understood as the most prominent feature of the 'divine frame of reference' in Luke–Acts. In so doing, I shall outline some important ideological features of the Lukan narrator. Furthermore, I shall also attempt to explain 'narrative reliability' in relation to both the Lukan narrator and other major characters. In short, this chapter will show the narrative relationship between the Lukan narrator (including leading characters) and the Holy Spirit; that is, the Spirit (within the 'divine frame of reference') is rhetorically employed for narrative reliability through both the Lukan narrator and major characters.

progress or development. On the contrary, these two volumes need to be read flexibly. Cf. the fact that this conventional expression of Luke–Acts has quite recently been challenged or at least reconsidered by focusing on the five aspects (i.e. authorial, canonical, generic, narrative and theological unity) by Parsons and Pervo (1993). According to them, except for authorial unity, there is no unity in Luke and Acts (see also Dawsey [1989: 48-66]; Parsons [1987: 24]). However, Marshall (1993: 180-82) critically reviews the arguments raised by Parsons and Pervo. For my criticism of Parson's view of the issue of the unity of Luke and Acts, see p. 91 n. 12. (2) On the genre: there are by and large four options from which we may choose: biography, historiography, *sui generis* and *genus mixtum*. Burridge's doctoral thesis (1992) examines the historical debate about the genre of the Gospels through 125 years of critical scholarship and suggests their genres be best considered Graeco-Roman βίος. His research sources, however, seem to be too dependent on Graeco-Roman biography (cf. Sterling [1992]), although he extends the genre/ definition of βίος in an effort to embrace more possible genres scattered in other ancient literature. In addition, when we acknowledge the fact that genre 'functions as a set of expectations, a kind of contract between author and reader to guide interpretation of the text' (Burridge 1992: 53), it is doubtful that all ancient readers understand Gospels as forms of Graeco-Roman βίος, regardless of their age, gender, location, ethnic origins, social status and so forth. In regard to the question of genre, I thus suggest that Luke–Acts be considered as a biblical *narrative* (see also Chapter 5). In other words, the literary form of Luke–Acts as a biblical *narrative* allows us to examine Luke–Acts in the context of the literary repertoire it takes up from the Jewish Bible. Accordingly, my literary point of departure does not begin with genre concepts, but with the undeniable background of 'biblical narrative'. This position is supported by Kurz (1993: 2); see also Johnson (1977: 21); Brawley (1990: 163, 234 n. 1); Roth (1997: 14).

2. *Definitions and 'Narrative Communication Situation'*

A narrator might simply be understood as a storyteller by whom a story as a whole (through its events and characters) is represented and evaluated in terms of his or her point of view. I shall now examine the 'point of view' of the narrator of Luke–Acts as a literary device of the implied author. For analysis, I shall adopt Rimmon-Kenan's analytic model, as it has been modified by other literary critics.[3] For instance, Rimmon-Kenan, modifying Uspensky's five 'planes' of point of view, offers three 'facets' of point of view or 'focalization', to unveil the narrator: (1) perceptual facet, (2) psychological facet and (3) ideological facet (1983: 71-85). Each facet, however, is not mutually exclusive. In other words, each facet is, in one sense or another, interdependent upon the others to disclose properly the narrator, who is called a 'whispering wizard'.

Before pursuing my task, I need to clarify some definitions related to the term narrator in regard to the 'narrative communication situation'. According to Rimmon-Kenan (87), 'the flesh-and-blood author is subject to the vicissitudes of real life', while 'the implied author of a particular work is conceived as a stable entity, ideally consistent with itself within the work'. Further 'the narrator can only be defined circularly as the narrative "voice" or "speaker" of a text', while 'the implied author is—in opposition and by definition—voiceless and silent'. In a similar vein, we are able to distinguish between narratee, implied reader and real reader. On the other hand, however, the notion of implied author or implied reader, according to Rimmon-Kenan (88), 'must be depersonified and is best considered as a set of implicit norms rather than as a speaker or a voice (i.e. a subject)'.[4] Hence, she argues that both implied author and implied reader must be excluded as participants in the 'narrative communication situation', which thus consists of the following four participants: the real author, the narrator, the narratee and the real reader.

On the other hand, however, the 'narrative communication situation'

---

3.   Rimmon-Kenan (1983: 71-74), like Gérard Genette, prefers the term 'focalization' to that of 'point of view'. Three dimensions of the narrative formulated by Rimmon-Kenan are story, text and narration. Cf. Rimmon-Kenan's definition and other parallel terms used by other literary critics, see 3, 133 n. 2.

4.   Contra Chatman (1978: 151).

becomes more complex if the reader's *reading process*[5] is taken into consideration, that is, the dynamic interaction between text and reader.[6] In other words, meaning of or response to a text cannot be actualized without the reader's conscious reading process. Thus, the concept of implied author or implied reader, although voiceless and silent in the text, should not be excluded, because these concepts are inferred from the narrative through the reader's reading process. Thus, these concepts, I believe, could be used effectively in the model of narrative communication.

Hence, 'Luke', the real author (though it is impossible to reconstruct the real author completely) communicates *through* the implied author (though it is voiceless and silent) and thence *through* the narrator. Nevertheless, the implied author, although voiceless and silent, can be inferred from the overall narrative through the reading process, whereas the narrator[7] is the voiced speaker of and in the narrative. In short, therefore, the participants in the 'narrative communication situation' are as follows:

Diagram 1. *The Dynamic Interaction[8] between Text and Reader[9]*

the real→ the implied→ the narrator→ the text ←the narratee ←the implied ← the real
author   author   reader   reader
(Luke)   (Theophilus)

5.   For instance, see Iser (1974, 1978); Eco (1979); cf. Fish (1980); Tompkins (1980: ix-xxvi).

6.   On the interaction between text and reader, I am sympathetic to Iser's dialectic theory and practice which have been criticized by (postmodern) critics. Moore (1989a: 102; 1989b: 86-89) criticizes Iser's inconsistency between the theory and the practice by quoting some literary critics: 'In theory Iser affirms the pertinence of individual reader-response, yet in his readings of specific works all such individuality is bracketed: "Although Iser wants to present reading as a process which balances text and reader, he always presents the reader in the firm grip of the text" (Berg, "Psychologies", 259). "His concept of the reader is not different from Ingarden's in that both are essentially normative" (Barnouw, "Critics", 222)'. Cf. Rimmon-Kenan's position (1983: 119): 'the "reader" is seen in this book as a construct, a "metonymic characterization of the text" (Perry 1979, p. 43), an "it" rather than a personified "he" or "she"'.

7.   The narrator in Luke–Acts is not clearly identified as male or female. Here after for convenience, however, I shall use a masculine pronoun to refer to the Lukan narrator.

8.   In Diagram 1, I do not make room for the extratext as literary repertoire, which can be inferred from the concepts of implied author and implied reader who

I shall now turn to the Lukan narrator's point of view, which consists of three facets.[10] This analytical frame enables us to appreciate not only the narrator's way of seeing, but also his fundamental norm or value-system. In the narrative, some characters also function as significant 'character-narrators' (called intradiegetic or internal narrator) like Jesus in the Gospel and Peter or Paul in Acts. My focus now, however, is on the narrator of the whole narrative (called generally extradiegetic or external narrator).[11] So if we can adequately grasp the significance of the external narrator[12] as a narrative-director, we may more effectively

are aware of the social symbolic universe, i.e. the ideology embedded in the text. Cf. Robbins's textual communication model (1995: 278).

9. My definition of 'reader' in Luke–Acts, unless otherwise stated, is a 'hybrid reader', who is 'part ancient, part modern' and 'part reader, part critic', a heuristic construct; see Darr (1992: 25). Thus, the possible meanings of the narrative of Luke–Acts are conveyed in the process of dynamic interaction between the text and the reader: 'a text can only come to life when it is read' argued Iser (1971: 2); yet without a text nobody can be a reader at all.

10. See Rimmon-Kenan (1983: 71-85). Cf. the 'typology of narrator' (94-103).

11. There are, however, two types of the extradiegetic narrator in Luke–Acts: (1) the first-person narrator as organiser and participating observer (by a single form in the prefaces in both the Gospel [1.1-4] and Acts [1.1-2]; by a plural form in the 'we' sections [16.10-17; 20.5-15; 21.1-18; 27.1–28.16] in Acts), and (2) the third-person narrator as omniscient narrator.

12. For the study of the Lukan narrator(s), not technical, yet helpful is Kurz (1993: 45-72, 73-110). See also Sheeley (1992: 149-59) and Parsons (1993: 45-83): both deal with the narrator of Luke–Acts by applying Rimmon-Kenan's theoretical analysis in terms not of the 'point of view of the narrator', but of the 'typology of the narrator'. Sheeley's main concern in his thesis is the identification and function of the 'narrative asides' in Luke–Acts; this study contains helpful insights (38-39, 175-76, 182-85): 'One of the most important results of this study has been the recognition of the way in which asides are used by the narrators of Luke–Acts to affirm their own authority as storytellers... In Luke–Acts especially, each narrator is attempting to persuade the reader to accept his world-view, and the asides provide the commentary and guidance which challenge and persuade the reader' (183). On the other hand, Parsons (1993) seeks to examine the literary characteristics of the narrator(s) in an effort to distinguish the narrator of the Gospel from that of Acts by applying the literary critic Chatman's two-fold feature of the narrative, i.e. 'story' and 'discourse', and he argues, 'at least on the discourse level, there are significant differences between Luke and Acts' (82). This is interesting, yet not wholly convincing because (1) he is not much concerned with the somewhat different narrative settings or stages that cause the narrator's typology (for instance, the narrator's use of the 'voice of Jesus in the Gospel' and 'that of his followers in Acts' could be

understand the chief interest of my study: how and why does the Lukan narrator make the Holy Spirit appear on the narrative stage?[13] Having this chief concern in mind, I shall now exhibit the narrator's point of view in relation to the Holy Spirit.

3. The Lukan Narrator's Point of View with Special Reference to the Holy Spirit

What is a 'point of view'? We can say that it is the perspective or the *Weltanschauung* of a narrator or a character in the narrative (Chatman 1978: 151-52). If so, how do we analyse the point of view of the narrator? This requires us to explore three facets in the narrator's point of view[14] that are not mutually exclusive, but overlapping. Thus, I shall first explain the definition of each facet and then elucidate how the Lukan narrator's point of view is expressed with special reference to the Holy Spirit. This analysis for understanding the narrator will also be

distinct); (2) he notices that there are both similar (e.g. 51, 52, 56, 59, 74) and different narrative devices, yet he gives too much emphasis to the different ones; (3) if we applied his critique to Lk. 1–2 and Lk. 9–19, there would be at least two more storytellers even in the Gospel; (4) in addition, he fails to point out one of the most consistent literary devices throughout Luke–Acts, namely, the 'reliability' of the narrator and his narrative in general. He leaves out the criterion of 'reliability' for the reason that 'The idea of an unreliable narrator seems to be a rather modern (in some cases postmodern) development in literary theory and since most biblical narrative critics agree that the Gospels (as well as all other literature of antiquity) show little or no evidence of literary unreliability, this analysis will not address that category' (p. 49 n. 19). However, the literary manner of showing or telling reliability in Luke–Acts should be noted. It is my observation that the narrator in Luke *and* Acts consistently employs the 'divine frame of reference' such as angels, visions, heavenly voices, scriptural citations and esp. the Holy Spirit to reinforce the narrative reliability *at the discourse level* (see below). Cf. on the unity of narrators in Luke–Acts, the more balanced view of Sheeley (1992: 137). See also Darr (1993: 43-59) who tries to see the reliable narrator as a 'specialized character' who is constructed by a 'text-specific reader'.

13. The answer to this question will be provided in its detailed and various aspects in Chapters 4 and 5.

14. It is Uspensky (1973: 6) who distinguishes five different 'planes' of point of view: spatial (location of the narrator), temporal (the time of the narrator), phraseological (speech pattern), psychological (internal and external to the characters) and ideological (evaluative norms).

highlighted in the broad concept of the 'divine frame of reference' in Luke–Acts. Meanwhile, I shall also notice how the narrator (or the implied author) employs the *divine* frame of reference with a view to making major characters reliable and authoritative. This implies that the narrator (or the implied author) enjoys the literary power and freedom that enable the narrator to utilize and record such reference, especially the Holy Spirit as a *divine* character.[15]

3.1. Perceptual Facet

The perceptual point of view encompasses both space and time, which have usually been treated separately. In terms of space as the location of the narrator, the narrator of Luke–Acts, like other Gospel narrators, is considered *omnipresent*. The literary critic Chatman (1978: 103) demonstrates this attribute as 'the narrator's capacity to report from vantage-points not accessible to characters, or to jump from one to another, or to be in two places at once'. Put differently, the narrator possesses a panoramic or simultaneous view, that is, a bird's-eye view to report and evaluate any events and characters in the narrative world. On the other hand, the narrator, in terms of time, tells the story *retrospectively*. Rimmon-Kenan (1983: 78) explains this as follows, 'an external focalizer has at his disposal all the temporal dimensions of the story (past, present and future), whereas an internal focalizer is limited to the "present" of the characters'. This means, according to Culpepper (1983: 28), 'The narrator therefore speaks from some point in the future within the narrative world and interprets Jesus as no contemporary observer would have been able to do'.

I note, therefore, the literary quality of the Lukan narrator's omnipresence,[16] which creates the 'environment' of the divine Spirit.[17] If I

---

15. See §§4 and 5 in Chapter 4.

16. For instance, the narrator of Luke–Acts reports simultaneously both Zechariah's service inside the sanctuary of the Lord and the prayer of the people waiting outside the sanctuary (Lk. 1.10, 21; see also 1.65; 4.5, 9; 5.15-16; 9.28-36; 24.13-14). Another example is found in Lk. 23.45 in the way in which the narrator tells us of the incident occurring inside the temple, i.e. the curtain of the temple was torn in two, while he also describes Jesus' death with his last saying on the cross in Golgotha, namely outside the temple. Likewise in Acts, the narrator portrays two different simultaneous scenes: 'About noon the next day, as they [two slaves and one soldier from Cornelius] were on their journey and approaching the city [Joppa], Peter [in Joppa] went up on the roof to pray' (Acts 10.9; see also 2.41; 4.4; 5.21-22; 8.1, 26-40; 9.31; 11.19; 19.1).

may say that heaven is the 'external environment' of the Holy Spirit (Lk. 3.21-22), there is also the 'internal environment' of the Spirit, i.e. God's people's (human) heart or spirit. It is noted here that only the narrator, with two exceptions (cf. John the Baptist by an angel of the Lord in Lk. 1.15 and Paul by Ananias in Acts 9.17),[18] directly reports characters' endowment or possession of the Spirit by employing the Greek phrases, 'be filled with' and 'be full of' the Holy Spirit: Elizabeth (Lk. 1.41), Zechariah (Lk. 1.67), Jesus (Lk. 4.1), the disciples (Acts 2.4; 4.31), Peter (Acts 4.8), Stephen (Acts 6.5; 7.55), Paul (Acts 13.9) and Barnabas (Acts 11.24).[19] In other words, through his transcendental vantage-point, the Lukan narrator has both power and authority, not only to report the original place of the Holy Spirit, but also to inform his readers about certain characters who are inspired by the Holy Spirit.[20]

On the other hand, however, the Lukan narrator, while using a retrospective manner of description,[21] does not himself tell us directly of the Holy Spirit's activity before the time of the story related in Luke–Acts. However, the narrator uses the statements of reliable characters (1) to refer to the Spirit of the Lord long promised by the Jewish God (by Jesus in Lk. 24.49; by Peter in Acts 2.16-40) and (2) to refer to the Spirit who once talked to David and Isaiah long years ago (by Peter in

17. A further discussion about the circumlocution of the Holy Spirit will be given in §5.1.2.5 p. 161 in Chapter 4.

18. On such occasions, however, the following is to be mentioned: the perspective of an angel of the Lord as a (reliable) spiritual character in Lk. 1.15 can be seen as sharing the same ideology with the narrator (see §5.2.2.1 in Chapter 4); Ananias in Acts 9.17, unlike the narrator, is not said to report directly the incident of Paul's filling with the Spirit, but to predict it.

19. A detailed analysis of such phrases will be discussed along with their implications in §5.2.1.2 in Chapter 4.

20. The narrative shows that a few major characters (e.g. Jesus in Luke and Peter in Acts) can also report indirectly the 'original place' of the Holy Spirit: 'power from on high' (by Jesus in Lk. 24.49; cf. Isa. 32.15; Wis. 9.17) and 'at the right hand of God' or 'from the Father' (by Peter in Acts 2.33). It should be noted that both are representative characters who are filled with the Holy Spirit and thus share the narrator's ideological point of view.

21. In the Gospel, for example, the narrator informs the readers of Judas Iscariot's intrigue in advance, when Jesus chooses his twelve disciples from other followers for his mission: '...and Judas Iscariot, who became a traitor' (Lk. 6.16b). See also Lk. 4.13; 9.51; cf. Acts 1.18-19.

Acts 1.16; cf. 4.25; by Paul in Acts 28.25).[22] In fact, readers can perceive that the narrator not only endorses such reliable characters' own direct speeches, but also presents indirectly his ideological perspective through their utterances. In a sense, therefore, some major characters can be at times, although not always, regarded as the narrator's spokesmen.[23]

In short, my observation above leads me to postulate that the Lukan narrator is omnipresent and tells his story retrospectively, and particularly in relation to references to the divine Spirit.

3.2. *Psychological Facet*

Rimmon-Kenan (1983: 79), distinguishing the psychological dimension from that of perception, explains that 'Whereas the perceptual facet has to do with the focalizer's sensory range, the psychological facet concerns his mind and emotions'. So, the former concerns knowledge, conjecture, belief and memory, while the latter distinguishes objectivity (a neutral and uninvolved narrator) and subjectivity (a coloured and involved narrator). Accordingly, the external narrator, according to Rimmon-Kenan (79), objectively or neutrally 'knows everything about the represented world, and when he restricts his knowledge, he does so out of rhetorical considerations'. More strictly speaking, however, objectivity or neutrality is understood not as an absolute, but as a relative 'degree of objectivity'. In other words, any interest and evaluation by any narrators (even an external narrator) express their own ideology[24] or world-view.

Hence, my concern with the narrator's psychological point of view in Luke–Acts will be limited to his capacity to present inside views of characters, their intentions or thinking and so forth. In this sense, readers can perceive that the narrator in Luke–Acts is godlike, that is, he is *omniscient*. Through his omniscient perspective, the narrator provides readers with a great deal of information that is crucial for any readers to

---

22. For the definition of the Holy Spirit as the 'promise of the Father', see §5.1.1.4; for the speech of the Spirit, see §5.1.2.1 in Chapter 4.

23. See §3.3.2 in Chapter 3.

24. The facet of the narrator's ideology will be discussed in the next section. The term ideology here refers to 'a relatively coherent set of ideas amounting to a world-view, or outlook on life' and/or 'a set of such ideas special to a particular social class or group'. See Clines (1995: 9-25, esp. 10). See also p. 98 n. 33 in this chapter.

appreciate properly the value of characters and incidents in the story.[25] In relation to the Lukan narrator's psychological facet with the reference to the Holy Spirit, I should first point out the unique characteristic of the Holy Spirit as a character, that is, the 'trait of person-unlikeness' that enables the Spirit to be defined as a divine character.[26] In other words, the omniscience of the narrator allows him to report the 'speech' (Acts 8.29; 10.19; 13.2) and/or 'action' (Lk. 2.26; 3.21-22; Acts 2.4; 8.39; 13.4; 16.6, 7) of the invisible and enigmatic figure, the Holy Spirit.[27] In addition, readers understand the 'external appearance' of the Spirit, although allusive and metaphorical, only on the basis of the narrator's description (Lk. 3.21-22; Acts 2.2-3).[28]

The narrator, through his meta-perspective, also offers some important information about other spiritual characters and their actions, which cannot be seen in ordinary ways: the appearance, the origin and the name of an angel of the Lord along with his divine speech (Lk. 1.11, 13 to Zechariah; 1.26, 30 to Mary; 2.9-10 to shepherds; 22.43 to Jesus; Acts 5.19 to the apostles; 8.26 to Philip; 12.7-8 to Peter), the devil's test of Jesus by his speech (Lk. 4.1-13), Satan's entering into Judas (Lk. 22.3), the heavenly voice of God (Lk. 3.22 to Jesus; 9.35 to Peter, James and John; Acts 10.13, 15 to Peter), the heavenly voice of the resurrected and exalted Jesus (Acts 9.4, 7 to Paul) and visions (Acts

25. In the Gospel, the omniscient narrator gives readers inside views of the following characters: Zechariah (1.12), Mary (1.29; 2.51), the people (3.15), Jesus (5.22; 6.8; 9.47, 51; 11.17; 19.11; 20.23), the scribes and/or the Pharisees (6.7, 11; 7.49), a lawyer (10.29), a certain ruler (18.23), the disciples (18.34; 22.61 [Peter]; 24.37), the scribes and chief priests (20.19), Herod (23.8), Pilate (23.20) and the women (24.8). Likewise in Acts, the omniscient narrator discloses inside views: the cases of the Israelites (2.37), a man lame from birth (3.5), Paul (8.1; 17.16; 20.16), Cornelius (10.4), Peter (10.17, 19; 12.9), the jailer at Philippi (20.16), the tribune at Jerusalem (23.10), Festus (25.9) and the centurion in the ship (27.43).

26. For the 'person-unlikeness' of the Spirit, see §§4 and 5.1.2.3 in Chapter 4.

27. On several occasions, some reliable characters also depict the Spirit's speech (Acts 11.12 by Peter; Acts 21.11 by Agabus; cf. Acts 1.16; 28.25) and action (Lk. 12.12 by Jesus; Acts 20.22-23 by Paul; Acts 20.28 by Paul). In this sense, these characters are presented as those who share, although not completely, the same ideological perspective as the narrator (as long as their understanding or description of the Spirit is to be sanctioned in the narrative by the narrator). The relationship between the narrator and other reliable characters in terms of the narrator's ideology will be examined in §3.3.2 in this chapter.

28. For the issue of the 'speech', 'action' and 'external appearance' of the Holy Spirit, see §5.1.2 in Chapter 4.

9.10 to Ananias; 10.3 to Cornelius; 10.17, 19 to Peter; 16.9, 10; 18.9 to Paul; cf. Lk. 9.29-36; Acts 7.55).[29] It would thus be fair to claim that the narrator is omniscient, not only in informing the readers of characters' intentions, thoughts or feelings, but also in providing the readers with the speeches and actions of the divine Spirit and traits of other spiritual characters, used to express the will/plan of God as the matrix of the plot designed in Luke–Acts.[30] In this way, the narration, shaped by the Lukan narrator through the 'divine frame of reference', especially the Holy Spirit, shows both that the narrator is *omniscient* and *omnipresent*,[31] and that he is *reliable* and *authoritative*.[32] I shall now discuss the next crucial facet of the point of view.

29. For the analysis of both the angel of the Lord and the devil/Satan along with demons/evil spirits in comparison with the Holy Spirit, see §5.2.2 in Chapter 4; for the further discussion of an 'angel(s) (of the Lord)', 'heavenly voices' and 'visions', see §3.3.1 in this chapter.

30. For the plot of Luke–Acts, see Chapter 5.

31. When I say that the narrator is omniscient and omnipresent, I mean the quasi-omniscience and quasi-omnipresence of the narrator as the implied author's rhetorical device. Some critics now prefer the term 'degrees of privilege for the narrator' to that of omniscience or omnipresence. For the study, however, I employ the conventional terms for convenience while grasping the nuance. See Darr (1993: 46 n. 6).

32. Two scholars veto the reliability of the Lukan narrator: they are Dawsey (1986: 143-56) and Moore (1987: 451-52; 1989a: 30-34). Arguing that no reading can be ideologically neutral, Gunn (1990: 53-64), against the poetics of Sternberg, offers a critique of the concept of the reliable narrator especially in the Hebrew Bible. However, most Lukan critics reject this 'unreliability' and argue that the Lukan narrator, like other biblical writers, is reliable. See Tannehill (1986: 7); Sheeley (1992: 154); Darr (1992: 181-82; 1993: 44-46); Parsons (1993: 49 n. 19); Shepherd (1994: 40 and *passim*). Cf. Brown's comment (1994: I, 8) on Luke's omission of the Roman scourging in relation to Jesus' own prophecy that he would be scourged (Lk. 18.33; cf. 'they' in 23.26), saying that 'Luke is sometimes a careless editor'; yet, the implied reader would recognize 'they' as possibly referring to both the 'people of Israel' (i.e. the chief priests and the rulers and the people as the essentially responsible party seen in Lk. 23.13) and the 'Gentiles' (i.e. Roman soldiers as the formally responsible party seen in Lk. 18.32-33) as reflected in Acts 4.25-27. We should also note Culpepper's explanation of 'narrative reliability' (1983: 32): 'The reliability of the narrator must be kept distinct from both the historical accuracy of the narrator's account and the "truth" of his ideological point of view'. Thus, he further adds '"Reliability" is a matter of literary analysis, historical accuracy is the territory of the historian, and "truth" is a matter for believers and theologians' (32).

3.3. *Ideological Facet*

Centrally important to the narrator's point of view is his ideological or evaluative viewpoint.[33] Rimmon-Kenan (1983: 81), quoting Uspensky's definition, explains the ideological facet as the 'norms of the text', which 'consists of "a general system of viewing the world conceptually", in accordance with which the events and characters of the story are evaluated (Uspensky 1973, p. 8)'. From his 'super position', the narrator is able to govern and evaluate all components, like characters and incidents, described in the narrative world. Culpepper (1983: 32) rightly explains this in what follows:

> No narrator can be absolutely impartial; inevitably a narrator, especially an omniscient, omnipresent, omnicommunicative, and intrusive one, will prejudice the reader toward or away from certain characters, claims, or events and their implications. More than that, no story can be very meaningful unless the readers are introduced to its value system or provided with some way of relating it to their own.

At this point, we should consider the conflict-world embedded in Luke–Acts as the causal nexus of the plot in order to grasp more clearly the Lukan narrator's ideology or theological world-view. There are two ultimate poles of conflict in the narrative: one is the side of God; the other the side of Satan. This ideological conflict reflected in Luke–Acts does not permit any characters to hold an interim locus between the two, although one character may shift from one pole to the other (for instance, Judas Iscariot [Lk. 6.12-16 and 22.3-6] and Saul [Acts 8.1-3; 9.1-2; 9.19-22 onwards]). In this way, the Lukan narrator attempts to

---

33. For the definition of 'ideology', see p. 95 n. 24. 'Lukan theology' belongs to the 'ideology of the implied author' in Luke–Acts. In other words, Lukan theology is the 'religious-ideology' or the 'biblical-ideology' delineated in Lukan writings as the expression of the narrator's point of view. Here Moore's view is helpful (1989a: 56; emphasis original): 'A synonym that expresses the meaning of *theology* in this context and that strips it of extraneous connotations is an evangelist's *ideological point of view*, denoting the systems of assumptions and convictions against which everything in the story (the set of persons, events, and places) is evaluated—or to put it another way, in terms of which everything in the story is presented'. Similarly, Clines suggests 'theology' is a 'subset of ideology' while acknowledging that the former has been, most of the time, conventionally used in biblical studies: 'This terminology ['theology'] makes sense, of course, since many of the ideas in the Bible are directly about God and most others have at least a theological element in them' (1995: 13).

challenge his readers to accept his "world-view" by using all sorts of rhetorical devices[34] in Luke–Acts.

The narrator's ideological point of view in Luke–Acts claims to encompass *God's point of view* through which he evaluates or comments on characters, depicted through inside views or outward behaviour (for instance, see Zechariah and Elizabeth in Lk. 1.6; Simeon in Lk. 2.25; Herod's death in Acts 12.23). Hence, by presenting characters as God's agents, the Lukan narrator clearly favours some characters and disfavours others. For instance, the narrator, by focusing on the person and work of Jesus (Acts 1.1-2), first introduces the birth, ministry, death, resurrection and ascension of Jesus as the Son of the Most High (Lk. 1.32 by an angel of the Lord; see also Lk. 2.40, 52) within the geographical setting of Palestine, and then continues to record in his second volume the spreading of this message by his disciples filled with the Holy Spirit into Gentile territory. Concerning the narrator's favour towards Jesus, Kingsbury (1991: 13) rightly points out,

> The authoritative narrator, we said, regards Jesus as authoritative and aligns himself with him. For his part, Jesus is the 'sign' of God. In Jesus, God himself is at work to accomplish his plan of salvation. According to Luke's conception of reality, therefore, God is viewed as the supreme arbiter of what is good or bad, right or wrong, true or false. Correlatively, since God makes himself present in Jesus, Jesus becomes the measuring rod against which all other characters are to be judged. Those who align themselves with Jesus 'serve the purpose of God' (16.15; Acts 13.36).

Therefore, the narrator of Luke–Acts holds, in short, a theocentric and christocentric ideology.[35] Thus the narrator's ideology is presented as a

---

34. For the general characteristics of narrator's rhetorical devices, see Rhoads and Michie (1982: 35-62). Cf. Booth's discussion (1991: 16-20) of 'the voices of the author': (1) direct addresses or commentary (e.g. Lk. 3.1-2; Acts 2.43-47), (2) explicit judgments (e.g. Lk. 7.29-30; Acts 12.23), (3) inside views (e.g. Lk. 7.49; Acts 25.9), (4) the reliable statements of any dramatized character (e.g. Lk. 1.6; Acts 6.5) and (5) all evidences of the author's meddling with the natural sequence, proportion, or duration of events (e.g. Lk. 9.51; 13.22; 17.11; 18.31; 19.11, 28; Acts 2.41-47; 4.32-35; 5.42; 6.7; 8.1-3; 9.31).

35. See also the narrator's use of the term, 'fall asleep' when he depicts Stephen as dead (Acts 7.60) in a manner similar to Jesus who uses that expression in the case of the dead daughter of Jairus (Lk. 8.52). For Jesus' ability to perceive the inside views of characters, see Lk. 5.22; 6.8; 9.47; 11.17, 38-39; 20.23; 22.21-22, 31-32, 34; 24.38. See also Lk. 10.18, 20; 19.30-31; 21.8-28; 22.10-12 for Jesus'

reliable and *authoritative* force to challenge the readers' ideology in their reading process. In other words, the Lukan narrator appeals to his readers for the reliability and authority of his narrative on the ground that he is on God's side and that of his Messiah, Jesus.

Hence, the narrator (and some major characters as intradiegetic narrators) also utilizes and/or depends upon the external reference to an angel(s) (of the Lord), visions, heavenly voices, scriptural citations and, above all, the Holy Spirit.[36] In regard to these rhetorical components, Darr (1992: 50-53) notes that the 'divine frame of reference' even encompasses the narrator.[37] Most importantly, he rightly and persuasively points out the significant role of the Holy Spirit as a meta-reference in understanding the whole narrative, particularly in association with major characters and in validating the cited Scripture. Thus, he (52-53) suggests,

> In this narrative, the divine point of view is invariably expressed or *authenticated through the auspices of the Holy Spirit*. Each protagonist is confirmed as such by an overt action of the Holy Spirit. Even the Lukan Jesus is validated in this manner... Moreover, every speech that purports to represent the divinity (especially prophetic or predictive words) must bear *the Spirit's stamp of approval*, or else it remains subject to suspicion... [E]ven the promises, predictions, and prefigurations found in scripture are placed *under the aegis of the Spirit*. That is, a *pneumatic (and christological) hermeneutic* is used to control how the writings are applied to the present narrative. The scriptures alone are not sufficient to legitimate anything; they too must be 'accredited' in each case by the Spirit, or by a figure who has the Spirit's sanction (emphasis added).

omnipresence (?). In fact, the resurrected Jesus, like the Holy Spirit, is portrayed as a character who transcends space and time (see Lk. 24.31, 51; Acts 1.9; 9.3-7; 23.11).

36. For the narrator's use of the Holy Spirit, see §5 in Chapter 4. Cf. Brawley's view (1990: 115) on the Holy Spirit as another epithet for God rather than as a different character. Yet he also acknowledges the difference between the two, but does not develop it further; see also p. 30 n. 49 in Chapter 1.

37. Cf. Powell's observation (1993: 24): 'The reader, then, is expected to accept not only that God's point of view is true and right, but also that God's point of view be expressed reliably through angels, prophets, miracles, dreams, and Scripture'. Darr, however, also mentions a 'hierarchy of viewpoints' in the divine frame of reference in which 'the narrator as god-like persona' is the 'most significant, all-encompassing frame of reference' (1992: 50).

It can thus be claimed that the Lukan narrator, in terms of ideology, represents not only a *theocentric* and *christocentric* position, but also a *pneumocentric* point of view that reinforces his evaluation or judgment of any characters and incidents.[38] Hence, the narrator tells the reader not only of the incidents of the coming of the Holy Spirit (e.g. Lk. 3.22 and Acts 2.1-4), but also of the characters who are inspired by the Holy Spirit (e.g. Elizabeth, Zechariah, John the Baptist, Jesus and so on).

As mentioned earlier, the Lukan narrator employs not only the Holy Spirit, but also an angel(s) (of the Lord), heavenly voices, visions and scriptural citations in the 'divine frame of reference'. In what follows, I shall note how frequently the Lukan narrator employs this divine frame of reference and then examine to what extent (some major) characters in Luke–Acts are associated with it. In so doing, I shall notice that the narrative reliability of characters is linked with their relationship to the divine frame of reference. In other words, if characters are engaged with the divine frame of reference in a positive way, that is, endorsed by the narrator, this functions as a literary indicator that they are reliable characters who share the same (triune) ideology with the Lukan narrator.

3.3.1. *The Divine Frame of Reference*[39]
3.3.1.1. *An Angel(s) (of the Lord).*[40] Out of 47 occurrences referring to an ἄγγελος in Luke–Acts, 32 cases are appropriate here and noted in the following Table (1).

---

38. This triune perspective of the Lukan narrator will be explained further in terms of the plot of Luke–Acts; see §3 in Chapter 5. Cf. Darr's claim (1992: 180 n. 9): 'One complexity of Luke–Acts, of course, is that the major agent—God—remains "offstage". The divine will is expressed in and through the omniscient narrator, Jesus, and especially the Spirit'; Powell (1991: 57; emphasis original): 'The book of Acts is *theocentric*. God is presented as the director of history, and the hope of humanity is presented as dependent on God's promises. Acts is also *christocentric*, for God exalts Jesus to become "Lord of all" (2.36; 10.36). Finally, Acts is *pneumocentric* (spirit-centered) for the exalted Lord Jesus pours out the Holy Spirit on his followers so that they might become his witnesses'.

39. I shall deal with the 'Holy' Spirit separately in more detail in terms of the most obvious 'direct definition' of the divine Spirit in Luke–Acts (see §5.1.1.1 in Chapter 4); in this subsection, I shall thus offer Table 4 which shows the Lukan characters who are filled with or full of the Holy Spirit (see below). On the other hand, due to the fact that the Lukan narrator utilizes evil spirits/demons who *ironically* identify who Jesus is, they seem to be categorized as a part of the 'divine

Table 1. *Angel(s) (of the Lord)*

Speaker	Any Related Characters	Passage (Singular or Plural)
narrator	Zechariah	Lk. 1.11 (S)
narrator	Zechariah	Lk. 1.13 (S)
narrator	Zechariah	Lk. 1.18 (S)
narrator	Zechariah	Lk. 1.19 (S)
narrator	Mary	Lk. 1.26 (S)
narrator	Mary	Lk. 1.30 (S)
narrator	Mary	Lk. 1.34 (S)
narrator	Mary	Lk. 1.35 (S); cf. 1.38; 2.21
narrator	shepherds	Lk. 2.9 (S)
narrator	shepherds	Lk. 2.10 (S)
narrator		Lk. 2.15 (P); cf. 2.13
Jesus		Lk. 9.26 (P)
Jesus		Lk. 12.8 (P)
Jesus		Lk. 12.9 (P)
Jesus		Lk. 15.10 (P)
Jesus		Lk. 16.22 (P)
Jesus		Lk. 20.36 (P)
narrator	Jesus	Lk. 22.43 (S)
narrator	the apostles	Acts 5.19 (S)
Stephen	Moses	Acts 7.30 (S)
Stephen	Moses	Acts 7.35 (S)
Stephen	Moses	Acts 7.38 (S)
Stephen		Acts 7.53 (P)
narrator	Philip	Acts 8.26 (S)
narrator	Cornelius	Acts 10.3 (S); cf. 10.7, 22; 11.13
narrator	Peter	Acts 12.7 (S)
narrator	Peter	Acts 12.8 (S)
narrator	Peter	Acts 12.9 (S)
narrator		Acts 12.10 (S)
Peter		Acts 12.11 (S)
narrator	Herod	Acts 12.23 (S)
Paul		Acts 27.23 (S)

frame of reference'. However, they, unlike the (reliable) 'divine frame of reference', are characterized as the agents of Satan, i.e. acting as 'opponents' *against* both God and Jesus, including his disciples in the narrative. See §5.2.2.2 in Chapter 4.

40. See also §5.2.2.1 in Chapter 4.

It is only the Lukan narrator (20 times) who directly records the appearance and speech or action of an angel(s) (of the Lord) in relation to several characters.[41] On such occasions, an angel (of the Lord) functions as God's spiritual agent who reveals God's will/plan to his people concerning the birth of John the Baptist in Lk. 1.13 and Jesus in Lk. 1.30-35; 2.10-11, and the proclamation of the gospel in Acts 8.26-27 (cf. 27.23-24); as a divine helper to Jesus in Lk. 22.43;[42] as a divine director to the apostles in Acts 5.19-20, particularly to Peter in Acts 12.7-8, and to Cornelius in Acts 10.3-4; as a divine judge to Herod in Acts 12.23. On the other hand, the internal narrators as characters tend to talk *about* angel(s), either prospectively by Jesus or retrospectively by Stephen, Peter and Paul.

The narrator thus utilizes an angel in an attempt to show the reliability and authority of his narrative, and makes some characters engage with an angel to portray them as reliable characters who are, so to speak, now guided by the special agent sent by God. In other words, they are depicted as the characters who are joining the side of the narrator's ideology.

3.3.1.2. Heavenly Voices. Thirteen cases, out of 37 references to voice, are noted in the following Table (2).[43]

Table 2. *Heavenly Voices*

Speaker	Voice-Sender	Voice-Receiver	Passage
narrator	God	Jesus	Lk. 3.22
narrator	God	Peter, James, John	Lk. 9.35
Stephen	God	Moses	Acts 7.31
narrator	Jesus	Paul	Acts 9.4
narrator	Jesus	Paul	Acts 9.7
narrator	God	Peter	Acts 10.13
narrator	God	Peter	Acts 10.15
Peter	God	Peter	Acts 11.7
Peter	God	Peter	Acts 11.9
Paul	Jesus	Paul	Acts 22.7

41. Similarly, various direct reports about the coming of the *Holy* Spirit along with his action and speech are made by the Lukan narrator with only one exception in Acts 21.11 (by Agabus). See §5.1.1.1 in Chapter 4.

42. For textual variants of Lk. 22.43, see p. 173 n. 180 in Chapter 4.

43. Most of the reference referring to human beings' voice (e.g. Lk. 1.44—Mary; Acts 2.14—Peter); cf. demon's voice in Lk. 8.18; unclean spirits' voice in Acts 8.7.

Speaker	Voice-Sender	Voice-Receiver	Passage
Paul	Jesus	Paul	Acts 22.9
Ananias	Jesus	Paul	Acts 22.14
Paul	Jesus	Paul	Acts 26.14

Table 2 shows that the Lukan narrator directly reports the incident in which some characters hear the divine voice from heaven or out of the cloud.[44] Through this heavenly voice, the narrator not only reveals (to his readers) both God's (in Luke and Acts) and the risen Jesus' (in Acts) will, but also confirms apologetically that his narrative is reliable and authoritative. What should be noted here is that the heavenly voice focuses on the identity of Jesus (Lk. 3.22; 9.35) and then guides the direction of Jesus' disciples' witness-mission not only to Jews, but also to Gentiles (Acts 9.4, 7; 10.13, 15). As a result, the characters, Jesus, Paul and Peter, who receive and respond to such a voice from heaven appear to work as reliable characters as God's and/or Jesus' witnesses. It should also be noted that Jesus as the 'receiver of God's voice' in Luke becomes the 'sender of his own voice' to his disciples after his resurrection in Acts. So Jesus' disciples in Acts are depicted as the resurrected and exalted Jesus' witnesses (Acts 1.8, 22; 2.32; 3.15; 5.32; 10.39, 41; 22.15, 20; 26.16).[45]

3.3.1.3. *Visions.* In Luke–Acts, 10 occasions among 13 (cf. Lk. 1.22; 24.23; Acts 12.9) indicating a vision need to be examined in the following Table (3).

Table 3. *Visions*

Speaker	Any Related Characters?	Passage
Peter	The young men	Acts 2.17 (Joel 2.28)
narrator	Ananias	Acts 9.10
narrator	Cornelius	Acts 10.3
narrator	Peter	Acts 10.17
narrator	Peter	Acts 10.19

44. For God's voice from heaven in the Hebrew Bible, see Deut. 4.36; 5.22-26; Isa. 6.4, 8; Ezek. 1.25, 28; cf. Ezra 6.13; Ps. 29.3-9. See also in Rev. 4.1; 10.4, 8; 11.12; 12.10; 14.13; 18.4; 21.3.

45. Jesus' disciples, after being given Jesus' authority and power, are said twice to proclaim the Kingdom of God in Lk. 9.1-6; 10.1-16. However, the portraits of them in the remaining Gospel narrative as 'coward witnesses' (i.e. before receiving the Spirit) should be distinguished from those as 'bold witnesses' in Acts (i.e. after receiving the Spirit). See Chapter 5.

Speaker	Any Related Characters?	Passage
Peter	Peter himself	Acts 11.5
narrator	Paul	Acts 16.9
narrator	Paul	Acts 16.10
narrator	Paul	Acts 18.9; cf. 22.18, 21; 23.11
Paul	Paul himself	Acts 26.19

Table 3 shows us again that the Lukan narrator describes the characters' receiving a divine vision (Acts 10.17; 16.9, 10) or hearing speech in a vision (Acts 9.10; 10.3; 18.9).[46] And the vision, like heavenly voices, reveals to Jesus' disciples the places where they as Jesus' witnesses should go: among the Gentiles who would have been ignored by the disciples without God's revelation through such visions. These visions are construed as divine and trustworthy, as visions from God (Acts 16.10), the risen Jesus (Acts 9.10; cf. 16.7; 18.9) and the Holy Spirit (Acts 10.19; cf. 16.6). Hence Paul is depicted as recounting the heavenly vision to King Agrippa (Acts 26.19).

By recounting these visions, the narrator implies that his narrative is reliable and authoritative. Also the characters, who see such visions and obey them, are presented as reliable. In addition, the narrator utilizes visions with a view to showing that the long-time promise of Joel's inspired prophecy (i.e. 'your [God's] young men [viz. Ananias, Cornelius, Peter and Paul] shall see visions'), attributed to Peter, has been accomplished.

3.3.1.4. Scriptural Citations. The Lukan narrator's use of scriptural citations (mainly the LXX)[47] also develops his ideological perspective. However, the narrator rarely presents the Jewish Bible directly, but more often presents quotations through the speeches of reliable characters.[48] Here I shall examine the narrator's skilful use of scriptural

46. For the vision of the Almighty or God in the Hebrew Bible, see Gen. 15.1; 46.2; Num. 12.6; 24.4, 16; Lam. 2.9; Ezek. 1.1; 8.3; 40.2. For a vision functioning as God's revelation, see also 2 Sam. 7.17; 1 Chron. 17.15; 2 Chron. 32.32; Isa. 1.1; 21.2; Ezek. 11.24; Dan. 2.19; 7.2; 8.2, 15, 17, 26; 9.21; 10.1, 7; Obad. 1.1; Nah. 1.1.

47. For general characteristics of Luke's use of the Jewish Bible, see Clarke (1922: 66-105); Ringgren (1986: 227-35); Barrett (1988: 231-44). For the recent academic debate on the Lukan use of the Old Testament, see Bock (1987: 13-53) and Kimball (1994).

48. Quite recently, Arnold (1996: 300-323) examines the Lukan use of the Jewish Bible through a new literary perspective and rightly points out this issue, saying, 'Luke uses Old Testament quotations in the speeches of his leading characters

citations in Luke and Acts respectively, and then bring out some implications for his ideological point of view. Although there are some trace-
able allusions[49] to the Jewish Bible in Luke–Acts, I shall focus on the
explicit quotations, whether they are *verbatim* citations or paraphrased,
which are introduced with Lukan citation-expressions such as 'it is
written', 'it is said', 'Moses wrote' and so on.

Table 4. *Scriptural Citations in Luke*

Speaker	Passage in Luke	Original Text	Quoted Expression
narrator	2.23	Exod. 13.2; cf. 13.12, 15	'it is written'
narrator	2.24	Lev. 12.8	'what is stated in the law of the Lord'
narrator	3.4-6	LXX Isa. 40.3-5	'it is written'
Jesus	4.4	LXX Deut. 8.3	'it is written'
Jesus	4.8	Deut. 6.13	'it is written'
the Devil	4.10-11	LXX Ps. 90.11-12	'it is written'

(Peter, Stephen and Paul) to express his point of view about those characters' (302);
'Luke has artfully used the Old Testament to express his ideological point of view'
(308). However, his research in regard to the Lukan scriptural citations has only
dealt with the Book of Acts and has not understood scriptural citations within the
'divine frame of reference', which expresses, I believe, the Lukan narrator's
ideological purpose.
    49. The allusions and the speakers who narrate them in Luke: 1.17 by an angel
of the Lord (Mal. 4.5-6); 1.48 by Mary (LXX 1 Sam. 1.11); 1.50 by Mary (Ps.
103.17); 1.76 by Zechariah (Mal. 3.1); 1.79 by Zechariah (Isa. 9.2); 2.24 by the narrator (Lev. 12.8); 2.52 by the narrator (1 Sam. 2.26); 3.22 by the narrator (Ps. 2.7;
Gen. 22.2; Isa. 42.1); 7.22 by Jesus (Isa. 35.5-6 and/or 61.1); 8.10 by Jesus (LXX
Isa. 6.9); 9.35 by the narrator (Ps. 2.7; Isa. 42.1; Deut. 18.15); 9.54 by James and
John (2 Kgs 1.10); 10.15 by Jesus (Isa. 14.13, 15); 12.53 by Jesus (Mic. 7.6); 13.27
by Jesus (Ps. 6.8); 13.35a by Jesus (Jer. 22.5); 13.35b by Jesus (Ps. 118.26); 19.38
by the disciples (Ps. 118.26); 20.9 by Jesus (Isa. 5.1-2); 21.27 by Jesus (Dan. 7.13);
21.34-35 by Jesus (Isa. 24.17); 22.69 by Jesus (Ps. 110.1); 23.30 by Jesus (Hos.
10.8); 23.34 by Jesus (Ps. 22.18); 23.46 by the narrator (Ps. 31.5). In Acts: 2.30 by
Peter (Ps. 132.11; cf. Ps. 89.3-4; 2 Sam. 7.12-13); 3.13 by Peter (Exod. 3.15); 4.11
by Peter (Ps. 118.22); 4.24 by Peter and John (Exod. 20.11; cf. Ps. 146.6); by
Stephen, 7.5 (Gen. 48.4; cf. 17.8); 7.14 (LXX Gen. 46.27; cf. Exod. 1.5); 7.18 (LXX
Exod. 1.8); 7.27-29 (LXX Exod. 2.13-15); 7.32 (Exod. 3.6; cf. 3.15); 7.35 (Exod.
2.14); 7.33-34 (Exod. 3.5, 7, 8a, 10a); 7.37 (LXX Deut. 18.15); 7.40 (Exod. 32.1; cf.
32.23); 13.18 by Paul (LXX Deut. 1.31); 13.19 by Paul (Deut. 7.1); 13.36 by Paul
(1 Kgs 2.10); 14.15 by Barnabas and Paul (Exod. 20.11; cf. Ps. 146.6); 17.31 by
Paul (Ps. 9.8; cf. 96.13; 98.9); 28.28 by Paul (LXX Ps. 66.3). Cf. Bratcher (1987:
17-24, 28-37).

Speaker	Passage in Luke	Original Text	Quoted Expression
Jesus	4.12	LXX Deut. 6.16	'it is said'
Jesus	4.18-19	LXX Isa. 61.1-2	'it was written' (by the narrator)
Jesus	7.27	Mal. 3.1	'it is written'
Jesus	10.26	Deut. 6.5; Lev. 19.18	'What is written in the law?'
Jesus	18.20	Exod. 20.12-16	'You know the commandments'
Jesus	19.46a/19.46b	Isa. 56.7b/Jer. 7.11	'it is written'
Jesus	20.17	Ps. 118.22	'What then is this that is written' (RSV)
some Sadducees	20.28	Deut. 25.5	'Moses wrote'
Jesus	20.37	Exod. 3.6	'Moses showed'
Jesus	20.42-43	LXX Ps. 109.1	'David says'
Jesus	22.37	Isa. 53.12	'what is written'
Jesus	24.46	no exact passage;[50] cf. Isa. 53; Hos. 6.2	'it is written' (cf. 24.27)

As we can see in Table 4, the Lukan narrator cites the Jewish Bible mostly in the speeches of the reliable character, Jesus (13 out of 17), whereas the narrator himself cites Scripture only twice. The other two cases are quoted by the devil and some Sadducees, who try to test Jesus by saying 'it is written' (Lk. 4.10) and 'Moses wrote' (Lk. 20.28). In these cases, the narrative, however, suggests through Jesus' re-citations of Scripture ('it is said' in Lk. 4.12; 'Moses showed' in Lk. 20.37) that their quotations are misused and misunderstood. This means that they do not possess Jesus' (or the narrator's) ideological or hermeneutical point of view. In other words, the narrator and the Spirit-filled Jesus are understood to cite Scripture and apologetically use it to defend John's

50. 24.46: 'and he said to them, 'Thus it is written, that the Messiah is to suffer and to rise from the dead on the third day"...' In fact, it is hard to trace the concept of messianic suffering on the basis of the Jewish interpretation of their scriptures (cf. the suffering of the innocent righteous: Pss. 22; 31; 69; 118; Isa. 53; for the background of the Hebrew Bible in relation to the passion of Jesus, see Brown [1994: II, 1452-65]). This text highlights, therefore, the Lukan narrator's ideological or theological view on the Jewish Bible, i.e. christocentric application of the Jewish Bible. Thus, Fitzmyer elucidates (1985: 1558), 'This is the Lukan way of casting the OT data; it is his global christological use of the OT (see p. 200). Luke has his own way of reading the OT and here puts it on the lips of Christ himself; a (Christian) interpretation of the OT thus surfaces in this episode and will be continued in Acts'.

identity (Lk. 3.4-6), Jesus' own messianic identity (Lk. 2.23; 4.4, 8, 12, 18-19; 10.26-27; 20.37) and his teaching (Lk. 18.18-20; 19.46; 20.17, 42-43; 22.37; 24.46). The most frequent introductory expression of the narrator and Jesus is 'it is written' (12 times; once used 'it is said'). Jesus also attributes the quotation twice to the Old Testament figures, Moses and David (see also the use of 'the prophet Isaiah' by the narrator in Lk. 3.4a and 'Moses' by the Sadducees in Lk. 20.28).

Table 5. *Scriptural Citations in Acts*

Speaker	Passage in Acts	Original Text	Quoted Expression
Peter	1.20a/20b	LXX Ps. 68.26/ Ps. 108.8	'it is written'
Peter	2.17-21	LXX Joel 3.1-5	'this is what was spoken through the prophet Joel'
Peter	2.25-28	LXX Ps. 15.8-11	'David says'
Peter	2.31	LXX Ps. 15.10	'David spoke of'
Peter	2.34-35	LXX Ps. 109.1	'David says'
Peter	3.22-23	LXX Deut. 18.15-16	'Moses said'
Peter	3.25	Gen. 22.18; cf. 12.3; 26.4; 28.14	'all the prophets... predicted'
Peter and John	4.25-26	LXX Ps. 2.1-2	'God who said by the Holy Spirit through our ancestor David, your servant'
Stephen	7.3	Gen. 12.1	'God said to Abraham'
Stephen	7.6	Gen. 15.13	'God spoke'
Stephen	7.7	Gen. 15.14; Exod. 3.12	'... said God'
Stephen	7.42-43	LXX Amos 5.25-27	'it is written'
Stephen	7.49-50	Isa. 66.1-2	'the prophet says'
narrator	8.32-33	LXX Isa. 53.7-8	'the passage of the scripture'
Paul	13.22	Ps. 89.20	'Samuel said'
Paul	13.33	Ps. 2.7	'it is written'
Paul	13.34	LXX Isa. 55.3	'God has spoken'
Paul	13.35	LXX Ps. 15.10	'God has said'
Paul	13.41	LXX Hab. 1.5	'what the prophets said'
Paul and Barnabas	13.47	LXX Isa. 49.6	'the Lord has commanded us, saying'
James	15.16-18	LXX Amos 9.11-12	'it is written'
Paul	23.5	Exod. 22.28	'it is written'
Paul	28.26-27	LXX Isa. 6.9-10	'The Holy Spirit was right in saying to your ancestors through the prophet Isaiah'

In Acts, the narrator (who only once directly cites Scripture in Acts 8.32-33) now further uses the Jewish Bible through the speeches of several Spirit-filled characters, Peter (7 times), Peter and John (1), Stephen (5), Paul (7), Paul and Barnabas (1) and James (1). Their use of scriptural citations is apologetically designed (for both the real narratee-characters and the implied reader) to vindicate Jesus' messianic identity and work (Acts 2.25-28, 31, 34-35; 3.22-23, 25; 8.32-33; 13.22, 33, 34, 35), and the coming of the Holy Spirit (Acts 2.17-21) as expressions of God's salvation plan. The implied author, through this 'proof of promise and fulfilment' based on Scripture, also attempts to justify the way of witness of Jesus' disciples to the Gentiles (Acts 13.47; 15.16-17; 28.28; cf. Lk. 2.32), while rebuking the 'stiff-necked Jews' (Acts 7.42-43; 28.26-27; cf. 4.25-26). In addition, like Jesus, both Stephen and Paul are once said to cite Scripture in order to defend themselves against Jews (Acts 7.49-50 against 6.13; 23.5 against 23.4).

In Acts, characters use these terms when they quote the Jewish Bible: 'it is written' (Acts 1.20; 7.42; 13.33; 15.16; 23.5; cf. 8.82), 'Joel, David, Moses, Samuel says/said' (Acts 2.25, 31, 34; 3.32; 13.22; cf. 2.17), 'God/the Lord said' (Acts 7.3, 6, 7; 13.34, 35, 47), 'by the Holy Spirit' or 'the Holy Spirit was right in saying' (Acts 4.25; 28.25b; cf. 1.16) and '[unnamed] prophet[s] predicted/says/said' (Acts 3.25; 7.49; 13.41). In comparison with the Gospel, the implied author adds the last three expressions and we note especially the references to the Holy Spirit as inspiring David and Isaiah.

On the basis of my examination of the Lukan quotations of the Jewish Bible in Luke–Acts, I can draw out the following points. (1) The narrator presents some leading characters (e.g. Jesus, Peter, Stephen and Paul) as sharing the narrator's ideology in their citations of Scripture in their speeches. They can thus be regarded as reliable characters. (2) A christocentric use of the Jewish Bible is closely associated with being filled with the Holy Spirit (i.e. Jesus in Luke; Peter, Stephen and Paul in Acts; see also Spirit-filled characters in Lk. 1-2 along with their use of Old Testament allusions). (3) The Lukan quotations of the Jewish Bible express the 'proof from promise and fulfilment' (cf. Lk. 1.1), which focuses on Jesus' messianic identity in most cases and also vindicates his disciples' witness to the Gentiles (cf. Lk. 2.32; 3.6; 7.9).[51] And (4)

---

51. Bock (1994a: 280-307) supports my observations: 'the two major themes of Old Testament fulfilment are Christology [Messiah–Servant–Prophet] and mission [to the Gentiles]' (305). Cf. Arnold concludes (1996: 323), who, 'Luke's skilful use

the narrator's use of Old Testament quotations is designed to suggest that the Lukan narrative is in continuity with the Jewish Bible and furthermore its fulfilment. These four points can also be recognized within other elements of the divine frame of reference in Luke–Acts.

3.3.2. *The Lukan Narrator and Reliable Characters*
I have already explored the Lukan narrator's use of the divine frame of reference to express his ideological point of view. As noticed earlier in connection with each element of the divine frame of reference, some leading characters in Luke–Acts are presented as sharing the same ideology. Hence such characters can be considered reliable and authoritative. That is, if a character assimilates or transforms their ideology to the narrator's, he or she becomes a reliable character.[52] In a sense, the Lukan narrator functions as an ideal character who can freely express the divine frame of reference.

The Tables 1-5 above and 6-7 below list some related characters who are linked with the divine frame of reference.

Table 6. *Characters Who are Filled with or Full of the Holy Spirit*[53]

Characters	Speakers	Passage
John the Baptist	an angel of the Lord	Lk. 1.15
Elizabeth	narrator	Lk. 1.41

of Old Testament quotations reveals not only the missionary purpose of the apostolic speeches historically, but also the polemical and theological purpose of the Book of Acts literally'.

52. Kissling thus claims (1996: 20), 'When a character's speech and/or actions always represent the narrator's point of view and always have the narrator's moral and ideological approval, that character is said to be a thoroughly reliable character'. For a more comprehensive approach to the reliability of characters, we should no doubt take into account the narrator's whole presentation of characters (i.e. 'direct definition', 'indirect presentation' [e.g. speech, action, external appearance and environment], 'repetition and similarity', 'comparison and contrast' and 'implication'). Nevertheless, the 'divine frame of reference' is, I believe, the most convenient and effective index in testing the narrative reliability of characters in Luke–Acts.

53. In Table 6, I only provide the characters who are 'filled with' or 'full of' the Holy Spirit, because these expressions are conceived as Lukan-favoured terms. For further argument, see §5.2.1.2 in Chapter 4. It is also true, however, that any characters who are positively related to the divine Spirit can be categorized as reliable characters. For other (named and unnamed) characters not listed in Tables 6 and 7, see Appendix III.

Characters	Speakers	Passage
Zechariah	narrator	Lk. 1.67
Jesus	narrator	Lk. 4.1
Peter	narrator	Acts 4.8
Paul	Ananias	Acts 9.17
Paul	narrator	Acts 13.9
Stephen	narrator	Acts 6.5
Stephen	narrator	Acts 7.55
Barnabas	narrator	Acts 11.24
Jesus' disciples	narrator	Acts 2.4
Jesus' disciples	narrator	Acts 13.52
Jesus' disciples (including their group members)	narrator	Acts 4.31
seven men[54]	the twelve apostles	Acts 6.3

Table 7. *Characters Associated with the Divine Frame of Reference*

Character	'Holy' Spirit	Angels	Voices	Visions	Citations
Jesus[55]	1	1	1		13
Peter[56]	1	4	4	3	8
Paul[57]	2	1	6	4	8
John the Baptist	1				
Zechariah	1	4			
Elizabeth	1				
Mary	(cf. Lk. 1.35)	4			
Stephen	2 (cf. Acts 6.3, 5)				5
Barnabas	1 (cf. Acts 13.2, 4)				1
Philip	(cf. Acts 8.29, 39)	1			
Cornelius	(cf. Acts 10.44-47)	1		1	
James	(cf. Jesus' apostles)		1		1
John	(cf. Jesus' apostles)		1		1
Ananias				1	

54. They are Prochorus, Nicanor, Timon, Parmenas and Nicolaus, including Stephen and Philip.
55. See also Jesus' relationship with the divine Spirit: Lk. 1.35; 3.22; 4.1, 14, 18; 10.21; Acts 1.2; 2.33; 10.38; with the vision without an explicit reference: Lk. 3.21-22; 9.28-36; 10.18-22.
56. See also Peter's relationship with the divine Spirit: Acts 8.17; 10.19; 11.12.
57. See also Paul's relationship with the divine Spirit: Acts 13.2, 4; 16.6-7; 19.6, 21; 20.21-22.

Character	'Holy' Spirit	Angels	Voices	Visions	Citations
Jesus' apostles and/or disciples	3 (cf. Acts 11.15, 17; 15.8)	1			
seven men	1				
shepherds		2			
Moses	(cf. Num. 11.17, 25)	3	(cf. Exod. 3)		

Table 7 demonstrates that Jesus in Luke, and Peter and Paul in Acts are designed as the most reliable characters when we compare them with other characters in terms of the frequency of their positive relationship to the 'divine frame of reference'. In addition, this is true if we contrast a character before he is engaged with the 'divine frame of reference' with him after he is related to it. For instance, we can contrast the narrative reliability of Peter in Luke (esp. Lk. 22.54-62) with that in Acts (esp. after Acts 2 onwards) as a contrast between the coward and false witness to Jesus and the bold and true witness to Jesus.[58] Similarly, we can contrast Saul as the witness against Jesus with Saul as the witness for (the sake of) Jesus.

Another important aspect is that characters[59] who are associated

58. Peter's confession of his master Jesus as Christ in Lk. 9.20 (cf. 22.31-32) can be understood as ironically reliable.

59. Like the narrator, reliable characters in Luke–Acts are presented as possessing a triune perspective: (1) Peter: theocentric (Lk. 9.1-6; Acts 2.22-24, 32; 10.34-43), christocentric (Lk. 9.1, 20; Acts 2.21-22; 3.6; 4.10; 5.31-32; 10.34-43) and pneumocentric (Acts 2.4; 4.8; 8.14-17; 10.19-23); (2) Paul: theocentric (Acts 13.5, 44, 46; 16.10; 18.5; 19.8; 20.21, 24; 24.14-16; 28.23, 31), christocentric (Acts 9.15, 20, 22; 13.23, 33; 16.7, 31; 17.3; 18.5; 20.21; 26.23; 28.23; 28.31) and pneumocentric (Acts 9.17; 13.2, 4, 9; 16.6; 19.5-6; 19.21; 20.22-23); (3) John the Baptist: theocentric (Lk. 1.15a, 16, 66, 76; 3.2), christocentric (Lk. 1.17, 76; 3.16-17; 7.27) and pneumocentric (Lk. 1.15); (4) Zechariah: theocentric (Lk. 1.6, 64, 68) and pneumocentric (Lk. 1.67); (5) Elizabeth: theocentric (Lk. 1.6, 58), christocentric (Lk. 1.43) and pneumocentric (Lk. 1.41); (6) Mary: theocentric (Lk. 1.28, 30, 46-55) and pneumocentric (Lk. 1.35); (7) Stephen: theocentric (Acts 7.1-53, 55), christocentric (Acts 7.52, 56; 22.20) and pneumocentric (Acts 6.5, 10; 7.55); (8) Philip: theocentric (Acts 8.12), christocentric (Acts 8.5, 12, 35) and pneumocentric (Acts 6.3, 5; 8.29, 39); (9) Simeon: theocentric (Lk. 2.28), christocentric (Lk. 2.26, 28) and pneumocentric (Lk. 2.25, 26, 27); (10) Anna: theocentric (Lk. 2.37-38) and christocentric (Lk. 2.38). Cf. Jesus: theocentric (Lk. 1.32, 35; 2.40, 49, 52; 3.22; 4.18-19; 6.12; 9.11, 48; 10.16, 22; 11.20; 22.29, 70), christocentric (Lk. 9.44, 58;

positively with the divine frame of reference function not only as God's human agents, but also as *Jesus' prophetic witnesses* who are portrayed as advancing the way of witness, proclaiming the gospel *to non-Jews* as well as Jews. This expresses the religious/theological ideology of both the Lukan narrator and his major characters.[60] As a result, Lukan readers hardly distinguish the messages of such leading characters in their speeches from that of the narrator, and construct the plot or the major theme of Luke–Acts through both. In short, the divine frame of reference[61] is deliberately designed to make reliable and authoritative the leading characters who are often presented as witnesses inspired/empowered by the Holy Spirit.[62]

4. Conclusion

My discussion of the three facets of the Lukan narrator's point of view with special reference to the Holy Spirit brings us to the following conclusion: the Lukan narrator's point of view is omnipresent and retrospective (in the perceptual dimension), omniscient (in the psychological dimension), and reliable and authoritative (in the ideological dimension). More specifically, I have pointed out that the Lukan narrator's ideology is theocentric, christocentric and pneumocentric, and he evaluates or judges any characters and incidents in these terms. In this sense, if any characters' speeches or actions are approved or sanctioned by the narrator, the readers, consciously or unconsciously, consider them reliable and authoritative. It is my contention, therefore, that the most discernible literary index in Luke–Acts that makes the narrator and characters reliable is their linking with the 'divine frame of reference',

12.50; 13.32-33; 17.25; 18.31-33; 22.15; 24.25-27, 44-49) and pneumocentric (Lk. 1.35; 3.16, 22; 4.1, 14, 18; 10.21).

60. Cf. §2.1. in Chapter 6.

61. Cf. Darr, who explains (1992: 53), 'Much like the narrator's perspective, the divine frame of reference provides the audience with a consistent and highly authoritative guide for constructing and/or evaluating characters and their roles in the action'.

62. The major characters (i.e. the Apostles: Peter, Stephen, Philip, Barnabas and Paul) as the 'men of the Spirit' in Acts, following the model of Jesus, are characterized as charismatic witnesses to proclaim/preach the gospel/the word of God boldly and to perform signs and/or wonders, which result in a series of response of 'acceptance and rejection. Cf. Johnson (1977: 58-59); O'Reilly (1987: 15-18; 161-90). For a detailed discussion, see §3 in Chapter 5.

i.e. an angel(s) (of the Lord), heavenly voices, visions, scriptural citations and, especially, the Holy Spirit. In this way, the reader is encouraged to grasp that not only the Holy Spirit (and other elements of the
divine frame of reference), but also characters who are inspired and
guided by the Holy Spirit are characterized as God's (divine and
human) reliable agents revealing/initiating, developing and accomplish-
ing/confirming his purpose/plan in the development of the narrative of
Luke–Acts.

Chapter 4

CHARACTER, PRESENTATION AND THE HOLY SPIRIT

1. *Introduction*

In the following first two sections of this chapter, I shall provide the narrative theories of 'character' and 'characterization'. On this basis, I shall examine briefly whether the Holy Spirit can be seen as a literary character and then apply the theory of characterization to the Holy Spirit in Luke–Acts in the rest of this chapter and the next: Chapter 4 analyses the Holy Spirit in terms of Lukan presentation (i.e. the Spirit as 'being'), whereas Chapter 5 deals with the Spirit in the light of the overall plot of Luke–Acts (i.e. the Spirit as 'doing'/'functioning'). In Chapter 4, I shall often compare the presentations and the immediate roles of the 'Holy Spirit' in Luke–Acts with those of the 'Spirit of the Lord/God' in the Jewish Bible as literary repertoire, which will thus draw out the similarities *and* differences between them.

2. *The Narrative Theory of Character*

Abrams (1993: 23) defines the literary term 'character' as follows:

> Characters are the *persons* presented in a dramatic or narrative work, who are interpreted by the reader as being endowed with moral, dispositional, and emotional qualities that are expressed in what they say—dialogue—and by what they do—the action (emphasis added).

His definition, together with other explanations based on other literary critics' theories (e.g. 'flat' and 'round' characters as two types of characters; 'showing' and 'telling' as two methods of characterization), has frequently been adopted by biblical critics interested in literary or narrative criticism.[1] Nevertheless, the theories both of character and

---

1.   Quite recently, however, biblical scholars influenced by current non-biblical literary studies on character begin to be more interested in the concept of character

characterization are complicated and are still debated among non-biblical literary critics. There are two interrelated ongoing literary debates on character: (1) the question about the modes of identity (Are characters understood as words or persons?) and (2) the question about the relation of characters to the plot (Are characters interpreted as function or as being *per se*?).

2.1. *Word or Person?*

> 'Emma Woodhouse, handsome, clever, and rich. [...]' Already I am caught. How is it possible to refuse the illusion that Emma Woodhouse was a woman whom I can discuss with as much unself-consciousness as the woman next door? At the very moment I refer to *her* (her: third person, feminine), I have already tacitly removed her from the novel, credited her with an independent life, and assumed a mimetic theory of character (Weinsheimer 1979: 185; emphasis original).

On a character's mode of identity or existence in a narrative, there are by and large two opposing literary opinions: one view is derived from mimetic criticism, the other from semiotic criticism. It is claimed in mimetic criticism that characters are equivalent to people in life, whereas in semiotic criticism they are viewed as segments of a closed text and thus dissolve into textuality (Weinsheimer 1979: 195, 208).[2]

Among literary critics, the former position, launched by Aristotle,[3] has long been acknowledged as valid until the rise and effect of 'New Criticism' (e.g. G.W. Knight [1928], L.C. Knights [1934], T.S. Eliot [1950]) in both England and America and of structuralism (e.g. V. Propp [1928], R. Barthes[4] [1966; cf. 1970, 1973], T. Todorov [1965]) or semiotics (e.g. A.-J. Greimas [1966], C. Bremond [1973]) in France.[5]

---

including characterization than the other literary aspects and thus to analyse it in detail. See Gowler (1989: 54-62; 1990: 29-75; 1994: 213-51); Shepherd (1994: 51-89); Williams (1994: 54-88). Notice also several articles edited by Malbon and Berlin (1993): esp. see Burnett 1-28; McCracken 29-42; Darr 43-60; Bach 61-80.

2.   See also Rimmon-Kenan (1983: 33). Mudrick (1960/1961: 211) labelled the former the 'realistic' argument, and the latter the 'purist' argument.

3.   Aristotle (Butcher 1943: 436) also indicated that the work of poetics is in nature mimetic. However, his understanding of character is plot-centred and thus is not seen as an independent and necessary aspect in literature.

4.   It is worth noting that Barthes (1990: 19) later reshaped his early 'formalist-structuralist' view of character and thus made allowances for a special independent voice, i.e. the 'voice of seme' as signifier.

5.   For this critical survey, see Hochman (1985: 13-27).

The representative work of the mimetic school is *Shakespearean Tragedy* (1904) written by A.C. Bradley, who discussed Shakespeare's characters as real human beings apart from their narrative context. His position was later harshly criticized in the article entitled 'How Many Children Had Lady Macbeth?' (1933) by L.C. Knights, who insisted that any attention to Lady Macbeth's character or other imaginable thoughts *out of context* misinterpreted the original play. What we should be concerned with, according to Knights, is the 'language of the play and the structure of the imagery' within the given narrative context (Hochman 1985: 16, 22).

Later, structuralists or semiologists, in terms of their own philosophical premises, attempted to deal with characters as 'ciphers that perform the functions needed to realise a schematic paradigm of narrative elements that underlies the "surface" of the story' (Hochman 1985: 23).[6] Characters are nothing but words or signs on a printed page. This extreme position, however, is not always accepted even by other literary structuralists like Chatman. For instance, against the extreme structuralistic view of character, Chatman (1978: 118) argued,

> The equation of characters with 'mere words' is wrong on other grounds. Too many mimes, too many captionless silent films, too many ballets have shown the folly of such a restriction. Too often do we recall fictional characters vividly, yet not a single word of the text in which they came alive; indeed, I venture to say that readers generally remember characters that way.

In so doing, Chatman (126) defined character as a 'paradigm of (personal) traits':

> 'trait' in the sense of 'relatively stable or abiding *personal quality*', recognizing that it may either unfold, that is, emerge earlier or later in the course of the story, or that it may disappear and be replaced by another (emphasis added).

---

6.   Shepherd (1994: 59-60) rightly points out the paradox of the anti-mimetic logic of structuralism: 'if people are no more than signs within a system of signs, how can structuralists object to a mimetic understanding of character? Characters would function exactly as people function—both merely move the action along. At this point, the ideology behind structuralism leads to an inescapable contradiction, where mimeticism is not really mimetic, but semiotic, while semioticism is really mimetic'.

It is also worth noting Wilson's analysis of character. In the article, Wilson (1979: 730) distinguishes *Homo fictus* and *Homo sapiens* and calls character a 'bright chimera'.[7] What we need to draw attention to here is the argument concerning his four possible theoretical paradigms of character based on Aristotle's classification of causes. Thus, he (730) claims,

> Briefly, these positions are: (1) that characters are products of the author's mind—memories, encapsulations of his experience or else (one might say) split-off slivers of his mind or self; (2) that characters are functions of the text in which they appear—embodiments of theme and idea—to be considered much as tokens, pieces, or counters in a game; (3) that characters are entirely artificial, constructs to be analysed in terms of the compositional techniques that have gone into their making; (4) that characters are, for the purposes of critical reading, to be considered *as if* they were actual persons, and the emphasis in criticism—its sole business, in fact—to discuss the response they engender in an intelligent reader (emphasis original).

Accordingly, Wilson (731-38) labels each position as (1) the efficient cause, (2) the material cause, (3) the formal cause and (4) the final cause, and then comments on each position's main argument, along with both their positive and negative aspects.

It is noticeable that this character-classification in terms of causes is closely connected with the three interpretative dimensions, i.e. author, text and reader. Accordingly the four positions outlined by Wilson can be reshaped into the following: (1) author-centred character analysis, (2) plot-centred character analysis ('doing' or 'function'), (3) character-centred character analysis ('being' or 'presentation') and (4) reader-centred character analysis.

Bearing these positions in mind, Wilson attempts to show the significance of readers as a final cause in constructing characters by taking *the concept of consciousness* into account. On character-analysis, he

7.   Both terms *Homo fictus* and *Homo sapiens* referring to two modes of character are first used by Forster (1927: 87) and further analysed by Hochman (1985: 59-85). In regard to the common ground between narrative world and real world, Martin (1986: 120) points out, 'The ultimate reference of fact and fiction is *our experience*, and it is entirely consistent with experience to say that I understand Huck Finn more or less well than I understand my next door neighbor. Our sense that fictional characters are uncannily similar to people is therefore not something to be dismissed or ridiculed but a crucial feature of narration that requires explanation' (emphasis added).

thus goes a step further than Chatman in that he posits an intimate relationship between 'character in literature' and 'people in life'.[8] In a similar vein, although he does not discuss the concept of consciousness, Weinsheimer asserts the necessity of making a balance between two extreme views drawn from semiotic and mimetic criticisms. Thus, he (1979: 208, 210) concludes,

> What we require is a Janus-faced critic who can do justice to both texts and persons: *to the textualized persons, personified texts that are characters*... [W]e have seen that both theories, despite the fact that they are mutually contradictory, must be true. *Characters are both people and words*. No other account of their status is satisfying or complete (emphasis added).

To sum up, it is thus claimed that characters portrayed by words in literature are generated by readers' consciousness or experience so as to become living people. This implies that characters are truly embedded in the text *and*, at the same time when the text is read by readers, they come alive and even remain in readers' conscious world.

Hence characters in Luke–Acts, as in other biblical narratives, are conceived as textualized persons or personified texts. In other words, characters like Jesus or Paul described in Luke–Acts are considered to be 'paradigms of *personified* traits' or even '*personified* signs' designed by Luke and then re-constructed as 'real people' by readers (through their reasonable and imaginative consciousness) in their reading process. It is thus '*person-likeness*' (such as human attributes of 'thinking', 'speaking', 'acting' or possessing 'names' etc.) as a literary character-index that signifies whether or not such and such 'paradigms of traits' or 'signs' form a 'character'. For instance, a 'temple' or a 'miracle' possibly possesses a paradigm of traits or a symbolic sign, but is not a 'character', because both are devoid of a literary character-index, namely 'person-likeness'.

---

8.   Wilson, in the last section of his article (1979: 748), thus, insists, 'Doubtless, there is a genuine relation between fictional and actual consciousness'. In fact, the importance of reader's consciousness or experience in the process of retrieving character from literature is already pointed out by Harvey (1965: 54). See also Hochman's view (1985: 36): 'What links characters in literature to people in life, as we fabricate them in our consciousness, is the integral unity of our conception of people and of how they operate'. Cf. Tompkins (1980: ix-xxvi).

2.2. *Doing or Being?*

What is character but the determination of incident? What is incident but
the illustration of character? (James 1948: 13).

Another recurring question about characters concerns their relationship
to the plot of the narrative. Like the debate on characters' modes of
existence as either words or persons, this question of characters' relationship to the plot has been answered in two extreme ways: one view is
to see characters as plot functionaries; the other as autonomous or
independent beings apart from the plot.

On the former position, Aristotle paved the way for the emphasis on
what characters *do*, rather than on what they *are* in the narrative. Thus
he (Butcher 1943: 427) states: 'Hence the incidents and the plot are the
end of all tragedy; and the end is the chief thing of all. So without
action there cannot be a tragedy; there may be one without character...
The plot, then, is the first principle, and as it were, the soul of a tragedy:
character holds the second place'. This position, although on the basis
of a different rationale from Aristotle's, has been reinforced by Formal-
ists and Structuralists such as Propp and Greimas. Propp, a Russian
formalist who examined the Russian folktale, claimed that characters in
folktale are defined by the 'spheres of action' in which they participate.
As a result of that study, he classified the role of characters into seven
functions: (1) the villain, (2) the donor, (3) the helper, (4) the sought-
for-person and (her) father, (5) the dispatcher, (6) the hero and (7) the
false hero. He also observed that one character may play more than one
role and that one function may be taken by more than one character
(Greimas 1983: 200-201).

Greimas, as a semio-structuralist, has developed Propp's study of
'character-function' not in relation to the Russian folktale, but in relation to stories in general, as a universal 'narrative-grammar', and has
defined six *actants*: (1) sender, (2) object, (3) receiver, (4) helper, (5)
subject and (6) opponent. He distinguished *actants* as six universal
function-agents from *acteurs* as specific action-actors in the given
narrative. Thus, the same *actant* (function-agent) can be presented by
more than one *acteur* (action-actor), and the same *acteur* can be
assigned to more than one *actant* (Greimas 1983: 198-215).[9]

In short, these approaches to understanding characters in literature
see characters as derivative products of plot and thus these approaches

9.   See also Rimmon-Kenan (1983: 34-36); Brooks (1984: 15-17).

tend to eschew analysing characters as independent actors or beings. This approach is underpinned by philosophical positions that are fundamental to structuralism and semiotics.

In opposition to the view of structuralism, Chatman has argued for a character-theory that makes independent room for characters as autonomous beings apart from the plot. Basically he has claimed to distinguish between folktales and modern fictions so as to 'recognize the existence of an existent or quality dimension at the level of story' (1972: 73). In fact, in his article, Chatman frequently mentioned the new shift in *modern* fiction to a *modern* character that needs a different approach to both aspects. Thus, at the end of his argument, he (78) concluded,

> It would be a fundamental misconception to assume that there is only a difference of degree and not of kind between the simplest narrative—the folk tale or fairy-tale—and modern fiction. But this clearly seems to ignore the shift in interest in a sophisticated reading-public, *from 'what happens' to 'whom does it happen to?'* Indeed, fiction of the twentieth century by the Woolfs and the Prousts clearly discounts the importance of 'What happens' (emphasis added).[10]

To a great extent Chatman's claim is convincing in relation to modern fiction and has influenced other literary critics such as Hochman and Rimmon-Kenan.

Moreover Harvey (1978: 63-78), building upon the work of Todorov and van Dijk, has distinguished two kinds of narrative: (1) 'character system narrative' and (2) 'plot system narrative'.[11] In this respect, as Chatman argued, modern fiction has begun to delineate characters as autonomous beings that become more interesting and important subjects than the other literary factors. It is thus appropriate to grasp a tendency in literature that could be presented in either a plot-centred narrative or a character-centred narrative, while we should take Henry James's famous dictum into consideration. In other words, it would be

---

10. Throughout the article, it is noticeable that his argument for character is based on the new literary trend of character or characterization in fictions of the twentieth century. The following terms are thus found in his article: 'more recent fiction' (60), 'fictions of the twentieth century' (60, 78), 'modern characters' (60), 'very recent fiction' (60), 'the modern fictional character' (61) and 'modern literature' (77).

11. However, in the article, he only laid emphasis on characterization within the system of character-centred narrative.

better or even necessary to analyse characters in accordance with the nature of narratives, i.e. as either 'being' or 'doing'.

On the other hand, however, it should also be noted that characterization is, after all, dependent upon readers as the final cause. This implies the possibility that readers' or critics' may choose either approach or both for their analysis of characters, regardless of the types of narrative.[12] Nevertheless, although it is hard to ignore or avoid readers' interests in looking at characters, two different types of characterization are, in practice, appropriate to all types of narrative.

Thus, we might reflect on the narrative type of Luke–Acts: is Luke–Acts a plot-centred narrative or a character-centred one? At first glance, Luke–Acts, like other biblical narratives, seems to be character-centred, plotted through several chief characters such as Jesus, Peter and Paul. When we examine these biblical characters, however, we are quite disappointed by the fact that identifying descriptions, such as appearance, age, habit, psychology and so forth, are rarely indicated in contrast to modern fiction. Elucidating characterization in ancient biblical narratives in a manner similar to that in modern fiction, therefore, can be unsatisfactory and problematical. In other words, we may say that the implied author of Luke–Acts, unlike that of modern fiction, presents major and minor figures, not for their own sakes, but with a view to focusing on delivering and assuring the narrative's total message: the plan of God as the matrix of the plot of Luke–Acts.[13]

If we regard the Holy Spirit as a character in Luke–Acts (see below), it is thus more natural to analyse the function of the Holy Spirit in terms of the overall plot. In noticing this, however, I shall also discuss the Holy Spirit as an actor presented in each immediate context, not only because the Spirit is portrayed as an actor, but also because this analysis is new and valuable in appreciating the divine Spirit. So, for my study, I shall apply both aspects to characterizing the Holy Spirit in Luke–Acts. Prior to this, I shall, in the following section, introduce two literary-critical approaches to characters as autonomous beings and adopt a more appropriate method for my study.

---

12. Cf. Rimmon-Kenan (1983: 36), who suggests, 'Hence it is legitimate to subordinate character to action when we study action but equally legitimate to subordinate action to character when the latter is the focus of our study'.

13. See §3 in Chapter 5.

3. *The Narrative Theory of Characterization*

The literary approach to characterization has, to some extent, shifted recently from a text-centred definition to a reader-centred one, influenced by reader response criticism. For instance, for structuralists, characterization refers to investing 'an identified character with an attribute or set of attributes (also called 'traits', 'qualities' or 'characteristics') which add descriptive material of a particular sort to the argument node' (Harvey 1978: 63).[14] However, the recent emphasis on the reader highlights the final initiative in establishing characterization, that is, characters are constructed or generated through the text by readers. Nevertheless, these two different points of view in characterization should not be viewed as contradictory, but as supplementary to each other. In what follows, I shall now discuss two methods of understanding characters: character-classification and character-presentation.

3.1. *Character-Classification*
Forster distinguished 'flat characters' from 'round characters', and has had a great influence on the discussion of characters in fiction. A flat character (also called a type or a caricature) is constructed around a 'single idea or quality' and can thus be defined in one sentence. In contrast, a round character, like real people in life, is 'complex in temperament and motivation' and is presented as developing in the course of narrative (1927: 67-78).

In spite of Forster's pioneering contribution, his division of characters into two types has now been criticized. His rigid dichotomy between flat and round characters, critics say, is too reductive. It is hard to argue that there are only two types of characters; there are some characters that are 'complex but undeveloping (e.g. Joyce's Bloom) and others which are simple but developing (e.g. the allegorical Everyman)' (Rimmon-Kenan 1983: 40-41).

Harvey (1965: 52-73) perceived the limitation of Forster's polarization of characters and thus attempted to show that characters exist on a continuum of the 'perspective of depth'. Nevertheless, for convenience,

---

14. See also Rimmon-Kenan (1983: 59). Cf. Rhoads and Michie 'Characterization refers to the way a narrator brings characters to life in a narrative' (1982: 101); Williams 'Thus, characterization refers to the elements in a narrative text which state or present the traits of a particular character' (1994: 60).

he also suggested three types of characters: (1) protagonists, (2) background characters and (3) a wide variety of intermediate characters that belong to the boundary between the protagonists and the background characters. His position, on the other hand, has also been criticized by Hochman (1985: 86-89). Thus, Hochman claims,

> Any adequate account of character in literature must try to define the various aspects and modes of such characters' existence both in themselves and within the texts that generate them. Such definition must isolate a range of qualities inherent in characters, and that range must be much wider than Forster's single polarity of 'flat' and 'round' and still more comprehensive than the scheme that Harvey provides (88).

As a result, Hochman (1985: 89), influenced by the view of J. Ewen,[15] proposed eight categories with each of their polar opposites, which attempt to take into account a large range of qualities and possibilities in characterization.[16]

Stylization	↔	Naturalism
Coherence	↔	Incoherence
Wholeness	↔	Fragmentariness
Literalness	↔	Symbolism
Complexity	↔	Simplicity
Transparency	↔	Opacity
Dynamism	↔	Staticism
Closure	↔	Openness

Therefore, Hochman has attempted to avoid reductivism in evaluating characters in (modern) literature and to describe characters' qualities according to their degree in the light of these eight polar axes.

For the analysis of characters in biblical narratives, scholars have used or modified several models of character-classification. For instance, for character-classification in the Gospel of Mark, Rhoads and Michie (1982: 101) have distinguished the dominant characters (Jesus, the disciples and the authorities) from the minor characters (other groups of people). Culpepper (1983: 101-44) has introduced Harvey's model, yet not fully applied it to the Gospel of John: the major characters (Jesus,

---

15. Ewen, while noticing that characters exist on a continuum of complexity, suggested three axes in evaluating the traits of characters in literature: (1) complexity, (2) development and (3) penetration into the inner life (Rimmon-Kenan 1983: 41-42).

16. Hochman (1985: 89-140) has thus dealt with these eight categories as a comprehensive model for evaluating characters in literature.

the Father, the disciples and the Jews) and the minor characters (John the Baptist, Jesus' mother, Nicodemus, the Samaritan woman, the royal official, the lame man, the brothers of Jesus, the blind man, Mary, Martha, Lazarus, Pilate and Mary Magdalene). For the characters in the Gospel of Luke, Kingsbury (1991: 9) suggested four distinct categories: the major characters (Jesus, the religious authorities, the apostles and disciples, and the crowds or the people), the minor characters (the righteous and devout in the infancy narrative, those living on the margins of society to whom Jesus ministers and who exhibit faith in him, and those during the passion who do not distance themselves from Jesus but serve or acclaim him), other characters (John the Baptist, Pilate and Herod Antipas) and the transcendent beings (God, angels, Satan, demons and the figure of the narrator).

On the other hand, Shepherd, on the basis of Hochman's eight categories as 'aspects and modes' of characters' existence, has recently evaluated the Holy Spirit as a character, and he is reluctant to name the Holy Spirit either as a major or minor character. Thus he (1994: 78) states, 'With Hochman's scheme, we have a highly detailed, nuanced system for describing the many facets of a character. This scheme will prove useful as a model for describing the character of the Holy Spirit in Luke–Acts.' Shepherd's study, however, raises questions about the application of Hochman's categories to the characterization of the Holy Spirit in Luke–Acts. The underlying question is this: On what basis or rationale can we judge the Holy Spirit in each category? For instance, in the category of Stylization/Naturalism, Shepherd, *unlike in the other categories*, has, as an exception, taken the Greek Old Testament as a ruler to define whether or not the role or portrait of the Holy Spirit is stylized. But it would be more consistent to consider the Spirit of the Lord/God in the Jewish Bible as a reference-value for each category in comparison with the Holy Spirit in Luke–Acts. More problematical is the fact that the 'aspects and modes' of the Holy Spirit as a character in each category (esp. stylization–naturalism; coherence–incoherence; wholeness–fragmentariness; complexity–simplicity; transparency–opacity) could be defined in different ways. For instance, in the category of Coherence/Incoherence, if the Holy Spirit is examined in terms of the portrait of the prophetic Spirit, the Holy Spirit is a highly coherent character. On the other hand, if the Spirit is evaluated in the light of the relationship with baptism, laying on of hands, faith, speaking in tongues and the coming of the Spirit, the Holy Spirit can be seen as an incoherent character. In fact, Shepherd, in his concluding chapter, has admitted the fuzziness of Hochman's model: 'The system is by no means exact, but I have attempted to place the Spirit within each category' (1994: 250).[17]

In the following subsection, therefore, I shall explain another way of evaluating characters in literature,[18] which I shall adopt in analysing the Holy Spirit as an autonomous being in Luke–Acts.

3.2. *Character-Presentation*

Characters are presented in two ways by the narrator: 'showing' and 'telling' (Booth 1991: 3-16). These two ways are re-shaped by Rimmon-Kenan. Under this subsection, I shall introduce Rimmon-Kenan's method for analysing characterization and then use it later as one of the dimensions for the character-building of the Holy Spirit in Luke–Acts. The following is, thus, a summary taken from Rimmon-Kenan's presentation of characterization (1983: 59-70).[19]

Rimmon-Kenan's analysis of characterization consists of two basic types of textual indicators of character, i.e. 'direct definition' and 'indirect presentation', along with a reinforcement of characterization as 'analogy'. Thus, she explains (1983: 59-60, 67):

> The first type ['direct definition'] names the trait by an adjective (e.g. 'he was good-hearted'), an abstract noun ('his goodness knew no bounds'), or possibly some other kind of noun ('she was a real bitch') or part of speech ('he loves only himself '). The second type ['indirect presentation'], on the other hand, does not mention the trait but displays and exemplifies it in various ways, leaving to the reader the task of inferring the quality they imply... I treat analogy as a reinforcement of characterization rather than as a separate type of character-indicator (equivalent to direct definition and indirect presentation) because its characterizing capacity depends on the prior establishment, by other means, of the traits on which it is based.

17. See also p. 32 n. 54 in Chapter. 1.

18. Shepherd, following Gowler's scheme, also uses the model of 'character-presentation' for the characterization of the Spirit; nevertheless, he does not properly apply this to the Spirit. See his summary of this analysis, 1994: 247-50.

19. Cf. Alter's 'scale of characterization' (1981: 116-17): 'Characters can be revealed through the report of actions; through appearance, gestures, posture, costume; through one character's comments on another; through direct speech by the character; through inward speech, either summarized or quoted as interior monologue; or through statements by the narrator about the attitudes and intentions of the personages'.

For characterization, direct definition as the most obvious form is, thus, of importance in evaluating not only characters who are described, but also the narrator (and possibly other characters) who portrays characters directly. Here readers should take the narrator's or the characters' relative reliability into account in building their characterization of the characters in each narrative context. For instance in Luke–Acts, the narrator's or Jesus' direct definition of characters lies at the highest level of reliability in understanding characters, whereas the group of religious leaders' definition of characters should not be taken at face value.[20]

On the other hand, indirect presentation displays or exemplifies characters' traits in several different ways. It is less explicit than direct definition, and therefore, possibly less concrete. Nevertheless, indirect presentation, such as 'action', 'speech', 'external appearance' and 'environment', is useful and even indispensable in building a character. But this aspect, too, needs to take into account each character's or narrator's degree of reliability and explicitness.[21]

Another significant factor for characterization is the mode of analogy that reinforces the establishment of characters' traits in several ways. In regard to analogy, Rimmon-Kenan proposes three elements: 'analogous names', 'analogous landscape'[22] and 'analogy between characters'. In

20. Cf. §3.3.2 in Chapter 3.

21. Williams (1994: 61-67), based on Rimmon-Kenan's analysis, enumerated the various means of characterization from the most explicit to the most covert: (1) the narrator may directly state the traits of a character; (2) the narrator may express an evaluation of what a character is like without directly stating a trait; (3) a character may directly state the traits of another character; (4) a character may express an evaluation of what another character is like without directly stating the person's traits; (5) a character may express an evaluation of another character through the use of a drastic action that speaks for itself; (6) the narrator may show the traits of a character by presenting the character's inward thoughts; (7) the narrator may show the traits of a character by presenting the character's actions; (8) the narrator may show the traits of a character by presenting the character's speech; (9) the narrator may show the traits of a character by presenting the character's appearance; (10) the narrator may highlight the traits of a character through the use of analogy; (11) the narrator may influence the reconstruction of a character's traits through the order of presentation.

22. Although Rimmon-Kenan attempts to distinguish 'environment' from 'landscape' in character-presentation (i.e. the former is related to story-causality, whereas the latter is not), it should be admitted that the difference is arbitrary on some occasions; in my study, therefore, the aspect of 'analogous landscape' will be included in that of 'environment'.

other words, through analogy, characterization is reinforced or further explained. Furthermore, Rimmon-Kenan, quoting Barthes, points out the significance of the 'proper name' for the construction of a character (1983: 39).[23] She thus raises a question, 'How are elements combined into unifying categories under the aegis of the proper name?', to which she replies, 'The main principles of cohesion, it seems to me, are repetition, similarity, contrast, and implication (in the logical sense)' (1983: 39).[24]

Thus, I shall reflect on this aspect and apply it in a modified form together with the mode of analogy to the character-presentation of the Holy Spirit in Luke–Acts. Accordingly, my two-fold model of character-presentation is set out in the following:

Diagram 1

Character-Presentation I

Direct Definition   Indirect Presentation

Speech   Action I and II   External Appearance   Environment

Character-Presentation II: Analogy

Repetition and Similarity   Comparison and Contrast

In the following section, I shall briefly show on what basis the Holy Spirit in Luke–Acts can be seen as a character, that is, as a literary figure. Then, I shall examine the Spirit in detail as a character by means of the model presented above.

23. Rimmon-Kenan treated the topic, 'How is character reconstructed from the text?', not in chapter 4, 'Text: characterization' (59-70), but in chapter 3, 'Story: character' (29-42). This is due to her distinct definition and application of 'story' and 'text' (see chapter 3). Nevertheless, some ideas in chapter 3 are important and applicable to the process of characterization, esp. in relationship to the mode of analogy.

24. For my application of Rimmon-Kenan's model to the Holy Spirit in Luke–Acts, I do not make separate room for 'implication' since the expressions of 'Holy' Spirit, 'God's' Spirit/the Spirit 'of the Lord' and the Spirit 'of Jesus' are better regarded as 'direct definitions' than as 'proper names'. Cf. Thompson, who argues that 'God' is not a name (1993: 189); contra Polzin (1993: 212).

4. The Holy Spirit As a Divine Character

It has already been argued that God in the biblical narratives can be seen as a literary figure, that is, a character.[25] In a similar vein, the Holy Spirit can also be considered a character because the Holy Spirit is portrayed as 'person-like'.[26] For instance, the Lukan narrative tells us that the Holy Spirit *reveals* (Lk. 2.26), *inspires* (Lk. 2.27), *leads* (Lk. 4.1), *teaches* (Lk. 12.12), *speaks* (Acts 1.16; 4.25; 8.29; 10.19-20; 11.12; 13.2; 21.11; 28.25), *gives utterance* (Acts 2.4), *forbids* (Acts 16.6-7), *testifies* (Acts 20.23), *oversees* (Acts 20.28; cf. 15.28) and so forth. This implies that the Holy Spirit as a character (i.e. as an active figure) participates in incidents and thus plays a role in interaction with, and conflict against, other characters within the plot of Luke–Acts.

On the other hand, it is also true that the Holy Spirit, like God, possesses some traits that ordinary people cannot share, that is, 'person-unlikeness'. To illustrate, the external appearance and environment of the Holy Spirit are so enigmatic that even the omniscient and omnipresent narrator[27] cannot describe them in coherent ways (e.g. the

---

25. For instance, the characterization of God in the Hebrew Bible is discussed by Sternberg (1985: 322-41). For the subject in Luke–Acts, Tannehill insists (1986: 29), 'To this extent God functions as a character in the plot, although hidden from human view'; Brawley (1990: 111) also views God as a character, 'God is a character whom the reader constructs out of the intersection of information, action, traits, and evaluation'. See also Darr (1992: 51); Thompson (1993: 177-204); cf. Kingsbury's dual opinions on it (1991: 11): 'Narratively, therefore, God is not to be counted as one of the characters of Luke's gospel story. From another perspective, however, God is the chief "actor" throughout the whole of Luke's double work'.

26. Defining the Holy Spirit as a character has been undertaken very recently in a comprehensive way by Shepherd (1994). Cf. Kock: 'In the Acts of the Apostles the chief protagonist is neither Peter nor Paul, but the Holy Spirit' (1970: 888); Hill: 'The Spirit is the main hero of the story. In terms of structuralist analysis of the story, it is not the apostles who are the "actors", while the Holy Spirit is the "adjuvant", but rather the opposite. The apostles, the co-workers and successors are energised and directed by the Spirit' (1984: 23). According to Shepherd, there are two features of Luke's text that present the Holy Spirit as a character: 'it [Luke–Acts] presents the Spirit as an actor in the story, and it involves the Spirit in inter-action and even conflict with other characters' (1994: 90). However, Shepherd does not properly discuss the 'person-unlikeness' of the Holy Spirit as a character because of his sole interest in the Spirit as (person-like) actor in Luke–Acts (see 90-93).

27. See §3 in Chapter 3.

Spirit's external appearance: as a dove in Lk. 3.22; as fire in Acts 2.3-4;
the Spirit's environment: allusions to heaven as God's throne in Lk.
3.22; 1.35; 4.18; 11.13; Acts 2.33). In addition, the narrator frequently
refers to other characters as people who 'are filled with the Holy Spirit'
and 'are full of the Holy Spirit'[28] (i.e. as an intermediate agent), thus
referring to the 'human environment' of the Holy Spirit. Also the Holy
Spirit as a character is said to be acted upon by God or the resurrected
Jesus. On several occasions, the narrator also portrays the Holy Spirit as
one who transcends time: who was in the past (with David in Acts 1.16;
with the Jewish ancestors in Acts 7.51; with Isaiah in Acts 28.25) *and* is
now in the eschatological present as promised (Acts 2.17, 33, 38; cf.
Lk. 11.13; 12.12).

Hence, the Holy Spirit can be seen as a character who holds two
dialectic paradigms of traits, i.e. those of 'person-likeness' *and* 'person-
unlikeness'. In a word, the Holy Spirit in Luke–Acts is to be understood
as a *divine character*.

5. *The Character-Presentation of the Holy Spirit in Luke–Acts*

I shall now examine the narrative description of the Holy Spirit as a
character in Luke–Acts by modifying Rimmon-Kenan's model under
the following two subsections of character-presentation, I and II. In the
process, I shall note at least two aspects: (1) based on each immediate
context, I shall highlight the narrator's or characters' presentation of the
Holy Spirit and explore anticipating implications in connection with
it,[29] and (2) this presentation of the Holy Spirit in Luke–Acts will be
compared with that of the 'Spirit of the Lord/God' in the Jewish Bible
as literary repertoire[30] so that plausible connotations can be provided.

28. I shall further discuss these metaphorical phrases in §5.2.1.2 in this chapter.

29. It will be noticed that the character-presentation of the Holy Spirit (as an
actor) from this section onwards in Chapter 4 cannot be separated from the
character-function of the Holy Spirit (as an agent) delineated in Chapter 5 as
theoretically seen in §2.2 in this chapter. In this light, part of my argument derived
here will be comprehensively discussed in the overall plot of Luke–Acts in the next
chapter.

30. See Chapter 2 and Appendix I.

5.1. *Character-Presentation I*

My first analysis of the character-presentation of the Holy Spirit comprises (1) direct definition and (2) indirect presentation, which is made through (2-1) speech, (2-2) action I, (2-3) action II, (2-4) external appearance and (2-5) environment. It is readily observed that the Holy Spirit is, on almost all occasions, described by reliable and authoritative figures such as the narrator (in Luke–Acts), Jesus (in Luke) and Peter and Paul (in Acts).

5.1.1. *Direct Definition.* In what follows, I shall explore several expressions for the Spirit in Luke–Acts as direct definitions: (1) 'Holy' Spirit, (2) 'God's' Spirit/the Spirit 'of the Lord', (3) the Spirit 'of Jesus' and (4) other definitions like the 'promise of my [Jesus']/[the] Father, 'power from on high', 'witness' and 'gift', while taking into consideration their immediate narrative contexts. So I shall offer relevant and important implications of the characterization of the Spirit based on each direct definition.

5.1.1.1. *'Holy' Spirit.* The word πνεῦμα occurs 106 times[31] in the narrative of Luke–Acts (36 in the Gospel; 70 in Acts).[32] Among these occurrences, *holy* as the most obvious direct definition of the Spirit

---

31. Like in the Jewish Bible as literary repertoire (see Chapter 2; cf. Excursus), the term *pneuma* is used to denote (a) breath (3 times)—Lk. 8.55; 23.46; Acts 7.59, (b) anthropological spirit (5 times)—Lk. 1.17 [Elijah], 47 [Mary], 80 [John the Baptist]; Acts 17.16 [Paul]; 18.25 [Apollos], (c) angelic spirit (4 times)—Lk. 24.37, 39; Acts 23.8, 9, (d) evil spirit (20 times)—Lk. 4.33, 36; 6.18; 7.21; 8.2, 29; 9.39, 42; 10.20; 11.24, 26; 13.11; Acts 5.16; 8.7; 16.16, 18; 19.12, 13, 15, 16 and (e) the divine Spirit (74 times). Unlike the Jewish Bible, however, Luke–Acts has no case in which *pneuma* refers to wind (cf. πνοή used in Acts 2.2).

32. Cf. the fact that the Western text of the book of Acts includes 6 additional references to the divine Spirit: 11.17 (του μη δουναι αυτοις πνευμα αγιον πιστευσασιν επ αυτω); 15.7 (ανεστησεν τω πνευματι Πετρος και), 29 (πραξετε φερομενοι εν τω αγιω πνευματι), 32 (πληρεις πνευματος αγιου); 19.1 (ειπεν αυτω το πνευμα υποστρεφειν εις την Ασιαν); 20.3 (ειπεν δε το πνευμα αυτω); see also the addition of τω αγιω to πνευματι in 6.10. All these additions reinforce the roles or function of the Spirit found in the Alexandrian text (for this subject, see Chapter 5): the Spirit verifies a certain group as God's restored people (11.17); the Spirit inspires reliable characters (Peter in 15.7; Judas and Silas in 15.32); the Spirit encourages the believers (15.29); the Spirit guides or directs Paul for the witness-mission (19.1; 20.3). See Black (1981: 160-78); Head (1993: 434-35).

occurs 54 times both in articular forms, τὸ ἅγιον πνεῦμα[33] and τὸ πνεῦμα τὸ ἅγιον,[34] and in an anathrous form, πνεῦμα ἅγιον.[35] Alternative terms such as the 'Spirit' (Lk. 2.27; 4.1b, 14; Acts 2.4b; 6.3, 10; 8.18, 29; 10.19; 11.12, 28; 19.21; 20.22; 21.4; cf. Mt. 4.1; 12.31; 22.43; Mk 1.10, 12), 'my [God's] Spirit' (Acts 2.17, 18; cf. Mt. 12.28), the 'Spirit of the Lord' (Lk. 4.18; Acts 5.9; 8.39; cf. Mt. 3.16; 12.28; 10.20) and the 'Spirit of Jesus' (Acts 16.7) are regarded as references to the Holy Spirit if we take each narrative context into consideration.[36] As a result, the occurrences of πνεῦμα (106 in Luke–Acts) referring to either the 'Holy' Spirit or the divine Spirit are 74 times (17 in Luke; 57 in Acts).[37] Nevertheless, we should notice different expressions referring to the Spirit in order to draw some relevant implications from them (see below).

I shall now explore the *Holy* Spirit in detail in terms of the direct definition of the Spirit in Luke–Acts. For my analysis, three aspects will be considered: (1) Who narrates or describes the *Holy* Spirit? (2) In what narrative contexts does the *Holy* Spirit appear? and (3) What are

33. This term is found in Lk. 12.10, 12; Acts 1.8; 2.38; 4.31; 9.31; 10.45; 13.4; 16.6 (9 times). In Luke–Acts except Acts 2.33, when the Holy Spirit is used in the genitive case (Acts 1.8; 2.33, 38; 4.31; 9.31; 10.45; 13.4; 16.6), Luke always prefers to employ the term τοῦ ἁγίου πνεύματος rather than τοῦ πνεύματος τοῦ ἁγίου, which could be understood as either 'of the Holy Spirit' or 'of the Spirit of the Holy One'. In some sense, therefore, it implies that the Holy Spirit particularly in Acts is considered an 'individual figure'. Cf. Mowery 1986: 26-45. Mowery attempted to provide the reasons why Luke uses different articular variants referring to the Holy Spirit on the basis of the Gospel sources and Lukan redactional tendency. But as he admitted, this solution cannot be seen as satisfactory (34, 36).

34. This term is found in Lk. 2.26; 3.22; 10.21; Acts 1.16; 2.33; 5.3, 32; 7.51; 10.44, 47; 11.15; 13.2; 15.8, 28; 19.6; 20.23, 28; 21.11; 28.25 (19 times). Cf. Mt. 12.32; Mk 3.29; 12.36; 13.11.

35. This term is found in Lk. 1.15, 35, 41, 67; 2.25; 3.16; 4.1a; 11.13; Acts 1.2, 5; 2.4a; 4.8, 25; 6.5; 7.55; 8.15, 17, 19; 9.17; 10.38; 11.16, 24; 13.9, 52; 19.2 [2 times] (26 times). Cf. Mt. 1.18, 20; 3.11; Mk 1.8.

36. If the pronoun ἦν in Acts 8.16 is counted, the number of the references to the divine Spirit becomes 75. Cf. 12 in Matthew and 6 in Mark. Bullinger (1979: 26-41) tried to distinguish between *pneuma hagion* (as divine 'gifts' or 'operations') and *to pneuma to hagion* (as the 'Holy Spirit') in the New Testament; however, his grammatical explanation of exceptional cases is far from convincing (35).

37. See also Table 3 later in this subsection. Cf. among 145 references to *pneuma* in Pauline letters, the 'Holy Spirit' occurs 17; the 'Spirit of God'/'His Spirit' 16; the 'Spirit of Christ' or its equivalent 3; see Fee (1994: 14-15; 831-45).

the implications of the term *holy*? The first two questions will be answered by providing Tables 1 and 2 below, whereas the last will be taken into consideration in connection with other expressions and roles of the divine Spirit in the Jewish Bible.

Table 1. *'Holy' Spirit in Luke*

	I	II	III	IV	V	VI	VII	VIII	IX	X	XI	XII	XIII	XIV	Total
A			1			1			2			3			7[38]
B						1	1						1		3[39]
C		1													1[40]
D	1											1			2[41]
Total	1	1	1			2	1		2			4	1		13

Table 2. *'Holy' Spirit in Acts*

	I	II	III	IV	V	VI	VII	VIII	IX	X	XI	XII	XIII	XIV	Total
A				1	3			5		1		8			18[42]
B		1				2									3[43]
E				1			1	4			1		1		8[44]
F								1	1	1	1				4[45]
G													1		1[46]
H												1			1[47]
I									1						1[48]
J														1	1[49]
K						1				1					2[50]
L											1				1[51]
M						1									1[52]
Total		1		2	3	4	1	10	2	3	3	9	2	1	41

38. Lk. 1.41, 67; 2.25, 26; 3.22; 4.1; 10.21.
39. Lk. 11.13; 12.10, 12.
40. Lk. 3.16.
41. Lk. 1.15, 35.
42. Acts 1.2; 2.4; 4.8, 31; 6.5; 7.55; 8.15, 17; 9.31; 10.44, 45; 11.24; 13.2, 4, 9, 52; 16.6; 19.6.
43. Acts 1.5, 8; 11.16.
44. Acts 1.16; 2.33, 38; 5.3; 10.38, 47; 11.15; 15.8.
45. Acts 19.2; 20.23, 28; 28.25.
46. Acts 7.51.
47. Acts 9.17.
48. Acts 21.11.
49. Acts 8.19.
50. Acts 4.25; 5.32.
51. Acts 15.28.
52. Acts 19.2.

[Context]
I.   Announcement of the birth of John and Jesus
II.   Prophecy about Jesus as the Baptizer with the Holy Spirit or Prophecy of the baptism with the Holy Spirit
III. Anointing of Jesus
IV.   Jesus' earthly ministry
V.   The Holy Spirit as a witness director
VI.   Receiving the Holy Spirit (for witness or witness context in general)
VII. The Holy Spirit as a gift given to God's people
VIII. The coming of the Holy Spirit
IX.   Revelation by the Holy Spirit
X.   Guide and encouragement of the Holy Spirit for God's people
XI.   Prophecies by Old Testament figures
XII. Being filled/full with/of the Holy Spirit, which contexts are in close relation to VI.
XIII. Rebuking the false witness to the Holy Spirit or resisting the Holy Spirit
XIV. False recognition of the Holy Spirit

[Speaker]
A. Narrator
B. Jesus
C. John the Baptist
D. An angel of the Lord
E. Peter
F. Paul
G. Stephen
H. Ananias
I. Agabus
J. Simon Magus
K. Peter and other apostles
L. The apostles and elders of Jerusalem
M. The disciples from Ephesus

From tables 1 and 2 above, we notice that the Spirit (of the Lord/God) promised by Scripture is understood (by the Lukan narrator, Peter and Paul) as the *Holy* Spirit (esp. see VIII), who *frequently appears in witness to Jesus contexts*, particularly in Acts (according to the narrator, Jesus, Ananias and an angel of the Lord; see V; VI; XII).[53] Apart from the narrator, there are only three characters in the Gospel who refer to the Holy Spirit: an angel of the Lord, Jesus and John the Baptist. Before their births, an angel of the Lord announces both Jesus and John as those who will be filled with the Holy Spirit (Lk. 1.15, 35). Thus, this

---

53. For my comprehensive discussion, see Chapter 5.

narrative indicator, that is, the expression 'being filled with the Holy Spirit', helps readers to trust the future speeches and actions of Jesus and John. In addition, their future ministry is also endorsed as God's sovereign work through the prophetic statements of other reliable Spirit-filled characters[54] such as Elizabeth (1.41), Mary (1.35), Zechariah (1.67) and Simeon (2.25-27) in the opening two chapters in the Gospel.

The close relationship between characters' being 'filled with' or 'full of' the Holy Spirit and their 'reliability' is more obvious when we compare the speeches and actions of Jesus' disciples in the Gospel with those in Acts. In this way, some characters are represented as sharing the same ideology with the Lukan narrator when they are filled with or full of the Holy Spirit. In other words, the narrator's literary technique of using the phrase 'being filled with' or 'being full of' the Holy Spirit functions as an index for character reliability in Luke–Acts. But certain characters are presented as speaking more authoritatively about the Holy Spirit than other reliable characters (43 out of 54 times): the narrator (25 times), Jesus (6 times), Peter (8 times from Acts 2 onwards) and Paul (4 times from Acts 9 onwards).

We can also see that there is no essential difference in relation to statements about the *Holy* Spirit between the narrator and other reliable characters[55] such as an angel of the Lord, Jesus, John the Baptist, Peter, Paul, Stephen, Ananias, Agabus, Peter and the other apostles, and the apostles and elders.[56] On the other hand, Simon Magus's statements about the *Holy* Spirit in Acts 8.18-19 are distinguished from those of the former characters: (1) He is said to have thought that to give and/or to receive the Holy Spirit is a human action. (2) Based on this misunderstanding, he is represented attempting to obtain such authority

---

54. For the narrative reliability of characters in Luke–Acts, see §3.3.2 in Chapter 3.

55. The instances in which the Spirit is presented as 'holy' apart from the narrator are as follows: I (by an angel of the Lord), II (by John the Baptist), VII (by Jesus; Peter), IX (by Paul; Agabus), X (by the apostles and elders in the Jerusalem Church), XI (by Peter; Paul; Peter and other apostles), XIII (by Peter; Stephen) and XIV (by Simon Magus).

56. In fact, the narrator gives to his readers other narrative information that makes those characters trustworthy. For instance, before Ananias's delivering his message to Paul (Acts 9.17), he, characterized as a 'disciple' in Damascus, changed his view of Paul from enemy (Acts 9.13-14) to friend (Acts 9.17) and obeyed the Lord's command given in a vision. See also the depiction of Agabus by the narrator in Acts 11.28 and 21.10.

(τὴν ἐξουσίαν) by offering money to Peter and John. In response to Simon, Peter is represented rebuking and correcting him by identifying the Holy Spirit as 'God's gift' (see also Acts 2.38; 11.17).[57] The story shows that there is a difference between 'seeing' the effects[58] of 'receiving the Spirit' as outsiders and 'receiving the Spirit' as insiders.[59]

With respect to the third question, I want first to consider the term *Holy* Spirit in Luke–Acts in comparison with the expressions for the divine Spirit in the Jewish Bible. It is obvious that the most frequent expression for the divine Spirit in Luke–Acts (or in the New Testament) is the *Holy* Spirit, whereas in the Jewish Bible, it is *God's* Spirit as in tables 3 and 4.

Table 3. *The Expressions for the Divine Spirit in Luke–Acts*

Term	Holy Spirit	Spirit	the Spirit of the Lord	My [God's] Spirit	the Spirit of Jesus	Total
Frequency: (Luke + Acts)	54 (13 + 41)	14 (3 +11)	3 (1 + 2)	2 (0 + 2)	1 (0 + 1)	74 (17 + 57)

Table 4. *The Expressions for the Divine Spirit in the Jewish Bible (MT and LXX)*[60]

Term	the Spirit of the Lord	My/His/Your [God's] Spirit	the Spirit of God	His/Your [God's] holy Spirit	Your [God's] good Spirit	Holy Spirit	the Spirit and other expressions	Total
Frequency (MT/LXX + Old Testament Apocy.)	25 (24 + 1)	23 (21 + 2)	13 (13 + 0)	6 (3 + 3)	2 (2 + 0)	1 (0 + 1)	44/41 (35/32 + 7)	114/111 (98: MT/95: LXX + 14: Old Testament Ap.)

In Luke–Acts, the terms 'Spirit of the Lord' and 'my [God's] Spirit' are found only five times. And three out of five cases are employed in the context of Old Testament quotations by Jesus in Lk. 4.18 and Peter in Acts 2.17, 18. Moreover, the reference to the 'Spirit of the Lord' in Acts 8.39 is ambiguous in relation to whether the word 'Lord' here

---

57. See §5.1.1.4 in this chapter.

58. For the effects of 'receiving the Spirit', see §5.2.1.1 in this chapter.

59. See another example in Acts 2.1-36. Peter's perception (as an insider) of the coming of the Holy Spirit on the day of Pentecost is differently understood by others (outsiders) as intoxication due to new wine. Peter and other circumcised believers rightly discern the coming of the Holy Spirit upon the Gentiles in Acts 10.44-47; 11.15-17.

60. Cf. Table 3 in Chapter 2.

denotes God or the risen Jesus.[61] That is, expressions for the divine Spirit shift from *God's* Spirit in the Jewish Bible to the *Holy* Spirit in Luke–Acts (and in the New Testament).

Nevertheless, it should also be noted that the role of the *Holy* Spirit in Luke–Acts is very similar to that of *God's* Spirit in the Jewish Bible, when we consider immediate contexts.[62] Furthermore, as noticed earlier, Luke identifies God's Spirit promised by Joel with the Holy Spirit on the day of Pentecost (Acts 2.4, 16, 18, 22, 38). This identification is also supported by reliable characters' mentioning the Holy Spirit who speaks or inspires the Old Testament figures, David (Acts 1.45; 4.25; cf. 2 Sam. 23.2) and Isaiah (28.25; cf. Isa. 61.1-3). This means that the references to the Holy Spirit in Luke–Acts indicate God's presence and power especially in the contexts in which major witness-characters are presented as carrying out God's purpose/will (e.g. Lk. 3.22; 4.14, 18; Acts 6.10; 8.29; 9.17; 10.38; 19.21). In so doing, the Holy Spirit in Luke–Acts is represented as revealing, initiating and supporting God's plan/counsel as in the Jewish Bible (Acts 8.15-17; 10.44-48; 11.15-18; 15.8). It should also be remembered that the term קרשׁ or ἅγιος in the Jewish Bible is closely linked with Yahweh himself.[63] At the same time, Luke–Acts also mentions twice the holiness of God in Lk. 1.49 through Mary: '*holy* is his [God's] name' (ἅγιον τὸ ὄνομα αὐτοῦ) and in Lk. 11.2 through Jesus: '*hallowed* be your [God's] name' (ἁγιασθήτω τὸ ὄνομά σου). In this sense, we may say that the Holy Spirit in Luke–Acts is another expression of God's Spirit, that is, *God's holy* Spirit, although the latter term is found only six times (Isa. 63.10, 11; Ps. 51.13; Wis. 1.5; 9.17; Sus. 1.45).[64]

It should also be noted that the same term *holy* is employed in directly characterizing Jesus: 'therefore the child [Jesus] to be born will be *holy*; he will be called Son of God' (διὸ καὶ τὸ γεννώμενον ἅγιον κληθήσεται υἱὸς θεοῦ) according to the angel of the Lord (Lk. 1.35);[65] 'I know who

---

61. See §5.1.1.2 in this chapter.

62. Cf. §5.2.1.1 in this chapter.

63. See §2.1.2.6 in Chapter 2.

64. It is, therefore, understandable that the DSS frequently use the expressions 'His Holy Spirit', 'Thy Holy Spirit' and the 'spirit *of holiness*' in 1QS, 1QM, CD and 1QH (13 out of 20 references to God's Spirit). For this, see my excursus. For the common use of the 'Holy Spirit' in targums, see p. 231 n. 154 in Chapter 5.

65. Shelton comments (1991: 17), 'the Holy Spirit is the reason (*dio*) Jesus would be called holy'.

you [Jesus] are, the *Holy* One of God' (οἶδά σε τίς εἶ, ὁ ἅγιος τοῦ θεοῦ) according to the demon (Lk. 4.34); 'the *Holy* and Righteous One' (τὸν ἅγιον καὶ δίκαιον)[66] according to Peter (Acts 3.14); '(the name of) your [God's] *holy* servant Jesus' (τοῦ ὀνόματος τοῦ ἁγίου παιδός σου Ἰησου) according to the apostles (4.27, 30; cf. 2.27; 13.35). It is worth noting in Luke–Acts that Jesus is *directly called holy* five times, whereas God only twice. Thus, we can say that 'holiness' characterizes the Spirit, God *and* the Messiah Jesus.[67]

Finally, we should not miss that this *Holy* Spirit can be contrasted with *evil* or *unclean* (see four different qualifications used: ἀκάθαρτος, πονηρός, ἀσθένεια and πύθων) spirit(s).[68] So any individuals who are incorporated into God's restored community through believing in Jesus as God's Messiah and/or receiving the gift of the Holy Spirit (Acts 2.38-39) are called 'saints' (οἱ ἅγιοι) in Acts 9.13, 32, 41; 26.10 (see also 26.18).[69] In this sense, the *Holy* Spirit is related to religio-ethical human behaviour (Acts 5.3, 9; 9.31; 20.28; cf. 2.42-47; 4.31-37; note also the contexts in the Jewish Bible where the references to God's *holy* Spirit occur: Isa. 63.10, 11; 51.13; Wis. 9.17-18; cf. Ezek. 36.27 within 36.20-28),[70] although this aspect is not highlighted in Luke–Acts.[71]

I thus conclude that the *Holy* Spirit as the most obvious direct defini-

66. The term δίκαιος is used four times in Luke–Acts in referring to Jesus (Lk. 23.47; Acts 3.14; 7.52; 22.14). Recently, Doble (1996), criticizing Kilpatrick's interpretation of the word (esp. in Lk. 23.47) as 'innocent' (70-72), suggests its meaning as 'righteous' or 'just' echoed in the Wisdom of Solomon. And he argues that δίκαιος in reference to Jesus is understood as a 'christological descriptor', which is fulfilled in Jesess Jesus' death, i.e. Jesus is depicted 'not as *a* δίκαιος but rather as *the* δίκαιος' (159; emphasis original).

67. Procksch (1964: 103) notes, 'The holiness of the Spirit is inseparable from that of Christ'.

68. See §5.2.2.2 in this chapter.

69. In respect of the relationship between Jesus and other human-inspired characters in terms of 'holy', both of them are alike characterized as God's (holy) agents, particularly functioning as prophetic witnesses. Nevertheless, Jesus as God's unique agent is also depicted in Luke–Acts as the Davidic-regal king (e.g. Lk. 1.32-33), the eschatological Mosaic-Isaianic prophet (e.g. Lk. 4.18-21; Acts 3.22-24) and the anointed holy servant (e.g. Acts 4.27, 30; see also Jesus' authority to forgive sins in Lk. 5.24 and the salvific function of Jesus' name in Acts: see Chapter 5.

70. Cf. the 'cleansing' and 'sustaining' functions of God's Holy Spirit in the DSS in my excursus.

71. See also p. 230 n. 151 in Chapter 5.

tion in Luke–Acts has the following implications: (1) The Holy Spirit is almost always characterized by the reliable narrator or characters (e.g. an angel of the Lord, Jesus, Peter and Paul). (2) The *Holy* Spirit is seen as *God's holy* Spirit and is frequently presented in witness contexts; namely the Holy Spirit is considered *God's holy agent* who reveals His plan/counsel in supporting and empowering Jesus and his witnesses.[72] In this sense, their work empowered by the *Holy* Spirit is construed as God's holy mission. (3) This *Holy* Spirit shares his attribute of holiness not only with God, but also with Jesus, the Messiah; in this light, we can understand why the Spirit is once described directly as the Spirit *of Jesus* (Acts 16.6-7).[73] And (4) those who receive the *Holy* Spirit are regarded as God's (eschatological) holy people,[74] obeying God (cf. Acts 5.32) and having nothing to do with Satan or evil spirits (cf. Acts 13.9-11; 8.18-24).[75] In addition, some characters who are filled with or full of the *Holy* Spirit are presented as God's (holy) human agents who reveal or accomplish his plan/purpose, functioning as reliable witnesses to the Kingdom of (holy) God and (holy) Jesus.

5.1.1.2. *'God's' Spirit/the Spirit 'of the Lord'*. The direct definition 'God's Spirit' is found only twice in Luke–Acts. On the day of Pentecost, Peter interprets the coming of the Holy Spirit by quoting the LXX Joel 3.1-5a.[76] Here, the term 'my Spirit' is utilized twice in Acts 2.17, 18 and thus the Spirit is understood as *God's Spirit* because the prophet Joel delivered the message by means of direct discourse in which God himself speaks, viz. λέγει ὁ θεός as in Acts 2.17. In other words, the descent of the Holy Spirit at Pentecost, according to Peter (and the implied author), is to be viewed as fulfilling the outpouring of God's Spirit prophesied by Joel.[77]

---

72. Cf. Procksch, who comments (1964: 104), 'As the Holy Spirit, He is everywhere thought to be grounded in God, so that ἅγιον takes on almost the meaning of divine'.

73. See §5.1.1.3 in this chapter.

74. Cf. the term 'Spirit of holiness', frequently used in the Qumran Literature in which the community members are self-defined as a (eschatological) 'House of Holiness': see my excursus and Moule (1978: 22-23).

75. See Lake (1933a: 102).

76. On the significance of Peter's citation of Joel, see §4.6.1.1 in Chapter 5.

77. Cf. the divine Spirit in Mark, which is never called 'God's Spirit/the Spirit of God' or the 'Spirit of the Lord', but always the 'Holy Spirit' or simply the Spirit; in Matthew, the expressions, 'Spirit of God' (3.16) and 'Spirit of [your] Father' (10.20) are found.

Likewise, the term 'Spirit of the Lord' is found only three times: Lk.
4.18; Acts 5.9; 8.39. In Lk. 4.18-19, the 'Spirit of the Lord' is mentioned by Jesus in the context of a direct citation of Isa. 61.1-2 with a
little divergence from the LXX version. This implies that Jesus' endowment with the Spirit in the Gospel explains the portrait of Jesus as
God's Spirit-empowered agent, especially as the prophetic Messiah
anointed in/with the 'Spirit of the Lord/God'.[78] In Acts 5.9, the 'Spirit
of the Lord' appears in the narrative context of Peter's rebuke of Ananias and Sapphira who have lied to the Holy Spirit: '"Ananias", Peter
asked, 'why has Satan filled your heart to lie to the *Holy* Spirit?...'
(5.3a) and 'How is it that you have agreed together to put the Spirit *of*
the Lord to the test?' (5.9a). The Lord here can be viewed as God in the
light of Peter's additional remarks: 'You did not lie to us but to *God*'
(5.4). Finally the term occurs in Acts 8.39 (cf. the term Holy Spirit in
8.29);[79] however, it is not clear whether the 'Lord' in this context refers
to God or the risen Jesus (cf. Jesus as 'Lord' in the immediate context:
9.10, 11, 13, 14, 15, 17).[80]

---

78. For further discussion, see §4.4 in Chapter 5.

79. Because of the possible confusion between the angel of the Lord in 8.26 and
the Holy Spirit in 8.29, the Western text rephrases verse 39 as follows: 'the Holy
Spirit fell on the eunuch, and the angel of the Lord snatched Philip away' (πνεῦμα
ἅγιον ἐπέπεσεν ἐπὶ τόν εὐνοῦχον, ἄγγελος δὲ κυρίου ἥρπασεν τὸν Φίλιππον).

80. The word κύριος as an absolute form is used in Luke (104 times) as the title
of God (37) and Jesus (23; esp. see Lk. 1.43, 76; 2.11; 24.3; cf. 20.42, 44). In Acts
(107 times), although this word also denotes either God (27; esp. 2.39; 3.22; 4.26;
cf. 5.9) or Jesus (59), and both (16; e.g. 1.24; 5.14; 8.22; 9.31; 16.14, 15), the
narrator uses it more for the exalted Jesus: 'Lord, Jesus' (19 times: 1.21; 4.33; 7.59;
8.16; 9.17; 10.36; 11.17, 20; 15.11, 26; 16.31; 19.5, 13, 17; 20.21, 24, 35; 21.13;
28.31); the 'Word of the Lord' (11 times: 8.25; 11.16; 13.44, 48, 49; 15.35, 36;
16.32; 19.10, 20; 20.35); the 'name of the Lord' (4 times: 9.28; 19.13, 17; 21.13).
On the Christology of Luke–Acts, Moule (1966: 160) has argued that the divine
'Lord' is not applied to Jesus in the Gospel with two exceptions in 1.43 and 1.76.
On the contrary, Jones has insisted (1974: 91), 'he [Luke] makes no distinction
between the earthly and the exalted Lord'. In regard to this issue in terms of literary
criticism, it can be pointed out that the narrator of Luke–Acts, from the outset,
relates the narrative in the light of a post-resurrection perspective as his ideological
point of view. After Jesus' resurrection and ascension, and his pouring out of the
Holy Spirit, however, the narrator more often refers to Jesus as the Lord. Cf.
O'Neill (1955: 155-74); de Jonge (1988: 97-111); Marshall (1976: 97-110);
Buckwalter (1996: 173-228).

5.1.1.3. *The Spirit 'of Jesus'*. The 'Spirit' in Acts 16.6 is re-introduced in the next verse as the 'Spirit of Jesus' (τὸ πνεῦμα Ἰησοῦ)[81] by the reliable narrator. In his commentary, Bruce (1988: 307) asked the right question, yet did not attempt to provide a full explanation:

> In saying that this second prohibition was imposed by 'the Spirit of Jesus', does Luke suggest some significance in the change of terminology? It was the same Spirit who forbade them to 'speak the word in Asia', but the fact that on this occasion he is called 'the Spirit of Jesus' may indicate that his guidance was now given *through a prophecy uttered expressly in the name of Jesus* (emphasis added).

This direct definition of the 'Spirit of Jesus' is striking when we acknowledge that there is no comparable expression used in the Jewish Bible and other intertestamental literature.[82] The fact that Jesus is directly characterized in Luke–Acts as God's Spirit-filled (Lk. 1.35; 3.16; 4.1, 14, 18; 10.21; Acts 1.2; 10.38) and holy (Lk. 1.35; 4.34; Acts 3.14; 4.27, 30) agent *par excellence* may help to understand the expression. It is also worth noting that after his resurrection *Jesus himself* promises to send his disciples the Holy Spirit: 'And see, I [*Jesus*] am sending upon you what my Father promised (καὶ [ἰδοὺ] ἐγὼ ἀποστέλλω τὴν ἐπαγγελίαν τοῦ πατρός μου); so stay here in the city until you have been clothed with power from on high' (Lk. 24.49; cf. Acts 1.4-5, 8; Lk. 3.16). Moreover, Peter's interpretation of the coming of the Holy Spirit at Pentecost (esp. see Acts 2.33: 'Being therefore exalted at the right hand of God, and having received from the Father the promise of the Holy Spirit, he [*Jesus*] *has poured out this* that you both see and hear')[83] reveals that this is the day of fulfilment not only of the coming of the Spirit as God long promised (Joel 2.28-32; Acts 2.16-21), but

---

81. Because of this unusual expression (nowhere else found in the New Testament), some manuscripts correct it to the more common 'Holy Spirit' (arm^mss Epiphanius) or 'Spirit of the Lord' (C*, it^gig); nevertheless the term 'Spirit of Jesus' is strongly attested by P^74, ℵ, A, B, C^2, D, E, 33, 69, 81*, 326, 467, vg, syr^p.h, cop^bo, arm^mss; see Metzger (1975: 442). Cf. the 'Spirit of Jesus Christ' (Phil. 1.19); the 'Spirit of Christ' (Rom. 8.9; 1 Pet. 1.11); the 'Spirit of his son' (Gal. 4.6).

82. As Turner (1994b) noticed, there are three expressions that might seem to be parallel: the 'Spirit of Elijah' (*Targ.* 2 Kgs 2.9-10); the 'Spirit of Moses' (Philo, *Gig.* 24, 26; *Num. R.* 13.20); the 'Spirit of the Messiah' (*Gen. R.* 2.4). And he rightly pointed out (433), 'In none of these cases does "the Spirit of X" mean "Spirit with the personality of X", far less that the named person impresses his character on the Spirit transferred to others'. Cf. Sir. 48.12; Bel 1.36; Sus. 1.44-46.

83. See §4.6.1.1 in Chapter 5.

also of (John the Baptist's prophetic words about Jesus [Lk. 3.16; cf. Acts 10.44-48; 11.15-16; 19.4-6] and) Jesus' own words about his sending the promise of his Father (Lk. 24.49; Acts 1.4-5), that is, Jesus is now seen not only as God's Spirit-filled agent, but also as the Spirit-baptizer/dispenser,[84] and this may explain why he is called 'Lord' (Acts 2.36).[85] This new understanding of Jesus as the Spirit-dispenser is unparalleled in intertestamental literature (cf. 1QIs^a 52.15; 1QS 4.21; CD 2.12; 11Q13; Isa. 11.1-2; 1QS^b 5.25; *Pss. Sol.* 17.37; 18.7; *Targ. Isa.* 11.2; 42.1-4; *1 En.* 49.3; 66.2), except in one case found in *T. Jud.* 24.3: 'He [the Messiah] will pour out the Spirit of Grace upon you', but this is regarded by critics as a Christian interpolation (Turner 1982: 181-82).

It is noted that the exalted Jesus and the Spirit are also depicted as playing parallel roles[86] especially in relation to Jesus' witnesses in Acts, as the earthly Jesus promises the disciples in the Gospel (12.12; 21.15): the Spirit (Acts 4.8-12; 6.10; 8.29; 10.19; 13.2-4; cf. 19.21) and the exalted Jesus (Acts 8.9-10; 22.17, 21; 23.11; 26.14-18) are alike presented as empowering Jesus' disciples for witness.[87] In this light, the exalted Jesus now has the power and authority to direct and empower his disciples either through the Holy Spirit, that is, the Spirit of Jesus, or

84. See Zwiep (1997: 184).

85. Turner raises the issue of 'divine Christology' in terms of the divine Spirit (1994b: 436): 'The argument of this essay is that the understanding of Jesus as sharing in God's lordship of the Spirit—that is, of the Spirit extending the presence and activities of the risen Lord to disciples in and through diverse charismata—can be traced to the earliest forms of Christianity we may claim to know anything about, and that this understanding was liable to provide a decisive impulse toward '"divine" Christology' and to open up the way to the worship of Jesus with the Father as the One God'. See also Turner (1982: 168-90). His argument is also supported by Buckwalter (1996: 193-205).

86. God is sometimes described as the Spirit in the Jewish Bible (e.g. Gen. 6.3; Isa. 30.1; 31.3; 40.13; Pss. 106.33; 139.7; Zech. 6.8; Mic. 2.7): see §2.1.2 in Chapter 2.

87. Buckwalter thus suggests (1996: 201), 'Luke's Spirit-Christ doublet in Luke 12.12/21.15 is expressive of what the Spirit will do on behalf of Christ in the mission of the church and in the fuller sense of what Christ himself will actively do alongside the Spirit. These categories are not mutually exclusive, for they parallel the work of Yahweh and his Spirit as depicted in the Old Testament'. See also Krodel (1978: 36); O'Toole (1981: 484); cf. Lampe (1977: 72).

through himself like God (Exod. 4.12; Num. 22.35, 38 [cf. the LXX Num. 23.7]; Isa. 50.4; 51.16; Jer. 1.9; Mic. 6.5).[88]

This picture of Jesus as Lord *functionally* equal to Yahweh[89] is further reinforced by two other Lukan features in a manner similar to that in the Jewish Bible: (1) the use of christophanies (Acts 9.4-6, 10-12, 15-16; 18.9-10; 22.7-10, 18-21; 23.11; 26.14-18) through visions or dreams, and (2) the frequently used expression: the 'name of Jesus' (cf. Lk. 21.12; 24.47).[90] Thus, 'everyone who calls on the name of the Lord shall be saved' in Acts 2.21, cited from Joel 3.5a, can be construed as a reference to the 'name of the Lord Jesus' as saviour: 'Repent, and be baptized every one of you in the name of Jesus Christ so that your sins may be forgiven; and you will receive the gift of the Holy Spirit' (2.38; cf. 4.12; 9.14, 21; 16.31; 22.16). So Buckwalter rightly comments (1996: 196), 'The Joel passage takes on significant christological meaning in that Peter transfers in v. 21 the agency of salvation from God (Yahweh) to Jesus. As Lord of the Spirit, Jesus now pours out the promised Spirit upon believers'.[91]

In sum, the Holy Spirit in Luke–Acts is seen as the 'Spirit of the Lord/God' as in the Jewish Bible, although this term is found only five times. This implies that the Holy Spirit is depicted as representing the

88. Thus, Stälin points out (1973: 247), 'der Geist steht zu dem erhöten Christus im selben Verhätnis wie im Judentum zu Gott'. Cf. Fitzmyer, who comments (1981: 230), 'Here [Acts 16.7] the Spirit is…a substitute for the risen Christ himself, when he is no longer physically present to his followers'; Zwiep (1997: 182 n. 3).

89. For this issue, see O'Toole (1981: 471-98): 'for Luke Jesus acts as does the Father, and Jesus can do what the Father does' (487); Buckwalter (1996: 204): 'Luke's perception of Jesus' relation to the Spirit seems closely reminiscent of OT monotheism: as the Spirit of God was largely the point of contact between Israel and Yahweh in the OT, so is the Spirit, according to Luke–Acts, primarily the point of contact between Jesus and the church, and Jesus and the world'.

90. For the word ὄνομα indicating Jesus, see 'in the name of Jesus Christ (of Nazareth)' (2.38; 3.6; 4.10; 8.12; 10.48; 16.18); 'in the name of Jesus (of Nazareth)' (4.18, 30; 5.40; 9.27, 29; 22.16; 26.9; cf. 3.16; 4.7, 12, 17; 5.28; 9.21); 'in the name of the *Lord* Jesus' (8.16; 19.5, 13, 17); 'for the sake of the name/my name; for the name of the *Lord* Jesus' (5.41; 9.16; 21.13); 'forgiveness of sins through his [Jesus'] name' (10.43); 'and have your sins washed away, calling on his [Jesus'] name' (22.16). Cf. ὄνομα, used only twice in Acts (15.14, 17), referring to God's name.

91. See also Bock (1987: 164-67); Haenchen (1971: 179, 186); Lincoln (1984/85: 206).

power and presence of the Jewish God through God's human agents in order to signal God's purpose or will especially in the witness contexts. At the same time, the Spirit plays roles parallel to the risen Jesus and is characterized in relation to the resurrected Jesus, empowering and guiding his disciples/witnesses to bear witness primarily to the risen Jesus as Lord and Saviour.

5.1.1.4. Other Definitions. Apart from the terms, *Holy* Spirit, *God's* Spirit/Spirit *of the Lord* and Spirit *of Jesus* as direct definitions, there are four other instances in Luke–Acts in which the Holy Spirit is defined in a direct way:

> And behold, I [Jesus] send *the promise of my Father* (τήν ἐπαγγελίαν τοῦ πατρός μου) upon you [the apostles]; but stay in the city, until you are clothed with *power from on high* (ἐξ ὕψους δύναμιν) (by Jesus; Lk. 24.49 in RSV; cf. Acts 1.8; 8.19).
>
> While staying with them, he [Jesus] ordered them [the apostles] not to leave Jerusalem, but to wait there for *the promise of the Father* (τήν ἐπαγγελίαν τοῦ πατρὸς). 'This', he said, 'is what you have heard from me; for John baptized with water, but you will be baptized with *the Holy Spirit* not many days from now'. (by Jesus; Acts 1.4-5).
>
> And we are *witnesses* (μάτυρες) to these things, and so is *the Holy Spirit* (καὶ τὸ πνεῦμα τὸ ἅγιον) whom God has given to those who obey him (by Peter and the other apostles; Acts 5.32).
>
> And I [Peter] remembered the word of the Lord, how he had said, 'John baptized with water, but you will be baptized with *the Holy Spirit*'. If then God gave them *the same gift* (τήν ἴσην δωρεὰν) that he gave us when we believed in the Lord Jesus Christ, who was I that I could hinder God? (by Peter; Acts 11.16-17; see also 2.38; 8.20).

The *promise of my/[the] Father* (τήν ἐπαγγελίαν τοῦ πατρός μου) in Lk. 24.49 and Acts 1.4 is the direct definition of the Holy Spirit made twice by the reliable character, the risen Jesus. The definition could already be anticipated by the implied reader from the early part of the Gospel (11.13; 12.12;[92] cf. 21.15). Furthermore, Acts 1.4-5 confirms that the Father's promise is identical with the Father's gift of the Holy Spirit (see also 2.33, 39; 17-21). As noticed earlier, however, the promise, first established by God, is also given through Jesus as the Son of the Most High: 'I [*Jesus*] send the promise of my Father upon you'

---

92. For my comment on each passage alongside its parallel contexts in Mark and Matthew, see n. 117 in Chapter 5.

(Lk. 24.49; see also Acts 2.33; cf. Lk. 12.12; 21.15).[93]
The Holy Spirit is also defined by the risen Jesus as *power from on high* in Lk. 24.49, which is later reiterated in Acts 1.8. The image of 'clothing' with a quality is also found in the LXX (Pss. 34.26; 92.1; 108.18; 131.9, 16, 18; Prov. 31.25; Wis. 5.18; 17.3).[94] In particular, 1 Chron. 12.18 relates that the Spirit clothes Amasai to make an inspired speech. Elsewhere, the Lukan narrative tells us through reliable characters that the Holy Spirit and divine power are intimately related to each other (Lk. 1.17, 35 [by an angel of the Lord]; 4.14 [by the narrator], 18 [by Jesus]; Acts 1.8 [by Jesus]; 10.38 [by Peter]).[95] It is through this divine power that Jesus' disciples are empowered to witness, beginning from Jerusalem to all nations (Lk. 24.47-49; Acts 1.8; cf. 8.19), as Jesus himself had been empowered by the Spirit for his witness ministry from Galilee to Jerusalem.[96]

Furthermore, the Holy Spirit himself is portrayed as a (confirming) *witness* by the reliable character, Peter in Acts 5.32. In other words, the Spirit is seen as not only the divine 'promise' and 'power' for the disciples who are to be involved in witness-mission, but also *the Spirit of witness* himself (cf. Lk. 12.10-12; 24.46-49; Acts 1.8; 4.31; 6.10; 7.55; 15.8; 20.23 see also Lk. 1-2).[97] This intimate connection between the Holy Spirit and the theme of witness in Luke–Acts will be discussed thoroughly in the next chapter.

The last direct definition of the Holy Spirit made by Peter in Acts 11.16-17 suggests that the same *gift* of God granted to Jewish believers (Acts 2.38; 8.20) is also given to Gentile believers. Thus, three important implications can be considered: (1) This definition indicates that the Holy Spirit cannot be manipulated by human beings, but is

93. See Fitzmyer (1981: 228-29, 230); Nolland (1993: II, 1220). For further discussion concerning Jesus as the Spirit-Baptizer/Dispenser/Sender, see §§4.5 and 5 in Chapter 5.

94. See my Table 4 in Chapter 2.

95. Contra Menzies (1991a: 124-30). His view of the relationship between the Holy Spirit and miraculous power, esp. healing and exorcism is rightly criticized by Turner (1991: 124-52). See also Shelton (1991: 57-58, 157).

96. Cf. a successive pattern for responsible leadership in relation to Spirit-endowment in the Jewish Bible: from Moses to Joshua (or to 70/72 elders); from Saul to David; from Elijah to Elisha: see n. 25 in Chapter 2.

97. See Barrett (1994: 291); Bruce thus comments (1990b: 18; see also 28), 'Luke's second volume is the record of the apostles' witness, and at the same time it is the record of the Spirit's witness'.

graciously given to them by God[98] (see Peter's rebuking Simon Magus for his wilful intention to obtain the power of the Holy Spirit in Acts 8.18-19). (2) The scope of 'everyone who calls on the name of the Lord shall be saved' in Acts 2.21//Joel 2.32 (see also 2.39) is not confined to Jews, but extended to Gentiles. Accordingly, the gift of the Holy Spirit, which is given to those who believe in Jesus and/or obey God (Acts 5.32), now becomes a (universal) gift regardless of ethnic origins. In some sense, therefore, an incident recounting the reception by people of the Holy Spirit along with other similar phrases, particularly outside Jerusalem, is construed as an apologetic confirmation or divine mark by which the narrator tells us that certain groups are welcomed as God's people (e.g. Acts 8.14-17; 10.44-18; 11.15-18; 19.1-7; cf. 15.8, 28; see Chapter 5). (3) The Holy Spirit as the gift of God is closely connected with believing in God's anointed Jesus (Acts 2.38-39; 9.15-17; 10.38-43; 11.17; 19.4-6; cf. 8.12-17). In other words, the bestowal of the Holy Spirit upon people is seen as part of God's ongoing redemptive work through Jesus. To receive the Holy Spirit in this context of Acts 2.38 is indeed depicted as one component of the Lukan symphony of salvation,[99] i.e. repentance, being baptized in the name of Jesus, God's forgiveness of sins, receiving the Holy Spirit as a (confirming) gift.[100]

In regard to the literary repertoire of Luke–Acts, we can see that the direct definitions of the Holy Spirit in Luke–Acts echo or reflect some features of God's Spirit in the Jewish Bible. The definitions, 'promise of my [Jesus']/[the] Father [God]' (Lk. 24.49a; Acts 1.4) and 'gift of God' (Acts 11.17; cf. 5.32b: 'the Holy Spirit whom God has given to those who obey him'),[101] interpret the Holy Spirit as the promised or

---

98. In the close relation of prayer to receiving the Spirit in Luke–Acts, it is God as the final or ultimate cause who wants to endow his people with the Holy Spirit in response to their sincere prayers (cf. Lk. 11.13). See n. 84 in Chapter 5.

99. See Marshall (1970: 97).

100. In my opinion, however, the implied author of Luke–Acts is *primarily* interested in the Holy Spirit as the source of empowering witness throughout the narrative, which *also* connotes the new relationship to the exalted Jesus as the Lord. This is the reason why major characters as witnesses are explicitly depicted as being filled with or inspired by the Spirit. See my detailed argument in Chapter 5. Cf. Marshall, who comments on the meaning of the gift of the Holy Spirit (1970: 200): 'It therefore seems likely that Luke especially understood the gift of the Holy Spirit as equipping the church for mission, and consequently that he regarded the essence of being a Christian as the activity of mission'.

101. This Lukan presentation of the Holy Spirit echoes the Qumran community's

realized gift of God's Spirit (cf. Lk. 11.13; Acts 2.38; 8.20; 10.45) to
his restored people, as predicted in the Jewish Bible (Joel 2.28-29; Isa.
44.3b; 59.21; Ezek. 36.27; 37.14a; 39.29; Prov. 1.23; Num. 11.29;
Zech. 12.10; cf. 'my [God's] blessing' in Isa. 44.3). Although the
definition of the Spirit as 'power from on high' (Lk. 24.49b) is not
explicitly found in the Jewish Bible, this connotation can be derived
from the following references: the '*power* of his Spirit' in Bel 1.36;
'might' in Isa. 11.2; a 'Spirit *from on high*' in Isa. 32.15; Wis. 9.17. In
fact, this understanding is widely embedded in the Jewish Bible.[102] The
Holy Spirit as 'witness' [μαρτύς] in Acts 5.32a indirectly reminds us of
the context of the LXX 2ʹ Esd. 19.30/the MT Neh. 9.30: καὶ ἐπεμαρτύρω
αὐτοῖς ἐν πνεύματί σου ἐν χειρὶ προφητῶν σου (cf. Acts 7.51; 10.43;
Neh. 9.20; Zech. 7.12; Ps. 106.33).[103]

Except for the word 'holy', the direct definitions of the Spirit in
Luke–Acts are not made by the narrator, but by Jesus and Peter
(including the other apostles once). Nevertheless, their direct definitions
of the Spirit as the 'promise of my/[the] Father' [by Jesus], 'power from
on high' [by Jesus], 'witness' [by Peter and the other apostles] and the
'gift of God' [by Peter] can be regarded as reliable (by implied readers),
because both Jesus and Peter from Acts 2 onwards are portrayed as
trustworthy characters who share the same ideological point of view of
the narrator.[104] In summary, the Lukan understanding of the Holy Spirit
is the Spirit that God promised to give in the past, which is now realized
as God's (universal and eschatological) gift to his people, and that the
risen Jesus also promised to his disciples/witnesses as witnessing power
for their ministry.

5.1.2. *Indirect Presentation*
5.1.2.1. *Speech*. Not many utterances of the Holy Spirit as a character
are noticed; nevertheless, we need to draw attention to seven instances

---

understanding of God's Spirit as an eschatological gift (e.g. note the expression 'the
Spirit which Thou hast given to me' in 1 QH 6.11-12; 12.11-12; 13.18-19; 16.12).
See my excursus.

102. See §2.1.2.3 in Chapter 2.
103. Cf. the direct definitions of God's Spirit in the Jewish Bible (apart from
'holy'): 'wisdom'; 'understanding, counsel, might, knowledge, the fear of the Lord/
fidelity'; 'justice'; 'compassion and supplication'; 'good'; 'immortal'; 'kindly'. See
Appendix I.
104. See §3.3.2 in Chapter 3.

found only in Acts in which the Holy Spirit speaks to reliable characters: Philip (Acts 8.29; cf. 6.5), Peter (Acts 10.19; 11.12), the Antioch Church leaders named Barnabas, Simeon, Lucius of Cyrene, Manaen and Saul as prophets and teachers (Acts 13.1-2) and a prophet named Agabus (Acts 21.11). Also important to note are the immediate contexts in which the Spirit is depicted as a directly speaking actor, three times by the narrator and once each by Peter and a prophet named Agabus.

Then *the Holy Spirit said to* (εἶπεν δὲ τὸ πνεῦμα τῷ) Philip, 'Go over to this chariot and join it' (by the narrator; Acts 8.29).

While Peter was still thinking about the vision, *the Spirit said to* (εἶπεν) him [Peter], 'Look, three men are searching for you. Now get up, go down, and go with them without hesitation; for I have sent them' (by the narrator; Acts 10.19).

The Spirit told (εἶπεν) me [Peter] to go with them and not to make a distinction between them and us (by Peter; Acts 11.12).

While they were worshipping the Lord and fasting, *the Holy Spirit said* (εἶπεν), 'Set apart for me Barnabas and Saul for the work to which I have called them' (by the narrator; Acts 13.2).

He [a prophet named Agabus] came to us and took Paul's belt, bound his own feet and hands with it, and said, 'Thus *says the Holy Spirit* (λέγει), "This is the way the Jews in Jerusalem will bind the man who owns this belt and will hand him over to the Gentiles"' (by Agabus; Acts 21.11).

In the first four narrative contexts the narrator and Peter attribute the ongoing witness-mission to the Holy Spirit who is portrayed as a direct speaker. The Spirit is, so to speak, characterized as an authoritative or reliable mission director participating in the decisive moments of the 'way of witness' by speaking to (and guiding) the disciples (Philip, Peter and the church leaders at Antioch) *particularly in relation to the Gentile mission*, which would have been ignored or not been launched unless the Spirit had given direct instructions to them: an Ethiopian eunuch on the road going down from Jerusalem to Gaza; Cornelius as a centurion of the Italian Cohort in Caesarea; both the Jewish and the Gentile community in Asia Minor. Hence, the implied reader at each context can recognize that the witness-mission plan beyond the territory of Palestine anticipated in Lk. 2.32; 24.47-49; Acts 1.8 will be set forth and accomplished according to God's counsel (Acts 15.14; cf. Isa. 49.6) in the sense that not the human characters, but the divine reliable character, God's Holy Spirit, is now actively and forcefully taking charge of directing the way of mission in Acts (cf. 15.8, 28; 16.6-7;

19.21), as did Jesus as God's agent in the Gospel (e.g. 4.14, 31, 43-44; 8.1, 22; 9.51; 13.22; 19.28).

We should also notice that Philip, Peter and Paul, commanded by the Spirit, are said to bear witness primarily to Jesus, rather than directly to God, as has been anticipated in Lk. 24.48 and Acts 1.8: 'he [Philip] proclaimed to him [an Ethiopian eunuch] the good news about Jesus' (Acts 8.35); 'Jesus as the Lord of all and God's anointed judge' (Acts 10.36-44, esp. 44, 38, 42); 'the promised Savior, Jesus' (Acts 13.23, 38-39). In other words, the Spirit's driving aim for witness-mission involves recipients in revealing who Jesus is and what Jesus has done. In this sense, we may say that the Spirit is indirectly characterized as a christological mission director who prompts the disciples to witness to Jesus.

The Holy Spirit also speaks through the prophet named Agabus in revealing Paul's future to be faced in Jerusalem.[105] Agabus is depicted as saying 'thus says the Holy Spirit' and the Holy Spirit's statement in Acts 21.11 warns about Paul's impending imprisonment,[106] which echoes Jesus' own predictions of his passion (Lk. 9.22, 44; 18.32; cf. 12.50).[107] This inspired and revelatory prophecy of Agabus is said to be accomplished in the subsequent narrative in Acts 21.27-36.[108]

There are two cases in Acts in which Peter and Paul are represented asserting that, even in the past, the Holy Spirit spoke through Old

---

105. Agabus' symbolic action is reminiscent of Old Testament prophets (e.g. Isa. 20.2-6; Jer. 13.1-7; 19.1-13; Ezek. 4.1-17). In addition, the narrator's use of 'thus says' (τάδε λέγει) also echoes the LXX in which, however, there is no exact parallel to 'thus says the Holy Spirit' in Acts. Instead, there is the formula of 'Thus says the Lord'. See Amos 3.11; 5.16; Obad 1.1; Hag. 1.2; Zech. 1.16; Isa. 3.16; Jer. 2.31; Ezek. 4.13; see also Josephus, *Ant.* 11.26; cf. Rev. 2.1, 8, 12, 18; 3.1, 7, 14. See Johnson (1992: 370).

106. Paul himself is said to have decided through the Spirit to go to Jerusalem and to Rome in Acts 20.22-23 (by Paul's own words); cf. 19.21 (by the narrator's statement). For a detailed analysis of this issue, see §4.6.3 in Chapter 5.

107. The implied reader can discern some narrative echoes between Jesus in the Gospel and Paul in Acts, and perceive the boldness of Spirit-filled witnesses before their forthcoming suffering (cf. Lk. 12.10-12; 21.15). In regard to the revelatory role of the Spirit, see both the Jewish Bible (see §§2.1.2 and 4.1.2 in Chapter 2) and the DSS (1QS 8.15-16; CD 2.12-13a; 1QH 12.11-12; 13.18b-19; 14.12b-13; for the ability of interpreting dreams or visions, see also Gen. 41.38; Dan. 4.8, 9, 18; 5.11, 14).

108. See also n. 278 in Chapter 5.

Testament reliable figures, David (cf. 1 Sam. 16.13) and Isaiah (cf. Isa. 6.1-8).

> Friends, the Scripture had to be fulfilled, which *the Holy Spirit* through David *foretold* (ἣν προεῖπεν τὸ πνεῦμα τὸ ἅγιον διὰ στόματος Δαυὶδ) concerning Judas, who became a guide for those who arrested Jesus (by Peter; Acts 1.16; cf. 4.25).
>
> Some were convinced by what he had said, while others refused to believe. So they disagreed with each other; and as they were leaving, Paul made one further statement: *'The Holy Spirit was* right *in saying to* your ancestors through the prophet Isaiah (καλῶς τὸ πνεῦμα τὸ ἅγιον ἐλάλησεν διὰ Ἡσαΐου)...' (by Paul; Acts 28.24-25).

In the first example, David's statement, according to Peter,[109] is not only attributed to the Holy Spirit (see below), but is also interpreted as prophetically referring to Judas. The necessity of Judas's action is emphasized, so that not even his betrayal stands outside the purpose of God. In the second example, Isaiah's prophecy about 'your ancestors' is used prophetically about these Jews who do not believe Paul's teaching. In this way, the narrator also shows that his narrative is reliable and authoritative not only by utilizing the divine character of the Holy Spirit, but also by quoting Scripture (e.g. Ps. 69.15; Ps. 2.1; Isa. 6.9). In addition, this suggests that the Holy Spirit is a divine character[110] who once spoke at the times of David and Isaiah, *and* has given utterances and acted during the ministries of Jesus and his disciples for the Lukan community.[111]

The reference that presupposes the speech of God's Spirit in the

---

109. In fact, Peter, at this narrative time of Acts 1.16-22, has not yet received the Holy Spirit as a narrative rhetorical index to 'reliability' for characters. Nevertheless, unlike in the Gospel, from the beginning of Acts, the narrator tends to portray Peter as the (reliable) representative of the twelve apostles from the narrator's retrospective point of view, which also fulfils Jesus' prayer for Peter (Lk. 22.32). Both Peter's (Acts 1.15-22) and Paul's (Acts 28.25-28) reading and interpretation of Scripture echoes that of Jesus in the beginning and end of his ministry in the Gospel (Lk. 4.16-21; 24.27, 44-45). For Peter's new status in Acts, Tannehill says (1994: 20), 'Peter is taking over a major function of the departed Jesus'; Shepherd also adds (1994: 158), 'Peter is presented to the reader as a reliable commentator, since he expresses Jesus' view that all the events leading up to this point in the story were in fulfilment of prophecy'.

110. See also §5.1.2.3 in this chapter.

111. More basically, these two passages demonstrate the narrator's ideological point of view that such faithful figures, David and Isaiah, speak their utterances inspired by the Holy Spirit.

Jewish Bible[112] is found in David's words in 2 Sam. 23.2 (cf. 1 Kgs 22.24//2 Chron. 18.23): 'The spirit of the Lord spoke (ἐλάλησεν) through me, his word was upon my tongue', which explains that David's last words are inspired by God's Spirit and thus sanctioned by God as indicated in the next verse: 'The God of Israel has spoken, the Rock of Israel has said to me'. This shows that the author of 2 Samuel uses this expression in order to make David's last words reliable and authoritative. Thus Luke not only adopts this rhetorical expression, but also develops it further in his narrative.

From my examination of the speeches of the Holy Spirit along with their related contexts in Luke–Acts, I can infer the following four important characteristics: (1) The Holy Spirit is depicted by the reliable narrator and characters as a trustworthy character who speaks to guide at decisive narrative moments the mission, especially in association with launching the witness to Jesus among Gentiles—*the Holy Spirit as a christocentric mission director*. (2) The Holy Spirit also speaks to reveal Paul's personal impending imprisonment through Agabus's prophecy—*the Holy Spirit as a reliable revealer* (see also Lk. 2.26). (3) The Holy Spirit is portrayed as *a reliable Scripture commentator* by Peter and Paul, who spoke to (or inspired) the Old Testament reliable figures, David and Isaiah, giving a message that is understood to be fulfilled in the narrative events. (4) The speech of the Holy Spirit is not found in the Gospel. It can be assumed that the narrator is reluctant to portray the Spirit as a speaking character until Jesus' ascension in Acts (see also the next subsection).

5.1.2.2. Action I. In this and following subsections, I am concerned with two ways of showing action in relation to the Holy Spirit: (1) the Spirit as acting and (2) the Spirit as acted upon. As in §5.1.2.1, the expressions for the former are attributed to the reliable narrator (7 times) or characters: Jesus (once), Paul (twice) and the Holy Spirit (once). I shall first look at statements about the Spirit's actions and then explore implications within the immediate contexts.

> [W]hen Jesus also had been baptized and was praying, the heaven was opened, and *the Holy Spirit descended upon him* in bodily form like a dove (καὶ καταβῆναι τὸ πνεῦμα τὸ ἅγιον σωματικῷ εἴδει ὡς περιστερὰν ἐπ' αὐτόν) (by the narrator; Lk. 3.21b-22a).

---

112. A 'spirit' is described by Micaiah as speaking to God, and as willing to entice Ahab by functioning as a 'lying spirit' in 1 Kgs 22.21//2 Chron. 18.20.

[F]or *the Holy Spirit will teach* (διδάξει) you at that very hour what you ought to say (by Jesus; Lk. 12.12).

All of them were filled with the Holy Spirit and began to speak in other languages, as *the Spirit gave* them *to speak out* (καθὼς τὸ πνεῦμα ἐδίδου ἀποφθέγγεσθαι αὐτοῖς) (by the narrator; Acts 2.4; my own translation).

When they [Philip and the Ethiopian eunuch] came up out of the water, *the Spirit of the Lord snatched* Philip *away* (πνεῦμα κυρίου ἥρπασεν τὸν Φίλιππον): the eunuch saw him no more, and went on his way rejoicing. But Philip found himself at Azotus, and as he was passing through the region, he proclaimed the good news to all the towns until he came to Caesarea (by the narrator; Acts 8.39-40).

Now get up, go down, and go with them [Cornelius's messengers] without hesitation; for *I* [*the Spirit*] *have sent* them (ἐγὼ ἀπέσταλκα αὐτούς) (by the Holy Spirit; Acts 10.20).

When they [Paul, Silas and Timothy] had come opposite Mysia, they attempted to go into Bithynia, but *the Spirit of Jesus did not allow* (οὐκ εἴασεν) them (by the narrator; Acts 16.7).

And now, *as a captive to the Spirit* (δεδεμένος ἐγὼ τῷ πνεύματι), I [Paul] am on my way to Jerusalem, not knowing what will happen to me there, except that *the Holy Spirit testifies* (διαμαρτύρεταί) to me in every city that imprisonment and persecutions are waiting for me (by Paul; Acts 20.22-23; cf. 5.32).

Keep watch over yourselves and all the flock, of which *the Holy Spirit has made* you *overseers* (ὑμᾶς τὸ πνεῦμα τὸ ἅγιον ἔθετο ἐπισκόπους), to shepherd the church of the Lord that he purchased with his own blood (by Paul; Acts 20.28; my translation).[113]

In addition, the narrator also describes the activity of the Holy Spirit in a passive form.

It *had been revealed* (κεχρηματισμένον) to him [Simeon] *by the Holy Spirit* that he would not see death before he had seen the Lord's Messiah (Lk. 2.26).

---

113. Two textual variants in Acts 20.28b are noted: (1) ἐκκλησία τοῦ θεοῦ in ℵ, B, 614, 1175, 2495; ἐκκλησία κυρίου in P⁷⁴, A, C*, D, E, Ψ, 33, 36, 453, 945, 1739, 1891; (2) διὰ τοῦ αἵματος τοῦ ἰδίου in P⁷⁴, ℵ, A, B, C, D, E, Ψ, 33, 36, 945, 1175, 1739, 1891; διὰ τοῦ αἵματος in the Byzantine text. Metzger (1975: 480-82) prefers the expression 'church of God' and interprets διὰ τοῦ αἵματος τοῦ ἰδίου as 'with the blood of his Own', regarding ἰδίου as the absolute use of ὁ ἴδιος equivalent to ὁ ἀγαπητός. See also NRSV: 'God' and 'with the blood of his own Son'; NASB: 'God' and 'His own blood'; KJV and NIV: 'God' and 'his own blood'.

So, *being sent out* (ἐκπεμφθέντες) *by the Holy Spirit*, they [Barnabas and Saul] went down to Seleucia; and from there they sailed to Cyprus (Acts 13.4).

They went through the region of Phrygia and Galatia, *having been forbidden* (κωλυθέντες) *by the Holy Spirit* to speak the word in Asia (Acts 16.6).

We can first notice that the Holy Spirit's action appears in the pivotal narratives of both Jesus' baptism and his disciples' Spirit-endowment through the narrator's statements (Lk. 3.21-22; cf. Lk. 4.18; Acts 2.1-4; 11.15-16), that is, as the prelude to each mission. We infer that the narrator designs these two episodes as introductions to the plot of Luke–Acts: Jesus in the Gospel and his disciples in Acts are represented as becoming inspired human agents of God.[114] The implied reader is thus prepared in the early part of both the Gospel and Acts by these remarkable manifestations of the Holy Spirit to trust them as reliable.

Secondly, by Jesus it is foretold that the Spirit will teach what his disciples should say in court (Lk. 12.12). Later, predicting persecution or witness, Jesus also promises that 'I [*Jesus*] will give you words and a wisdom that none of your opponents will be able to withstand or contradict' (Lk. 21.15). These two statements, which give parallel roles to Jesus and the Holy Spirit, make the reference to the 'Spirit of Jesus' in Acts 16.7 unsurprising (cf. Acts 2.33).[115] Jesus' prophecy is explicitly fulfilled in Acts 6.3-10 (see also 4.5-22; 5.17-42; cf. 9.31; 13.52).

Thirdly, the narrative depicts the Holy Spirit as testifying or revealing to Simeon and Paul their personal future history regardless of what they would expect. Each narrative then confirms the statement by the Spirit as reliable (see Lk. 2.27-35; Acts 21.27-36). In this sense, the Holy Spirit is regarded as reliable prophetic revealer in Luke–Acts (cf. Lk. 1.41-45; 67-80; 3.16-17; 4.18-19; Acts 19.21; 21.11).

Fourthly, the Holy Spirit as a character plays a marked role in guiding and directing the witness-mission of Jesus' disciples, especially to Gentiles: Philip according to the narrator in Acts 8.39;[116] Peter according to

---

114. These two contexts will be discussed in detail in light of the plot of Luke–Acts in Chapter 5.

115. The frequent phrase 'name of Jesus' in Acts probably refers to the reality and power of Jesus' presence. In this sense Acts 9.5, ' "Saul, Saul, why do you persecute me [Jesus]?" ', also implies that Jesus is present in the lives of his disciples. On this issue of Jesus' presence in Acts, see MacRae (1973: 151-67); Franklin (1975: 29-47); Maddox (1982: 139).

116. Note that the narrator employs the term 'Spirit of the Lord', which echoes

the Holy Spirit in Acts 10.20;[117] Barnabas and Saul according to the narrator in Acts 13.4; Paul, Silas and Timothy according to the narrator in Acts 16.7. Thus, it is in the contexts of disciples' witness-mission to Gentiles that the Holy Spirit is characterized as a mission-director, directly intervening in the disciples' missionary activity by means of speeches (see the previous subsection) *and* actions. Similarly, the Spirit is said to compel (δέω)[118] Paul to go to Jerusalem (Acts 20.22), in which Paul bears witness to Jesus (22.15; 23.11).

Fifthly, although only once mentioned by Paul, the Spirit is also represented as acting to provide church-supervisors (Acts 20.28; cf. 5.1-11; 9.31; 15.28). In other words, the Spirit is seen as working not only in guiding the disciples to the Gentile mission, but also as shepherding the members of the settled local church by appointing church elders.[119]

Finally, we should note that 8 out of 11 references to the action of the Holy Spirit are found in Acts (in addition, Lk. 12.12 also tells the future action of the Spirit). Thus, the Holy Spirit is depicted as a more dynamic character in Acts than in Luke. As mentioned earlier, this narrative phenomenon seems to be explained by Jesus' departure from earth in Luke 24 and Acts 1.

In the LXX, we can find the following action verbs in association with God's Spirit: γίνομαι (to come upon; 9 times: Num. 23.7; 24.2; Judg. 3.10; 11.29; 1 Sam. 19.20, 23; 2 Kgs 2.9; 2 Chron. 15.1; 20.14); ἀναλαμβάνω (to take up; 6: Ezek. 3.12, 14; 8.3a; 11.1a, 24a; 43.5a); (ἐφ)ἄλλομαι (to come/leap upon; 6: Judg. 14.6, 19; 1 Sam. 10.6, 10; 11.6; 16.13); (συν)ἄγω (to lead; 5: Ezek. 8.3b; 11.1b, 24b; 43.5b; Isa. 34.16); ἐπαναπαύω (to rest upon; 4: Num. 11.25b, 26; 2 Kgs 2.15;

---

the similar action of the Spirit in the Jewish Bible. See 1 Kgs 18.12; 2 Kgs 2.16; Ezek. 11.24; cf. Ezek. 2.2; 3.12, 14; 8.3; 11.1; 43.5.

117. This is one of the cases that the Holy Spirit directly speaks to characters in the narrative. See also Acts 8.29; 10.19; 11.12; 13.2; 21.11; cf. the Tyrian disciples' inspiration by the Spirit in Acts 21.4.

118. Louw and Nida (1989: I, 476; II, 57) put δέω in Acts 20.22 and ἀναγκάζω in Gal. 2.14 together in the same semantic domain: 'to compel/force' or 'to cause it to be necessary for' and translate this clause 'and now the Spirit compels me to go to Jerusalem'; cf. BAGD (178), which classifies the word as supernatural binding: 'bound by the Spirit' (cf. Lk. 13.16).

119. Like the whole narrative, this small narrative unit betrays one of Paul's (and the narrator's) ideological points of view, that is, the Ephesian Church leaders have been appointed not by men, but by the Holy Spirit.

1 Sam. 11.2); πορεύομαι (to go; 3: Ezek. 1.12, 20; 3.14b); (ἐπ)ἔρχομαι (to come upon; 3: Isa. 32.15; Ezek. 2.2a; 3.24a); ἐνδύω (to clothe; 3: Judg. 6.34; 1 Chron. 12.19; 2 Chron. 24.20); ἐξαίρω (to lift up; 2: Ezek. 2.2b; 3.14a); αἴρω (to raise; 2: 1 Kgs 18.12; 2 Kgs 2.16a); ἵστημι (to stand; 2: Ezek. 3.24b; Hag. 2.5); ῥίπτω (to cast/throw down; 1: 2 Kgs 2.16b); ἐπιμαρτυρέω (to bear witness; 1: Neh. 9.30); ἀφίστημι (to depart; 1: 1 Sam. 16.14a); συνεκπορεύομαι (to go out with; 1: Judg. 13.25); πίπτω (to fall upon; 1: Ezek. 11.5); (ἐπι)φέρω (to move; 1: Gen. 1.2); ὁδηγέω (to lead/guide; 1: Ps. 142.10 [ET: 143.10]).[120] Among these cases, the following verbs are to be noted: to take up (ἀναλαμβάνω), to lift up (ἐξαίρω) and to raise (αἴρω) versus to snatch away (ἁρπάζω) in Acts 8.39; to bear witness (ἐπιμαρτυρέω) in Neh. 9.30 versus to testify (διαμαρτυρέω) in Acts 20.22-23. In spite of different narrative contexts, however, the action of God's Spirit in the Jewish Bible and that of the Holy Spirit in Luke and Acts alike represent vividly and dynamically the power and presence of God: the Spirit enables God's chosen (charismatic) individuals to carry out God's will/purpose.[121] In so doing, any figures who are inspired or guided by the Spirit are depicted as God's reliable human agents. On the other hand, however, we should point out that the action (and speech) of the divine Spirit from Acts 2 onwards is frequently presented *as empowering Jesus' disciples to bear witness to the risen Jesus* in support of the Gentile mission (Acts 2.4-36; 8.29-40; 10.19-43; 16.6-32; 13.4-41; cf. Lk. 2.26; 12.8-12) and is also characterized as parallel to the action of the risen Jesus (cf. Acts 16.7; 2.33).[122]

5.1.2.3. Action II. In this subsection, I shall note the references to the Holy Spirit as a character who *is acted upon by* other characters, God or the risen Jesus. The references are found as follows:

[F]or John baptized with water, but you will *be baptized with the Holy Spirit* (ἐν πνεύματι βαπτισθήσεσθε ἁγίῳ) not many days from now (according to the resurrected Jesus; Acts 1.5; 11.16; cf. Lk. 3.16).

Now when Simon saw that *the Spirit was given* (δίδοται τὸ πνεῦμα) through the laying on of the apostles' hands, he offered them money (by the narrator; Acts 8.18; cf. 5.32; 11.17; 15.8; Lk. 11.13).

---

120. For the related action verbs in the MT, see Appendix I.
121. See §2.1.2 and Table 2 in Chapter 2.
122. See §§5.1.1.2 and 5.1.1.3 in this chapter.

The circumcised believers who had come with Peter were astounded that *the gift of the Holy Spirit had been poured out* (ἡ δωρεά τοῦ ἁγίου πνεύματος ἐκκέχυται) even on the Gentiles (by the narrator; Acts 10.45; cf. 2.17, 18, 33).

Unlike in §5.1.2.2, the Spirit is treated in these contexts as a 'thing' rather than as a 'person'; the Spirit is poured out like water (cf. Isa. 44.3) or given like a gift (cf. Wis. 9.17-18).[123] The expression 'to receive the Spirit' (as a gift or a thing) is also used in Acts 2.33, 38; 8.15, 17, 19; 10.47; 19.2. In other words, these references indicate that the Holy Spirit is characterized as a 'non-person like' character.[124] This trait of the 'person-unlikeness' of the Spirit can be further explored.[125]

First, the Holy Spirit is given no personal name[126] or age (unlike, John or Jesus or the angel, Gabriel; cf. the Jewish God as Yahweh) by the narrator or other characters.

Secondly, the physical appearance or environment of the Spirit is not clearly described or delineated.[127] The Spirit, unlike angels seen in Lk. 24.4 ('two men in dazzling clothes'); Acts 1.10 ('two men in white robes'); Acts 10.30 ('a man in dazzling clothes'), is never portrayed as having the bodily form of human beings; the Spirit's appearance is depicted as in bodily form like a dove, a wind and fire (see below). Moreover, the Spirit's 'transcendent environment' can be regarded as heaven like God's (see below), whereas the Spirit is said to dwell in

123. For the direct definition of the Spirit as 'gift' or 'promise', see §5.1.1.4 in this chapter.

124. Cf. Bultmann's double understanding of the Holy Spirit (1951: 155-56), i.e. 'animistic thinking pneuma' as an independent and personal power and 'dynamistic thinking pneuma' as an impersonal force. For other scholars' views of the nature of the Holy Spirit, see Table 3 in Chapter 1.

125. Cf. Sternberg (1985), who has pointed out the similarity and the difference between the divine and the human in terms of both character and characterization. For the discernible traits of the divine character, he indicated: the difficulty in applying 'physical appearance', 'social status', 'personal history', 'local habitation' to God (323); the constancy in God's character (324); the permanent ambiguation of God's character (325).

126. See n. 24 in this chapter.

127. See also Lk. 20.36 in which Jesus, in response to the Sadducees' test, gives an account of resurrected human beings like angles. Like demons or Satan (e.g. Lk. 22.3; Acts 5.3), however, the Spirit enters into or remains in human beings. For the similarities and differences of the Spirit to an angel(s) and to demons/Satan, see §5.2.2 in this chapter.

God's faithful people as 'immanent environment', so that the actions of these humans are treated as evidence of the Spirit's activity in inspiring them. Hence, the Lukan narrator often refers to people as filled with or full of the Holy Spirit.[128]

Thirdly, the Spirit, like God yet unlike human beings (except the resurrected Jesus, e.g. in Lk. 24.31, 51; Acts 1.9; 9.3-7), is represented as a character who transcends space and time: the Spirit can dwell in more than one place/person at once (e.g. '*all of them* were filled with the Holy Spirit' in Acts 2.4; 'the Holy Spirit fell upon *all* who heard the word' in Acts 10.44); the Spirit is said to speak at the times of David (Acts 1.16; cf. 1 Sam. 16.13; 2 Sam. 23.2) and Isaiah (Acts 28.25; cf. Isa. 6.1-8; 61.1-3), and Philip (Acts 8.29) and Peter (Acts 10.19; 11.2).

In fact, in the Jewish Bible, the Spirit's 'person-unlikeness' is more frequently found than the Spirit's 'person-likeness'. For instance, we can find only one reference (2 Sam. 23.2) in which 'the Spirit of the Lord' is described as speaking to a human character.[129] In almost all cases, the Spirit in the Jewish Bible is understood as God's mysterious force, mighty power or presence (see Chapter 2). Nevertheless, except the verb βαπτίζω,[130] the expressions 'to pour out upon' (ἐκχέω [ἐπί]) and 'to give' (δίδωμι) for Spirit-endowment used in Luke–Acts are also found in the LXX: Joel 3.1, 2; Zech. 12.10 (cf. Isa. 32.15; 44.3; Ezek. 39.29 in the MT) and Num. 11.29; Neh. 9.20; Isa. 42.1; Ezek. 37.14.[131]

As in the Jewish Bible, therefore, actions mediated through the Spirit in Luke–Acts are considered as God's power, gift or presence (cf. Lk. 11.13; Acts 5.32; 8.20). However, after Jesus' ascension, that is, from Acts 2 onwards, this Spirit is also conceived as the risen Jesus' ongoing activity upon or presence with his disciples/witnesses as he promised on earth (cf. Lk. 12.12; 21.15; 24.49; Acts 1.5; 11.16; 16.7). Thus, in the contexts above and other contexts in which the words πίμπλημι, πλήρης and πληρόω are used in relation to the Spirit, the Spirit is represented as the powerful activity or manifestation of God (mainly in the Gospel) and/or the risen Jesus (in Acts).

On the basis of the two dialectic traits of the Holy Spirit as a character, therefore, it is inadequate to define the Spirit either as a 'personal being' or as an 'impersonal force'. Put differently, the Lukan narrator

128. See §5.2.1.2 in this chapter.
129. See also Appendix I.
130. For this verb, see n. 77 in Chapter 5.
131. See also n. 159 in this chapter, and Appendix I.

does not seem to *tell* us whether the Spirit *is* person or not. Rather he *shows* that the *personal* activity of the Spirit dynamically participates in believers' affairs as signifying the divine (God's and/or the risen Jesus') intervention or manifestation.[132] The Spirit (like God) in Luke–Acts (and in the Jewish Bible) *is represented metaphorically as a character in the narrative*,[133] identified sometimes in terms unlike those appropriate to human characters as an enigmatic divine character.

5.1.2.4. *External Appearance*. There are only two instances in the narrative that readers might regard as descriptions of the external or physical appearance of the Holy Spirit. There is no explicit reference to God's Spirit's external appearance in the Jewish Bible. Both cases in Luke–Acts are, however, metaphorical, so it is hard to explain what exact implications about the Holy Spirit are to be drawn.

> [W]hen Jesus also had been baptized and was praying, the heaven was opened, and the Holy Spirit descended upon him in bodily form *like a dove* (ὡς περιστεράν). And a voice came from heaven, 'You are my Son, the Beloved; with you I am well pleased' (by the narrator; Lk. 3.21b-22).
>
> And suddenly from heaven there came a sound *like the rush of a violent wind* (ὥσπερ φερομένης πνοῆς βιαίας), and it filled the entire house where they were sitting. Divided tongues, *as of fire* (ὡσεὶ πυρός), appeared among them, and a tongue rested on each of them. All of them were filled with the Holy Spirit... (by the narrator; Acts 2.2-3).

In the first instance, the Holy Spirit is said to descend upon Jesus in bodily form as a dove in the context of Jesus' baptism. In this context, Luke, in comparison with Mark and Matthew, does not employ (omits?) the words 'he [Jesus] saw' in Mk 1.10 and Mt. 3.16, but stresses the physical manifestation of the coming of the Holy Spirit by using (adding?) the expression σωματικῷ εἴδει in Lk. 3.22,[134] implying that not only Jesus but all those present could see the descent.

Scholars dispute the significance of the association of the Spirit with a dove.[135] Among them, the most plausible views are considered in

---

132. See §5.2.1.1 in this chapter, and Chapter 5.
133. Cf. Turner (1981c: 50-58).
134. See Schweizer (1952: 265-66).
135. See Keck (1970: 41-67, esp. 57-67) and Gero (1976: 17-35); Marshall (1978: 153); Fitzmyer (1981: 483-84); Bock (1994b: 338-39). Keck insists that the original *adverbial* reference to the descent of the Spirit in Mark is later misunderstood *adjectivally* (63-67).

relation to Old Testament allusions: the symbol of a dove seems to link the Holy Spirit (1) with a 'new creation', recalling the LXX Gen. 1.2[136] and/or (2) with the 'new covenant' echoing Noah's dove in Gen. 8.8-12.[137] Although the above interpretations have weak points (Menzies 1991a: 149-50), these views are cogently based on probable Old Testament allusions. In the narrative, however, it is the voice from heaven that reveals the significance of the close relationship between Jesus and God.[138] Later, Jesus himself (and also Luke) interprets his Spirit-baptism as prophetic anointing for his messianic ministry (Lk. 4.14, 18; Acts 10.38).[139] What is obvious here is that the narrator shows the concrete and visible manifestation of the coming of the Holy Spirit upon Jesus at the opening of his messianic ministry.[140]

The second incident uses other metaphorical language in reporting the outpouring of the Holy Spirit on the day of Pentecost in Acts 2.1-4. The description of the coming of the Holy Spirit upon Jesus' disciples in regard to time, 'suddenly', and origin, 'from heaven', shows that this long-anticipated event (Lk. 3.16; 11.13; 12.12; 24.49; Acts 1.5, 8; cf. Num. 11.29; Joel 2.28-32) originates from God (cf. Acts 2.33).

The narrator here employs two different metaphorical phrases in referring to Jesus' disciples' receipt of the Holy Spirit: 'a sound like the rush of a violent wind' and 'divided tongues, as of fire'.[141] As we have

136. This position is sustained by Barrett (1947: 38-39); Dunn (1970a: 27); Allison (1992: 58-60). Cf. Marshall's cautious words (1978: 154): 'It is just possible that thoughts of the new creation brought about by the Spirit are in mind. We are not, however, told what the effect of the descent of the Spirit was'. It can be noted that Rabbinic tradition (*b. Ḥag.* 15a) links the Spirit to a dove as the power of creation (cf. *Gen. R.* 2.4, which simply refers to a bird).

137. This view is suggested by Baer (1926: 58); Lampe (1951: 36). Cf. Dunn (1970a: 27): 'Either way [i.e. alluding to Gen. 1.2 or Gen. 8.8-12] the dove would mean a new beginning, a new epoch in God's dealings with creation, even a new covenant—in the eschatological circumstances, *the* new covenant' (emphasis original; see also 27 n. 13). Johnson (1991: 71) explains the dove as the 'hovering' symbol in association with Lk. 1.35 and 2.14 possibly influenced by Gen. 1.2 (as a new creation) or 8.8 (as a new covenant).

138. See §4.3.2 in Chapter 5.

139. For Jesus' sermon in the Nazareth synagogue, see §4.4 in Chapter 5.

140. See Greeven (1968: 63-72).

141. Cf. some occasions in the Jewish Bible (1 Kgs 19.11-12; 2 Kgs 2.11; 2 Sam. 22.8-15; Isa. 66.15; cf. *4 Ezra* 13.10; *1 En.* 14.8-15) in which both wind and fire are used in reference to God's power. See Johnson (1992: 42) and Barrett (1994: 113-14). Cf. several language parallels in Philo and *Targ. Ps.-J.*; see n. 130 in Chapter 5.

shown earlier in Chapter 2, the word *rûaḥ* or *pneuma* is frequently used
in referring not only to the 'divine Spirit', but also to mighty 'wind'
particularly in the Hebrew Bible and the LXX.[142] Although the Greek
word for wind in Acts is πνοή, the close etymological relationship
between the 'Spirit' and 'wind' should not be neglected.[143] In other
words, we can assume that likening the coming of the Holy Spirit upon
Jesus' disciples to a 'violent wind' suggests God's overwhelming and
mysterious power coming upon them. The divine Spirit is also said to be 'divided tongues, as of fire'.
'Divided tongues' in Acts 2.3 (cf. *1 En.* 14.8-15; 71.5) seem to be
related to 'began to speak in other tongues' in verse 4, which are possibly identified as each 'native language' in 2.8-11. This implies in this
present context that the pentecostal Spirit is understood as the Spirit for
world-wide mission among Jews beyond Palestine (cf. 8.14-17; 10.44-
48; 11.15-18; 19.1-7).[144] 'Fire' is often found in the context of theo-
phany in the Jewish Bible.[145] Above all, John the Baptist is depicted
using the imagery of both wind and fire in connection with the
promised baptism with the Holy Spirit in a context of future judgment
(Lk. 3.16): 'he will baptize you with the Holy Spirit and with fire' and
'the wind blowing the chaff away and the fire consuming it'. The
coming of the Holy Spirit at Pentecost fulfils Jesus' prophetic words
(Lk. 24.49; Acts 1.5) as well as John's prophecy (Lk. 3.16.-17) and is
interpreted as God's eschatological gift or promise given to his restored
people.[146]

142. See nn. 6, 38, 52 in Chapter 2. Note the references to God's 'wind' as an
overwhelming and mysterious power (e.g. Exod. 15.10; Ps. 147.18; Isa. 17.13;
27.8; 59.19; Hos. 13.15).
143. In the LXX, three words refer to wind: πνεῦμα, ἄνεμος and πνοή (e.g. Ezek.
13.13 in the judgment context).
144. See Haenchen (1971: 168). See also §4.5.2 in Chapter 5.
145. See Gen. 15.17 (fire/voice); Exod. 3.2 (fire/voice); 13.21-22 (cloud/fire);
14.24 (cloud/fire); Exod. 19.18 (cloud/fire); 24.17 (cloud/fire); Num. 14.14 (cloud/
fire); Deut. 4.12 (fire/voice), 24 (fire), 33 (fire/voice), 36 (fire/voice); 5.4 (fire); 10.4
(fire); 1 Kgs 19.12 (fire/wind); 2 Kgs 2.11 (fire/wind); LXX Ps. 17.9 (smoke/fire);
LXX Ps. 28.7 (voice/fire); Job 37.2-5 (thunder/lightning/voice); Ezek. 1.25-28
(voice/fire); Dan. 7.9-14 (fire/voice/languages). See Johnson (1992: 42) and
Menzies (1991a: 238 n. 1).
146. Note the Lukan alteration of μετὰ ταῦτα to ἐν ταῖς ἐσχάταις ἡμέραις in
Acts 2.17. I shall discuss this in detail in Chapter 5 along with other changes from
the LXX Joel 3.1-5a.

What we should not miss is that the narrator describes the appearance of the Spirit in the following narrative contexts: the coming of the Holy Spirit (1) upon Jesus, the witness *par excellence* to the Kingdom of God as the Son of God, the Messiah and the anointed prophet and (2) upon Jesus' disciples as his witnesses to the Kingdom of God *and* to Jesus as the risen Lord. In other words, the two pivotal scenes in Luke–Acts are described with vivid expressions referring to the concrete reality of the Holy Spirit as signalling God's intrusive presence or power working within Jesus and his disciples as God's human agents.

5.1.2.5. Environment. There are two realms in which the Holy Spirit is said to be: (1) a heavenly realm and (2) an earthly realm. The former is described in what follows.

> Now when all the people were baptized, and when Jesus also had been baptized and was praying, *the heaven was opened* (ἀνεῳχθῆναι τὸν οὐρανόν), *and the Holy Spirit descended upon* him in bodily form like a dove. And a voice came from heaven, 'You are my Son, the Beloved; with you I am well pleased' (by the narrator; Lk. 3.21-22; cf. Acts 2.1-4).
>
> And behold, I [Jesus] send the promise of my Father upon you; but stay in the city, until you are clothed with *power from on high* (ἐχ ὕψους δύναμιν) (RSV; by Jesus; Lk. 24.49).

The references above, i.e. 'heaven' according to the narrator (cf. Acts 10.11) and 'from on high' according to Jesus, suggest that the original dwelling place of the Holy Spirit is transcendent.[147] In other words, through the statements of the reliable narrator and characters, we can suppose that the environment of the Spirit is with both God the Father[148] (Lk. 10.21; Acts 7.48) and the exalted Jesus (Acts 7.55; 9.3-5; cf. Lk. 24.51; Acts 1.9-11). The phrase 'from on high' is used twice in association with God's Spirit in the Jewish Bible (Isa. 32.15; Wis. 9.17; cf. Ezek. 1.12-20). We should also remember that in the Jewish Bible this divine Spirit is very often referred to through God's possessive adjectives,[149] which means the 'environment' of the Spirit cannot be separated from that of Yahweh.

---

147. Cf. the fact that the resurrected Jesus is said to sit 'at the right hand of God', i.e. heaven, and from there he is said to pour out the Holy Spirit upon his disciples (Acts 2.33; cf. Pss. 110.1; 16.11).

148. For heaven as God's dwelling place in the Hebrew Bible and the LXX, see Deut. 26.15; Josh. 2.11; 1 Kgs 8.30, 39, 43, 49; 2 Chron. 6.21, 30, 33, 39; 2 Macc. 15.4; 3 Macc. 2.15.

149. See Table 3 in Chapter 2.

On the other hand, the 'immanent environment' of the Holy Spirit is shown through several expressions: 'be filled with', 'be full of', 'be baptized with' and so forth are used in indicating that the Holy Spirit is present in or at work *through reliable characters*, i.e. John the son of Zechariah, Mary, Elizabeth, Zechariah, Simeon and Jesus in the Gospel; Jesus' disciples (particularly Peter, Stephen, Philip, Paul, Barnabas and other disciples—13.52; 19.6) and God's people (2.38; 4.31; 5.32; 8.17; 10.45) in Acts.[150] Likewise, God's Spirit in the Jewish Bible dwells and remains in faithful Old Testament figures (e.g. Moses, Joshua, Saul, David, Elijah, Elisha and so forth).[151] After the day of Pentecost, however, the divine Spirit is not limited to specific leaders such as prophets, kings or craftsmen as in the Jewish Bible, but is regarded as the promised gift granted to 'everyone whom the Lord our God calls to him' (Acts 2.39b).[152] Nevertheless, the Lukan implied author mostly provides the immanent environment in close connection with the actions and speeches of leading characters in Luke–Acts: Jesus in the Gospel and his disciples/witnesses in Acts. In sum, these references to the Holy Spirit's (transcendent and immanent) environment highlight the Spirit as God's divine actor or agent. This divine Spirit as a character, unlike human characters, is usually indirectly characterized through the actions or speeches of major human characters who are inspired by the Spirit.[153]

5.2. Character-Presentation II

The second method of character-presentation of the Holy Spirit is made through the following two categories: (1) repetition and similarity, and (2) comparison and contrast.[154] In the first aspect, I shall examine repeated effects of and similar expressions for Spirit-endowment. In the second aspect, I shall first compare the Holy Spirit with an angel(s) (of the Lord) as a non-human agent(s), and then contrast the Spirit with other supernatural beings such as a demon(s)/an evil spirit(s) and/or the devil/Satan.

150. See also §5.2.1.2 in this chapter.
151. See Table 2 in Chapter 2.
152. For the significance of the coming of the Spirit on the day of Pentecost, see §4.6.1.1 in Chapter 5.
153. In other words, to characterize the Holy Spirit in Luke–Acts requires us to explore the role/function of the Spirit in relation to the activities of the major Spirit-inspired characters, i.e. in the development of the Lukan plot: see Chapter 5.
154. See §3.2 in this chapter.

5.2.1. *Repetition and Similarity*
5.2.1.1. *Repeated Effects of Spirit-Endowment.* As I have noted in §5.1, the Holy Spirit is normally presented indirectly in influencing human characters. In other words, the portrait of the Holy Spirit can be further clarified when I take into consideration the inspired human beings' bodily actions and/or speeches. In what follows, therefore, I shall briefly introduce several repeated effects on the Lukan-inspired characters and I shall make comparisons with those on characters in the Jewish Bible.

(1) The most frequent and immediate effect on human beings when they are inspired by the Holy Spirit is prophetic/revelatory inspired oracle and/or speech: Elizabeth in Lk. 1.41-45; Zechariah in Lk. 1.67-79; cf. Simeon in Lk. 2.28-32; Stephen in Acts 4.8; 7.55-56; Agabus in Acts 11.28 and 21.11; Paul in Acts 13.9-11; the Tyrian disciples in Acts 21.4. At times, this effect includes praise to God: Zechariah in Lk. 1.67-79; Cornelius's household in Acts 10.46; the Ephesian disciples in Acts 19.6; cf. Mary in Lk. 1.46-55.[155] Although this effect is not so prominent in the MT, similar prophetic/revelatory oracles/speeches are given to human characters: Azariah in 2 Chron. 15.1-7; Jahaziel in 2 Chron. 20.14-17; Zechariah in 2 Chron. 24.20. In addition, two cases are added in the LXX to highlight the relationship between God's Spirit and prophetic oracle: Balaam in Num. 23.7; Zechariah in Zech. 1.6.[156]

(2) A revelation or revelatory guidance is offered through the visions or dreams of characters endowed with the Spirit: Lk. 2.26-27 to Simeon; 4.1, 14 to Jesus; Acts 10.19 to Peter; 13.2 to the Antioch Church leaders; 16.6-10 to Paul and his companions; 20.23 to Paul. A similar effect is also found in the Jewish Bible: Gen. 41.38 to Joseph; Dan. 4.8, 9, 18; 5.11, 14 to Daniel (see also the revelatory function of the Spirit of the Lord/God in the DSS in Excursus).

(3) Speaking in tongues is another phenomenon represented as caused by the Spirit: Jesus' disciples in Acts 2.4; Cornelius and his household in Acts 10.44-46; the Ephesian disciples in Acts 19.6. Within the narrative contexts, 'speaking in tongues' functions as a legitimate or apologetic sign, testifying that a certain group of people can be regarded as God's people. Also 'speaking in tongues' is said to be closely related to 'praising God' or 'prophecy' according to Acts 10.46 and 19.6

155. Cf. Turner (1996a: 224).
156. For the concept of prophecy in diverse contexts, see Aune (1983); Forbes (1995); Turner (1996a: 185-200); Penney (1997b: 35-84).

respectively: λαλούντων γλώσσαις καὶ μεγαλυνόντων τὸν θεόν and ἐλάλουν τε γλώσσαις καὶ ἐπροφήτευον. Although we cannot find the exact term (γλῶσσα) referring to 'speaking in tongues' as an effect of endowment by the Spirit in the LXX, 'non-revelatory ecstasy' or 'unintelligible prophecy' might be understood as a similar effect of the Spirit: the seventy elders in Num. 11.25, 26; Saul in 1 Sam. 10.6, 10; 19.23; Saul's messengers in 1 Sam. 19.20. Like 'speaking in tongues' in Acts, this unintelligible prophecy also functions as signalling the presence of God's Spirit on human beings who then prophesy. Only Acts 2.4, 8 represents this ecstatic speech as intelligible to listeners.

(4) A miracle might be regarded as an effect engendered by the Spirit: Jesus in Lk. 4.18-41; Acts 10.38. In fact, the Spirit-filled Jesus and his disciples/witnesses are often said to perform miracles or 'signs and/or wonders';[157] yet, the narrator does not emphasize that Jesus' or his disciples' exorcism or healing is an immediate effect of the Spirit, although he presupposes the Spirit as the cause of miracles (cf. Lk. 1.17, 35; 4.14; 24.49; Acts 1.8; 10.38). And these miracles performed by Lukan characters through the Holy Spirit are presented as signalling the eschatological presence of the Kingdom of God, and functioning as part of their witness ministry for God's people, including non-Jews (e.g. Lk. 17.11-19; cf. Acts 14.8-18). The Jewish Bible, on the other hand, relates miracles as one of the most immediate effects of God's Spirit endowment: Judg. 3.10; 6.34; 11.29; 13.25; 14.19; 15.14; 2 Kgs 2.9-15; cf. Ezek. 3.12, 14; 8.3; 11.1, 24; 43.5; Mic. 3.8; Sir. 48.12; Bel 1.36. Also noted is that unlike those in Luke–Acts, Spirit-inspired characters in these contexts are mostly characterized as 'warriors', whose miraculous power obtains a victory/peace for the people of Israel against their enemies, that is, non-Jews.

(5) Charismatic gifts like wisdom and faith in Stephen (Acts 6.3, 5, 10) and Barnabas (11.24), and like joy in Jesus (Lk. 10.21; cf. the unborn John in 1.44, 15-16) and the disciples (Acts 13.52) might be considered the effects of the Spirit upon them. These charismatic gifts, however, in Luke–Acts are better seen as qualities (caused by the Spirit) rather than as immediate effects since they persist through time (cf. Gen. 41.38-39). The Jewish Bible relates that God endows several individuals with 'wisdom' or 'understanding' through his Spirit: Exod. 28.3; 31.3; 35.31; 34.9; Isa. 11.2-5; Sir. 39.6; Wis. 1.6; 7.7, 22; 9.17; cf.

157. See n. 147 in Chapter 5.

Dan. 5.11, 14. Hence, God's Spirit in the Jewish Bible is directly presented as the 'Spirit of wisdom/understanding' (Exod. 28.3; Deut. 34.9;
Wis. 7.7; Isa. 11.2; cf. Wis. 7.22-23). Charismatic 'faith' (cf. 1QH 7.6-
7; 12.11-12) or 'joy' (cf. 1QH 9.32), however, is not found there,
although we should note the reference to 'fidelity' in the LXX Isa. 11.2.
Along with these qualities, other human religio-ethical qualities are
seen as inspired by the Spirit in Acts (2.42-47; 4.31-37; 5.1-11; 6.3;
11.24) and the literary repertoire (Isa. 11.2-5; Pss. 51.11-13; 139.7;
143.10; Ezek. 36.26-27; Zech. 12.10; Neh. 9.20, 30).

In regard to the repeated effect of Spirit-endowment, we have seen
that there are some similarities and differences between Luke–Acts and
the Jewish Bible. Nevertheless, if we take into consideration their own
historical narrative contexts, similar effects should be highlighted. That
is to say, the Holy Spirit in Luke–Acts is undoubtedly defined as the
Spirit promised by God in the Jewish Bible (see especially the first
three effects in terms of the 'Spirit of prophecy' in Joel 2.28-29). However, the repeated effects of Spirit-endowment in the Jewish Bible are
almost always employed to indicate related characters as God's human
agents revealing or accomplishing his will or purpose in various ways,
whereas similar effects in Luke–Acts are mostly presented in the
witness-contexts and the Spirit-inspired characters are portrayed not
only as God's human agents, but also as (the risen) Jesus' witnesses.[158]

5.2.1.2. Similar Expressions for Spirit-Endowment. In this subsection, I
shall focus on the narrator's favourite expressions in referring to
characters' endowment with the divine Spirit. Of 74 references to the
divine Spirit in Luke–Acts, 50 cases[159] are concerned with characters'

---

158. Taking into account the narrative of Luke–Acts as one book written by one
author (cf. 56 books in the Jewish Bible), we may expect that the repeated effects of
the Lukan Holy Spirit are well presented in association with the whole *narrative
function* of the Spirit. In other words, the implied author of Luke–Acts utilizes the
repeated effects or roles of the Spirit in relation to the plot. This will be the issue
discussed in Chapter 5.

159. Out of 50, there are (a) 2 occasions where 'to anoint' (χρίω) is used in Lk.
4.18; Acts 10.38; cf. 1 Sam. 10.1; 16.13; Isa. 61.1; (b) 3 occasions where 'to
baptize' or 'to be baptized' (βαπτίζω) is used in Lk. 3.16; Acts 1.5; 11.16: for the
meaning of this verb, see n. 77 in Chapter 5; (c) 4 occasions where 'to pour out
upon' (ἐκχέω ἐπί) is used in Acts 2.17, 18, 33; 10.45; cf. Joel 3.1, 2; Zech. 12.10;
(d) 7 occasions where 'to receive' (λαμβάνω) is used in Acts 2.33, 38; 8.15, 17, 19;
10.47; 19.2; (e) 5 occasions where 'to give' or 'to be given' (δίδωμι) is used in Lk.
11.13; Acts 5.32; 8.18; 11.17; 15.8; cf. Num. 11.29; Neh. 9.20; Isa. 42.1; Ezek.

Spirit-endowment. From the references, three Greek expressions used in 14 cases are viewed as Lukan favourite and unique terms in referring to 'Spirit-endowment', i.e. 'to be filled with the Holy Spirit' and 'to be full of the Holy Spirit'.[160]

(1) To be filled with (πίμπλημι):[161]

[H]e [John] will *be filled with the Holy Spirit*. He will turn many of the people of Israel to the Lord their God (by an angel of the Lord; Lk. 1.15b-16a).

[A]nd Elizabeth *was filled with the Holy Spirit* and exclaimed with a loud cry, 'Blessed are you among women, and blessed is the fruit of your womb!' (by the narrator; Lk. 1.41a-42).

Then his father Zechariah *was filled with the Holy Spirit*, and spoke this prophecy. (by the narrator; Lk. 1.67).

And all of them *were filled with the Holy Spirit* and began to speak in other languages, as the Spirit gave them ability (by the narrator; Acts 2.4).

Then Peter, *filled with the Holy Spirit*, said to them... (by the narrator; Acts 4.8a).

37.14; (f) 3 occasions where 'to fall upon' (ἐπιπίπτω) is used in Acts 8.16; 10.44; 11.15; (g) 4 occasions where 'to come upon' is differently used in Lk. 1.35; Acts 1.8 (ἐπέρχομαι; cf. Isa. 32.15; Ezek. 2.2a; 3.24); Lk. 3.22 (γίνομαι ἐπί; cf. Num. 23.7; 24.2; Judg. 3.10; 11.29; 1 Sam. 19.20, 23; 2 Kgs 2.9; 2 Chron. 15.1; 20.14); Acts 19.6 (ἔρχομαι ἐπί); (h) 1 occasion where 'to be upon' (εἰμί ἐπί) is used in Lk. 2.25; (i) 7 occasions where two different prepositions ἐν (Lk. 2.27; 4.14; 10.21; Acts 19.21; cf. Dan. 4.8, 9, 18; 5.11, 14) and διά (Acts 1.2; 11.28; 21.4) are used. Cf. the use of ἐνδύω in Lk. 24.49. See Appendices I and II. Some different verbs are used to denote the same event, i.e. the coming of the Holy Spirit at Pentecost: to be clothed with in Lk. 24.49 by Jesus; to baptize in Acts 1.5 (and 11.16) by Jesus (cf. in Lk. 3.16 by John the Baptist); to come upon in Acts 1.8 by Jesus; to be filled with in Acts 2.4 by the narrator; to pour out upon in Acts 2.33 by Peter and 10.45 by the narrator; to give in Acts 11.17 by Peter; to fall upon in Acts 11.15 by Peter.

160. See also my discussion of each context within the plot-development of Luke–Acts in the next chapter. There is no reference ('πίμπλημι + genitive of Holy Spirit' and 'πλήρης + genitive of Holy Spirit') in the other Gospels (cf. Jn 1.14) and in the other writings in the New Testament (yet, the word πληρόω + genitive of Holy Spirit is once found in Eph. 5.18). In addition, these phrases are not exactly found in the LXX, either (cf. Job 14.1; Isa. 51.20; Dan. 3.19; Sir. 1.30; 19.26; 23.11; 48.12; 1 Esdr. 1.23; 3 Macc. 6.31).

161. Out of 22 occurrences in Luke–Acts, the phrase 'be filled with X' is found 15 times. Apart from references to the 'Holy Spirit', the phrase is always used with abstract nouns: 'wrath' (Lk. 4.28), 'awe' (Lk. 5.26), 'fury' (Lk. 6.11), 'wonder and amazement' (Acts 3.10), 'jealousy' (Acts 5.17; 13.45) and 'confusion' (Acts 19.28).

And when they had prayed, the place in which they were gathered together was shaken; and they *were all filled with the Holy Spirit* and spoke the word of God with boldness (by the narrator; Acts 4.31).

[H]e [Ananias] laid his hands on Saul and said, 'Brother Saul, the Lord Jesus, who appeared to you on your way here, has sent me so that you may regain your sight and *be filled with the Holy Spirit*' (by Ananias; Acts 9.17).

But Saul, also known as Paul, *filled with the Holy Spirit*, looked intently at him and said...(by the narrator; Acts 13.9-10a).

(2) To be full of (πλήρης):[162]

Jesus, *full of the Holy Spirit*, returned from the Jordan, and was led by the Spirit in the wilderness (by the narrator; Lk. 4.1).

Therefore, friends, select from among yourselves seven men of good standing, *full of the Spirit and of wisdom*, whom we may appoint to this task (by the twelve apostles; Acts 6.3).

And what they said pleased the whole community, and they chose Stephen, a man *full of faith and the Holy Spirit*, together with Philip, and Prochorus, Nicanor, Timon, Parmenas, and Nicolaus, a proselyte of Antioch (by the narrator; Acts 6.5).

But he [Stephen], *full of the Holy Spirit*, gazed into heaven and saw the glory of God, and Jesus standing at the right hand of God (by the narrator; Acts 7.55 in RSV; cf. NRSV).

When he came and saw the grace of God, he rejoiced and he exhorted them all to remain faithful to the Lord with steadfast devotion; for he [Barnabas] was a good man, *full of the Holy Spirit and of faith* (by the narrator; Acts 11.24).

(3) To be filled with (πληρόω):[163]

And the disciples *were filled with joy and with the Holy Spirit* (by the narrator; Acts 13.52).

---

162. This phrase 'be full of X' is used 10 times of which (1) 2 cases are used only with the Holy Spirit (Lk. 4.1; Acts 7.55), (2) 3 cases with both the Holy Spirit and other abstract nouns: 'full of the Spirit and of wisdom' (Acts 6.3), 'full of faith and of the Holy Spirit' (Acts 6.5) and 'full of the Holy Spirit and of faith' (Acts 11.24) and (3) the other 5 cases are found without reference to the Holy Spirit: 'a man full of leprosy' (Lk. 5.12), 'full of grace and power' (Acts 6.8), 'full of good works and acts of charity' (Acts 9.36), 'full of all deceit and villainy' (Acts 13.10) and 'full of rage' (Acts 19.28).

163. This verb occurs 25 times of which the formation 'to be filled with X' is used 3 times: (1) 'be filled with wisdom' (Lk. 2.40), (2) 'be filled with gladness' (Acts 2.28 quoted from Ps. 16.11) and (3) 'be filled with joy and the Holy Spirit' (Acts 13.52).

The use of both expressions, 'to be filled with the Holy Spirit' and 'to be full of the Holy Spirit', is unique to Luke–Acts and is found throughout the narrative of Luke (4 times) and Acts (10 times). This stylistic trait of the narrator is an important element for understanding not only the characters who are said to be endowed with the Holy Spirit, but also the immediate narrative contexts in which these expressions are used.

We can see that it is usually the reliable narrator who uses these expressions (11 out of 14). The phrases are also employed by the following reliable characters: an angel of the Lord (Lk. 1.15), Jesus' disciple, Ananias (Acts 9.10) and the twelve apostles (Acts 6.3). But it should be noted here that only the narrator connects these expressions with characters' inspired words. Apart from this point, there is no difference between the statements of the narrator and those of characters. Thus, I shall explore some implications derived from the references regardless of speakers, that is, whether the speaker is the 'external narrator' or an 'internal narrator'.

(1) The phrase 'to be filled with the Holy Spirit' is *not always, but often* tied with narrative contexts in which characters are presented as giving inspired speeches. Through their prophetic or inspired utterances, these characters act as witnesses to Jesus: Lk. 1.42; 1.67; Acts 2.4; 4.8a; 4.31; 13.10a.

(2) The words πλήρης and πληρόω with the Holy Spirit are *sometimes* employed along with other divine charismatic gifts or qualities such as 'wisdom' (Acts 6.3), 'faith' (Acts 6.5; 11.24) and 'joy' (Acts 13.52). Thus, the Spirit seems to cause or is at least in close connection with such spiritual qualities. However, we should avoid imposing dogmatic claims on these expressions[164] or distinguishing connotations for each expression,[165] since the narrative shows exceptions to these

---

164. See two inadequate explanations imposing dogmatic ideas on the phrases: Ervin (1968: 59-87) argues that the condition of 'the fullness of the Holy Spirit' indicates Christians' second blessing; on the contrary, Bruner (1970: 163) insists that the phrase 'be filled with the Spirit' refers to Christian conversion.

165. Stronstad (1984: 54-55): '[F]illed with the Spirit *always* describes inspiration... "Full of the Spirit" describes the Spirit's enabling, while "filled with the Spirit" describes prophetic inspiration' (emphasis added); cf. Shelton (1991: 137): 'It may be generally true that Luke uses "full of the Holy Spirit" to express the

simplistic suggestions (see Lk. 1.15; Acts 9.17; Acts 7.55).
(3) The narrator uses these two phrases freely, viz. in referring to (a) both individual (John, Elizabeth, Zechariah, Peter, Saul, Jesus, Stephen and Barnabas) and collective ('all of them [Jesus' disciples]' in Acts 2.4; 'they' [Jesus' disciples] in Acts 4.31) endowment with the Spirit, (b) both men and a woman (i.e. Elizabeth; cf. Mary in Lk. 1.35) and (c) both the period before (Lk. 1.15, 41, 67; 4.1) and after (Acts 2.4; 4.8, 31; 6.3, 5; 7.55; 9.17; 11.24; 13.9) the day of Pentecost. Nevertheless, the significance of Pentecost as the day of fulfilment of God's promised endowment by the Spirit[166] as predicted in Joel should not be ignored.[167] My contention is that there is both *continuity and discontinuity* in the

character of a disciple and "filled with the Holy Spirit" to indicate the empowering of an individual on a specific occasion to speak authoritatively... Both expressions, however, do occur in contexts in which inspired speaking is the major theme'. See also Shelton's other article on this matter (1988: 80-107), although much of his argument overlaps. Cf. Turner's rather cautious position (1981c: 45-63; 1994a: 103-22, esp. 108-10). However, Turner (1981c: 54-55) also explained the nuanced differences between 'be filled with' and 'be full of'. According to him, the former 'designates the intense presence, or abnormally strong activity of the defining quality *in a definite event of short duration*' (emphasis original), whereas the latter is 'to describe a quality manifest over a long period of time (weeks or more) rather than an immediate inspiration'. The following characters seem to be permanently endowed with the Spirit: John the Baptist (Lk. 1.15); Simeon (Lk. 2.25); Jesus (Lk. 3.22; 4.18; Acts 10.38); Jesus' apostles/disciples (Acts 1.8; 2.4); Stephen and the other Six (Acts 6.3, 5); Paul (Acts 9.17); Barnabas (Acts 11.25); cf. Old Testament figures: Moses (Num. 11.17); Joshua (Num. 27.18; Deut. 34.9); David (1 Sam. 16.13); Elijah (2 Kgs 2.16; Sir. 48.12); Elisha (2 Kgs 2.15; Sir 48.12).

166. However, such words as 'to pour out upon', 'to receive' and 'to fall upon' are only used in Acts after Pentecost. In addition, 'to baptize' in Lk. 3.16 and 'to give' in Lk. 11.13 are used in a future tense anticipating the outpouring of the Spirit at Pentecost and baptismal practice in Acts.

167. Contra Stronstad (1984: 53): 'The gift of the Spirit to the disciples on the day of Pentecost is not an isolated and unique event. It is but one of several occasions, both prior to and following Pentecost, when people are filled with the Spirit'. Cf. Shelton (1991: 16): 'For Luke, the difference between the experiences with the Holy Spirit for the pre- and post-Pentecost faithful is *not* primarily qualitative but quantitative... Therefore, when it comes to pneumatology, he blurs the epochs' (emphasis original). Yet, he admits at least the progress of salvation history: 'To him [Luke], salvation history is progressive, something like slowly turning up the volume on a radio' (25). See also Table 5 in Chapter 1.

presentation of Spirit-endowment from the Gospel to Acts or from the Jewish Bible to Luke–Acts.[168]

(4) These expressions are the narrator's literary indicators to the reader, suggesting that the characters who are inspired or empowered by the Spirit are thus considered to be the human agents of *God* (usually in the Gospel as is seen in the LXX) and of *Jesus* (usually in Acts: see Lk. 12.11-12; 21.15; Acts 16.7; cf. 8.39). In other words, the expressions imply that the characters are equipped with the Spirit of the *Lord*[169] to accomplish successfully and boldly their witness to the Lord God and the exalted Jesus.[170]

(5) These phrases are the repetitive literary indicators that the endowed characters are considered reliable and authoritative witnesses to God *and* Jesus. Thus, readers are encouraged to trust such characters and their inspired speeches, and to anticipate that their prophetic utterances will be fulfilled.

In regard to these Lukan favourite expressions, the verb (ἐμ/ἐν) πίμπλημι is found 7 times in the LXX: Exod. 28.3 (craftsmen); 31.3 (Bezalel); 35.31 (Bezalel); Deut. 34.9 (Joshua); Mic. 3.8 (Micah); Sir. 39.6; 48.12 (Elisha). The first three occasions have Yahweh as the subject of the verb; the following three cases, like in Luke–Acts, are used in a passive voice: καὶ Ἰησοῦς υἱὸς Ναυη ἐνεπλήσθη πνεύματος συνέσεως in Deut. 34.9; ἐὰν κύριος ὁ μέγας θελήσῃ πνεύματι συνέσεως ἐμπλησθήσεται in Sir. 39.6 (the psalmist in the future tense); Ἠλιας ὃς ἐν λαίλαπι ἐσκεπάσθη καὶ Ἐλισαιε ἐνεπλήθη πνεύματος αὐτοῦ in 48.12 (Elisha). As in Luke–Acts, the Old Testament figures who are full of God's Spirit are portrayed as God's human agents possessing such charismatic gifts or qualities as 'wisdom', 'ability', 'intelligence', 'knowledge', 'understanding', 'power', 'justice' and 'might'. Unlike in Luke–Acts, however, they are not depicted as the witnesses to the coming Messiah and the verbs in the LXX are not used in relation to inspired witnessing speeches, nor do they involve any female characters.

We have seen that the Lukan narrator often uses the words πίμπλημι, πλήρης and πληρόω, when he describes some characters' inspiration by the Holy Spirit. And through these expressions, he presents their narrative portrait as reliable and authoritative, not only as God's human agents, but also as witnesses to (the resurrected and exalted) Jesus. For

168. For my detailed discussion about this, see §§4.6.1.1 and 5 in Chapter 5.
169. For the use of κύριος in Luke–Acts, see n. 80 in this chapter.
170. See also §5.1.1.3 in this chapter.

this purpose, the Lukan narrator uses the metaphorical expressions, 'be filled with' and 'be full of' the Holy Spirit, more often and rhetorically[171] than Jewish writers.[172]

5.2.2. *Comparison and Contrast.* I shall here examine similarities and differences between the Holy Spirit, and an angel/angel of the Lord, on the one hand, and a demon/evil spirit or the devil/Satan, on the other, in Luke–Acts since both an angel and a demon, like the Holy Spirit, can be envisaged as non-human characters. I shall thus explore their characteristics by comparing and contrasting them with the Holy Spirit in order to make the character-presentation of the Holy Spirit clearer.

5.2.2.1. *An Angel(s) (of the Lord).* The word ἄγγελος is found 47 times in Luke (26) and Acts (21), referring to (a) an 'angel of the Lord/God' (Lk. 1.11; 2.9; Acts 5.19; 8.26; 10.3; 12.7, 23; 27.23), (b) an 'angel' denoting an angel of the Lord/God in the context (Lk. 1.13, 18, 19, 26, 30, 34, 35, 38; 2.10, 13, 21; 22.43; Acts 7.30, 35, 38; 10.7, 22; 11.13; 12.8, 9, 10, 11), (c) an 'angel' as a category of being (Acts 6.15; 23.8, 9), (d) 'angels' in the plural (Lk. 2.15; 4.10; 9.26; 12.8, 9; 15.10; 16.22; 20.36; 24.23; Acts 7.53),[173] (e) an angel as a 'guardian angel for a human'[174] (Acts 12.15 for Peter) and (f) human messenger(s) (Lk. 7.24, John's disciples; 7.27, Jesus' messenger referring to John the Baptist; 9.52, Jesus' disciples). Here, I shall not deal with the last two kinds.

'An angel of the Lord/God' in the Jewish Bible usually appears as a special agent of Yahweh (e.g. Exod. 3.2; 14.19; Num. 22.22-35; Judg. 2.1; 6.11-16; 1 Kgs 19.7; 2 Kgs 19.35; 1 Chron. 21.14-15; Ps. 34.7). In addition, occasionally it is hard to distinguish an 'angel of the Lord' from Yahweh in the certain contexts (e.g. Gen. 16.7-14; 21.17-19; 22.11-19; 31.11-13; Exod. 3.2-12; Num. 22.35, 38; Judg. 6.11-24; 13.3-25; cf. *Ant.* 5.284; 9.20; 5.277-84).[175] Both an angel of the Lord/God

---

171. See Table 6 in Chapter 3.

172. For other Spirit-reception verbs used in Luke–Acts and the LXX, see n. 159 in this chapter and Appendix I.

173. The plural form referring to angels in terms of *rûah* is particularly prominent in 1QM and 1QH (cf. Num. 16.22; 27.16 in the LXX); see my Excursus.

174. See also Mt. 18.10; cf. 'angels of the Presence' for the welfare of humans in *Jub.* 1.27; *T. Levi.* 3.4-8; 1QH 6.13; 1QSb 4.26. For more detail, see Davidson (1992b: 10).

175. See von Rad (1964: 76-80); C. Davis (1996: 29-38); see also n. 21 in Chapter 2.

and the Spirit of the Lord/God[176] play thus similar role as God's divine agents in the Jewish Bible.

Likewise in Luke–Acts, the narrative role of the angel is sometimes presented as identical with that of the Holy Spirit: Acts 8.26; 10.3, 7, 22; 11.13 (see also 8.29 [the Spirit]; 8.39 [the Spirit of the Lord]; 10.19 [the Holy Spirit]; 11.12 [the Holy Spirit]).[177] In addition, an angel is sometimes described as a *holy* angel (by Jesus in Lk. 9.26; by Cornelius's messengers in Acts 10.22; cf. 10.7; cf. a 'good angel' in Tob. 5.22; 2 Macc. 11.6; 15.23) and as his [Lord's] angel (by Peter in Acts 12.11; cf. 'my [God's] angel' in Exod. 23.23; 32.34). The term angel(s) *of God* found in Lk. 12.8, 9; 15.10; Acts 10.3; 27.23 (cf. Lk. 4.10) is also reminiscent of the Spirit *of God* in Acts 2.17, 18. However, except in Acts 10.3 and 27.23, the term is always used in a plural form, that is, the 'angels of God'. On the other hand, the angel *of the Lord*, like the Spirit *of the Lord*, always appears in a singular form: Lk. 1.11; 2.9; Acts 5.19; 8.26; 12.7, 23 (cf. Acts 12.11; Lk. 22.43). Unlike in the Jewish Bible, however, there is no instance in which an 'angel of the Lord' (ἄγγελος κυρίου) called Gabriel (Lk. 1.19, 26)[178] is identified with God himself. Rather, the angel's role (Acts 5.19-20; 8.26; 10.4-6; 27.23-24), like that of the Spirit (Acts 8.29; 10.19; 13.2-4), is parallel to that of the risen Jesus (Acts 18.9-10; 22.18, 21; 23.11; cf. Lk. 24.37): revealing the will/purpose of God by directing or guiding the way of witness for Jesus' disciples (see below).

More specifically, an angel, like the Holy Spirit,[179] is presented as

176. For the Spirit of the Lord/God as referring to God's will or dispositions in the Jewish Bible, see §2.1.2 in Chapter 2.

177. Josephus also once makes the angel of God identical with the divine *pneuma* in *Ant.* 4.108. For the frequent use of *rûaḥ* as a plural form referring to angelic beings in the DSS, see Excursus. Levison (1995: 464-93) recently argues that the divine Spirit in Jewish traditions can be interpreted as an angelic being, which may influence three relatively early Christians texts: the Fourth Gospel, the *Shepherd of Hermas* and the *Ascension of Isaiah*.

178. In Luke–Acts, there is only one proper name referring to the angel. In the Jewish Bible, however, the names of 'Gabriel' (Dan. 9.21-27; 8.15-26) and of 'Michael' (Dan. 10.13, 21; cf. Jude 9; Rev. 12.7) are found. Cf. 4 names in 1QM 9.14-16; *1 En.* 9.1, viz. Michael, Gabriel, Sariel and Raphael; 6 names in *1 En.* 20: Suruel, Raphael, Raguel, Michael, Saraqael and Gabriel; cf. 7 angels in Tob. 12.15. For the nature and function of angels especially in Qumran and *1 Enoch*, see Davidson (1992a).

179. The Holy Spirit also appears in the following contexts: (1) birth (e.g. Lk.

closely associated with the following five narrative contexts: (1) birth foretelling (Lk. 1.11-17; 2.9; cf. Judg. 13.3-5), (2) guidance and instruction (Acts 8.26; cf. Gen. 24.7, 40; Exod. 23.23; 1 Kgs 19.7; 2 Kgs 1.3, 15), (3) protection and deliverance (Acts 5.19; 12.7, 11; cf. Exod. 14.19; Ps. 34.7; Isa. 63.9), (4) destruction or judgment (Acts 12.23; cf. 2 Sam. 24.16; 2 Kgs 19.35; Ps. 35.5-6; *1 En.* 100.4) and (5) witness (Lk. 2.10-14; 4.10; 9.26; 12.8-9; 15.10; 24.23; cf. Job 38.7; Dan. 7.9-10, 13-14). In addition, like the Holy Spirit, the angel as God's divine agent is also presented as speaking and acting with a view to revealing God's will, particularly in witness-contexts (e.g. Lk. 1.13-20; 24.5-7; Acts 8.26; Acts 10.1-23; 27.23). And the provenance of an angel is said to be 'from heaven' (by the narrator in Lk. 22.43; see also 1.26; 2.15; cf. ['in/of heaven'] by Jesus in Mt. 18.10; 22.30; 24.36 ['in heaven'] by Jesus in Mk 12.25; 13.32; cf. Gen. 21.17; 22.11).

Most importantly, the narrator frequently makes an angel(s) appear in contexts associated with Jesus and his witnesses: (1) the birth of *Jesus* (Lk. 1.26-38; 2.8-12; cf. Gen. 16.11; Judg. 13.3-5), (2) the temptations of *Jesus* (Lk. 22.43;[180] Mt. 4.11; Mk 1.13; cf. 1QM 12.7-9; 17.5-8; 2 Macc. 10.29-30), (3) the coming of the *Son of Man* and the final judgment (Lk. 9.26; Mt. 16.27; Mk 8.38; cf. Dan. 7.9-10; 13-14), (4) the resurrection of *Jesus* (Lk. 24.4-7, 23; Mt. 28.2, 5-7; Mk 16.5; cf. 2 Macc. 3.26, 33-34) and (5) the witness-mission of *Jesus'* followers to Gentiles (Acts 8.26-40; 10.1-23; 11.13-18; 27.23).[181] In this light, an angel(s) in Luke–Acts functions as a witness to *Jesus* (before his birth and after his resurrection) and as a 'helper' to his disciples' witness-mission to *Jesus*.[182]

1.35), (2) guidance and instruction (e.g. Lk. 2.26-27; 4.1; Acts 8.29, 39; 10.19), (3) protection and deliverance (e.g. Lk. 12.12; Acts 2.38), (4) destruction and judgment (e.g. Acts 5.1-11) and mostly (5) witness (e.g. Lk. 4.18-19; Acts 1.8; 4.8; 5.32).

180. Some ancient manuscripts suggest that Lk. 22.43-44 is not part of the original text (Fitzmyer 1985: 1444; Nolland 1993: III, 1080-81): P[69], P[75], ℵ[1], A, B, T, W, syr, cop, arm etc.; other evidence includes the verses (Marshall 1978: 831-32; Brown 1994: I, 180-86; Bock 1996: 1763-64): ℵ*, ℵ[2], D, L, Θ, Ψ, 0171 etc. Because of this textual difficulty, the UBS committee retained the words yet within double square brackets: Metzger (1975: 177).

181. Cf. Davidson (1992b: 9-11).

182. The expression ἄγγελος κυρίου (Acts 5.19; 8.26; 12.7, 23) may refer to an 'angel of God' or an 'angel of the risen Jesus': Fletcher-Louis (1997: 51).

Thus, whereas both the angel and the Spirit of the Lord are regarded as God's divine agents in the Jewish Bible (and the DSS),[183] in Luke–Acts they are characterized not only in relation to God, but also in relation to God's 'Messiah and Lord', Jesus. Thus, Davidson (1992b: 11) rightly points out the function of angels in the Gospels:

> The Gospels present angels as exercising functions similar to what we may observe in the OT and intertestamental Jewish writings. These include mediating heavenly revelation, aiding the pious and assisting in the final judgment. *However, unlike the OT and other Jewish writings, the angelology of the Gospels is, like the Gospels as a whole, essentially christocentric.* The functions of angels relate directly to the life and ministry of Jesus. Specifically, angels mediate direct revelation from God only at two moments: Jesus' birth and his resurrection. In the interim, he himself is the pre-eminent disclosure of God (emphasis added).

Thus, the narrator employs not only the Holy Spirit, but also an angel of the Lord as a divine and reliable character in order to reveal God's salvation-plan carried out by Jesus and his witnesses. In other words, both divine characters in Luke–Acts represent the same religious ideology in close association with (the risen) Jesus (and his witnesses) as well as God. Thus, readers are encouraged to trust any characters who are guided by these two divine characters in the narrative. Moreover, these two divine characters are closely linked to both Jesus' and his disciples' witness-mission. The actions and speeches of both the angel and the Holy Spirit are particularly highlighted *before* Jesus' birth (in Lk. 1–2) and *after* Jesus' ascension (in Acts in general). During his earthly ministry, however, *Jesus himself* as the Messiah, Son of God is portrayed not only as *the man of the Spirit*, but also as *the holy agent of God* (Lk. 1.35; 4.34; Acts 3.14; 4.27, 30)[184] who is born through the power of the Holy Spirit (Lk. 1.35) in accordance with God's angel's announcement.[185]

---

183. See my discussion in Chapter 2.

184. Fletcher-Louis (1997: 34-107; 218-54) examines the angelomorphic earthly and risen life of Jesus in Luke–Acts in the light of Jewish angelomorphic traditions and then argues that the portrait of the earthly and risen Jesus can be explained as an angelomorphic figure (e.g. Acts 7; 9; 22; 26; cf. Lk. 24.13-43), i.e. 'angel-Christology'; for his definition of the word 'angelomorphic', see 14-15.

185. After being resurrected, Jesus is presented as a spiritual or divine character, rather functioning as the lord of the Spirit sharing God's power or authority. See §5.1.1.3 in this chapter.

As noticed earlier, however, an angel(s) of the Lord and the Holy Spirit are also differently presented in Luke–Acts: for instance, unlike the Holy Spirit, (1) there are multiple angels (Lk. 2.13, 15; 4.10; 9.26; 12.8, 9; 15.10; 16.22; 20.36; 24.23; Acts 7.53), including one distinguished by a proper name, Gabriel; (2) the narrator never refers to an angel(s) or an angel of the Lord with metaphorical terms like 'be filled with', 'be full of', 'be baptized with' and so forth; (3) the external appearance of the angel ('two men in dazzling clothes' by the narrator in Lk. 24.4 [cf. 24.23]); 'two men in white robes' by the narrator in Acts 1.10; 'a man in dazzling clothes' by Cornelius in Acts 10.30 cf. 6.15; Gen. 18.1-2; 19.1, 10, 12, 16; Dan. 8.15-16; 9.21) is portrayed like a human being, only more dazzling (cf. that of the Holy Spirit in Lk. 3.21-22; Acts 2.2-3).

In sum, I may conclude that the Lukan narrator employs both an angel(s) of the Lord and the Holy Spirit as God's (holy) agents to reveal his purpose/will as in the Jewish Bible. Unlike the literary repertoire, however, Luke–Acts highlights the role of the angel, like that of the Holy Spirit, particularly in association with Jesus the Messiah (as both the Mosaic prophet and the Davidic king)[186] and his disciples, witnessing to the risen Jesus as Lord.

5.2.2.2. Evil Spirits/Demons; the Devil/Satan. The character-presentation of the Lukan Holy Spirit is also highlighted in various ways by contrast with an evil/unclean spirit(s)[187] or a demon(s),[188] and ultimately the devil/Satan.[189] In the MT, unlike in Luke–Acts (or the New Testament),

---

186. For this portrait of Jesus, see Chapter 5.

187. In Luke–Acts, there are 20 occurrences in which four different qualifications are used with πνεῦμα: (1) ἀκάθαρτος (e.g. Lk. 4.36), (2) πονηρός (e.g. Lk. 7.21), (3) ἀσθένεια (e.g. Lk. 13.11) and (4) πύθων (e.g. Acts 16.16). Out of 20, half are used in a singular form (Lk. 4.33; 8.29; 9.39, 42; 11.24; 13.11; Acts 16.16, 18; 19.15, 16) and the other half in a plural form (Lk. 4.36; 6.18; 7.21; 8.2; 10.20; 11.26; Acts 5.16; 8.7; 19.12, 13).

188. Twenty-four occurrences of τό δαιμόνιον or ὁ δαίμων are found both as a singular (Lk. 4.33, 35; 7.33; 9.42; 11.14 [× 2]) and a plural form (Lk. 4.41; 8.2, 27, 30, 33, 35, 36, 38; 9.1, 49; 10.17; 11.15 [× 2], 18, 19, 20; 13.32; Acts 17.18). Among them, some are identical to an 'evil/unclean spirit(s)' in the immediate contexts (Lk. 4.33, 35, 41; 8.2, 29-38; 9.42; 11.15-18).

189. The devil (διάβολος) as the arch-demon is always used as a singular form (7 references: Lk. 4.2, 3, 5, 13; 8.12; Acts 10.38; 13.10), which is interchangeable with Beelzebul as the ruler of the demons (Lk. 11.15, 18; cf. 2 Kgs 1.2-3, 6, 16; *Ant.* 19.9) and/or Satan (σατανᾶς; σατᾶν) (Lk. 11.18-19; 10.18; 13.16; 22.3, 31;

an evil spirit (cf. Satan in Zech. 3.1; Job 1.6-12; 2.1-6; cf. 1 Chron. 21.1//2 Sam. 24.1) is viewed as the spirit caused by the Lord (1 Sam. 16.14, 15, 16, 23; 18.10; 19.9) and is thus characterized not as God's adversary, but as his agent, sometimes even identified with the 'Spirit of the Lord' (see 1 Sam. 16.23a).[190] References to evil spirits and/or Satan as God's adversary begin to be found during the intertestamental period possibly under the influence of Persian dualistic thought.[191] Nevertheless, in Jewish writings, references are integrated into Jewish monotheism: the evil spirit or Satan is not presented ontologically as God's (ultimate) opponent (e.g. the LXX 1 Kgs 22.21-23; 2 Chron. 18.20-23; 1 Sam. 16.14-23; 1QS 3.25; cf. Num. 22.22; 1 Kgs 11.14, 23, 25).

On the other hand, the word δαιμόνιον is used in Greek literature to denote 'a deity (Philo *Vit. Mos.* 1. 276), a lesser deity (Plutarch *Rom.* 51), a divine power or unknown supernatural force (Josephus, *J.W.* 1. 69), the human element in touch with the divine (Galen *De Placitis* 5.6.4) and an intermediary between humans and the gods (*Corp. Herm.* XVI. 18)' (Twelftree 1992: 164).[192] In Hellenistic literature the word δαίμων with its associated concepts is, thus, closer to the divine πνεῦμα in the New Testament (cf. ξένων δαιμονίων referring to 'foreign gods/ divinities' by people at Athens in Acts 17.18).

However, in Luke–Acts along with the other Gospels, the devil/Satan and related expressions represent the chief enemy of both God *and* the Messiah Jesus (e.g. Lk. 11.14-26; 13.16; Acts 10.38; cf. Lk. 4.18; 7.22). Likewise, the devil/Satan and his agents are depicted as non-human characters who impede the mission of Jesus' disciples (Acts 13.10; cf. Lk. 8.12). Unlike in the Jewish Bible, therefore, demons are envisaged as messengers or agents of Satan/Beelzebul (Lk. 11.15-18; cf. Mt. 25.41). Hence, the narrator of Luke–Acts, implicitly and explicitly, presents both the devil/Satan and demons/the evil/unclean spirits as the counterpart to the divine character(s) of the *Holy* Spirit and/or a *holy* angel(s) of the Lord (e.g. Acts 5.1-11; Lk. 9.26; Acts 10.22; 12.11). In other words, throughout Luke–Acts, Satan and his messengers are presented

---

Acts 5.3; 26.18), a transliteration of the Hebrew ‏שטן‎ (1 Chron. 21.1; Zech. 3.1-2; Job 1.6–2.7; the LXX Ps. 108.6; cf. 1QM 13.4, 11; *Jub.* 10.8). For the origin of the word Beelzebul, see Fitzmyer (1985: II, 920-21).

190. See §§2.1.1 and 3.1.1 in Chapter 2.

191. See Tob. 6.8 and my excursus.

192. For a neutral use of this term, see Josephus, *Ant.* 13.415; 16.76, 210; *War* 1.556, 628. See also Paige (1993: 269-72).

as the ultimate 'opponents' of both Jesus and his disciples, whereas the Holy Spirit and an angel of the Lord play the role of 'helper' to them.[193] This understanding is supported by direct definitions of the devil/ Satan/Beelzebul: the 'enemy [of God/the Lord]' (by Jesus in Lk. 10.19; cf. Acts 13.10) and the 'ruler of the demons' (by some people[194] in Lk. 11.15). The words 'evil' and 'unclean' spirits (20 times in Luke–Acts) are the most obvious direct definitions, and are contrasted with the word 'holy', which is mostly employed as a direct definition of the Spirit. The indirect presentation of a demon and/or the devil further confirms this contrast. The aim of the speech (Lk. 4.3, 6-7, 9-11, 33-34, 41) and action (Lk. 4.2, 5, 13, 35; 8.12; 9.42) of the devil or demons is nothing but to interfere with God's purpose/plan, particularly Jesus' messianic ministry as God's Son. In other words, their role is quite the reverse of that of the Holy Spirit. For instance, the devil (Lk. 4.5, 9) and the Holy Spirit (4.1) alike are said to lead (ἄγω in 4.1, 9; ἀνάγω in 4.5) Jesus; however, the motivation of each is quite differently presented: the devil leads/entices Jesus to test God, whereas the Spirit leads/ empowers Jesus to obey God.

However, the narrative at times shows that demons as supernatural beings have spiritual insight, which ironically enables them to reveal who Jesus is: the 'Son of God' in Lk. 4.3, 9, 41; the 'Holy One of God' in Lk. 4.34; the 'Son of the Most High God' in Lk. 8.28, and what Jesus would do: 'Have you come to destroy us?' in Lk. 4.34; cf. Lk. 4.18; 7.22; 11.20; 13.32-33; Acts 10.38.[195] Likewise, the devil is represented as knowing Scripture yet using it to test Jesus (Lk. 4.10-11).

---

193. For the narrative function of the Holy Spirit in terms of *actant*, see §5 in Chapter 5. For the conflict between Jesus and Satan as one of the leading motifs, see Page (1995: 87-135). See also Garrett's claim (1989: 59), 'even passing references to exorcisms and healings included in Lukan summary reports ought to be interpreted as [Jesus'] earthly, visible signs of victory over the invisible spiritual Enemy [Satan]'.

194. Their statement can be considered reliable (see Jesus' response in Lk. 11.17-19 in which what Jesus denies is not their definition of Beelzebul as the 'ruler of the demons', but their false claim in regard to Jesus' exorcism).

195. Jesus as victor over the devil and demons by casting out demons connotes, to be sure, the Kingdom of God in operation (Lk. 11.14-23), which will be consummated in the final judgment (cf. Isa. 24.21-22; *1 En.* 10.4-6). Jesus' exorcism is said to be carried out by Jesus' own authority *and* the power of the Holy Spirit (Lk. 4.18; Acts 10.38; cf. Lk. 11.20; Mt. 12.28). For Jesus' exorcism, see Page (1995: 164-79).

In spite of their supernatural recognition,[196] the narrative presents their primary concern as the destruction of Jesus' messianic mission and the prevention of people, especially his disciples, from believing in and following Jesus, that is, to interrupt the 'way of witness' to God and/or Jesus (Acts 13.10; cf. Lk. 8.12). Thus, not only the devil, but also any characters seduced by Satan are represented as acting against Spirit-filled characters and finally against God and/or Jesus (Lk. 4.33, 41; 7.33; 8.2, 27, 33, 36; 22.3; Acts 5.3). The function of demons/*evil* spirits or Satan is contrary to that of the *holy* Spirit in the narrative (e.g. Lk. 4.1-13; Acts 5.1-11).

In sum, the devil/Satan and demons/evil spirits, unlike the Holy Spirit, are characterized as anti-God and anti-Jesus, and hence, anti-the Holy Spirit,[197] while an angel(s) (of the Lord), like the Holy Spirit, is portrayed as divine reliable agent(s) functioning on behalf of God and (the risen) Jesus, especially in witness-contexts. In Luke–Acts, therefore, the characterization of the Holy Spirit has been elaborated or confirmed in comparison with an angel(s) (of the Lord) on the one hand; in contrast with the devil/Satan and/or demons/evil spirits on the other.

6. *Conclusion*

This chapter has aimed to provide narrative theories of both character and character-presentation through which we may analyse the Holy Spirit as a character in Luke–Acts. I have thus shown that the Holy Spirit can be envisaged as a literary figure possessing two dialectic paradigms, i.e. those of 'person-likeness' and 'person-unlikeness' (see §5.1.2.3). In short, the Holy Spirit is defined as an enigmatic *divine* character. It is not surprising, therefore, that the Holy Spirit, unlike human characters, is mostly characterized indirectly in relation to the actions or speeches of other (major) characters who are inspired by the Spirit.

196. McCasland (1944: 33-36) argues that these confessional statements about Jesus were understood as the demons' protection from the power of Jesus by identifying their opponent in advance; a different view has been suggested by Guelich (1989: 57) and Page (1995: 143): they represent demons' subordination to the exorcist.

197. Likewise, all Spirit-filled/inspired characters in Luke–Acts are to be viewed as anti-demons or anti-Satan; see §3.3.2 in Chapter 3. It is, however, Jesus (e.g. Lk. 4.35-36; Acts 10.38) and his followers (e.g. Lk. 9.6; 10.19-20; Acts 3.6-10; 16.18; cf. Lk. 9.49-50; Acts 19.13-16) who are said to cast out demons.

The following two aspects will be highlighted by summarizing the Lukan presentation of the Spirit: (1) the Spirit in Luke–Acts is characterized as the Spirit promised by God in the Jewish Bible and (2) this same Spirit is mostly presented in close association with the 'Messiah and Lord' Jesus (Acts 2.36) and his witnesses. We have seen that the divine Spirit in Luke–Acts is for the most part directly presented as *holy* (54 out of 74 occasions; cf. at most 6 out of 112 cases in the literary repertoire: Ps. 51.11; Isa. 63.10, 11; Wis. 1.5; 9.17; Sus. 1.45; cf. LXX Dan. 4.5, 6, 15; 5.11). This *holy* Spirit in Lukan contexts, however, is to be regarded as *God's holy Spirit* (Acts 2.17, 18). On the other hand, when we consider the direct definitions of the Spirit as the Spirit *of the Lord* (Lk. 4.18; Acts 5.9; 8.39; cf. Acts 2.36) and the Spirit *of Jesus* (Acts 16.7; cf. 2.33; also notice that Jesus is directly characterized as 'holy' on five occasions), and their implications, the Holy Spirit is related to the resurrected Jesus as well as God. Some definitions of the Spirit as the '*promise* of my [Jesus']/[the] Father' and God's '*gift*' highlight that the Holy Spirit in Luke–Acts is the gift promised by God in the Jewish Bible (cf. the resurrected Jesus' promise of the Spirit in Lk. 24.49). Other definitions of the Spirit as '*power* from on high' and '*witness*' are utilized in connection with the witness-mission *to (the risen) Jesus*; also the *Holy* Spirit frequently appears *in witness contexts to Jesus*.

The connotations of the direct definitions of the Spirit are also confirmed by the indirect presentation of the Spirit. For instance, the speech (e.g. to David in Acts 1.16; to Isaiah in Acts 28.25; 2 Sam. 23.2), action (e.g. Acts 8.39//Ezek. 2.2; 3.12; 1 Kgs 18.12; Acts 20.22-23//Neh. 9.30) and environment (e.g. Lk. 24.49//Isa. 32.15; Wis. 9.17) of the Holy Spirit generally reflect those of *God's Spirit* in the Jewish Bible. At the same time, however, the immediate contexts in which the Holy Spirit is presented are closely associated with *Jesus* and *his* disciples in their witness-mission. Most importantly, the Spirit is said *to speak or act* (at decisive moments) in directing or guiding Jesus' witnesses to testify about Jesus particularly to non-Jews and is thus characterized not only *as God's reliable mission commentator*, but also *as a mission director witnessing to Jesus*.

I have also elaborated the previous portrait of the Spirit in several ways. I have shown that the repeated effects of the Spirit on Lukan characters are presented as identical with or similar to those of God's Spirit, while also noting some differences or different degrees of emphasis: prophetic/revelatory inspired oracle and/or speech; revelatory guidance through visions or dreams; speaking in tongues; miracles; charismatic gifts like wisdom, faith and joy. Again, these effects in Luke–Acts are frequently reported in the witness-contexts of Jesus and his disciples. The Lukan favourite expressions of 'being filled with' or 'full of' the Spirit (cf. Deut. 34.9; Mic. 3.8; Sir. 39.6; 48.12) also indicate that those who are inspired by the Spirit are portrayed not only *as God's reliable human agents* for accomplishing his will or purpose, but also *as Jesus' witnesses testifying about his resurrection*.

In addition, the Holy Spirit is more clearly defined, on the one hand, in comparison with an angel(s) (of the Lord) as another *holy* agent of God (Lk. 9.26; Acts 10.22), and, on the other, in contrast with evil or *unclean* spirits or the devil/Satan. Likewise, the angel, like the Spirit, appears frequently as 'helper' in contexts associated with *Jesus* and *his* witnesses, whereas the demons or Satan, unlike the Spirit, are represented as 'opponent' to both of them in those contexts. In this sense, references to the angel express the theo-, christo- and pneumo-centric points of view, whereas references to evil/unclean spirit(s) or the devil/Satan express the anti-theo-, anti-christo- and anti-pneumo-centric points of view.

In regard to the Lukan presentation of the Holy Spirit, we may, therefore, conclude that there is both continuity *as God's holy Spirit* and discontinuity (or development) *as the Spirit of/from the risen Jesus* when compared with the Jewish Bible as literary repertoire. I now turn in the next chapter to explore in detail the 'doing'/'functioning' of the Holy Spirit as a character, that is, the plot-centred characteriza tion of the Spirit in Luke–Acts.

Chapter 5

PLOT, FUNCTION AND THE HOLY SPIRIT

1. *Introduction*

In Chapter 4, I provided the theoretical foundation for the characterization of the Holy Spirit and applied it by focusing on the Lukan presentation of the Holy Spirit. Now in this chapter, I shall further explore the Holy Spirit as a character by paying attention to the narrative function of the Spirit in terms of the Lukan plot on the basis of the reliable narrator's and characters' characterization of the Spirit in each immediate context.[1] So I shall first define the literary term 'plot' and suggest what the plot of Luke–Acts highlights in providing four notable features. Then, on the basis of my definition of a 'plot' and the 'plot of Luke–Acts', I shall analyse the characterization of the Holy Spirit in terms of the causal aspect of the plot in order to show the narrative function(s) of the Spirit (cf. Shepherd's thesis goal, 1994: 101, 246-47).

2. *Definition*

The literary critic Egan's article entitled 'What Is a Plot?' (1978) begins with the following statements, which show that a plot is defined at different levels of abstraction by critics:

---

1.   In this chapter, I want to distinguish the *narrative function* of the Spirit from the *immediate roles* or *characterization* of the Spirit: the former refers to the overall effect of the Spirit delineated in the process of the narrative, whereas the latter refers to the contextual results caused by the Spirit in immediate narrative situations (cf. §5.2.1.1 in Chapter 4). However, the immediate role and narrative function of the Spirit sometimes overlap, particularly in the two programmatic passages: Lk. 4.18-19 and Acts 1.8.

The term *plot* is used variously in poetics and critical literature. Perhaps most commonly it is used to mean an 'outline of events [Robert Scholes and Robert Kellogg]', a scenario, an 'articulation of the skeleton of narrative [R. Scholes and R. Kellogg]'. Thus, to answer 'What is the plot of X?' is to give an account of the main incidents. Other common uses differ from this primarily in their degree of abstraction from the narrative, leading to a more or less pronounced form/content distinction. At an intermediate stage of abstraction, 'plot' is seen as the *arrangement* of the incidents, or as the relationship both among incidents and between each incident or element and the whole. In this view, it is the 'pattern' or 'geometry' of the narrative... 'Plot' is 'causal completion [Wayne C. Booth]', which determines the sense of unity; it produces a synthetic whole carved from the infinite contingency of the world. It is the final end that all the parts are to serve; it is the soul of the work [R.S. Crane]. Seen with a diachronic rather than the above synchronic emphasis, 'plot' is the 'dynamic, sequential element in narratives [R. Scholes and R. Kellogg]'. As a process of causal completion, it is the source of movement from beginnings in which anything can happen, through middles where things become probable, to ends where everything is necessary [Paul Goodman]... 'Plot is the knowing of destination' [Elizabeth Bowen]... 'Plot is story', suggesting that the same answer is called for by the questions, 'What is the plot of X?' and 'What is the story of X?' [E. Bowen]... 'A story already represents items selected according to some elementary law of narrative logic which eliminates irrelevancies. And a *plot* is then a further refinement which organizes these items for maximum emotional effect and thematic interest [R. Scholes]' (455; emphasis original; authors' names added).

After noting these divergent opinions about plot,[2] Egan concludes that 'a plot is a set of rules that determines and sequences events to cause a determinate affective response' (470). He also attempts to take the reader's reading process into consideration for the proper appreciation of a plot.

Similarly, Matera (1987), after arranging various critical views on plot according to (1) 'arrangement of events in terms of causality' (Forster, Scholes and Kellogg, Ricoeur and Muir), (2) 'time and final causality' (Kermode, Crane, Ford and Brooks), (3) 'emotional effect which this ending should produce in the reader' (Friedman and Egan) and (4) 'interrelationship between discourse and story as plot-events' (Chatman), concludes that 'we can say that although literary critics nuance

---

2.   Cf. Brooks's comment on a plot (1984: 3, 37); Rimmon-Kenan (1983: 135 n. 12) regards 'plot as one type of story (the type which emphasises causality)'.

their approaches to plot, they agree that it has something to do with how discourse arranges events by time and causality in order to produce a particular affective or emotional response' (236).

In the light of these approaches,[3] I note that story refers to general and broad contents in a narrative, whereas plot refers to *a narrative-flow that is engendered by causality in orderly sequence, evoking an affective or emotional response in the reader.*[4] Hence, a plot may involve 'narrative structure' or 'narrative pattern' or 'major themes'. For my study, however, when I employ the term plot, it has a slightly different nuance or emphasis from these terms. Although these subjects often overlap, 'structure' refers to formal outline (e.g. the geographical structure or the salvation-history structure in Luke–Acts), 'pattern' identifies similar types among some narrative blocks (e.g. the promise-fulfilment pattern in Luke–Acts), 'theme' is relevant to topic or interest in a narrative (e.g. the salvation theme in Luke–Acts), whereas 'plot' refers to an orderly sequence unified by causality, which creates an emotional response in the reader. In this sense, a major theme is closely related to a plot as a sub-plot,[5] whereas a well-organized meta-theme can be seen as a plot.[6]

3. *The Plot of Luke–Acts*

In terms of my definition of a plot, what then is the plot of Luke–Acts? Kingsbury (1991: 34), without providing any definition of a plot, argues, 'At the heart of this gospel [Luke] plot is the element of con-

---

3.   For the plot of Mark's Gospel, Smith (1996: 90), in describing plot as an arrangement of incidents, has taken four factors into consideration: (1) the causal factor, (2) the affective factor, (3) the character factor and (4) the conflict factor. And he understands the Markan plot as a tragic one.

4.   Whereas purpose tends to deal with extrinsic elements of the narrative, plot concerns intrinsic features in the narrative.

5.   Abrams (1993: 161) says, 'the subplot serves to broaden our perspective on the main plot and to enhance rather than diffuse the overall effect'. We can think of Jesus' journey to Jerusalem (Lk. 9–19) and Paul's sea-voyage (Acts 13–28) as sub-plots in Luke–Acts.

6.   Again for this close relationship between theme and plot, see Culpepper's comment (1983: 98): 'The gospel's [John's] plot, therefore, is controlled by thematic development and a strategy for wooing readers to accept its interpretation of Jesus'; Sheeley points out (1992: 139), 'the use of themes as plot devices by the narrator'.

flict'.[7] Thus, he (1994: 377) reads the end of the Gospel as a resolution of the conflict: 'Accordingly, the resolution of Luke's gospel-story of conflict between Jesus and the religious authorities is found in the events associated with Jesus' crucifixion, resurrection, and ascension'. This understanding of the plot of the Gospel(s) and/or Acts in terms of conflict[8] is widely held by biblical critics.[9] Nevertheless, I venture to ask again what the plot of *Luke–Acts* is. I am not saying that the conflict view of Luke–Acts is entirely wrong, but this characterization of the plot seems to be so broad and general that it is applicable to most biblical narratives, even to many literary novels. Thus, at this point, I am inclined to say that *conflict is the causal nexus through which the Lukan plot is developed* (cf. the repeated pattern of acceptance and rejection of Jesus and his witnesses). In the expression of this conflict as the causal nexus of the plot, characters or incidents are evaluated from the Lukan narrator's point of view.[10] Moreover, conflict in the narrative goes beyond human levels in a cosmic struggle between God('s will/purpose) and Satan('s will/purpose) (cf. Lk. 11.14-26; Acts 26.18).[11] Accordingly 'conflict as the causal nexus of the plot' of Luke–Acts cannot properly be understood without reference to the 'counsel/plan/will of God' (ἡ βουλὴ τοῦ θεοῦ).[12] I thus label *the plan of God as the matrix of the plot of Luke–Acts*.

7.   See also Tyson (1983: 313; 1986).

8.   L. Perrine, *Story and Structure* (New York: Harcourt, Brace, Jovonovich, 4th edn, 1974), p. 44, defines conflict as 'a clash of action, ideas, desires, or wills'; quoted in Powell (1993: 42).

9.   See Bar-Efrat (1992: 94); Petersen (1978: 83); Via (1975: 100); Tannehill (1994: 34, 47); Gowler (1990: 179); cf. Brawley (1990: 70); Parsons (1987: 71-72, 78-83); Powell (1993: 42-44).

10.   See my Chapter 3.

11.   See Kingsbury (1991: 1-2).

12.   This phrase is found nine times in Luke–Acts (for the reference to God: Lk. 7.30; Acts 2.23; 4.28; 5.38-39; 13.36; 20.27; to human beings: Lk. 23.51; Acts 12.12, 42; cf. God's θέλημα in Lk. 22.42; Acts 13.22; 21.14; 22.14), whereas only three occur elsewhere in the New Testament (1 Cor. 4.5; Eph. 1.11; Heb. 6.17). Other terms used in the narrative are also noted: δεῖ (Lk. 2.49; 4.43; 9.22; 13.33; 17.25; 21.9; 22.37; 24.7, 26, 44; Acts 1.16, 21; 3.21; 4.12; 5.29; 9.6, 16; 14.22; 16.30; 17.3; 19.21; 20.35; 23.11; 24.19; 25.10); μέλλω (Lk. 9.31, 44; 22.23; 24.21; Acts 17.31; 26.22, 23); πληρόω (Lk. 4.21; 9.31; 21.24; 22.16; 24.44; Acts 1.16; 2.28; 3.18; 12.25; 13.25, 27, 52; 14.26; 19.21); τελέω (Lk. 12.50; 18.31; 22.37); other προ-compounds and related verbs such as προορίζω (Acts 4.28), προκαταγγέλλω (Acts 3.18; 7.52), προχειρίζομαι (Acts 3.20; 22.14; 26.16) and so forth. Cf.

Then, what is the plot of Luke–Acts?[13] It is my claim that *the plot of Luke–Acts is the way*[14] *of witness,*[15] *in seeking and saving God's people,*

God's βουλή, which is found 23 times in the LXX: 2 Esdr. 10.3; Jdt. 2.2, 4; 8.16; Pss. 32.11; 105.13; 106.11; Prov. 19.21; Wis. 6.4; 9.13, 17; Mic. 4.12; Isa. 4.2 (?); 5.19; 14.26; 19.17; 25.1, 7; 46.10; 55.8; Jer. 27.45; 30.14; 39.19. Most of all, the text of Isa. 46.10 is significant in affirming that God's counsel will be established in the future: '[God] declaring the end from the beginning and from ancient times things not yet done, saying, "My purpose shall stand, and I will fulfil my intention (καὶ εἶπα Πᾶσά μου ἡ βουλὴ στήσεται, καὶ πάντα, ὅσα βεβούλευμαι ποιήσω)." ' See Sterling (1992: 358 nn. 239-43) and Squires (1993: 1-14; esp. 1-3).

13. My understanding of the Lukan plot will be more evident in due course when I elucidate, for instance, the two most programmatic passages (so called 'narrative kernels') in Luke–Acts, i.e. Lk. 4.18-19 and Acts 1.8. Cf. Tannehill's remarks (1986: 2): 'Luke–Acts has a unified plot because there is a unifying purpose of God behind the events which are narrated, and the mission of Jesus and his witnesses represents that purpose being carried out through human action'. For the plot of the Gospel of Matthew, Matera (1987: 243) argues, 'the plot of Matthew's Gospel has something to do with salvation history, the recognition of Jesus' identity, his rejection by Israel, and with the preaching of the gospel to the Gentiles'; Powell (1993: 49) suggests, 'the main plot of Matthew's Gospel concerns the divine plan by which God's rule will be established and God's people will be saved from sin'. Smith's appreciation of the Markan plot reads (1996: 96), 'The action in Mark stems from Jesus' awareness that the Spirit of God has come upon him, and that he has a divine mission which he must fulfil in word and deed. The narrative then goes on to explore the different ways in which others react to this mission— especially the opponents and the disciples. Finally, underpinning these two threads is a cosmic struggle between Jesus, in whom God's Spirit dwells, and Satan and his demonic forces'.

14. For Luke's characteristic expression 'way', see Tinsley (1965: 107, 209-210): 'The Gospel of Luke and Acts are, in fact, two books about "the way": the "way of Christ" in the Gospel and the "way of Christians" in Acts' (209). The word ὁδός is found twenty times each in Luke and in Acts; 24 refer to literal 'way' (Lk. 2.44; 3.5; 8.5, 12; 9.3, 57; 10.4, 31; 11.6; 12.58; 14.23; 18.35; 19.36; 24.32, 35; Acts 1.12; 8.26, 36, 39; 9.17, 27; 14.16; 25.3; 26.13), 11 (as both singular and plural forms) are metaphorical (1.76, 'for you will go before the Lord to prepare his ways' [ὁδοὺς αὐτοῦ]; 1.79, 'the way of peace' [ὁδὸν εἰρήνης]; 3.4, 'the way of the Lord' [τὴν ὁδὸν κυρίου]; 7.27, 'your way' [τὴν ὁδόν σου]; 20.21, 'the way of God' [τὴν ὁδὸν τοῦ θεοῦ]; Acts 2.28—'the ways of life' [ὁδοὺς ζωῆς]; 13.10, 'the straight ways of the Lord' [τὰς ὁδοὺς τοῦ κυρίου τὰς εὐθείας]; 16.17, 'the way of salvation' [ὁδὸν σωτηρίας]; 18.25, 'the way of the Lord' [τὴν ὁδὸν τοῦ κυρίου]; 18.26, 'the way of God' [τὴν ὁδὸν τοῦ θεοῦ]) and 6 (only singular form in Acts) are technical ('the Way' [τῆς ὁδοῦ/τὴν ὁδόν], Acts 9.2; 19.9, 23; 22.4; 24.14, 22; cf. 1QS 9.17, 18; 10.21; CD 1.13; 2.6; 20.18). In addition, it should be noted that in

engendered by Jesus (in the Gospel) *and his witnesses* (in Acts), *through the power and guidance of the Holy Spirit in accordance with the plan of God.* This Lukan plot can also be presented in terms of Greimas's *actantial* model[16] as follows.[17]

Luke–Acts the journey motif (Lk. 9.51-19.44; Acts 13-28) as sub-plot is embedded in this plot. In this sense, ὁδός is dynamically used in relation to the Lukan plot both *literally* (i.e. geographical expansion of the gospel) *and metaphorically* (i.e. the instruction about God and/or Jesus for early Christians [cf. Lk. 20.21]). Quite recently, Strauss (1995: 278-305) has persuasively claimed that Luke drew his new exodus imagery not only from Deuteronomy (as already demonstrated by Evans, Drury and Moessner), but also from Isaiah and the Prophets to view Jesus as Davidic king and servant of Yahweh. For the significance of the book of Isaiah for the major themes in Luke–Acts, see Sanders (1993: 14-25; esp. 20-25).

    15. For the witness-motif in Luke–Acts, see μάρτυς—twice in the Gospel (esp. 24.48) and 13 times in Acts (esp. 1.8, 22; 2.32; 3.15; 5.32; 10.39, 41; 13.31; 26.16; 22.15, 20); μαρτυρία—one each in the Gospel and in Acts (esp. 22.18); μαρτύριον—3 in the Gospel and 2 in Acts (esp. 4.33); μαρτυρέω—1 in the Gospel and 11 in Acts (esp. 10.43; 14.3; 23.11); μαρτύρομαι—two in Acts (esp. 26.22); διαμαρτύρομαι—1 in the Gospel and 9 in Acts (esp. 2.40; 8.25; 10.42; 18.5; 20.21, 24; 23.11; 28.23). Witness, found in the passages in parentheses, is presented as 'evangelistic witness' to Jesus. For the comprehensive analysis of the concept of witness in the New Testament, see Trites (1977; 1992: 877-80); for the relationship of Jesus' followers to the Spirit in terms of the motif of witness, see 1992: 879. Soards (1994) has claimed that the speeches in Acts as a whole are to be viewed as witness: 'Thus, when one asks, What is "the meaning to be attributed to the speeches in the work as a whole?" one finds that the speeches unify the Acts account, and through them Luke advances his theme of divinely commissioned unified witness to the ends of the earth' (15; see also 194).

    16. See §2.2 in Chapter 4. The application of this *actantial* model to biblical studies has proved its value. For instance, see Barthes (1977: 125-41); Patte (1974: 1-26); Crespy (1974: 27-50); Stibbe (1992: 34-39; 123-25; 1993b: 189-206). Nevertheless, some weak points embedded in Greimas's *actant* model have been discerned. For instance, the concept and identity of subject and/or object as actants could be identified in different ways according to one's interest or point of view. For the problematical points in Greimas's model, see Scholes (1974: 103-106).

    17. Cf. Given's (1995: 360-63) application of the *actantial* model to the book of Acts: Jesus (as Sender), Word (as Object), Humanity/Judea, Samaria and to the end of the earth (as Receiver), the Holy Spirit (as Helper), Witnesses (as Subject) and Satan (as Opponent). As the plot develops, however, the Holy Spirit can also be characterized as Sender (Acts 13.2, 4; 8.29, 39; 10.20; 11.12; cf. Lk. 2.26; 4.1, 14) and even Opponent (Acts 21.4; cf. 16.6-7). cf. Jesus as Sender (Lk. 9.1-2; 10.1; 24.45-48; Acts 1.8; 9.15-17; 22.18, 21; 23.11; 26.15-18). See §5 in this chapter.

Diagram 1

SENDER	→	OBJECT	→	RECEIVER
God		to seek and save God's people by proclaiming the Kingdom of God and bearing witness to Jesus with powerful words and deeds		Jesus and his witnesses

↑

OPPONENT	→	SUBJECT	←	HELPER
Pharisees; teachers of the law; scribes; chief priests; elders; evil spirits/demons; [ultimately] Satan[18]		God's will/plan		the Holy Spirit

God is thus presented as the final and responsible cause of the plot: an off-stage character yet gathering his people[19] in accordance with his plan through the ongoing witness of Jesus and his witnesses as on-stage characters by empowering and directing them through his Holy Spirit. In the service of this plot, some 'opponents' are pictured in a series of conflicts with God's human agents as 'receivers' and the divine agent Holy Spirit as 'helper' in carrying out God's will or desire.

I now turn to highlight briefly four features of the plot of Luke–Acts, which will be unfolded in detail in the process of examining the references to the Holy Spirit.

(1) The plot of the 'way of witness' in Luke–Acts is closely inter-woven with that of the 'way for salvation'[20] (Lk. 1.76-79; 2.30-32; 3.4-

18. Jesus' disciples in the Gospel are also represented as 'opponents' to Jesus' way (Lk. 9.54-56; 18.15-17; 22.3, 14, 31, 45-46, 47-51).

19. The theme of 'falling and rising' (Lk. 2.34) is, in fact, less connected with the Gentiles than with the Israelites. In spite of this, the similar theme of 'gathering and sifting' a people is clearly applicable to both ethnic groups throughout the nar-rative of Luke–Acts (e.g. Lk. 1.51-53; 2.34; 4.17; 5.31-32; 10.1-16; Acts 2.37-41; 13.46; 18.6; 28.28). Lohfink (1975: 17-31) rightly argues that the theme of 'gather-ing and sifting' is found even in Lk. 1-2. Furthermore, he also insists that in the process of the Lukan narrative the Gentiles become part of 'restored Israel' (79, 95). On this theme, see also Brawley (1990: 78-85, esp. 83). Within the theme of 'falling and rising' or of 'gathering and sifting', another theme of 'reversal' could be delineated in the narrative.

20. The word 'salvation' (σωτηρία: Lk. 1.69, 71, 77; 19.9; Acts 4.12; 7.25; 13.26, 47; 16.17; 27.34; σωτήριον: Lk. 2.30; 3.6; Acts 28.28; cf. σωτήρ: Lk. 1.47; 2.11; Acts 5.31; 13.23) is not found in the other synoptic Gospels. For the Lukan

6; 5.32; 19.10; Acts 16.17; cf. Acts 6.7; 9.31; 12.24; 16.5; 19.20). Thus, the Spirit-empowered Jesus, during his ministry from Galilee to Jerusalem, proclaims the salvific message in mighty words and deeds (cf. Lk. 24.19; Acts 2.22; 10.38) by preaching repentance and forgiving sins, especially in healing disabled people (Lk. 5.20-26; 7.47-50; 8.48, 50; 17.19; 18.42). In a similar fashion, Jesus' witnesses, empowered by the Holy Spirit, proclaim, during their ministries from Jerusalem to Rome, the same message of salvation, yet this is developed by bearing witness to Jesus' resurrection and ascension (Acts 2.37-41; 4.10-12; 10.36-43; 13.26-39; 16.30-31; 17.3; 26.22-23; 28.23, 31). Within this plot, the Holy Spirit is occasionally depicted apologetically as a decisive 'divine verifier' to confirm certain groups ignored by the (Christian) Jews (i.e. the Samaritans in Acts 8.17; the Gentiles in 10.44-48; 11.17-18; the Ephesian disciples in 19.5-6) as God's people.

(2) The 'way of witness' is advanced as the way which proclaims[21] the Kingdom of God *and* who Jesus is: (a) the Kingdom of God[22] (e.g. Lk. 4.18, 43; 7.22; 8.1; 9.6; 10.11; 11.20-23; 16.16; Acts 1.3; 8.12; 14.22; 19.8; 20.25; 28.23, 31) and (b) Jesus' identity as Messiah and Lord (e.g. Lk. 1.32, 35, 43, 76; 2.11, 26, 30-32; Acts 2.36; 5.42; 8.4, 5, 12; 9.20; 10.37, 42; 11.20; 17.18; 18.25; 19.13; 28.31; note also the frequent use of the 'name of Jesus'[23] in Acts). In a sense, Jesus' proclamation of the Kingdom of God is also understood as Jesus' self-witness because his mighty words and deeds are presented as indications of his (unique) relationship to God the Father (Lk. 5.20-26; 9.48; 10.16; cf. Lk. 2.49; 4.43; 10.22; 22.70-71).[24] Thus, the Kingdom of God can be said to be the kingdom of Jesus (Lk. 1.33; 22.29-30; 23.42; cf. Acts 8.12; 19.8; 28.23, 31). Moreover, Jesus is presented as the Son of God

concept of salvation, see Marshall (1970: 94-102); Johnson (1993: 520-36); Turner (1996b: 133-36, 145); Bock (1994b: 33-34).

21. The word κηρύσσω occurs nine times in the Gospel (3.3; 4.18, 19, 44; 8.1, 39; 9.2; 12.3; 24.47) and eight times in Acts (8.5; 9.20; 10.37, 42; 15.21; 19.13; 20.25; 28.31). It should also be noted that other similar verbs such as εὐαγγελίζω (Lk. 4.43; 8.1; 9.6; 16.16; Acts 8.12; 11.20) and διδάσκω (Lk. 20.21; Acts 4.2, 18; 5.21, 42; 11.26; 18.11, 25; 20.20; 28.31) are closely linked with both the Kingdom of God and the person of Jesus as the content of witness.

22. The term Kingdom of God is found 45 times in the Gospel and 8 in Acts. See nn. 127, 129 in this chapter.

23. See n. 90 in Chapter 4.

24. For the intimate relationship of the Kingdom of God to the proclamation of Jesus as Lord and Messiah, see Marshall (1977/78: 13-16); Beasley-Murray (1986).

and the Son of Man who reveals or bears witness to both God the Father and himself.[25] Jesus' self-witness to his identity reaches its climax in his resurrection teachings (Lk. 24.27, 44), and these are confirmed by the narrator's accounts of his ascension and outpouring of the Holy Spirit on his disciples (Acts 2.33). In other words, Jesus is portrayed as the witness *par excellence* both to God and himself (Lk. 2.30-35), thus offering himself as the 'model of prophetic witness'[26] for his witnesses in Acts, and, at the same time, he becomes the core of the message that his witnesses are represented proclaiming to the ends of the earth (Acts 1.8; cf. Lk. 24.46-48).

(3) It is the Holy Spirit who is described as empowering and guiding both Jesus (Lk. 3.22; 4.1, 14, 18; Acts 1.2; 10.38) and his disciples/ witnesses (Lk. 24.49; Acts 1.8 and *passim*: esp. Peter, Stephen, Philip, Barnabas and Paul) to accomplish boldly their witness-mission under whatever circumstances. In addition, the Holy Spirit is depicted not only as a 'helper' for Jesus and his witnesses, but also as a 'sender'.[27] It is not surprising then that the Spirit is also characterized as a witness (Acts 5.32).[28] In Acts, after Jesus' ascension and his sitting at the right hand of God, the Holy Spirit can be understood as the Spirit of communication between the risen Jesus and his disciples/witnesses[29] (Lk. 12.11-12; 21.15; cf. Acts 6.10) in a manner similar to the relationship between God and the earthly Jesus (cf. Lk. 10.21-22; Acts 10.38): on the one hand, major Spirit-filled/-empowered/-guided characters are

---

25. In the Gospel, the narrator, in fact, indicates the people's Jesus-centred response: 'And a report about him [Jesus] began to reach every place in the region' (4.37). See also Lk. 5.15; 7.3, 17; cf. 8.39-40. Moreover, Jesus in Acts is introduced as a 'man attested to you *by God* (ἄνδρα ἀποδεδειγμεςνον ἀπὸ τοῦ θεοῦ)' (2.22). See also the narrator's Jesus-centred summary of the Gospel in Acts 1.1-2a: 'In the first book, Theophilus, I wrote about all that Jesus did and taught from the beginning until the day when he was taken up to heaven'.

26. Luke seems to identify the work of Jesus' witnesses with that of Old Testament prophets (Acts 10.43; cf. Lk. 10.24; 24.27). For Jesus as the prophetic model for his disciples/witnesses in Acts, see Johnson (1977: 60-78; 1991: 17-20; 1992: 12-14).

27. See n. 17 and §5 in this chapter.

28. See §5.1.1.4 in Chapter 4.

29. See Drumwright (1974: 6, 7); Turner argues (1980: 138), 'The Spirit of prophecy thus makes the 'absent' Lord 'present' to the community, not only through charismatic speech, but also through visions *of* Jesus' (emphasis original; see also 129, 136); cf. Conzelmann (1960: 184).

characterized as witnesses *to Jesus* and, on the other, the Spirit is also portrayed as the Spirit *of Jesus* (Acts 16.7). In other words, in the Gospel, Jesus as God's agent is empowered and sanctioned by God's Holy Spirit to announce and reveal God's counsel, whereas Jesus' disciples in Acts as the risen Jesus' witnesses are also empowered and sanctioned by the same Spirit, but now this Spirit is sent through or caused by the exalted Jesus (Acts 2.33-36; 9.17; cf. 16.7; 18.9-10; 22.18, 21; 23.11),[30] to accomplish God's plan. So the figures who are depicted as inspired, empowered and guided by the Spirit are also portrayed as leading characters who play crucial roles in the development of the plot of Luke–Acts.

(4) The plot depicts a geographical expansion, which is carried out by leading Spirit-inspired characters.[31] Thus, the narrator highlights the geographical settings in developing the plot, e.g. Jesus' witness from Galilee to Jerusalem in the Gospel and his disciples' witness from Jerusalem, through Judea and Samaria, and to Rome in Acts.[32] Jerusalem, thus, seems to be the geographical centre of Luke–Acts (or at least of the Gospel). Nevertheless, from the beginning, the gospel of or the witness to Jesus is to be delivered beyond the territory of Israel (Lk. 2.32; Acts 1.8; 2.5-11): the salvific witness is directed not only to Jews, but also to Gentiles (Lk. 2.32; 24.47; Acts 1.8), first through Jesus who is depicted as chosen, baptized/anointed and commissioned by God (Lk.

30. See §5 in this chapter.

31. Johnson (1991) has rightly pointed out, 'Luke uses geography to structure his story and to advance his literary and theological goals' (14): for instance, 'In the Gospel, the narrative moves *toward* Jerusalem... In Acts, the geographical movement is *away from* Jerusalem' (14-15; emphasis original). For more detailed discussion, see Scott (1994: 483-544). His main argument is that Luke's geographical horizon is a confluence of two worlds, i.e. the Jewish and the Graeco-Roman. It is helpful to note his claim found in his conclusion: 'Thus the Spirit-impelled witness which proceeds from Jerusalem—the center—to the ends of the earth is divided into three missions, according to the three sons of Noah which constitute the Table of Nations: Shem in the middle of the world, Ham to the South, and Japheth to the North' (544).

32. Cf. Alexander (1995: 17-49), who observes the similarities and the differences of the 'voyage as plot' in the Acts of the Apostles and Greek Romances while commenting on the 'travel-narrative' both in Luke and Acts: 'Luke's predilection for structuring his narrative in terms of journeying has already been demonstrated in the "travel-narrative" of the Gospel. In Acts it is of course seen most clearly in the Paul narrative, and it is this which has most obviously attracted comparison with Greek romance' (23).

4.18, 43; 9.48; 10.16; Acts 3.20, 26), and then through Jesus' followers who are similarly chosen, baptized (metaphorically and literally) and commissioned through the risen Jesus by God (Lk. 9.2; 10.1, 3; 22.35; 24.49; Acts 1.5, 8; 2.4; 9.17; 26.17). Most importantly, readers can see at almost every critical plot-stage of the mission in Acts (8.29, 39, 10.19; 11.12; 13.2, 4; 16.6, 7; 19.21; 20.22) that the Holy Spirit appears as a reliable mission-supporter and/or director who, on the one hand, empowers and guides the witnesses and, on the other, verifies certain groups as God's people. In this regard, the plot is developed through a geographical expansion caused both by God's divine agent, that is, the Spirit (including an angel [of the Lord]), and by God's human agents, that is, Spirit-inspired witnesses, in order to fulfil the plan of God.[33]

In sum, the four claims summarized above imply that the narrative function(s) of the Holy Spirit is one of the most crucial factors for readers in grasping the plot of Luke–Acts.

4. *The Characterization of the Holy Spirit in Relation to the Causal Aspect of the Plot*

As mentioned, the Lukan plot is expressed and developed through references to a geographical expansion of the gospel to and from Jerusalem to Rome, seen as an effect of witnessing by Jesus (in the Gospel) and his disciples/witnesses (in Acts). In other words, the causal stages of plot-development can be discerned through geographical references as the 'way of witness' advanced by Spirit-inspired characters. This geographically oriented plot can thus be divided into the following five causal stages[34] in an orderly[35] sequence:

33. In this sense, Jesus is depicted as both God's human agent (in the Gospel) and God's divine agent (in Acts). See §5.1.1.3 in Chapter 4.

34. This five-stage framework is applied in the analysis of the Fourth Gospel by Hitchcock (1923: 307-317) and Stibbe (1994: 35-36).

35. This orderly sequence of the plot usually follows a chronological order. The narrator, however, may change the chronological order of a story for his own 'narrative order'. For instance, the narrator places the short account about John's imprisonment just before the scene of Jesus' baptism (3.22-23; cf. Mk 6.17-18; Mt. 14.3-4) in an attempt to highlight the sole ministry of Jesus. Cf. 'narrative/discourse time', which refers to 'the order in which the events are described for the reader by the narrator' (cf. the 'story time', which 'refers to the order in which events are conceived to have occurred by the implied author in creating the world of the story'); see Powell (1993: 36).

I.   Beginning (Lk. 3.1–4.13): at the Jordan river and/or wilderness in
     Judea
II. Development towards the Central Point (Lk. 4.14–19.44): from
     Galilee to Jerusalem
III. Central Point (Lk. 19.45–Acts 2.13): in Jerusalem
IV. Development towards the End (Acts 2.14–28.15): from Jerusalem,
     through Judea and Samaria, and towards Rome
V.   Open-Ended Finale (Acts 28.16-31): Rome.

However, both Lk. 1.1-4 (Luke–Acts' preface as well as Acts' preface
in 1.1-2) and Lk. 1.6–2.52 (Luke–Acts' prologue) are not included in
the five stages, but treated as a two-fold introduction to the overall
plot.[36] Accordingly, the Lukan plot is outlined as follows:

Two-fold Introduction to the Plot

I. *Preface*:   As a reliable witness-narrative (Lk. 1.1-4)
II. *Prologue*: Witnesses to the unborn babies, John and Jesus, and the
                child Jesus in Jerusalem and his self-witness in the
                temple—Jesus as the light for revelation to the Gentiles
                and for glory to the people of Israel (Lk. 1.5–2.52; cf.
                Acts 26.23)

The Plot-Outline of Luke–Acts

I. *Beginning (Lk. 3.1–4.13)*
John the Baptist's witness to Jesus and Jesus' resistance to the Devil's
tests in Judea as preparation for his witness-mission
II. *Development towards the Central Point (Lk. 4.14–19.44)*
Jesus' witness-journey from Galilee to Jerusalem
     II-1. Jesus' witness in Galilee (Lk. 4.14–9.50)
     II-2. Jesus' witness-journey towards Jerusalem (Lk. 9.51–19.44)
III. *Central Point (Lk. 19.45-Acts 2.13)*
Jesus' self-witness, his reminding his disciples of his Father's promise,
and the coming of the Holy Spirit to the disciples in Jerusalem
     III-1. Jesus' teaching (Lk. 19.45-22.46)
     III-2. Jesus' arrest and trial (Lk. 22.47-23.43)
     III-3. Jesus' death (Lk. 23.44-56)
     III-4a. Jesus' resurrection I (Lk. 24.1-49)
     III-5a. Jesus' ascension I (Lk. 24.50-53)
     III-4b. Jesus' resurrection II (Acts 1.[1-2] 3-5)

36. Some scholars insist that the first two chapters of the Gospel were added as
a prologue to the Gospel narrative: Taylor (1926: 165-68); Cadbury (1927: 204-
209); Brown (1993: 38, 239-43).

III-5b. Jesus' ascension II (Acts 1.6-11)
    III-6. Jesus' sending the Holy Spirit (Acts 1.12-2.13)
IV. *Development towards the End (Acts 2.14-28.15)*
Jesus' witnesses from Jerusalem, through Judea and Samaria and to the
ends of the earth
    IV-1. Witnesses in Jerusalem (Acts 2.14-7.60)
    IV-2. Witnesses in Judea and Samaria (Acts 8.1-11.18)
    IV-3. Witnesses towards the ends of the earth (Acts 11.19-28.15)
        IV-3-1. Barnabas and Paul's witness in Antioch (Acts 11.19-
                12.25)
        IV-3-2. Paul's witness-journey in Asia Minor (Acts 13.1-14.28)
        IV-3-3. The council in Jerusalem which authorizes the mission
                to Gentiles (Acts 15.1-35)
        IV-3-4. Paul's witness-journey in Macedonia and Achaia (Acts
                15.36-18.17)
        IV-3-5. Paul's witness-journey in Asia Minor (Acts 18.18-
                20.38)
        IV-3-6. Paul's arrest and defence of his mission to Gentiles in
                Jerusalem[37] (Acts 21.1-26.32)
        IV-3-7. Paul's witness-journey towards Rome (Acts 27.1-28.15)
V. *Open-Ended Finale (Acts 28.16-31)*
Paul's witness in Rome

I shall first briefly discuss the two-fold introduction to the Lukan plot:
the preface (Lk. 1.1-4) and the prologue (Lk. 1.5-2.52) by calling
attention to the references to the Holy Spirit in the prologue, which
anticipate the characterization(s) of the Spirit presented in the main
story, 'plot'.

4.1. *Preface (Lk. 1.1-4): As a Reliable Witness-Narrative*
Unlike the other Synoptic writers, Luke begins his narrative (διήγησις)[38]
with a preface[39] (cf. 2 Macc. 2.19-32; Josephus, *Apion* 1.1; 2.1), as do

---

37. The narrative setting of Jerusalem in IV-3-3 and IV-3-6 has to do with
recapitulation of the Gentile mission and endorsements of it that further the plot of
geographical expansion.
    38. This term (cf. the verb διηγέομαι, which is found in Lk. 8.39; 9.10; Acts
8.33; 9.27; 12.17) in ancient literature has been used to embrace both oral and
written reports/accounts. 'A διήγησις is a longer narrative composed of a number of
events, differing from a διήγημα, which concerns a single event' in Hermogenes,
Progymnasmata 2; quoted in Tannehill (1986: 10); cf. Alexander (1993: 111).
    39. For Lk. 1.1-4 as the preface referring to the Gospel and Acts, see Cadbury
(1922: I, 492); Minear, (1973: 133); Bovon (1989: 41-42); Evans (1990: 120-21);
Fitzmyer (1981: 289); Maddox (1982: 1-6); Marshall (1991a: 278-80); Johnson

other Hellenistic writers on various subjects. This Lukan preface is of importance in perceiving the aim of his composition. By giving special attention to several words in the preface within the three-fold grammatical structure (i.e. 'Since...I decided...so that...'),[40] I shall highlight the four qualities that are used to suggest that Luke, as an able writer, offers assurance to his reader about his story.

In the causal clause (vv. 1-2) we note: (1) the reference to 'many' (πολλοί) predecessors, without indicating their means of communication whether oral or written and (2) the references to 'eyewitnesses (αὐτόπτης) and servants (ὑπηρέτης) of the word'[41] (cf. Acts 4.20; 26.16). 'Eyewitnesses' could refer to the apostles (e.g. Acts 1.22; 10.39) and 'servants of the word' could refer to other significant contemporary persons or groups (e.g. Acts 6.3; 11.19-20). Thus, the narrator suggests to the narratee that the unfolding story after the preface is compiled on the basis of what they have seen and heard, even though we cannot exactly identify who they are. Hence, the Lukan narrative is presented as playing a similar role towards its readers as did the 'eyewitnesses' and the 'servants of the word' towards their hearers. We can therefore assume that both the implied author and the implied reader are

(1991: 27); Shepherd (1994: 102); contra Conzelmann (1960: 15 n. 1); Schümann (1984: I, 4); Schweizer (1984: 11); Nolland (1989: I, 11f.); cf. Alexander (1993: 2 n. 1, 145-46). We can learn from previous scholarly researches (see Alexander 1986: 48-51; 1993: 1-10) that Lk. 1.1-4 should be considered neither as solely a *'theological* preface', nor as just a *'(conventional) historical* preface'. Rather we see general implications embedded in the preface, which expose a conceivable *narrative* purpose; see du Plessis (1974: 259-71; esp. 260); van Unnik (1973: 7-26; esp. 8); Johnson (1991: 27-30); Tannehill (1986: 9-12).

40. That is, (1) a causal clause (vv. 1-2), (2) a main clause (v. 3) and (3) a purpose clause (v. 4). Cf. Acts 15.24-25. See Dillon (1981: 218); Alexander (1993: 105, 137). Cf. Fitzmyer (1981: 288), who suggests that Luke introduces Greek periodic style in the preface including three parallel phrases between the protasis (vv. 1-2) and the apodosis (vv. 3-4).

41. Scholars tend to interpret οἱ αὐτόπται καὶ ὑπηρέται γενόμενοι τοῦ λόγου as 'one group' that plays a two-fold role (i.e. 'eyewitnesses who became servants of the word'); see Fitzmyer (1981: 294); cf. Dillon (1978: 270-71), who argues that this one group has functioned ('to see' and 'to proclaim') in two transitional stages and also suggests (216-17) that this second role advanced in the preface hints at continuous events driven by the Spirit in the mission-era of the church; and cf. Alexander's (1993: 120) interpretation of αὐτόπται: 'those with personal/first-hand experience: those who know the facts at first hand'.

to envisage the Lukan narrative as a form of 'witness-narrative', which is reliable and trustworthy.

In the main clause (v. 3), we note: ἔδοξε κἀμοὶ παρηκολουθηκότι ἄνωθεν πᾶσιν ἀκριβῶς καθεξῆς σοι γράψαι, κράτιστε Θεόφιλε. Most scholars connect the first three underlined words with the first verbal phrase παρηκολουθηκότι and the last underlined word with γράψαι. So this verse reads: 'it seemed good to me also, having investigated carefully (ἀκριβῶς)[42] everything (πᾶσιν)[43] from the beginning (ἄνωθεν),[44] to write an orderly (καθεξῆς)[45] account for you, most excellent Theophilus'. This main clause thus discloses the implied author's claims for his investigation and composition: accuracy ('carefully'), completeness ('everything'), thoroughness ('from the beginning') and orderliness ('orderly'). Claims to all these qualities in v. 3 ground the assertion about the

42. For this word in Luke–Acts, see also Acts 18.25; 23.15, 20; 24.22. Nolland (1989: I, 9) says this term 'should probably be linked to both, παρηκολουθηκότι, "investigated", and, γράψαι, "write"'.

43. Regardless of whether we take the pronoun to be neuter (referring to 'events' in v. 1) or to be masculine (referring to 'many' in v. 1 and/or 'eyewitnesses and ministers of the word' in v. 2), we can see that Luke claims to have made every possible effort to get the available sources for his work.

44. This term (cf. Acts 26.4-5) can mean either 'from the beginning' (Fitzmyer 1981: 298; Johnson 1991: 27) or 'for a long time' (Cadbury 1922: 502-503; Marshall 1978: 42). If the former, the scope of 'from the beginning' is still in question: does it refer to the 'Infancy Narrative', i.e. the births of John the Baptist and Jesus (Plummer 1900: 4; Schneider 1977: I, 39; Bock 1994b: 61) or to the preaching of John the Baptist (Fitzmyer 1981: 294; cf. Lk. 3.23; 23.5; Acts 1.1, 22; 10.37)? This word, suggests Alexander (1993: 130), can also mean 'thoroughly'. Whatever option we take, the point here is clear: the claim is to have taken every necessary trouble.

45. The understanding of this term (cf. Lk. 8.1; Acts 3.24; 11.4; 18.23) is diverse: for the scholarly discussion, see Fitzmyer (1981: 298-99) and Bock (1994b: 62-63). On the basis of both the nuanced views of Fitzmyer ('a literary systematic presentation') and Bock ('a promise-fulfilment structure with broadly chronological and geographic orientation'), I also want to relate this word to Lukan rhetorical design (cf. Acts 11.4), including the Lukan plot itself. With respect to this term, Johnson (1991: 30) claims that Luke, feeling dissatisfied *in part* with his forerunners, attempts to rearrange the gospel of Jesus in a more 'convincing sort of order'; Moessner (1992: 1513-14, 1517, 1523, 1528). Cf. Dillon who argues (1981: 208) for Lukan solidarity with previous works, noting the word κἀμοις; see also Alexander (1993: 135).

narrative's reliability used in an emphatic final position in the last clause (v. 4): ἀσφάλεια[46] (cf. Acts 2.36; 21.34; 22.30; 25.26) as addressed to Theophilus and, through Theophilus, to other readers or listeners. Thus Johnson (1991: 28) argues, 'The key word is *asphaleia*. It does not mean "truth" as opposed to "falsehood", as although Luke's predecessors had their facts wrong. *Asphaleia* refers rather to a mental state of certainty or security (Acts 5.23, and for the idiom 21.24). Luke's narrative is intended to have a "convincing" quality.[47] Thus the implied author, as a deft storyteller, designs this witness-narrative in an orderly (καθεχῆς) sequence to convince his narratee(s) of its reliability.[48]

In short, the Lukan preface (Lk. 1.1-4) is designed to engender confidence in the narrative of Luke–Acts as a whole and to introduce it to the readers as a 'reliable witness-narrative'.

4.2. *Prologue (Lk. 1.5–2.52): Witnesses to the Unborn Babies, John and Jesus, and the Child Jesus in Jerusalem and his Self-Witness in the Temple*

The Lukan reader may be surprised at the abrupt change of Lukan style right after the preface, Lk. 1.1-4. Two features need to be mentioned (Kurz 1987: 203-208). One is the shift from Hellenistic Greek to Septuagintal Greek;[49] the other is the transition in the manner of narration, that is, from the 'telling' of the first-person narration to the 'showing' of the omniscient third-person narration.[50] Luke–Acts seems to imitate the biblical narrative of the LXX and so implies a reliable narrative given by the omniscient third-person narrator.[51]

---

46. See Maddox (1982: 22); Minear (1973: 133).

47. Cf. Alexander (1993: 140): 'so that you may have assured knowledge'.

48. See Dillon (1981: 224). Cf. Fitzmyer (1981: 289, 291).

49. For the heavy Semitic flavour of the Greek (i.e. Septuagintal Greek, possibly including a few Aramaisms) of the prologue, see Cadbury (1927: 70-75); Brown (1993: 245-50); Fitzmyer (1981: 312); N. Turner (1955/56: 100-109).

50. This shift in Luke–Acts (cf. 'we' sections in Acts), unlike the narratives in the Hebrew Bible with the exception of Ezra and Nehemiah, is detected by Stemberg (1985: 86-87) in accusing Luke–Acts of an inconsistent point of view. In regard to such shifts in point of view as precedents for Luke–Acts, Kurz remarks (1987: 204-206) not only the Hebrew Ezra, but also 1 Esdras, Tobit and 2 Maccabees. For the literary distinction between 'telling' and 'showing', see Booth (1991: 3-20).

51. Gasque claims (1989a: 248), 'he [Luke] is intending to write *biblical narrative...* He wishes to show that the promises God gave to Israel of old were

We also notice several specially designed parallels between the account of the birth of John the Baptist and of Jesus.[52] But this parallelism expresses both similarities and differences in the forthcoming roles of John and Jesus. In several ways, Jesus (Lk. 1.32; 2.11) is depicted as superior to John the Baptist (Lk. 1.76). For the characterization of Jesus, all reliable Spirit-filled human characters (including the non-human character, an angel) in Lk. 1–2 are employed to pinpoint who Jesus is: the 'Lord' by the angel, Gabriel (1.17; cf. 1. 76-77; 7.27); the 'Son of the Most High' by Gabriel (1.32); the 'Son of God' by Gabriel (1.35; cf. by Jesus' own words in 2.49); 'Lord' by Elizabeth (1.43); 'Savior, who is the Messiah, the Lord' by the angel (2.11); 'your [God's] salvation' by Simeon (2.30; cf. by Anna in 2.38). In other words, *human characters are represented as inspired or guided by the Holy Spirit in their bearing direct or indirect witness to Jesus* who is to act as God's inspired agent *par excellence* for his salvific plan. It is also noted that the geographical settings in the prologue anticipate those given in the rest of the Gospel: desert (1.80), Judea (1.39, 65; 2.4), Galilee or Nazareth (1.26; 2.4, 39, 51) and Jerusalem (2.22, 25, 38, 41, 45; cf. Bethlehem: 2.4, 15). I shall now examine the seven references to the Spirit by focusing on the Spirit-filled/-inspired characters with attention to major elements of the plot proleptically embedded in the prologue: 1.15, 35, 41, 67; 2.25, 26, 27.

4.2.1. The Witness of the Unborn John, Elizabeth and Zechariah. The first reference to the Holy Spirit is found in the announcement of the angel, Gabriel, to Zechariah concerning his son to be born and named John:[53] 'even before his birth he will be filled with the Holy Spirit

---

fulfilled in Jesus and in the birth of the church' (emphasis original); Sterling avers (1992: 363), 'Luke–Acts represents *sacred narrative*' (emphasis original). Cf. Rosner (1993: 65-82), who argues that Luke and esp. Acts should be conceived as a continuous biblical history based on the linguistic influence of the LXX, many similar themes, the Old Testament models, the literary techniques and the theological understanding of history.

52. For the study of these parallels in the Birth Narrative, see Brown (1993: 248-53, 292-98, 408-10); Fitzmyer (1981: 313-15); Tannehill (1986: 15-44).

53. Brown (1993: 156-57) introduces the five elements in a biblical birth annunciation (Gen. 16.7-12; 17.1-21; 18.1-15; Judg. 13.3-23) that Luke alludes to: (1) the appearance of an angel of the Lord or the Lord, (2) fear or prostration of the recipient, (3) the divine message, (4) an objection or a request of the recipient for a sign and (5) a sign for giving assurance.

(πνεύματος ἁγίου πλησθήσεται)' in 1.15. This prophetic statement by
the angel delineates John's future mission, which is precisely related to
his inspiration by the Holy Spirit in a role similar to that of God's
empowered figure, Elijah: 'to make ready a people prepared for the
Lord with the spirit and power of Elijah' (1.16-17).[54] Prior to his adult
mission (Lk. 3.3-14, 16-17; cf. 7.27), the Spirit-inspired unborn John is
even portrayed as bearing witness to the unborn Jesus by leaping for joy
in his mother's womb (1.41, 44). Not only 'inspiration', but also 'joy'
may thus be attributed to the Spirit (cf. 10.21; Acts 13.52). So the Spirit
is characterized not only as inspiring John for his future witness to
Jesus, but also as indirectly causing the unborn baby John to leap for
joy in testifying about the unborn Jesus.

Then, when Mary visited her, Elizabeth herself is said to be filled
with the Holy Spirit (ἐπλήσθη πνεύματος ἁγίου) in 1.41 and to give
inspired speech in addressing Mary as the 'mother of *my Lord*' (1.43).
The Spirit is thus characterized as causing Elizabeth to give inspired
words in testifying to the unborn Jesus.

After John is born as promised by Gabriel, his father Zechariah is
also said to be filled with the Holy Spirit (ἐπλήσθη πνεύματος ἁγίου) in
1.67 and to give a prophetic speech of praise to God inspired by the
Spirit in disclosing his son's future mission as the forerunner-witness to
the coming Messiah (1.76-79; cf. 3.16-17 narrated by John himself;
7.27 by Jesus), which includes reference to God's act of redemption/
salvation (1.68, 69, 71, 77) for his people Israel through his forgiveness
(1.72, 78; cf. 1.50, 58): 'for you [John] will go before the Lord to
prepare his ways, to give knowledge of salvation to his people by the
forgiveness of their sins' (1.76b-77). It is important to note that Zechariah's inspired prophecy ends with the remark pointing to the Messiah
(referring to Jesus) as a 'rising star' (ἀνατολή),[55] coming from on high

---

54. The phrase 'spirit and power of Elijah', foreshadowing the role of John as
parallel to that of Elijah (cf. Mk 9.11-13; Mt. 17.10-13; Mal. 4.5; Sir. 48.10), is here
understood as a metonymic expression (see 2 Kgs 2.9-10, 15; Sir. 48.12; LXX 4
Kgdms 2.15).

55. It is debated whether the word refers to (1) 'branch, shoot' (Jer. 23.5; 33.15;
LXX 40.15; Zech. 3.8; 6.12; cf. Isa. 4.2) or (2) 'star or sun' with the verbal form
ἀνατέλλω (Num. 24.17; Mal. 4.2), although I prefer the latter due to the following
'shining' (ἐπιφᾶναι). The point, however, is clear that either term used in the
Hebrew Bible (cf. Ezek. 29.21) and Jewish Literature (esp. at Qumran: CD 7.18-19;
1QM 11.6; 4Q175; 4Q161) denotes the coming Messiah. See Fitzmyer (1981: 387);
Marshall (1978: 95).

(ἐξ ὕψους; cf. Lk. 24.49), and to his mission of guiding the people of Israel into the way of peace[56] (τοῦ κατευθῦναι τοὺς πόδας ἡμῶν εἰς ὁδὸν εἰρήνης) (1.78-79).

In both 1.41-45 and 1.67-79, therefore, the immediate effect of being filled with the Spirit is represented as people's 'prophetic-inspired speech/praise' as often found in the literary repertoire. Also noted is that Zechariah, Elizabeth and even the unborn John, who are filled with the Spirit, are characterized as bearing witness to Jesus and his future messianic mission in the way of peace/salvation.

4.2.2. *The Witness of Mary.* The angel of the Lord, Gabriel, is also represented appearing to Mary to announce God's message concerning Jesus whom Mary will bear: Jesus is the 'Son of the Most High' (1.32a) who will be given the throne of his ancestor David (1.32) and reign over the house of Jacob and his kingdom forever (1.33).[57] In this angelic annunciation, Mary is said to conceive through the Holy Spirit[58] and the power of the Most High, and thus (διό) her child is to be called 'holy, the Son of God' (1.35; cf. 3.22; 9.35; 'a savior, who is the Messiah, the Lord'[59] in 2.11).[60] The parallelism of 'Holy Spirit' and 'power

---

56. 'Peace' is described as part of 'salvation' or as salvation itself in Luke. See Lk. 2.14, 29; 7.50; 8.48; 10.5; 19.38; 24.36; Acts 10.36. Thus, O'Toole (1997: 476) rightly concludes, ' "[P]eace" for Luke is not only a result of salvation, the spiritual and psychological state that follows on the reception or effect of God's salvific activity; but rather another expression for salvation like forgiveness of sins'.

57. The Davidic messianic tone of Gabriel's witness to Jesus is taken up again in 1.27, 69; 2.4, 11; 18.39; 19.38; Acts 2.30. Hence Jesus is presented as a person in whom all Israel may hope (cf. 2 Sam. 7.9, 13-14, 16; 1 Chron. 17.11-14). See Fitzmyer (1981: 338-40); Bock (1987: 55-90). Strauss (1995: 87-125) has persuasively and thoroughly analysed the theme of Jesus as the Davidic Messiah not only in Lk. 1-2, but also in the rest of Luke–Acts.

58. It is not unusual in Jewish writings that God's Spirit is understood as the source of miraculous power (see Chapter 2); on the other hand, unique in the picture at 1.35 is the idea of *the conception of the Messiah by the Holy Spirit*, although there are a few references related to the messianic figure which mention the divine Spirit (Isa. 11.1-2; cf. 4.2-4; 42.1; *1 En.* 49.2; 62.2; *Pss. Sol.* 17.37; 18.7; *Targ. Isa.* 4.2). Thus, Brown (1993: 312; see also 29-32 and n. 15) notes, 'The real parallel for the conglomeration of ideas in 1.35 is not an OT passage but the early Christian formulations of Christology'.

59. This combination of titles 'Savior', 'Christ' and 'Lord' is so unique that we can not find it elsewhere in the New Testament. In the context, however, the dominant tone of such titles indicates Jesus as the Davidic messianic figure, which is to

of the Most High' (see 1QH 7.6-7; cf. *T. Levi* 16.3) thus implies that the Spirit is here envisaged as God's creative power, causing Mary's miraculous conception (Fitzmyer 1981: 350).[61]

Mary, the mother of Jesus, is said to address prophetic speech or praise to God in 1.46-55, and we may understand this as another expression of the influence of the Holy Spirit (1.35a).[62] Thus, *the Magnificat*, as prophetic canticle, not only offers praise to God for vindication of Mary and the faithful among the people of Israel, but also anticipates *the nature of Jesus' ministry*[63] conceived through the 'motif of reversal' and/or 'pattern of acceptance and rejection' (Lk. 2.34; 6.20-26; 9.24, 46-48; 10.21; 13.25-30; 14.7-11, 16-24; 16.15, 19-31; 18.9-14; 22.24-27).[64]

In relation to the causal aspect of the plot, the Holy Spirit is represented both as inspiring prophetic announcements about who Jesus is and what he would do, and as engendering miraculously Jesus' actual

be further defined by Luke (or to be clarified by the reader) in the rest of the narrative, esp. after Jesus' resurrection and ascension (Lk. 20.41-44; Acts 2.33-36).

60. On the Jewish parallel use of 'son of God' and 'son of Most High', see 4Q246, Col 2, lines 1 and 5-6, as Turner (1996b: 155-56) noted; against Leisegang's argument, he rejects pagan influence of divine procreation in 1.32-35, following the views of Brown and Fitzmyer.

61. It is not convincing to sharply dissociate (God's) power (δύναμις) as the source of 'exorcisms and miracles of healing' from the Holy Spirit as the source of 'prophetic speech' in Luke–Acts: see Lk. 1.35; 4.14; 24.49; Acts 1.8; 6.3-8; 10.38. Cf. Table 4 in Chapter 1.

62. The implied reader hardly fails to attribute *the Magnificat* to the inspiration of the Holy Spirit when he or she compares the other prophetic hymns (*the Benedictus* by Zechariah; *the Nunc Dimittis* by Simeon), especially considering the greetings by Elizabeth who honours Mary. Within the flow of the immediate context, the reader may go back to 1.35 to appreciate *the Magnificat* properly. See Shepherd (1994: 121); Menzies (1991a: 127); Turner (1996b: 143-44 n. 13).

63. For the opinion that the aorist verbs in vv. 51-54 are 'prophetic aorist', portraying Jesus' mission authorized by God, see Marshall (1978: 84); Plummer (1900: 33); Danker (1988: 43-44); Bock (1994b: 155). For the view that they refer to 'past events', to both God's past acts for Old Testament figures and the work of Jesus reflected by early Christians' original hymns, see Brown (1993: 352-53); Fitzmyer (1981: 361); Farris (1985: 120-21). On the other hand, Coleridge (1993: 92) comments that the working of God's power described here reaches beyond any time-spans—past, present and future. All these views thus support directly or indirectly my reading of 1.51-55 in terms of Jesus' future ministry.

64. See Tannehill (1986: 27-31).

conception. Hence readers are encouraged to have confidence in Jesus' ministry as the ministry of one who would effect God's plan.

4.2.3. *The Witness of Simeon and Anna.* Simeon, like Zechariah and Elizabeth (1.6), is described as an ideal Jew by the narrator: 'righteous and devout, looking forward to the consolation of Israel' (2.25a), and is also portrayed in relation to the inspiration of the Spirit: 'the Holy Spirit rested on him' (πνεῦμα ἦν ἅγιον ἐπ᾽ αὐτόν) in 2.25b;[65] the Spirit revealed (κεχρηματισμένον ὑπὸ τοῦ πνεύματος τοῦ ἁγίου) that he would see the 'Lord's Christ' before his own death (2.26); the Spirit guided him (ἦλθεν ἐν τῷ πνεύματι) to the temple (2.27). This explains how Simeon is able to see the Lord's Christ in the eight-day-old Jesus who is dedicated to God (2.28) and to deliver his prophetic oracle (2.29-32, 34-35). In terms of the causal aspect of the plot, therefore, the Spirit, as often seen in the Jewish writings, grants revelation, guidance and prophetic speech. As a result of these charismatic gifts, Simeon is aware of Jesus' messianic role; so Simeon, like other characters inspired by the Spirit in the narrative, is described as rightly bearing witness to who Jesus is and what his future mission will be.[66]

65. This Greek phrase καὶ πνεῦμα ἦν ἅγιον ἐπ᾽ αὐτόν (cf. Lk. 4.18 on Jesus; Num. 11.17 on Moses) implies a permanent endowment of the Spirit.

66. Simeon's two oracles (Lk. 2.29-32, 34-35), construed as a programmatic narrative device, are designed to shed light on the Lukan plot in the remainder of Luke–Acts. There are two pivotal implications to be examined. First, Simeon declares that he sees 'God's salvation' and in turn discloses God's plan of salvation, which would be open not only to Israelites, *but also to Gentiles* (Isa. 40.5; 42.6; 46.13; 49.6; 52.9-10): 'Master, now you are dismissing your servant in peace, according to your word; for my eyes have seen *your salvation*, which you have prepared in the presence of *all peoples* (πάντων τῶν λαῶν), *a light for revelation to the Gentiles and for glory to your people Israel* (φῶς εἰς ἀποκάλυψιν ἐθνῶν καὶ δόξαν λαοῦ 'Ισραήλ)' (Lk. 2.29-32); see Tannehill's (1986: 40, 43) comment; cf. Tiede (1988: 27). Secondly, Simeon uncovers and foretells the 'sign of Jesus' (not presented until Lk. 2.34-35) not only as a guarantee for authentic belief, but also as a stumbling block (cf. Lk. 7.23; 20.17-18 and Isa. 8.14-15) causing unbelief among some in Israel: 'This child is destined for *the falling and the rising of many in Israel* (πτῶσιν καὶ ἀνάστασιν πολλῶν ἐν τῷ 'Ισραήλ), and as a sign that will be opposed so that the inner thoughts of many will be revealed' (Lk. 2.34-35). This seems to prefigure the conflict and tension (cf. Lk. 1.51-53; 2.34-35; 3.16-17; 12.51-53) between Jesus and his opponents in the Gospel and between Jesus' disciples/ witnesses (chiefly seen as Peter, Stephen and Paul) and their opponents in Acts, which are pervasive in the subsequent narrative. Therefore, we cannot over-

In the prologue, there is one human character who is not (explicitly) described as inspired by the Spirit, yet who bears witness to Jesus: she is Anna, an old widow-prophetess, dedicated to fasting and praying in the temple, where she is said to testify about Jesus to the people longing for the redemption of Jerusalem (2.36-38). The reason why the narrator does not explicitly represent Anna's witness to Jesus as inspiration by the Spirit is not clear, but perhaps it is because Anna, unlike Mary, Elizabeth, Zechariah and Simeon, is not given a direct quotation. Also she is explicitly characterized as 'prophetess'[67] (cf. Acts 2.17; 21.10-11) and this may imply inspiration by the Spirit (cf. Zech. 7.12; Neh. 9.30).

4.2.4. Summary. In relation to the causal aspect of the plot, the Spirit in the prologue is characterized as *inspiring* the main characters (Elizabeth, Mary, Zechariah and Simeon; cf. Anna, Jesus himself[68]) *to*

emphasize the pivotal importance of Simeon's two oracles for grasping the plot of the whole narrative of Luke–Acts: it would lead readers to expect (1) a series of resistant or hostile responses of some Israelites to Jesus himself (cf. Lk. 7.1-10) and to Jesus' disciples/witnesses (e.g. Acts 4.5-7, 13-18; 5.17-18, 33; 6.8-15; 7.54-60; 8.1-3; 9.23-30; 12.1-5; 13.44-45) and thereby (2) a repeated theme of reversal (cf. 4.18-19; 5.31-32; 6.20-26; 7.22-23) through a pattern of 'acceptance and rejection' extended to the inclusion of Gentiles among God's restored people (Acts 10.44-48; 11.15-18; cf. 13.46; 18.6; 28.28).

    67. God used women called 'prophetesses' as his revelatory agents in the Hebrew Bible: Miriam (Exod. 15.20), Deborah (Judg. 4.4), Huldah (2 Kgs 22.14) and Isaiah's wife (Isa. 8.3), as observed by Nolland (1989: I, 122); cf. seven women have been designated in Jewish tradition as prophetess: Sarah, Miriam, Deborah, Hannah, Abigail, Huldah and Esther (*b. Meg.* 14a), see Ellis (1974: 84).

    68. When twelve-year-old Jesus speaks his first words in response to his mother's question in the Gospel, the sense of his own identity and mission in relation to his Father, God, is revealed: 'Why were you searching for me? Did you not know that I *must be* (δεῖ) in *my Father's house*?' (2.49; cf. 3.22; 9.35; 10.22; 22.29; 24.49). The key issue of this verse is how to interpret the phrase ἐν τοῖς τοῦ πατρός μου literally translated 'in the (things) of my Father'. Two interpretations have been accepted: (1) 'I must be about my Father's business' (cf. Mk 8.33; 1 Cor. 7.32-34; 1 Tim. 4.15) and (2) as preferable, 'I must be in my Father's house', supported by biblical and extrabiblical Greek texts, i.e. 'the neuter plural of the definite article followed by a genitive singular or plural' referring to 'the house/ household of X' as used in Gen. 41.51; Esth. 7.9; Job 18.19, see Fitzmyer (1981: 443-44); Brown (1993: 475-77). Either reading intimates Jesus' own identity and the meaning of his subsequent mission in the rest of the narrative.

bear witness to the unborn Jesus and the child Jesus through their prophetic speeches/praise.[69] The Spirit is also presented once as *revealing and guiding* Simeon *to see Jesus* in the temple. On the other hand, the account of John's *inspiration caused by the Spirit* in his mother's womb, and that of Jesus' *miraculous conception caused through the power of the Spirit* attributes their relationship to the Spirit as set forth in the subsequent narrative. In this way, the prologue as the 'prelude' to Luke–Acts foreshadows the characterization of both the Spirit and Spirit-filled characters appearing in the plot of the main narrative. Readers can also anticipate on the grounds of Simeon's reliable inspired speech that the mission of Jesus (and his witnesses) would encounter a series of conflicts with his (or their) opponents in a 'pattern of acceptance and rejection'. Readers thus become aware that the characterization of the Spirit in the prologue will be further clarified and developed in the process of the plot.

---

69. Some readers (e.g. Moessner [1988: 38, 40-41]; Moore [1987: 446-48]) might question the reliability of Mary's and Zechariah's inspired speeches in regard to the hope/salvation for 'Israel' through the Messiah, Jesus (1.54-55, 68, 71-73; cf. Anna in 2.38; 24.19-21). The implied reader, however, through their reading process, may construe this expectation not simply as 'nationalistic', but as 'universal'. This clue is already embedded in Simeon's inspired oracle (2.30-32, 34) and Jesus' sermon at Nazareth (4.24-27), that there are wilful Jews (e.g. 19.47) who are not to participate in God's redemption, whereas there are faithful/repentant Gentiles (e.g. 7.2-9) entering into this redemption as part of 'restored Israel' (cf. Acts 15.16-17). In addition, Jesus' death, as he predicted (9.22, 44; 18.31-33), is interpreted (by Jesus and the implied author) as an inevitable part of the (servant) Messiah's 'way of witness' in fulfilment of Scripture (24.25-27, 44-46; cf. Acts 3.18; 13.28-29). And the narrative claims that God raises Jesus from the dead and vindicates him as God's Messiah (Lk. 24.46; see also Acts 2.23-32, 36; 3.13, 15; 4.10-11; 5.29-32; 13.30-35). This means that God provides Israel with another opportunity of repentance in response to either the risen Jesus (e.g. Jesus' disciples in Lk. 24; Saul in Acts 9) or the disciples' witness to him (the replacement of Judas with Matthias for completing again twelve apostles seems to symbolize the restored twelve tribes in Israel in Acts 1.16-26; see also Lk. 22.28-30; cf. 1QS 8.1; see Johnson 1992: 39). In this respect, Mary's and Zechariah's speeches inspired by the Spirit can be sustained as reliable, although they are to be reshaped as the plot develops (see also Shepherd 1994: 119 n. 56; cf. Karris 1996: 745). In addition, the expectation of the 'rising and falling of many in Israel' (2.34) can also be seen as 'external prolepsis', beyond the narrative world of Luke–Acts. See Tiede (1988: 29, 34); Brawley (1990: 44-46); cf. Tannehill (1986: 40-41).

4.3. *Beginning (Lk. 3.1–4.13): John the Baptist's Witness to Jesus and Jesus' Resistance to the Devil's Tests in Judea as Preparation for his Witness-Mission*

In terms of the causal aspect of the plot, readers may identify the opening lines of Luke 3 as an actual beginning[70] of the narrative (cf. Acts 1.22; 10.37), which is reminiscent of that of some prophetic books in the Jewish Bible.[71] This plot-stage as 'beginning' exhibits two introductory episodes: (1) John the Baptist's witness to Jesus (3.1-20) and (2) Jesus' preparation for witness-mission (3.21-4.13).[72] The geographical setting for the narrative of John and Jesus is near the Jordan river (3.3; 4.1), and in the wilderness (3.2, 4; 4.1) of Judea (3.1).

There are four references to the Spirit (3.16, 22; 4.1a, 1b), which are all presented in association with Jesus: John's proleptic remark about the Spirit in 3.16 foreshadows Jesus' baptism, functioning as a literary type of repetition in terms of narrative-frequency (Tannehill 1996: 81-82),[73] which is further clarified in the plot-development (Acts 1.5; 11.16; cf. 19.4-5; 2.38; 1.8; Lk. 24.49); the descent of the Spirit in his baptism in 3.22; the empowerment and guidance of the Spirit in his test by the devil in 4.1. At the outset of the plot, the Holy Spirit is closely associated with Jesus' activity as God's agent: the Spirit is character-

---

70. Cf. Tyson (1991: 116) who proposes 'three beginnings' in Luke: (1) Lk. 1.1-4 as conventional introduction, (2) Lk. 1.5-2.52 as dramatic prologue and (3) Lk. 3.1-2 as scenic introduction. See also Tannehill's comment (1986: 52): '3.1-2 marks a major new segment of the narrative. Rather than establishing continuity with the previous episode, the narrator introduces a new character performing a new activity in a new place and time'.

71. Two factors are noted here: one is the way of presentation of John in introducing his father's name, Zechariah (e.g. Hos. 1.1; Joel 1.1; Zech. 1.1); the other is the familiar phrase 'the word of God came to a certain prophet', which indicates the beginning of a prophet's ministry (e.g. Hosea, Micah, Joel, Jonah, Zephaniah, Haggai, Zechariah and Jeremiah).

72. My division of 3.1-4.13 as a narrative unit is also held by Marshall (1978: 131); Fitzmyer (1981: 450); Bock (1994b: 331).

73. The narrative term 'frequency' (as analysed by Genette) is used to indicate the relation between the number of occurences of an actual event in the story and that of a narrated event in the text. There are three types of frequency: (1) 'Singulative'—telling once what happened once, (2) 'Repetitive'—telling x times what happened once, and (3) 'Iterative'—telling once what happened x times. In this sense, the narrator's making 'repetitive' a certain event may indicate that such an event is of significance for appreciating the story: Rimmon-Kenan (1983: 56-58).

ized as inspiring, empowering and leading Jesus as God's Messiah to prepare for his own mission as one appointed by God.

4.3.1. *John the Baptist's Witness to Jesus (Lk. 3.1-20)*. In terms of the narrative flow (cf. 1.15, 17), the first part of the narrative-context (3.3-20)[74] represents the Holy Spirit as causing John's prophetic witness to Jesus (1.76-77). In other words, in relation to the causal aspect of the plot, the Holy Spirit is here understood to inspire John's prophecy to Jesus as the mightier One who is coming and as the one who will baptize the people of Israel with the Holy Spirit and fire[75] (3.16; cf. Acts 19.4): the Spirit inspires/empowers John to witness to Jesus (1.15, 17).[76] The implied reader may retrospectively appreciate the significance of John's prophetic statement about Jesus' role as baptizer[77]

74. Luke, on the one hand, like in Mk 1.2 and Mt. 3.3, substitutes αὐτοῦ for τοῦ θεοῦ ἡμῶν in attempting to identify κύριος in 3.4 with Jesus (1.17, 76; cf. 7.27; 1.43; 2.11) rather than with God (Fitzmyer [1981: 461, 385-86]); on the other hand, however, Luke's use of the quotation from Isa. 40.3-5, unlike that in Mk 1.2-3 and Mt. 3.3, provides the whole quotation of the LXX Isa. 40.3-5 in order not to omit the words in v. 5: 'all flesh shall see the salvation of God' in Lk. 3.6 (cf. 2.30).

75. Unlike in Mk 1.8, the term 'fire' is found in Luke here and Mt. 3.11. On the other hand, 'fire' is not used in Jesus' own prediction of the coming Spirit in Acts (1.5; 11.16). Scholarship is divided on whether the phrase 'he will baptize you with the Holy Spirit and fire' (αὐτὸς ὑμᾶς βαπτίσει ἐν πνεύματι ἁγίῳ καὶ πυρί) implies two distinct baptisms (i.e. Spirit-baptism for the righteous and fire-baptism for the unrepentant) or a single baptism (i.e. one Spirit-and-fire baptism). The latter view is grammatically more convincing: there is not only the single preposition ἐν which governs both Spirit and fire, but also the single object 'you' (ὑμᾶς) to be baptized. If the phrase means the former, it should contain ἤ. Dunn (1970a: 12 nn. 11-12) points out that the image of fire itself has a dual function in referring to judgment (Isa. 31.9; Amos 7.4; Mal. 4.1; *Jub.* 9.15; 36.10; *1 En.* 10.6, 12-13; 54.6; 90.24-27; *4 Ezra* 7.36-38; *Pss. Sol.* 15.6-7; 1QH 6.18-19) and purification (Isa. 1.25; Zech. 13.9; Mal. 3.2-3; 1QH 5.16). This 'single baptism of Jesus' is also defended by Marshall (1978: 146-47); Fitzmyer (1981: 474); Turner (1996b: 177-79); Bock (1994b: 322-24).

76. John's portrait of one paving the way (1.76, 79; 3.4-6; 7.27) for Jesus, thus, presents an exemplary role of witness for Jesus' disciples/followers who will continue and extend the 'way of the Lord/salvation' (Acts 9.2; 19.9, 23; 22.4; 24.14, 22; 16.17).

77. The verb βαπτίζω is used four times in the LXX: Isa. 21.4; 2 Kgs 5.14; Jdt. 12.7; Sir. 31.35; see Foakes-Jackson and Lake (1920: 333-34). However, the exact meaning of 'baptize' in 3.16 has been disputed. Turner (1996b: 180-84), introducing particular scholars' understanding of the word βαπτίζω ('to immerse'

with the Holy Spirit (cf. Acts 1.5; 11.16; 19.4) when encounting an episode about the coming of the Spirit on the day of Pentecost (Acts 2.1-4, 33; cf. 10.44-48; 11.15-16; 19.4-7). At the present stage of the reading-process, however, the reader cannot fully understand what John's characterizing of the Messiah as the Spirit-baptizer connotes, because there are no telling parallels to Lk. 3.16, as Turner (1982: 168-90; 1994b: 413-36) notes, in the Jewish Bible and other Jewish writings.[78]

Nevertheless, the implied reader may connect John's prophetic and revelatory witness in Lk. 3.3-17 with the preceding information of John's inspiration by the Holy Spirit, although there is no direct

argued by Webb; 'to deluge with' or 'to overwhelm with' by Marshall and once by Turner [1981c: 50-53]; 'to initiate' by Dunn) and evaluating them negatively, avers that this word rather connotes 'to cleanse', effecting both judgment and salvation (thus Turner [1980: 48-52; 208-210] shifts from his old view). Turner's view seems to be valid particularly in solving the crux of the unparalleled image of a messianic figure in Judaism who otherwise is to be understood by John as the one pouring out the divine Spirit. It is true that his argument (to see Jesus as the Davidic Messiah who restores the people of Israel by cleansing them with the Spirit-and-fire baptism, i.e. the Spirit has soteriological function) goes well with Acts 1.5-8 and 11.15-18; cf. 2.38. However, this position cannot sufficiently (1) explain the pivotal passages of Lk. 24.49 and Acts 1.8 (i.e. 'Jesus' baptizing with the Holy Spirit' is tantamount to 'Jesus' sending of the Holy Spirit' as supported in Acts 1.5; 2.33; cf. Lk. 2.16; 11.13; 12.12; 21.15, thus indicating 'Spirit-empowering for witness-mission') and (2) reflect the implied author's literary design in terms of 'order' and 'frequency', esp. a repetitive pattern that requires readers' prospective and retrospective reading. Turner (1996b: 186-87), perceiving this dilemma, thus suggests 'we need at least potentially to distinguish between the views attributed to the Baptist (or other characters) within the narrative and those of the narrator/implied author himself... [H]e [John] is aware that the salvation historical events took a rather different "shape" from what might have been expected by extrapolation from traditional hopes'. For the meaning of 'baptize' in Luke–Acts, I take both views of Marshall and Turner as complementary to each other: the former is applicable to Jesus' charismatic followers as witnesses since Pentecost (Lk. 24.48-49 and Acts 1.8); the latter to ordinary people as God's restored community (Acts 2.38-39).

78. Cf. Dunn (1972: 89-92) who has attempted to connect John the Baptist's understanding of the Messiah as bestowing the Holy Spirit to the idea in 1QIs[a] 52.14-15 and CD 1.12 (cf. *T. Levi* 18.6-8 and *T. Jud.* 24.2-3, which are excluded as Christian interpolations); yet he has concluded, 'it is quite probable that it was John the Baptist who *finally* linked the eschatological outpouring of the Spirit to the Messiah and who *first* spoke of the Messiah's bestowal of the holy Spirit under the powerful figure...of a baptism in Spirit-and-fire' (92; emphasis added).

reference to the Spirit with regard to John from 1.15 onwards.[79] Hence, John's ministry and role must be conceived as those of a reliable and inspired witness[80] to Jesus in that the Spirit is represented as causing or empowering him to speak and act. John, after finishing this role, is left behind in giving way to Jesus.

4.3.2. *Jesus' Preparation for Witness-Mission* (*Lk. 3.21–4.13*). The narrator now begins to focus on the adult Jesus by linking closely the beginning of both the accounts of Jesus' baptism and his test with the Holy Spirit. In the Lukan account, unlike in Mark and Matthew, John is removed from the narrative stage before Jesus' baptism. In this way, Luke seems to dissociate John's initiative as a baptist from Jesus' baptismal experience of the Holy Spirit.[81] Luke rather adds Jesus' own praying right after the baptism and just before the descent of the Holy Spirit[82] upon him. This implies that the coming of the Spirit upon Jesus in his baptism is pictured as God's response (cf. the expression 'the heaven was opened' in 3.21b)[83] to Jesus' prayer:[84] the coming of the

79. Here, we should note that only John and Jesus are uniquely described as being associated with the Holy Spirit even from their mothers' womb, without parallels (esp. concerning the coming Elijah and/or Messiah) in the Jewish Bible and other related literature. Due to their unmatched relationship to the Holy Spirit, the narrator, as we may suppose, need not further mention the Spirit during their ministries apart from the essential narrative stage of Jesus' ministry, as messianic preparation (Lk. 3.21-22; 4.1-13) and verification (4.14-19). On the other hand, however, when John loses his narrative-setting in the 'wilderness' (Lk. 1.8, 3.2, 3; 7.24), he appears to lose his identity or role as a witness to Jesus (cf. Lk. 7.17-20).

80. Cf. Darr's comment (1992: 66): 'John is a product of (Luke's) ideal Judaism, and his responsibility is to bring the rest of Israel into line with that ideal so that divine revelation will be recognized'.

81. See also the introduction of the adult John as the 'son of Zechariah' instead of as 'John the Baptist' (3.2; cf. Mk 1.4; Mt. 3.1).

82. Only Luke employs the term 'Holy Spirit' when describing Jesus' baptism in 3.22; cf. the 'Spirit' in Mk 1.10 and the 'Spirit of God' in Mt. 3.16. See §5.1.1.1 in Chapter 4.

83. The picture of heaven's opening draws on God's dramatic action and/or his revelation in Jewish writings: Ezek. 1.1; Isa. 24.18; 64.1; Gen. 7.11; Mal. 3.10; *3 Macc.* 6.18; *T. Levi* 2.6-8; 18.6-7; *T. Jud.* 24.2; *Apoc. Bar.* 22.1; *Apoc. John* 47.30; cf. Acts 7.56; 10.11. See Nolland (1989: I, 160); Bock (1994b: 337).

84. The implied author expresses a particular interest in the relationship between the Spirit and prayer: (1) God's people are frequently granted the Spirit by God in response to their prayers (Lk. 11.13; Acts 1.14; 2.11, 47; 4.29-31; 8.15-17; 9.11, 17;

Spirit is said to be caused by God in response to Jesus' prayer to him. Thus the narrator describes the descent of the Spirit upon the adult Jesus: 'the Holy Spirit descended upon him (καταβῆναι…ἐπ' αὐτόν)[85] in bodily form like a dove' (3.22a), which is placed between the narration of the opening of heaven (3.21) and of the heavenly voice (3.22b; cf. 9.35): 'You are [my] Son, the Beloved; with you I am well pleased' (σὺ εἶ ὁ υἱός ὁ ἀγαπητός, ἐν σοὶ εὐδόκησα).[86] In the present scene, the role of the Spirit is not explicitly delineated; we might assume that the coming of the Spirit like a dove[87] characterizes Jesus as God's agent, heralding the Kingdom of God as a new (covenantal) age. Also the adult Jesus, conceived through the Spirit, is additionally inspired by the Spirit, which indicates that the adult Jesus is understood to be inseparable from the inspiration of God's Holy Spirit in his forth-coming messianic mission.

10.1-4, 44-48; 13.2; cf. Wis. 7.7; 8.20-21; 9.4; Sir. 39.6-7): it is interesting to observe that as a textual variant of Lk. 11.2b, the clause ἐλθέτω ἡ βασιλεία is replaced with that of ελθετω το πνευμα σου το αγιον εφ ημας και καθαρισατω ημας ('May your Holy Spirit come upon us and purify us') in some minor manuscripts (162, 700), Marcion and some patristic writers (Gregory of Nyssa and Maximus the Confessor); (2) the Spirit is at times characterized as inspiring God's people to praise or pray to God (Lk. 1.46-55, 68-79; 2.28-32; 10.21-22; Acts 7.55-60; 10.46; cf. 2.4, 11). Lampe (1957: 169) describes prayer in Lukan writings as 'the means by which the dynamic energy of the Spirit is apprehended'; Shelton (1991: 87) comments, 'Spirit-empowerment is prefaced with and realized by prayer'. See also Smalley (1973: 64); Penney (1997a: 48-53); for the prayer-motif in Luke–Acts, see Trites (1978: 168-86). Cf. Crump (1992), who attempts to show that Jesus' unique role as the Messiah in relation to God and his people is discerned through his manner of prayer.

85. Luke, as does Mt. 3.16 (cf. 'into' [εἰς] in Mk 1.10), uses 'upon' (ἐπ') for the description of Jesus' endowment with the Holy Spirit, which does not, however, seem to have any significant impact on the scene. See Fitzmyer (1981: 484); Bock (1994b: 340).

86. This divine voice, i.e. God's voice addressing Jesus alone (see 'you' as the subject of God's address, as in Mk 1.11; cf. Mt. 3.17 where the heavenly voice is said to address Jesus' companions: 'this one') is reminiscent of both Ps. 2.7 (cf. Acts 4.25-26; 13.33) and Isa. 42.1 (possibly with 41.8 and 44.2; cf. Lk. 9.35 [ὁ υἱος μου ὁ ἐκλελεγμένος]; 23.35 [ὁ χριςτὸς τοῦ θεοῦ ὁ ἐκλεκτός]) in defining Jesus both as the regal Davidic-messianic figure and the Chosen Servant as the representative of the people of Israel (implied in both subsequent scenes in 3.23-38 and 4.1-12). See Bock (1987: 99-105); Fitzmyer (1981: 480-83; 485-86).

87. See §§5.1.2.2 and 5.1.2.4 in Chapter 4.

On the other hand, it can also be suggested that the content of the divine voice connotes the meaning/significance of the descent of the Spirit upon Jesus. Lk. 3.22 shows that God's voice (3.22b), following immediately after the coming of the Holy Spirit upon Jesus (3.22a), verifies Jesus as the (Davidic) regal Messiah (Ps. 2.7; cf. *Pss. Sol.* 17.23-24; 4Q174), anticipated in the prologue (1.27, 32-35, 69; 2.11), but also as endorsing Jesus as the servant Messiah (Isa. 42.1; cf. Acts 3.13, 26; 4.27, 30), who has a unique relationship to God. In this sense, *God's* Spirit is characterized in relation to *God's* voice, which verifies Jesus as the regal-Davidic servant Messiah.[88]

After the episode of Jesus' baptism, the narrator informs the reader of Jesus' age (about thirty years old) and his genealogy (3.23-38), which ends with the phrase the 'son of God', possibly pointing to Jesus' significance as the new Adam and faithful Son of God (see below).[89] This implicit indication is clarified by the subsequent narrative scene about Jesus' test by the devil.

Before recounting three temptations of Jesus, the narrator provides the double reference to the Spirit. By the phrases 'Jesus, full of the Holy Spirit (πλήρης πνεύματος ἁγίου),[90] returned from the Jordan' and 'led by the Spirit' (ἤγετο ἐν τῷ πνεύματι),[91] the narrator defines the Spirit as the empowering cause of Jesus' movement into the wilderness

88. In the reading process, the characterization or role of the Holy Spirit in 3.21-22 needs to be complemented or clarified in meaning when readers engage the subsequent episodes related to the Spirit, particularly on the grounds of Jesus' own understanding (Lk. 4.18-19) and that of Peter (Acts 10.38), i.e. the Spirit empowers Jesus for his (messianic) witness-mission.

89. See Danker (1988: 98); Schürmann (1984: 210-12); Johnson (1991: 71-72); Nolland (1989: I, 174); Bock (1994b: 348-50); Marshall (1978: 161).

90. See §5.2.1.2 in Chapter 4. On this phrase in 4.1, Turner (1996b: 202) suggests, 'It is probably intended by the narrator as a *general* characterization of Jesus' relationship to the Spirit in the ministry, from Jordan onwards' (emphasis original).

91. The comparison and its implication based on the different phrases used in Mk 1.12 (τὸ πνεῦμα αὐτὸν ἐκβάλλει) and Mt. 4.1 (ἀνήχθη...ὑπὸ τοῦ πνεύματος) against Lk. 4.1b have been overemphasized by Schweizer (1968: 404-405; i.e. the Lukan Jesus is portrayed as the Lord of the Spirit, whereas the Jesus in Mark and Matthew as simply the pneumatic Lord); this view is rightly criticized with a rather different nuance by Turner (1980: 81-83; 1996b: 202-204) and Menzies (1991a: 155-57), noting that (1) Luke's verb ἤγετο is used in a passive form; (2) the phrases of ἐν τῷ πνεύματι and ὑπὸ τοῦ πνεύματος are used in Luke as functional equivalents (cf. Lk. 2.26-27).

where he is tested by the devil. This description explains that Jesus' activity is inseparable from the power of the Spirit after his reception of the Spirit in his baptism. In regard to Jesus' powerful self-witness[92] as God's true Son based on quotations from Scripture,[93] the narrative also implies that the Holy Spirit inspires Jesus to resist the devil's tests (cf. 4.14). Thus, Marshall (1978: 169) rightly comments on Lk. 4.1 in relation to the Spirit as follows: 'The role of the Spirit is primarily guidance, but there is no reason to exclude the thought of his powerful inspiration which (for Luke) enabled Jesus to overcome the tempter'.[94] This temptation scene thus intimates that Jesus' conflict with the devil results in confirmation of himself as the 'Son of God' with the 'help' of the Holy Spirit and ends with the devil's temporarily leaving Jesus (cf. Lk. 22.3). In summary, the Spirit is presented as empowering, guiding and inspiring Jesus to encounter patiently and overcome successfully the three temptations of the devil, and so himself to bear witness as God's true son and faithful agent.

4.3.3. *Summary*. The 'Beginning' stage starts with John who fulfils his role as a (forerunner) prophetic-witness to Jesus, *inspired by the Spirit* as predicted in Lk. 1.15, 17, in preparing for the 'way of the Lord' (cf. 1.76-77; 7.27),[95] Jesus (3.15-17). The four remaining references to the

92. Readers may perceive that the account of Jesus' tests by the devil serves to confirm Jesus' self-identity. In contrast with both Adam (Gen. 3) and the people of Israel (Exod. 14.10-17; 16; Deut. 8), who are said to rebel and grieve God's holy Spirit (Isa. 63.7-14; cf. Acts 7.51), Jesus is represented as the new Adam and the true/faithful Son of God under the auspices of the Holy Spirit.

93. For the relationship between the Spirit-inspired characters and scriptural citations, see §3.3.1.4 in Chapter 3.

94. See also Fitzmyer (1981: 513): 'He conquers the devil, because he is filled with the Spirit...Luke not only notes Jesus' endowment, but makes it clear that his experience in the desert was under the aegis of God's Spirit'; Lampe (1957: 170); Shelton (1991: 58-60); Turner (1996b: 204), noting Luke's use of imperfect ἤγετο in comparison with Matthew's aorist, claims, 'Jesus was continually led 'in the Spirit' *while he was in the wilderness locked in his conflict with the devil'* (emphasis original). Furthermore, he (208-209) attempts to connect the influence of the Holy Spirit in Jesus' victory in the tests in 4.1-13 with 'ethical empowering' under the Isaianic New Exodus motif (esp. Isa. 42.1-9; 49.1-13; 50.4-11; 52.13-53.12; cf. Isa. 63.10-11; 11.1-2).

95. In the process of the plot, the message of John's preaching, 'a baptism of repentance for the forgiveness of sins' (3.3) along with 'good news' (3.18) to the people, is presented as taken over by the coming Messiah Jesus (5.17-32; 24.47; cf.

Spirit found in this stage are then used in association with the adult Jesus. So the Spirit is characterized as inspiring, empowering and leading Jesus to make him ready to inaugurate his public 'way of witness' to salvation: Jesus is *inspired (or verified) as God's unique agent* (i.e. the regal-Davidic servant Messiah) *by the Spirit* at the Jordan river; *empowered and guided by the Spirit* in order to overcome the tests by the devil in the wilderness of Judea, *which thus shows how the Spirit-inspired Jesus himself testifies* as God's faithful Son. In this way, the Spirit-inspired Jesus is singled out as the most active and reliable character (in witnessing to God and himself). The narrator thus sets forth the basic frames of the narrative function of the Spirit in relation to Jesus' messianic task, which will be clarified further in the next plot-stage.

4.4. *Development towards the Central Point (Lk. 4.14–19.44): Jesus' Witness-Journey from Galilee to Jerusalem*

The narrator sets forth the second plot-stage by introducing the beginning of Jesus' public ministry in Galilee (4.14; cf. 23.5; Acts 10.37) and ends it by reporting that Jesus (and his followers) arrives at Jerusalem (19.44; cf. Acts 13.31) as the destination of his journey (9.51; 13.22; 17.11; 18.31; 19.11, 28). The stage can thus be divided into two narrative subsections set by a geographical shift from Jesus' mission in Galilee[96] (4.14-9.50) and his witness-journey towards Jerusalem (9.51–19.44).[97]

Six references to the Spirit are found in this second stage: 4.14, 18; 10.21; 11.13; 12.10, 12. The first three references are associated with Jesus, whereas the last three are used in foreshadowing the future

Acts 2.38; 26.20), and developed by him and his followers (4.18-19; 7.22-23; Acts 2.38; 4.10-12; 10.36-43; 26.23).

96. There is one exceptional episode that shows that Jesus and his disciples cross the lake of Galilee to the region of the Gerasenes, i.e. 'which is opposite Galilee', in Lk. 8.20. Nevertheless, it is remarkable to notice that Jesus' mission depicted in Lk. 4.14–9.50 is almost never outside of Galilee in contrast to Mark and Matthew (e.g. Mk 8.27 and Mt. 16.13 against Lk. 9.18; Mk 9.30 against Lk. 9.43). Note the so-called 'Great Omission' of Lk. 6.20–8.40 from Mk 6.45–8.26.

97. In the central section of the Gospel, the so called 'travel narrative', the ending, unlike that of the beginning (9.51), has been diversely identified: 18.14, 30, 34; 19.10, 27, 40/41, 44, 48. For scholars' positions with their arguments, see Resseguie (1975: 3-36); Nolland (1993: II, 525-31); Bock (1994b: 957-64).

A Dynamic Reading

ministry of his disciples. I shall particularly focus on the episode in the Nazareth synagogue described in 4.16-30, for this programmatic narrative unit[98] generates the narrative function of the Spirit for the causal aspect of the plot, so, in relation to Jesus' whole earthly witness-mission initiated and developed at this plot-stage and accomplished in the next.

4.4.1. *Jesus' Witness, his Disciples' Future Witness and the Spirit.* The narrator, before presenting Jesus' sermon in the Nazareth synagogue, provides the reference to the Spirit in a summary statement (4.14-15) about Jesus' public ministry in Galilee: 'And Jesus returned in the power of the Spirit (ἐν τῇ δυνάμει τοῦ πνεύματος) into Galilee' (RSV; 4.14a). On the one hand, this verse suggests that the Spirit leads Jesus to Galilee (cf. 2.27; 4.1); on the other, the next verse suggests that the Spirit is also seen as inspiring Jesus to teach: 'And he taught in their synagogues, being glorified by all'. In addition, the expression 'power of the Spirit'[99] may indicate the essential nature of the Spirit: the Spirit is presented as (God's)[100] δύναμις (cf. 1.35; 4.36; 24.49; Acts 1.18; 4.33; 6.3-10). This implies that Jesus' power (and authority: 4.32, 36; 5.24; 7.8; 9.1; 10.19; Acts 8.19) is inseparable from the power of the Spirit (caused by God), particularly in relation to his performing healings and exorcisms (4.36; 5.17; 6.19; 8.46; 9.1; 10.13, 19; 19.37; Acts 2.22). This view is then supported not only by Jesus' own understanding of his Spirit-empowered commission by God (4.18-19; see below), but also by Peter's retrospective summary statement about Jesus' whole earthly ministry: 'That message spread throughout Judea, beginning in Galilee after the baptism that John announced: how God anointed Jesus of Nazareth with *the Holy Spirit and with power*; how he went about *doing good and healing* all who were suppressed by the devil, for God was with him' (Acts 10.37-38). Hence, the Spirit, in this context, is not only characterized as guiding and inspiring Jesus to go to

98. Cf. Luke's 'narrative order' of this episode as the introductory statement for Jesus' public ministry in comparison with Mk 6.1-6 and Mt. 13.53-58. For the significance of Lk. 4.16-30 in the overall picture of the Gospel (and even of Acts), see the following scholarly works to mention a few: Hill (1971: 161); Tannehill (1972: 51-75); Combrink (1973: 39); Sloan (1977: 1); Schreck (1989: 399-400); Siker (1992: 73-90); Kim (1993: 57); Prior (1995: 15 and chapter 7).
99. See §5.1.1.4 in Chapter 4.
100. See §2.1.2 in Chapter 2.

and teach in Galilee, but also defined as God's power in relation to Jesus' activity.

In the second reference to the Spirit, the nature of Jesus' identity and mission is more vividly characterized in close relation to the Spirit through his scriptural citation[101] of Isa. 61.1-2 along with 58.6d, as described in Lk. 4.18-19. In this way, the narrator re-interprets the significance of Jesus' baptism in the Spirit and unfolds the essential narrative function of the Spirit in relation to the causal aspect of the plot: empowering Jesus for his messianic witness through his mighty words and deeds (cf. 24.19; Acts 2.22).

4.18   The Spirit of the Lord is upon me
        because he has anointed me
            to preach good news to the poor.
        He has sent me
            [to heal the broken hearted]
            to proclaim liberty to the captives and sight to the blind
            to set at liberty the oppressed (Isa. 58.6d)
4.19   to *proclaim* the acceptable year of the Lord.
            [and the day of vengeance of our Lord][102]

By this citation of Isa. 61.1-2, Jesus himself (and the narrator) understands his Spirit-baptism at the Jordan as prophetic anointing[103] to carry

101. The citation of the LXX Isa. 61.1-2 (plus 58.6d) in Lk. 4.18-19 includes some changes: (1) two omissions from Isa. 61.1 (ἰάσασθαι τοὺς συντετριμμένους τῇ καρδίᾳ: 'to heal the broken hearted') and 61.2 (καὶ ἡμέραν ἀνταποδόσεως: 'and the day of recompense of our God'), (2) one addition at the end of Lk. 4.18 from the LXX 58.6d (ἀποστεῖλαι τεθραυσμένους ἐν ἀφέσει: 'to set the oppressed at liberty') and (3) one change at 4.19 from the word καλέσαι ('to announce') to κηρῦξαι ('to proclaim'). For this alteration with regard to the understanding of the Holy Spirit in this context, Menzies (1991a: 161-77) ascribes it to Lukan redaction; by contrast, Turner (1996b: 215-26) refers it to Lukan special sources (i.e. not to Q).

102. [Brackets] mean an omission from Isa. 61.1-2; underlined words an addition; *italics* a verbal change.

103. The nature of 'Jesus' anointing' with the Spirit is primarily 'prophetic' (cf. Isa. 61.1-2 [Isaiah himself?] and Lk. 4.24-27 [Elijah and Elisha; cf. 7.16; Acts 3.22]), yet also 'messianic' within the overall image of Jesus in Luke–Acts (2.11; 3.22; Acts 4.27; 5.42; 9.22; 17.13; 18.5). Thus, Nolland (1989: I, 196) points out, 'Luke thinks in both prophetic and messianic terms...though in the immediate pericope the prophetic thought is predominant'. Cf. Fitzmyer (1981: 529-30), who denies a Servant or a royal image, but argues that Jesus is presented as a prophetic figure as well as the 'herald' of good news in Isa. 52.7 who appears as one 'anointed with the Spirit' in 11Q13 18. Bock (1987: 109-11) and Strauss (1995:

out his messianic mission: God has endorsed and commissioned him (4.43; 10.16, 22; 11.20; 22.29; cf. 8.39; 9.20; 20.9-18) as the prophetic Messiah *empowered by God's Spirit* (see Acts 10.38). It is probable that the first clause in 4.18a is an introductory statement that is then explained in the following clause (see also Jesus' summary statement about his commission by God in 4.43). Regardless of either punctuation,[104] the Spirit is thus characterized as empowering Jesus: (1) to preach good news to the poor, (2) to proclaim liberty (ἄφεσις)[105] to the captives and sight to the blind, (3) to set at liberty (ἄφεσις) the oppressed and (4) to proclaim the acceptable year of the Lord.[106] At first glance, this characterization of the mission of Jesus seems to restrict it to his preaching/ proclamation or teaching; however, the continuing narrative suggests his performing miracles should also be included (cf. 4.31-44; 5.15; 6.17), for his authoritative words are to be actualized through his mighty works (e.g. 5.20-26; 7.22; 8.42-56). In other words, Jesus' healings and exorcisms are viewed as part of his preaching the good news to the poor (e.g. 7.22) or proclaiming the Kingdom of God (e.g. 11.20). The words 'poor', 'captives', 'blind' and 'oppressed' are thus understood as both literal and metaphorical.[107] In this way, Jesus can be identified with the Spirit-empowered Isaianic prophet,[108] actualizing

231) aver that Lk. 4.18-19 also contains kingly motifs as well as prophetic.

104. Agreeing with Turner (1996b: 221 n. 22), I follow the UBS text, which places a stop after the word πτωχοῖς (cf. both Marshall [1978: 183] and Menzies [1991a: 163 n. 3], who prefer to put a stop after ἔχρισέν με).

105. Jesus' messianic mission is here tied to the Jubilee theme of 'liberation' or 'release' from various types of oppression (Isa. 58.6; 61.1; Lev. 25; cf. 1 Esd. 4.62; 1 Macc. 10.34; 13.34). See Sloan (1977: 4-27; 38-41). Cf. Turner (1996b: 226-32), who argues that 4.18-27 is pre-Lukan tradition (i.e. not Luke's redaction) and then attempts to connect the interpretation of Isa. 61.1-2 in 11Q13, 4Q521 and 4Q431 with that of Lk. 4.18-27 in order to appreciate Jesus within the context of Jewish eschatological Jubilee and New Exodus hopes.

106. For the use of the verbs, εὐαγγελίζομαι and κηρύσσω, in Luke–Acts, see n. 21 in this chapter.

107. Cf. Simeon's portrait of Jesus as 'a *light* for revelation to the Gentiles and for glory to your people Israel' (2.32); see also Paul's witness: 'he [Jesus] would proclaim *light* both to our people and to the Gentiles' (Acts 26.23b). For this theme, see Hamm (1986: 458-71). Jesus' mission is seen to continue through his witnesses, esp. Paul (see Acts 26.17-18: 'I [the risen Jesus] am sending you *to open their eyes* so that they may turn *from darkness to light* and from the power of Satan to God').

108. This Isaianic prophet is also congruent with Moses (Lk. 7.16—Deut. 18.15; Acts 2.22//7.36; 3.20-24; 7.22//Lk. 24.19) and Elijah (Lk. 7.11—1 Kgs 17.9-10; Lk.

Isa. 61.1-2 in his present salvific mission by proclaiming the Kingdom
of God and God's salvation to the Israelites by means of miraculous
deeds[109] and authoritative words.[110] The Spirit therefore is understood
to empower Jesus for his whole ministry commissioned by God as the
Davidic(regal)-messianic figure (1.32-35; 2.11; 3.22a based on Ps. 2.7),
the Chosen Servant (3.22b based on Isa. 42.1) and the eschatological
prophetic (Isaianic, Elijianic and Mosaic) Messiah (4.18-19 based on
Isa. 61.1-2 and 58.6; cf. Acts 3.22).[111]

The Nazareth episode thus reveals that the narrator not only re-
interprets the meaning and significance of Jesus' baptism in the Holy
Spirit by linking Jesus' citation of Isa. 61.1-2 to his anointing experience, but also understands the phrase 'Holy' Spirit (3.22; cf. the 'Spirit'
in Mk. 1.10; the 'Spirit of God' in Mt. 3.16) as the 'Spirit of the Lord'
or 'God's Spirit'.[112] If we take into consideration the import of this episode in the immediate contexts and the rest of the plot, we can discern
that the narrator attempts to represent, not exclusively but mainly, both
Jesus' reception of the Spirit at the Jordan and his entire public ministry
in the light of the prophetic empowering for mission: the Spirit equips
Jesus as God's agent *par excellence* to carry out his messianic witness.[113] In other words, the Holy Spirit is characterized as God's Holy
Spirit who empowers and guides Jesus during his whole ministry to

7.15–1 Kgs 17.23) in the subsequent narrative. In regard to this, Allison (1993: 39-
45) argues that some overlapping traits between Moses and Elijah exist even in the
Hebrew Bible (1 Kgs 17–19; 2 Kgs 1–2) and also later in Jewish traditions (e.g.
Pes. R. 4.2). In addition, he (69-71) also claims several features of this Mosaic
image are found in the Deutero-Isaianic servant.

109. For various miracles seen as 'offering salvation', see esp. Lk. 5.17-26; 7.11-
17; 8.16-39, 42-28; 49-56; 17.11-19; 18.35-43.

110. Jesus' own speech inspired by the Spirit (4.17-21) is depicted as gradually
realized at this plot-stage: to preach good news to the poor/captives/blind in proclaiming or teaching the Kingdom of God (4.32, 43-44; 5.3, 17; 6.6, 20-49; 8.1;
9.11a; 13.10, 22; cf. Jesus' forgiving sins in 5.20; 7.43-50), and performing healings (4.39, 40; 5.13, 24-25; 6.10, 18-19; 7.10, 15, 21-22; 8.2, 43-48, 54-55; 9.11b;
13.11-13; 14.3-4; 17.12-14; 18.35-43; cf. 19.37) and exorcisms (4.35, 41; 8.32-33;
9.41-42; 11.14, 20; cf. other miracles in 5.5-6; 8.24-25; 9.16-17).

111. Marshall (1970: 125-28): 'The result has been to show that Luke took up a
view of Jesus which saw Him not merely as a prophet but as the final prophet, the
Servant and the Messiah' (128; see also 1976: 54); Turner (1996b: 233-50).

112. See §5.1.1.1 in Chapter 4.

113. Bruce 1973: 167-78.

bear witness to God (and himself) in accordance with God's will/plan (cf. 4.43; 7.16; 8.39;10.16, 22; Acts 10.38).

It is thus not surprising that the narrator, from the Nazareth episode onwards, does not mention the Holy Spirit in relation to Jesus' activity with one exception in 10.21a: 'At that same hour Jesus rejoiced in the Holy Spirit and said' (Ἐν αὐτῇ τῇ ὥρᾳ ἠγαλλιάσατο ἐν τῷ πνεύματι τῷ ἁγίῳ καὶ εἶπεν). This clause appears to link the preceding seventy (-two)[114] disciples' mission (10.17-20) to Jesus' following praise to God (vv. 21-22). In the immediate context, the Holy Spirit is characterized as causing Jesus to be joyful (cf. Lk. 1.44; Acts 13.52)[115] and to give inspired speech/praise (or prayer) in response to God's mighty acts. It should not, however, be missed that Jesus' Spirit-inspired joy, on the one hand, results from the successful mission of the disciples sent through *his* power and authority (10.19; cf. 9.1-2);[116] his inspired

114. The manuscripts are evenly divided between 'seventy' and 'seventy-two'; see Metzger (1975: 150-51). Either case, however, suggests the geographical expansion in the subsequent narrative especially in Acts. The twelve disciples of Jesus are, as it were, to replace the twelve tribes of Israel, while the number of seventy (cf. Exod. 24.1; Num. 11.16-17, 24-25) or seventy-two (the LXX Gen. 10; *3 En.* 17.8; 18.2-3; 30.2) implies the world-wide mission based on the Jewish 'Table of Nations'. For details, see Marshall (1978: 414-15); Fitzmyer (1985: 845-46); Scott (1994: 524-25).

115. The verb ἀγαλλιάω is found four times in Luke–Acts and is used in similar contexts in 1.47 [Mary]; Acts 2.26 [David] with one exception at Acts 16.34. Cf. the rabbinic evidence, 'the Holy Spirit rests only on a joyful man' (*y. Suk.* 5.55a, 54), possibly influenced by the LXX Ps. 51.13-14 (MT; 50.13-14), cited in Menzies (1991a: 180 n. 4). See also §5.2.1.1 in Chapter 4.

116. Turner (1980: 86-88; 1996b: 265 n. 164) overstates that the phrase in 10.21a implies the Spirit's work in the disciples *before Pentecost*; Shepherd (1994: 139; see also 131 n. 90) follows his view in saying that 'The joy sparked by the Spirit underscores the presence of the Spirit among the seventy(-two) disciples'. See Menzies' (1991a: 182 n. 3) critique of Turner's view. It is not impossible to argue that the disciples may feel the presence/power of the Spirit when they are said to perform healings and exorcisms. However, the following evidence suggests that the narrator is reluctant to connect the disciples' works with the Spirit *before Pentecost*: (1) he explicitly mentions '*Jesus*' power and authority' as the source of their mission (9.1; 10.19; see also the expression '*Jesus*' name' in 10.17; cf. 'a man' [τινα] who is not following Jesus and his disciples is also said to cast out demons in Jesus' name in 9.49); (2) they are not yet described as fully reliable characters in the Gospel as in Acts (e.g. 9.41; 18.34; 24.38; see §3.3.2 in Chapter 3); (3) in relation to 11.13 (the gift of the Spirit as God's answer to human prayer), it is noted that the disciples in the Gospel are described as those who fail to pray (9.28, 32;

speech, on the other, bears witness to himself as Son who has the authority of God the Father: 'All things have been handed over to me by my Father; and no one knows who the Son is except the Father, or who the Father is except the Son and anyone to whom the Son chooses to reveal him' (10.22; cf. 5.24; 9.48; 10.16). In this way, this reference to the Spirit in 10.21 thus not only confirms Jesus' (unique) relationship to God, but also foreshadows the intimate relationship between (the risen) Jesus' power and authority and the Spirit in connection with the future witness-mission of Jesus' disciples in the next two stages. This might be the reason why the narrator offers the unusual reference to the Spirit in relation to Jesus' activity in the midst of his ministry.

In addition, the narrator also provides three anticipating references to the Spirit in relation to Jesus' disciples: 11.13 and 12.8-12(×2).[117]

22.39, 45-46; in contrast, see Jesus' prayer in 5.16; 6.12; 9.18, 28-29; 11.1; 22.41-45; 23.34, 46; cf. 22.31-32 and the disciples' prayer in Acts, e.g. 1.14; 2.47; 3.1; 4.24-31; 7.55-60; 8.15; 9.11; 10.9, 19; 13.1-2) in spite of their asking Jesus how to pray in the Gospel (11.1). So in terms of the plot-development, the narrator reserves the reference to the Spirit (and prayer) in relation to Jesus' disciples until after his departure.

117. I briefly note the contexts in 11.13 and 12.8-12 in comparison with the other Synoptic writers: (1) Lk. 11.13 shows that Jesus, while teaching his disciples how to pray, refers to the specific good gift, namely the Holy Spirit (cf. Mt. 7.11—'good things' in a different narrative context). In other words, the Lukan implied author sees 'receiving the Spirit' as the highest gift from God (cf. Acts 2.38; 8.20; 11.16-17) and closely associates it with prayer as seen throughout the narrative of Luke–Acts (see nn. 84, 116). On the other hand, by redaction criticism, most scholars explain the Holy Spirit in Lk. 11.13 as the Lukan redactional modification for the more original variant of 'good things' preserved in Mt. 7.11. See Fitzmyer (1985: 915-16); Menzies (1991a: 180-85). (2) Jesus' mentioning of the Holy Spirit to his disciples is also delineated in his account of the blasphemy against the Holy Spirit in Lk. 12.12. This Lukan context of 'blasphemy' is different from that of Mk 3.28-30 and Mt. 12.31-32; cf. 12.22-30: (i) In Luke, Jesus addresses his saying *to his disciples*, whereas both in Mark and Matthew he delivers it to his enemies, namely the scribes in Mark and the Pharisees in Matthew. (ii) In addition, blasphemy against the Holy Spirit in Luke is parallel to *the betrayal of Jesus* (e.g. Judas Iscariot in Luke; cf. the reference to both Jesus' prayer for Peter's faith and his prediction about Peter's disowning him in 22.31-34) or a *false witness* (e.g. Ananias and Sapphira in Acts) in times of trial, whereas in Mark and Matthew it applies to Jesus' casting out of demons through the Holy Spirit, i.e. God's power is regarded as Jesus' demon-possession (Satan's power). Cf. the context of the 'Beelzebul controversy', which is relocated in Lk. 11.14-26 by using the 'finger of God' instead of the 'Holy Spirit'. On this alteration of Luke, Menzies (1991a) claims, like

Noted is that these references to the Spirit are all given *directly by Jesus* to his disciples. In 11.13 the Holy Spirit is characterized as God's gift (cf. Acts 2.38; 8.20; 11.16-17),[118] caused by God the heavenly Father in response to his sons' (i.e. God's people's) earnest prayer (11.5-13; cf. Jesus' prayer in 3.21-22). On the other hand, Jesus, in 12.8-12, is said to mention the role of the Spirit as 'teaching'[119] his disciples 'what they ought to say' in future witness-contexts (τὸ γὰρ ἅγιον πνεῦμα διδάξει ὑμᾶς ἐν αὐτῇ ὥρᾳ ἃ δεῖ εἰπεῖν; cf. 21.15). In this sense, the characterization of the Spirit in relation to both the present mission of Jesus and the future mission of his witnesses is presented as analogous: the reception of the Spirit will be caused by God in answer to their prayer and the Spirit will inspire them to speak and act in their witness-mission.

Schweizer, that Luke intentionally dissociates the work of the Holy Spirit from miraculous power, saying 'Luke does, however, attribute healings and exorcisms to the δύναμις of God (Lk. 4.36; 5.17; 6.19; 8.46; 9.1; Acts 4.7; 6.8)... This would appear to indicate an important distinction between Luke's use of δύναμις and πνεῦμα'. (125; see also 196-98). However, his argument does not seem to be convincing, because there are several explicit references (e.g. Lk. 1.17, 35; 4.14; 24.49; Acts 1.8; 10.38) to evidence the intimate association between power and the Holy Spirit, although Menzies is even there forced to suggest 'a highly nuanced way' between the two. Turner (1996b: 255-59) thus rightly criticizes Menzies' argument with a probable explanation of the Lukan replacement of the Holy Spirit by the 'finger of God' (δακτύλῳ θεοῦ) in terms of the Lukan tendency to depict Jesus as the Mosaic prophet-messiah in the New Exodus motif (Exod. 8.19; cf. Isa. 49.24-25; 63.10; Ezek. 8.1-2); see also the frequent Lukan use of the expression in Lk. 1.66; Acts 4.28, 30; 7.50; 11.21; 13.11; cf. the 'arm of the Lord' in Lk. 1.31; Acts 13.17; for this explanation, see also Johnson (1991: 181-83). At any rate, it should be emphasized that the Lukan understanding of the blasphemy against the Holy Spirit closely links with the contexts of witness against Jesus in times of trial. Likewise, I may explain 'a mouth and wisdom' (στόμα καὶ σοφίαν) in Lk. 21.15 as fulfilled in Jesus' witnesses not only through revelatory visions given by (the exalted) *Jesus* ('for I [Jesus] will give you...'; cf. Acts 9.10, 15; 18.10-11; 22.18, 21; 23.11; cf. Exod. 4.12, 15), but also through the *Holy Spirit* as is seen in Lk. 12.12 ('for the Holy Spirit will teach you...'; cf. Acts 4.8-14; 6.3, 10; cf. 26.24-32). These two passages also hint at the intimate relationship and parallels between the activity of the exalted Jesus and that of the Holy Spirit in the future, i.e. in the witness-mission of Jesus' disciples in Acts (in terms of '*actant*', both the risen Jesus and the Holy Spirit in Acts are seen as 'sender' and 'helper'). See §5 in Chapter 5.

118. See §5.1.1.4 in Chapter 4.
119. See §5.1.2.2 in Chapter 4.

4.4.2. *Summary*. This plot-stage focuses on Jesus' Spirit-inspired public ministry, commissioned by God, launched in and moved from Galilee to Jerusalem. At the outset of this stage (4.14), the Spirit is characterized as *guiding and inspiring Jesus to go and teach* in Galilee; later (10.21), the Spirit is presented *as giving him joy and causing him to give an inspired speech or praise to God.* Most importantly, the narrator explains the characterization of the Holy Spirit in relation to Jesus' whole messianic witness-mission on earth by providing 4.18-19 as a paradigmatic narrative index: *the Spirit empowers him as God's agent for bearing witness to God and himself*[120] *through mighty words and deeds.*[121] Then, the narrator also prepares the coming plot-stages by connecting the other references to the Spirit in this stage with the future witness-mission of Jesus' disciples (11.13; 12.10, 12):[122] *the Spirit will be given/caused by God in response to their prayer and inspire their speeches in witness-contexts.* This characterization of the Spirit in relation to Jesus' disciples will thus be clarified further in terms of the causal aspect of the next plot-stages.

4.5. *Central Point (Lk. 19.45–Acts 2.13): Jesus' Self-Witness, his Reminding the Disciples of the Father's Promise and the Coming of the Holy Spirit in Jerusalem*
This central stage consists of six thematic episodes that all take place in the temple (19.45, 47; 20.1; 21.37, 38; [22.53]; 24.53) or Jerusalem

---

120. This stage shows that Jesus' mighty words and deeds function as witnessing to both God (5.26; 7.16, 29; 8.39a; 9.43; 13.13; 17.15; 18.43; cf. 19.37-38) and himself (4.14-15, 37; 5.15; 7.3, 17; 8.39b; see also 24.44-48; Acts 2.22).

121. From 'beginning' to 'central point', the references to the Spirit (10 times) are always used in relation to Jesus (cf. 11.13 and 12.10-12 are narrated *by Jesus*). Jesus is thus depicted not only as a Spirit-led/inspired character, but also as a Spirit-bearer (in the later stage, he will be viewed as a Spirit-sender who fulfils John's witness to him, i.e. as a Spirit-baptizer).

122. The narrator shows that Peter is first chosen and commanded by Jesus to 'catch people' (Lk. 5.10). Peter and the other members of the twelve disciples are also recorded as chosen by Jesus (Lk. 6.12-16). This means that the twelve disciples as witnesses *have seen and heard* what Jesus is doing and saying. In this regard, this type-scene provides the pattern of 'being caught oneself (i.e. by Jesus) first and catching others (i.e. 'bearing witness' to Jesus) later' (Lk. 24.13-35, 44-48; Acts 1.21-22; 9.1-22). Meanwhile, Jesus addresses and shows to the would-be disciples that following him (i.e. being a witness and then bearing witness to Jesus) requires sacrifice and suffering, which might even lead to death (Lk. 9.23-27; 14.26-27, 33; 18.28-30; cf. Acts 7; 12.2 and *passim*).

(22.10; 23.7, 28; 24.13, 18, 33, 52; Acts 1.4, 12; 2.5): (1) Jesus' teaching (19.45-22.46), (2) his arrest and trial (22.47-23.43), (3) his death (23.44-56), (4) his resurrection (24.1-49; Acts 1.3-5), (5) his ascension (24.44-56; Acts 1.6-11) and (6) Jesus' disciples' waiting for the coming of the Holy Spirit (Acts 1.12-2.13). In these contexts,[123] explicit references to the Spirit occur six times, all found in Acts: 1.2, 5, 8, 16; 2.4a, 4b.

At the beginning of Acts, the narrator summarizes the Gospel by reminding the reader of Jesus' earthly ministry and indicating that Jesus' post-resurrection teaching to his apostles was given/caused by the inspiration of the Spirit: 'I wrote about all that Jesus did and taught from the beginning until the day when he was taken up to heaven, after giving instructions through the Holy Spirit to the apostles whom he had chosen (ἐντειλάμενος τοῖς ἀποστόλοις διὰ πνεύματος ἁγίου οὓς ἐξελέξατο ἀνελήμφθη)' (1.1b-2).[124] The Spirit is thus presented here as inspiring Jesus' post-resurrection instructions to the apostles. This suggests that, after his resurrection, both Jesus' witnessing to himself (Lk. 24.44-47; Acts 1.3) and his commissioning his disciples (Lk. 24.48-49; Acts 1.4, 8) are inspired by the Spirit.

---

123. From the outset of Jesus' journey towards Jerusalem the implied author appears to design such episodes in order to highlight the account of Jesus' ascension as the final goal of his earthly ministry (for some parallels between Lk. 9 and Acts 1, see Talbert [1974: 114-15; 61-62]). The account of Jesus' ascension is also regarded as a narrative centre that interlaces the Gospel with Acts (Parsons [1987: 185; see also 198]: 'The ascension, then, describes the journey of Jesus into heaven and the journey of the church into the world'); Maddox (1982: 10); cf. Prior (1995: 24), who names the ascension as 'hinge' in offering an architectonic narrative chart for Luke–Acts, which, as he admits, does not embrace the early part of Lk. 1–4.13. It is at this linchpin of the plot-development that the (implicit and explicit) references to the Holy Spirit occur.

124. Among scholars the opinions on the syntactical role of 'through the Holy Spirit' in Acts 1.2 (διὰ πνεύματος ἁγίου is placed between ἐντειλάμενος and ἐξελέξατο) are divided: Conzelmann (1987: 3); Barrett (1994: 69); Shelton (1991: 119); Menzies (1991a: 200); Dunn (1996: 6) opt for the former: 'giving instructions through the Holy Spirit', whereas Marshall (1991a: 57); Schneider (1980: 192); Haenchen (1971: 139) prefer to take this phrase with '(the apostles) whom he had chosen through the Holy Spirit'. Cf. Johnson (1992: 24), who, in an intermediate position, suggests 'that it modifies both, which is probably what the author intended it to do...Luke sees all of Jesus' activities as directed by the Spirit (Luke 4.1, 14, 18, 36; 10.21)'.

However, readers should not miss the implicit reference to the Spirit found twice in the Gospel and once in Acts: the 'promise of my/the father' in Lk. 24.49a, Acts 1.4 and 'power from on high' in Lk. 24.49b, which shed light on exploring the narrative function of the Spirit in relation to the causal aspect of the next plot-stages.

4.5.1. *The Promise of my/the Father, Power from on High and the Holy Spirit*

> Then he [Jesus] opened their minds to understand the Scriptures, and said to them [Jesus' disciples], 'Thus it is written, that the Christ should suffer and on the third day rise from the dead, and that repentance and forgiveness of sins should be preached in his name to all nations, beginning from Jerusalem. You are witnesses (ὑμεῖς μάρτυρες) of these things. And behold, I send *the promise of my Father* (τὴν ἐπαγγελίαν τοῦ πατρός μου) upon you; but stay in the city, until you are clothed with *power from on high* (ἐξ ὕψους δύναμιν)' (Lk. 24.45-48; RSV).
>
> And while staying with them he [Jesus] charged them [Jesus' disciples] not to depart from Jerusalem, but to wait for *the promise of the Father* (τὴν ἐπαγγελίαν τοῦ πατρὸς), which, he said, 'you heard from me, for John baptized with water, but before many days you shall be baptized with *the Holy Spirit*'. So when they had come together, they asked him, 'Lord, will you at this time restore the kingdom to Israel?' He said to them, 'It is not for you to know times or seasons which the Father has fixed by his own authority. But you shall receive *power* (δύναμιν) when *the Holy Spirit* has come upon you; and you shall be my witnesses (μου μάρτυρες) in Jerusalem and in all Judea and Samaria and to the end of the earth' (Acts 1.4-8; RSV).

At first glance, it is not clear what the right connotation of the 'promise of my Father' and/or 'power from on high' is at the end of the Gospel. The reader, however, is compelled to identify the 'promise of my Father' and/or 'power from on high' with the Holy Spirit when coming to the beginning of Acts (1.4-5, 8; cf. 2.33, 39; 9.17; cf. Isa. 32.15).[125] In this way, the implied author attempts to show that the disciples, like Jesus (Lk. 3.21-22; 4.18-19), are to be empowered by the Spirit (Acts 1.5, 8)[126] in order to continue to develop his way of witness. So, the Spirit is characterized as the Spirit promised by God (cf. God's gift in

---

125. See §5.1.1.4 in Chapter 4.

126. Acts 1.5, 8 implies that Jesus (and the narrator) interprets John's prophecy about his baptism in Lk. 3.16 in terms of empowering the disciples to witness through the Spirit (cf. Peter's understanding in Acts 2.33, 38; 11.16-18; see below).

Lk. 11.13; see Joel 2.28-32//Acts 2.16-21 in the next stage), and is characterized as God's power (see Lk. 1.35; 4.14; Acts 10.38). This empowerment by the Spirit of the disciples implies that their witness will be sanctioned by God (cf. the 'promise *of my Father*' and 'power *from on high*'; see also Acts 2.22). In other words, their witness to Jesus to the ends of the earth (cf. Isa. 49.6; 24.16; 45.22; 48.20; 62.11) is to be advanced in accordance with the plan of God (e.g. Acts 8.29; 11.17-18; 13.4; 15.8; 16.6-7; 19.21; cf. 27.23-24).

These contexts, however, do not indicate the present role of the Spirit, but point forward to the *future* role/function of the Spirit in relation to Jesus' disciples unfolded in the next stages. In relation to the causal aspect of the plot, the reader is thus prepared to expect that the Spirit, already characterized as empowering Jesus in the previous stage, will be presented as empowering the disciples to bear witness to the resurrected Jesus (see 'in *his* [Jesus'] name' in Lk. 24.47; '*my* [Jesus'] witnesses' in Acts 1.8)[127] in proclaiming the salvific message (i.e. 'repentance and forgiveness of sins'[128]) and performing miracles (for this connotation of 'power', see my discussion in Lk. 4.14, 18-19)[129] to the ends of the earth.

---

127. For instance, in Acts witness is chiefly used as 'my [Jesus'] witness', 'witness for Jesus' and 'witness for what God has done for/through Jesus' (see 1.8, 22; 2.32; 3.15; 5.32; 10.39, 41; 22.15, 20; 26.16; cf. 13.31; 14.3; 23.11). In addition, it could be assumed that Jesus' disciples/witnesses would teach about Jesus in relation to the Kingdom of God (see Acts 8.12; 28.23, 31; possibly 19.8; the other references to the Kingdom of God as the message of Jesus and his witnesses are found in Acts 1.3; 14.22; 20.25; cf. 1.6).

128. This message is consistently conveyed by John the Baptist, Jesus and his witnesses throughout Luke–Acts: Lk. 3.3, 8; 5.32; 10.13; 11.32; 13.3, 5; 15.7, 10; 16.30; 17.3-4; 24.47; Acts 2.38; 3.19; 5.31; 8.32; 10.43; 11.18; 13.24, 38; 17.30; 19.4; 20.21; 26.18, 20.

129. This two-fold ascension narrative thus discloses two essential points for the development of the plot: (1) Jesus' witness-mission is to be taken over by his disciples/witnesses. In this transition, Jesus' mission for the Kingdom of God (45 references to the Kingdom of God in the Gospel are found in 1.33; 4.5, 43; 6.20; 7.28; 8.1, 10; 9.2, 11, 27, 60, 62; 10.9, 11; 11.2, 17, 18, 20; 12.31, 32; 13.18, 20, 28, 29; 14.15; 16.16; 17.20a, 20b, 21; 18.16, 17, 24, 25, 29; 19.11, 12, 15; 21.10, 31; 22.16, 18, 29, 30; 23.42, 51; in Acts there are 8: see n. 127) is to be given through his disciples' witness to the risen and exalted Jesus as already anticipated in Lk. 9.1-6 and 10.1-20. (2) Jesus' commission to his disciples reveals that their forthcoming mission to proclaim the message of 'repentance and forgiveness of sins' should not be confined to Jews, but be extended to 'all nations' (εἰς πάντα τὰ ἔθνη

4.5.2. *The Coming of the Holy Spirit: Narrator's Description*. The final
episode in the central stage presents the narrator's account of the coming of the Holy Spirit on the day of Pentecost (Acts 2.1-13).[130] This
episode consists of two parts: the first part (Acts 2.1-4) introduces the
audible and visible phenomena of the coming of the Holy Spirit and the
disciples' reception of the Holy Spirit at Pentecost;[131] the second (Acts
2.5-13) recounts the reaction of the crowd at Jerusalem. In the second
part, the Spirit is presented as causing the disciples to speak in other
tongues 'the mighty works of God' (τὰ μεγαλεῖα τοῦ θεοῦ in Acts
2.11).[132] 'And they[133] were all filled with the Holy Spirit (καὶ

in Lk. 24.47) and the 'ends of the earth' (ἕως ἐσχάτου τῆς γῆς in Acts 1.8), which
echoes the prediction by the reliable and inspired character Simeon in the early part
of the Gospel (2.30-32; cf. 4.24-27). The exact meaning of 'the ends of the earth' in
Acts 1.8 does not seem to indicate simply Rome, although the narrative ends with
the episode about Paul's arrival and bearing witness in Rome (*Pss. Sol.* 8.15 refers
to Rome by the phrase ἤγαγεν τὸν [Pompey the Great] ἀπ᾽ ἐσχάτου τῆς γῆς; cf.
Deut. 28.49; Ps. 134.6-7; Isa. 8.9; 14.21-22; Jer. 10.12; 16.19; 1 Macc. 3.9): the
phrase may refer to Rome as one example (not as an end in itself) of the ends of the
earth when we have in mind the narrative features in Acts 28 properly seen as
an open-ended account. See Barrett (1994: 80); Johnson (1992: 26-27); Dunn
(1996: 11).
    130. It has been disputed among scholars whether the Lukan account of Pente-
cost is affected by Jewish Sinai traditions, i.e. Jesus' giving the Spirit instead of
Moses' giving the Law to establish a new covenant. There is, in fact, possible evidence (*Jub.* 1.1-2; 6.19; 1QS 1.8-2.18; 4Q266; cf. 2 Chron. 15.10-12; Exod. 19.1)
about the celebration of Moses' giving of the law at Sinai on the day of Pentecost
before the destruction of the temple. The probable relationship between the account
of Pentecost in Acts and the Sinai traditions is also sustained by the similar visible
and audible phenomena (e.g. 'sound/wind', 'fire', 'voice', 'language' etc.) depicted
in these two episodes: e.g. Philo, *Dec.* 32-36, 44-46; *Spec. Leg.* 2.188-89; *Targ.
Ps.-J.* on Exod. 20.2; *b. Shab.* 88b. See Lake (1933b: 115-16); Betz (1967: 93); Le
Déaut (1970: 263-66); Dunn (1970a: 47-49); Dupont (1979: 39-45); Haenchen
(1971: 174); Maddox (1982: 138); Turner (1996b: 279-85). Contra Lohse (1968:
48-50); Noack (1962: 80); Marshall (1977: 347-49); Menzies (1991a: 229-41);
Barrett (1994: 111-12): the latter scholars, arguing that only after the destruction of
the Temple did the Jews begin to commemorate the giving of the law at Pentecost,
have thus claimed that the Lukan pentecostal episode did not intend to establish a
'new covenant' motif in replacing the law given by Moses with the Spirit by Jesus.
For Jesus as 'new Moses', see also n. 161 in this chapter.
    131. See §5.1.2.4 in Chapter 4.
    132. Turner (1992b: 76; following G. Haya-Prats and R. Pesch) suggests that 'to
speak with other tongues' (i.e. *xenolalia*) in Acts 2 be regarded as 'invasive

ἐπλήσθησαν πάντες πνεύματος ἁγίου) and began to speak in other tongues, as the Spirit gave them utterance' (Acts 2.4; RSV).

Two anticipating features are taken into account in relation to the causal aspect of the plot: (1) the disciples' speaking in other tongues (ἤρξαντο λαλεῖν ἑτέραις γλώσσαις in Acts 2.4; cf. διαμεριζόμεναι γλῶσσαι in Acts 2.3), caused by the Spirit, is identified as their ability to speak each 'native language' (ἰδίᾳ διαλέκτῳ) in Acts 2.8, 11 (Haenchen 1971: 168).[134] In addition, the expression 'Jews from every nation under heaven'[135] (Acts 2.5) implies the missiological significance (Acts 2.9-11) of the pentecostal gift as already embedded in Lk. 24.47 ('to all nations') and Acts 1.8 ('to the ends of the earth'). This thus foreshadows the world-wide mission empowered or directed by the Spirit (see the next stages).[136] (2) The narrator describes the disciples' reception (or baptism; see Acts 1.5) of the Spirit at Pentecost by using the phrase 'filled with the Holy Spirit' (ἐπλήσθησαν πνεύματος ἁγίου),[137] which echoes each occasion in which John (Lk. 1.15), Elizabeth (Lk. 1.41) and Zechariah (Lk. 1.67) are said to be inspired by the Spirit to

charismatic praise' directed to God, as also in Acts 10.46 and 19.6 (see also 1996b: 271-72). Contra Menzies (1991a: 211 n. 3) who interprets it as a missiological 'proclamation'.

133. It is not clear to whom the word πάντες in Acts 2.1 and 2.4 is referring. While it could refer either to the twelve apostles (cf. Dupont [1979: 37-38], who regards 'all' as the twelve apostles along with the persons mentioned in Acts 1.14), just restored by substituting Matthias for the betrayer Judas (Acts 1.26), or to the 120 persons mentioned in Acts 1.15 (e.g. Barrett [1994: 112]; Marshall [1991a: 64]). The former (especially Peter), however, appear to be the centre of attention from this incident onwards (see Acts 2.14-40, 42-43; cf. Acts 1.5, 8).

134. Cf. Johnson (1992) who has noticed the literary parallelism found after each coming of the Spirit upon Jesus and his disciples between the account of the genealogy of Jesus in Lk. 3.23-38 and that of the table of nations in Acts 2.9-11 and suggested, 'The parallelism fits the pattern of Luke's story: Jesus is the prophet who sums up all the promises and hopes of the people before him; in his apostolic successors, that promise and hope (now sealed by the Spirit) will be carried to all the nations of the earth' (47).

135. For a detailed thesis on the 'nations in Luke–Acts' (Lk. 2.1-2; 24.46-47; Acts 1.8; 2.5-11; 17.22-31) along with its two-fold background in the Jewish and the Greek worlds and its literary significance throughout the overall narrative, see J. Scott (1994: 483-544; as far as Acts is concerned, however, he admits that the narrative is fundamentally oriented to the Jewish world, esp. Gen. 10).

136. Thus, Baer (1926: 103) claims, 'der Pfingstgeist ist der Missionsgeist'.

137. See §5.2.1.2 in Chapter 4.

testify to the unborn Jesus. The same phrase used in Acts 2,[138] as that in Luke 1, may thus indicate that the narrator's interest in the disciples' reception of the Spirit at Pentecost centres on their witness to the resurrected Jesus as also anticipated in Lk. 24.47 ('in his name') and Acts 1.8 ('my witnesses'). These two features in relation to the role/function of the Spirit (i.e. empowering for the world-wide mission and the witness to Jesus) will be clarified and developed further in Peter's speech in Acts 2.14-40 and confirmed in the process of the next two stages.

4.5.3. Summary. In this third stage, the Spirit is presented not only implicitly *as empowering Jesus* (as indicated in Lk. 4.18-19) to testify about himself in the temple or Jerusalem through teaching (esp. Lk. 20.41-44; 21.8-28; 22.15-22), trial (Lk. 22.69-70; 23.3), death (Lk. 23.34, 43; cf. 23.47) and resurrection (Lk. 24.38-39; Acts 1.3), but also explicitly *as inspiring Jesus' post-resurrection teaching to the apostles* (Acts 1.2; cf. Lk. 24.25-27, 44-49). Most illuminating in regard to *the future function of the Spirit is the Spirit's empowering the disciples to bear witness to the resurrected Jesus* (Acts 1.8; cf. Lk. 24.49) *and to God's Kingdom* (Acts 1.3; 8.12; 14.22; 19.8; 20.25; 28.23, 31). And this is signified with the narrator's description, which represents the Spirit *as causing the disciples to speak in tongues* (Acts 2.4).

As noticed, the double account of Jesus' ascension in the Gospel and Acts is designed with reference to the Spirit in this 'Central Point' as a climactic plot-axis proleptically highlighting the (successive) 'way of witness'.[139] Jesus' inspired witness is to be taken up by his disciples/witnesses under the same empowerment caused by the Spirit.[140] However, readers should not miss that the commission to the disciples in Lk. 24.46-49 and Acts 1.8 is given directly by the risen Jesus (cf. Acts 1.2) as the continuation of God's plan (Acts 15.8-9, 4-18; cf. Isa. 49.6; 24.16; 45.22; 48.20; 62.11). The narrator will thus unfold the sub-

138. Nevertheless, the uniqueness of the coming of the Holy Spirit at Pentecost should also be discerned (e.g. unique expressions of the phenomena in Acts 2.1-3) in terms of the plot-development (see my discussion of Peter's interpretation of this event in the next stage).

139. Shelton (1991: 120) concludes, 'The witness theme provides the important transition between Luke's Gospel and Acts'; see also Penney (1997a: 120).

140. This scene echoes the Old Testament transfer of the Spirit in relation to the sharing or succession of 'leadership': from Moses to the elders (Num. 11.16-25); from Moses to Joshua (Deut. 34.9; cf. Num. 27.15-23); from Elijah to Elisha (2 Kgs 2.9, 15); cf. from Saul and David (1 Sam. 10.10; 16.13-14). See §2.1.2 in Chapter 2.

sequent plot-stages on the basis of Jesus' three-fold geographical outline in Acts 1.8 (i.e. the disciples' witness in Jerusalem [2.5–7.60], in
Judea and Samaria [8.1–11.18], and to the ends of the earth [11.19–
28.31]). In this sense, Acts 1.8, as the programmatic plot-index for the
rest of Acts,[141] justifies not only the forthcoming Gentile mission as fulfilment of God's plan, but also expresses the narrative function of the
Spirit as empowering the disciples for their witness to Jesus.

**4.6. Development towards the End (*Acts 2.14–28.16*): Jesus' Followers'
Way of Witness from Jerusalem, through Judea and Samaria, and to the
Ends of the Earth**
This long plot-stage (Acts 2.14–28.16) is discernibly shaped and developed in terms of geographical expansions (see Acts 8.1; 9.31; 10;
11.19; 13; 16; 19.21; 28.16) in association with the increasing conflict
between Jesus' witnesses (mainly Peter, Stephen, Barnabas and Paul)
and their opponents, especially the contemporary Jewish authorities
(Acts 4.1, 5-6; 5.17; 6.12) and their followers (Acts 6.9; 9.23; 13.45;
17.15; 21.27; 23.12-13).

In such contexts, the narrator refers to the Holy Spirit 50 times (2.17,
18, 33, 38; 4.8, 25, 31; 5.3, 9, 32; 6.3, 5, 10; 7.51, 55; 8.15, 17, 18, 19,
29, 39; 9.17, 31; 10.19, 38, 44, 45, 47; 11.12, 15, 16, 24, 28; 13.2, 4, 9,
52; 15.8, 28; 16.6, 7; 19.2a, 2b, 6, 21; 20.22, 23, 28; 21.4, 11). So I
shall continue to explore the characterization of the Holy Spirit in relation to the causal aspect of the plot in the following three subsections:
(1) witnesses in Jerusalem, (2) witnesses in Judea and Samaria and
(3) witnesses towards the ends of the earth, and provide a summary at
the end of each subsection. This examination, like those of the previous
plot-stages, will call attention to several leading characters who act as
Jesus' witnesses. While doing so, I shall also note how the key passages
of both Lk. 24.46-49 (cf. 12.11-12; 21.12-15) and Acts 1.8, and Acts
2.38-39 are represented as fulfilled in the subsequent narrative. Hence, I
shall demonstrate that *the primary characterization of the Spirit* is consistently presented *as the empowering and guiding cause of those who
bear witness to Jesus for the salvific mission through their speaking*

141. Haenchen (1971: 145-46) comments on Acts 1.8, 'Luke has in fact described
the contents of Acts through the words of Jesus in verse 8…now the whole action
of Acts becomes the fulfilment of Jesus' word, and this is much more than a mere
table of contents; it is a promise!' See also Johnson (1992: 10-11); Dunn (1996:
10-11).

prophetic words and performing signs and wonders, and that the same Spirit, from Acts 2.38-39 onwards, is also at times viewed *as the verifying cause of recognizing certain groups as incorporated into God's (eschatological) people.* Moreover, on several occasions, the Spirit is characterized *as God's supervising or sustaining cause of those who are already Christians in settled communities.*

4.6.1. *Witness in Jerusalem (Acts 2.14–7.60).* In this subsection, I shall focus on Peter's first inspired speech since it is not only designed as the programmatic paradigm[142] for the mission of Jesus' witnesses, but also discloses the significance of the coming of the Holy Spirit at Pentecost. Then I shall also deal with the passages related to Stephen in order to see how reference to the Spirit is effectively employed to highlight his witness to Jesus.

4.6.1.1. *The Witness of Peter (and the Other Apostles).* Peter's reliable witness in Jerusalem (2.14, 22; cf. 1.12; 2.5, 46; 3.1, 11-12; 4.5, 10, 16; 5.16, 28) about the resurrected and ascended Jesus begins with his own *pesher*[143] on Joel 3.1-5a (LXX), used to explain the previous account of the coming of the Holy Spirit at Pentecost. The speech interprets the 'mighty works of God' (2.11) as those taking place in Jerusalem as Jesus had promised (1.5, 8). As the representative of the twelve Spirit-filled disciples at Pentecost, Peter, in response to the crowd's charge that the disciples 'had drunk too much wine' (2.13, 15), immediately bears witness to the resurrected Jesus by citing three explicit Old Testa-

---

142. The Nazareth episode in the Gospel and that of Pentecost in Acts are seen as two crucial programmatic narrative units in Luke–Acts. The similarities found between the two accounts are as follows: (1) both associate the beginning of the respective missions of Jesus and his disciples with the reception of the Holy Spirit, (2) both are supported by Scripture (Isa. 61.1-2; Joel 2.28-32) to demonstrate the present situations in Lk. 4 and Acts 2 as times of eschatological fulfilment of the Jewish Bible and (3) both foreshadow the forthcoming rejection by some Jews and inclusion of Gentiles. See Menzies (1991a: 162 n. 1). In this way, the narrative function of Peter's speech (Acts 2.14-42) recalls in several ways that of Jesus' sermon at Nazareth (Lk. 4.16-30). See Talbert (1974: 15-19); Tannehill (1994: 29-32). Nevertheless, the uniqueness of Jesus' identity and his messianic mission should not be underestimated (see Lk. 9.20, 48; 10.16, 22; 20.39-44; 24.25-27; Acts 2.36; 4.12; 10.42-43): see Hengel (1981: 67-71, 87); cf. Dunn (1991: 178-81).

143. For *pesher* interpretation ('this is that', so called 'charismatic midrash'; cf. Acts 2.16) once used in the Qumran community, see Longenecker (1975: 38-45, 212); Ellis (1974: 7-8); Evans (1983: 150).

ment passages in his speech: (1) Joel 3.1-5a (LXX) in 2.17-21, (2)
Ps. 15.8-11 (LXX) in 2.25-28, 31 (cf. Pss. 132.11; 89.3-4; 2 Sam. 7.12-
13 in 2.30) and (3) Ps. 109. 1 (LXX) in 2.34-35. Within this witness-
speech inspired by the Spirit (2.4), Peter quotes Joel 3.1-5a with several
alterations[144] for interpreting the significance of the present coming of
the Holy Spirit. The following four important implications of the characterization of the Spirit can be taken into consideration in relation to
the causal aspect of the plot.

(1) The pentecostal gift of the Holy Spirit is represented as an
eschatological sign. The future expectation of the outpouring of the
Spirit prophesied by Joel is said to be fulfilled on the day of Pentecost
and is construed as the eschatological Spirit by replacing the Joel
phrase with 'in the last days' (2.17).[145] Above all, the words σημεῖα and
τέρατα in 2.19 highlight the significance of the coming of the Spirit as
an eschatological climax to signal the imminent arrival of the Day of
the Lord. In this sense, the Spirit is represented *as the cause of these
(eschatological) signs and wonders*,[146] which anticipate a series of
eschatological manifestations in Luke–Acts.[147] Jesus' Spirit-inspired

144. In Peter's citation of Joel 3.1-5a (LXX), six main changes need to be noted:
(1) the replacement of LXX μετὰ ταῦτα ('after these things') by ἐν ταῖς ἐσχάταις
('in the last days') in 2.17; (2) the addition of λέγει ὁ θεός ('God says') in 2.17;
(3) the double insertion of μου, 'my (God's) men-servants and my (God's) maidservants', in 2.18; (4) the addition of καὶ προφητεύσουσιν ('and they shall prophesy') in 2.18; (5) the addition of ἄνω, σημεῖα and κάτω in 2.19; (6) the omission of
Joel 3.5b ('for on Mount Zion and in Jerusalem there will be deliverance, as the
Lord has said, among the survivors whom the Lord calls'). On the 'alterations' in
Acts 2.17-21, see Rese (1969: 46-55); Bock (1987: 156-69); Menzies (1991a: 213-
23; on textual problems, see 213 n. 2); Turner (1996b: 268-70). Scholarly views on
the tradition-history of 2.17-21 along with the other speeches in Acts dispute
whether they are drawn from traditional sources (e.g. Bruce [1974: 53-68]; Gasque
[1974: 232-50; 1989b]; Turner [1996b]) or created by Luke (e.g. Dibelius [1936:
xv]; Haenchen [1971]; Zehnle [1971]; cf. Menzies's argument on redactional
emphasis [1991a]).

145. In later Judaism (e.g. *Midr. Ps.* 14.6; *Deut. R.* 6.14), the deluge of the Spirit
described in Joel is seen to apply to the future messianic times. See Bock (1987:
166, 346 n. 39). Cf. VanGemeren (1988: 83-90).

146. The narrator, on some occasions, however, attributes these miracles to
'Jesus' (Acts 9.34; 14.3) or 'Jesus' name' (Acts 3.6, 16; 4.10, 30; see also n. 177)
and 'God' (Acts 15.12).

147. The collocation of 'signs and wonders' is found in Acts 2.19, 22, 43; 4.30;
5.12; 6.8; 7.36; 14.3; 15.12. This collocation also refers to the miracles of Moses in

witnesses (2.43; 4.30; 5.12; 6.8 [Stephen]; 14.3; 15.12 [Paul and Barnabas]; cf. simply by 'signs' in 8.6, 13 [Philip]) are thus characterized as performing 'signs and/or wonders' in a manner similar to the Spirit-empowered Jesus (2.22; cf. the cosmic signs described in the crucifixion in Lk. 23.44//Acts 2.20).[148]

(2) The gift of the Spirit at Pentecost is not said to be limited to a few charismatic leaders, but to be universally open to God's people. The pentecostal Spirit is upon 'all flesh' (πᾶσιν σάρκα in 2.17; Joel 3.1). This can also be seen as fulfilling Moses' desire for a bestowal of God's Spirit upon 'all the Lord's people' (πάντα τὸν λαὸν κυρίου) described in Num. 11.29. We should have in mind, however, that 'all flesh' or 'all the Lord's people', whom both Moses and Joel wish to be endowed with the Spirit in each context, refer only to the Jewish people. Even Peter, who declares the pentecostal gift as the promise to 'all that are far off, every one whom the Lord our God calls to him' (2.39), does not appear to consider 'non-Jews' as participating in God's eschatological community until later, when he receives visions to visit Cornelius's house at Caesarea.[149] Nevertheless, proleptically Peter's words can apply to the forthcoming mission to the Gentiles.[150]

In this context, the Spirit is presented as God's gift or promise of

the wilderness (7.36; cf. in the LXX: Exod. 4.8, 9, 17, 28, 30; 7.3, 9; 10.1, 2; 11.9-10; Num. 14.1J-12; Deut. 4.34; 6.22; 7.19; 11.3; 26.8; 29.3; Pss. 77.43; 104.27; 134.9). Cf. the word 'signs' is used to denote the future cosmic phenomena associated with the Day of the Lord (Lk. 21.11, 26). In this respect, the collocation of 'signs and wonders' or 'signs' used in Luke–Acts indicates the divine acts not only heralding the Kingdom of God, but also anticipating the expected arrival of the Day of the Lord within the scheme of eschatological gradation. See O'Reilly (1987: 161-90); cf. Bock (1987: 167).

148. Hence, the main Spirit-filled characters in Acts are characterized as the *Endzeit* prophetic witnesses performing 'signs and/or wonders' who continue the salvific mission taken over from Jesus.

149. In Acts 10.44-47 and 11.15-18, see the parallels with the account in Acts 2: 'the circumcised believers'/'we' (10.45; 47) vs 'the Gentiles'/'these people' (10.45); 'them'/'the Gentiles' (11.15, 18) vs 'us'/'we' (11.15, 17). See also the words, 'the circumcised believers'/'the apostles and the believers who were in Judea' vs 'the Gentiles'/'uncircumcised men' in 11.1-3. After his visit to Cornelius' house, Peter thus proclaims before the other apostles and the elders at Jerusalem, 'And God, who knows the human heart, testified to them by giving them the Holy Spirit, just as he did to us; and in cleansing their hearts by faith he has made no distinction between them and us' (Acts 15.8-9).

150. Cf. Haenchen (1971: 179).

salvation given to those who will be baptized in the name of Jesus Christ for the forgiveness of their sins (Lk. 24.49; Acts 2.38-39). In regard to the characterization of the Holy Spirit, the implied author, from Acts 2 onwards, thus appears to juxtapose the two-fold universal scheme in accordance with two kinds of recipients: (a) Jesus' disciples/witnesses (Lk. 24.46-49; Acts 1.8) and (b) God's people (Acts 2.38-39). In other words, the Spirit is characterized, on the one hand, as empowering and guiding Jesus' disciples (Acts 2.4, 14; 4.8, 31 [Peter and other apostles]; 6.5, 10 [Stephen]; 8.29, 39 [Philip]; 9.17-22 [Saul]; 10.19; 11.12 [Peter]; 13.2-3, 4 [Barnabas and Paul]; 16.6-7; 19.21 [Paul]); on the other, as verifying certain groups of people as God's (eschatological) community (8.14-17 [Samaritans]; 10.44-48; 11.14-18; 15.8 [Cornelius's household]; 19.1-7 [the Baptist's Ephesian disciples]).[151] Thus, this pentecostal Spirit is said to produce a double *effect*[152] on recipients in generating and developing two programmatic verses of Acts 1.8 and 2.38-39 side-by-side.[153]

---

151. These two seemingly incongruent elements concerning the characterization or role of the Spirit in Luke–Acts can be traced back to the Jewish Bible: the former is linked with Joel 2.28-32; the latter with Ezek. 36.22-28 (cf. Ezek. 37.14, 24-28; Isa. 44.3-4; *Jub.* 1.20-23). These two future expectations of the Spirit, however, should be appreciated within the Jewish hope of the future restoration (or salvation) of Israel (cf. Isa. 32.15; 43.10-12; 49.6) along with the anointed messianic figure (Isa. 11.1-5). In this sense, these two elements, although not employed equally, can be regarded as two original pictures of one Spirit embedded in the Hebrew Bible; cf. McQueen (1995: 56; see also 47-48) and Keener (1997: 9). In contrast, Menzies (1991a: 47-49; 316-18) argues that only the former (i.e. Joel's prophecy with Jewish intertestamental literature) has been adopted by Luke (i.e. 'prophetic pneumatology' as a *donum superadditum*), and the latter (i.e. Ezekiel's prophecy with 1QH and *Wisdom of Solomon*) by Paul (i.e. 'soteriological pneumatology'). The problem with his argument is that he always dissociates the Lukan understanding of the Spirit from that of Paul (and from the 'charismatic pneumatology' of the primitive church, i.e. the community of Mark, Matthew and Q), and fails to notice aspects of the characterization of the Spirit in Acts.

152. Hence, the (Jesus' disciples') 'way of witness' to Jesus empowered and guided by the Spirit should also be appreciated in conjunction with the 'way of salvation' confirmed by the Spirit for people, regardless of whether they are Jews or Gentiles.

153. Nevertheless, it should be noted as well that Luke's overall plot is shaped and advanced by the actions and/or speeches of the main Spirit-filled characters (e.g. Jesus in Lk. 3.21-22; 4.1, 14, 18-21; Peter and/or the apostles in Acts 2.4; 10.19; 11.12; Stephen and/or Philip in Acts 6.3, 5, 8, 10; 7.55; 8.29, 39; Paul and/or

(3) The characterization of the Spirit of Pentecost draws on the repertoire of the Spirit of the Lord/God in the Jewish Bible.[154] Luke highlights this point by inserting the phrases, 'God says' (2.17), 'my' (God's) menservants and 'my' (God's) maidservants (2.18), 'and they shall prophesy' (2.18), so that the Holy Spirit (2.4; cf. 10.47; 11.15) is portrayed as causing God's human agents to give inspired/prophetic speeches that reveal *God's* will or plan. The double addition of 'my' also emphasizes that those who 'see visions'/'dream dreams' in the rest of Acts are God's Spirit-filled servants: Stephen in 7.55-56; Saul in 9.3-10; Ananias in 9.10-16; Cornelius in 10.3-6, 10-16; Peter in 11.5-10; Paul in 16.9-10; 18.9; 23.11; 27.23-24. Like the 'Holy Spirit' in the

Barnabas in Acts 9.17; 13.2, 4; 16.6, 7; 19.21; 20.22-23), rather than by inspired people in general (e.g. the Samaritans or the Cornelius household). This impels me to claim that the *primary* function of the Holy Spirit in terms of the Lukan plot is viewed as empowering and guiding Jesus and his witnesses for God's salvation plan. See §5 in this chapter.

154. The traditional Jewish understanding of the Spirit has been designated as the term 'Spirit of prophecy' (רוח נבואה) on the basis of the Jewish literature (*Jub.* 31.12), esp. of targums (*Targ. Onq.* Gen. 41.38; Num. 11.25, 26, 29; 24.2; 27.18; *Targ. Ps.-J.* Gen. 41.38 [= *Targ. Onq.*]; 45.27; Exod. 33.16; Num. 11.17, 25 [= *Targ. Onq.*], 26 [= *Targ. Onq.*], 28, 29 [= *Targ. Onq.*]; 24.2 [= *Targ. Onq.*]; 27.18 [= *Targ. Onq.*]; *Targ. Neb.* Judg. 3.10; 1 Sam. 10.6, 10; 19.20, 23; 2 Sam. 23.2; 2 Kgs 2.9; Isa. 61.1; Ezek. 3.22; 8.1; 11.5; 40.1); nevertheless, we should note that the term 'Holy Spirit' (רוח קודשה) has also been generally used (*Targ. Onq.* Gen. 45.27; *Targ. Ps.-J.* Gen. 6.3; 27.5, 42; 30.25; 31.21 [= *Targ. Neof.*]; 35.22; 37.33; 43.14; Exod. 31.3 [= *Targ. Neof.*]; 33.16; Deut. 5.21; 18.15, 18; 28.59; 32.26; *Targ. Neb.* Isa. 40.13; 42.2; 44.3; 59.21; Ezek. 36.27) and occasionally even preferred to the 'Spirit of prophecy' in *Frag. Targ.* (Gen. 27.1; 37.33; 42.1 [= *Targ. Neof.*]; Exod. 2.12 [= *Targ. Neof.*]; Num. 11.26) and *Targ. Neof.* (Gen. 41.38; 42.1; Exod. 31.3; 35.31; Num. 11.17, 25 [×2], 26, 28, 29; 14.24; 24.2; 27.18; see also the marginal gloss in Gen. 31.21; Exod. 2.12). See Schäfer (1970: 304-14; 1972: 23-26); Menzies (1991a: 99-104); Turner (1996b: 86-89). In this sense, we can agree that the targumists have equated the 'Spirit of the Lord/God' in the Jewish Bible with either the 'Holy Spirit' or the 'Spirit of prophecy'. However, in Luke–Acts (and elsewhere in the New Testament, only except in Rev. 19.10), Luke has never employed the terminology 'Spirit of prophecy', he has, instead, used the term 'Holy Spirit' as expressing several concepts corresponding with the Jewish understanding of God's Spirit in general. The Lukan textual evidence thus suggests that the 'Spirit of prophecy' is not the proper term in naming the divine Spirit in Luke–Acts (or the New Testament), although the Jewish idea embedded in the term can be used. Cf. Table 4 in Chapter 1.

Gospel and 'God's Spirit' in the Jewish Bible,[155] the Spirit at Pentecost in Acts 2 (and in the rest of the narrative) is thus said to cause the following (conventional) roles or effects: 'prophetic speech or praise' (2.4; 4.8, 25, 31; 6.10; 10.46; 11.28; 13.9; 19.6; 21.4, 11; cf. 1.16; 28.25), 'revelation' through visions or dreams (see above), 'wisdom' (6.3, 5, 10; 9.31; 13.9; 16.18; cf. Lk. 21.15) and a 'religio-ethical form of life' (5.3, 9; 9.31; 6.3-10; 11.24; 13.52; cf. 2.42-47; 4.31-36).[156] Nevertheless, the characterization of the pentecostal Spirit develops the concept of God's Spirit in Jewish writings (see below).

(4) The pentecostal Spirit is also interpreted in relation to the risen and exalted Jesus. This can partly be discerned in the Gospel references to the Spirit and Jesus' promise to his disciples (Lk. 21.15 ['I (*Jesus*) will give you words and a wisdom'; cf. Lk. 12.12]; 24.49 ['I (*Jesus*) send the promise of my Father']). The narrator also connects John the Baptist's witness to Jesus as the One who will baptize God's people in the Holy Spirit (Lk. 3.16), although 'baptism' is understood metaphorically with regard to the pentecostal outpouring of the Spirit (Acts 1.5; 11.16).[157] Jesus is presented as the baptizer/dispenser of the pentecostal Spirit (Acts 2.33).

To this end, the implied author hightens the status and/or role of Jesus by means of Peter's two additional LXX citations, which refer to the resurrected and ascended Jesus. This relationship of Jesus to the Spirit should thus be understood in the light of the new view of the exalted Jesus sitting at the right hand of God (cf. Lk. 19.12; 20.42-43; 22.69). First, Peter (and the narrator/Luke) portrays Jesus as the Davidic Messiah[158] by citing Ps. 16.8-11. This LXX citation is then interpreted as supporting Jesus' bodily resurrection within Peter's Christian hermeneutical application of the cited passage (Acts 2.29-31).[159] Secondly, he further claims to demonstrate that Jesus is Lord by

---

155. See Chapter 2 and esp. §5.2.1.1 in Chapter 4.

156. Cf. Turner (1996b: 349-52); Menzies (1991a: 224 n. 2).

157. See Tannehill (1994: 40).

158. This concept can be traced in *Pss. Sol.* 17.32 ('their king shall be the Lord Messiah') and 18.7 ('under the rod of discipline of the Lord Messiah'); cf. an expectation of two 'anointed' figures described in 1QS 9.10-11 (a 'messiah of Israel'); CD 12.22-23 (a 'messiah of Aaron'). See Hurtado (1992: 107).

159. Bock (1987: 172-81), noticing six differences between the LXX translation and the MT, has named the use of Ps. 16 in Acts 2.25-31 as a 'powerful messianic and Christological text' explained by a 'powerful Christian exposition'.

citing Ps. 110.1 (as quoted by Jesus in Lk. 20.41-44) in terms of Jesus' ascension (to be David's Lord) and exaltation to the right hand of God (Acts 2.33). As a result, Jesus, according to Peter, should be declared not only 'Messiah' (God's agent), but also 'Lord' (co-regent) (2.36).[160] In between the two LXX citations, Peter declares, 'Being therefore exalted at the right hand of God, and having received *from the Father* the promise of the Holy Spirit, he (*the exalted Jesus*) has *poured out* this (*the Holy Spirit*) that you both see and hear' (Acts 2.33).[161] According to Peter, it is the exalted Jesus who sends (i.e. metaphorically baptizes his people in) the pentecostal gift of the Holy Spirit (Lk. 3.16//Acts 1.5; Lk. 24.49//Acts 1.5, 8; 11.16).[162] In other words, the exalted Jesus, sitting at the right hand of God in heaven and thus sharing the power and authority to send the Spirit of God, is characterized as 'Lord of the Spirit' (cf. 16.7; 8.39) in terms analogous to

---

160. See Bock (1987: 184); cf. Turner (1996b: 276).

161. Some scholars (e.g. Lindars [1961: 43-44]; Dupont [1973: 219-27]; Turner [1980: 121-26; 1982: 176-79; 1996b: 285-89] have argued that Acts 2.33 (while Lincoln [1981: 157-58] has mainly dealt with the relationship between Eph. 4.8 and Ps. 68.18, he has also suggested that the Psalm would be a possible background for the Lukan account of Pentecost, i.e. Jesus as 'new Moses') was influenced by Ps. 68.18 (cf. the Jewish interpretation of the Psalm in association with Moses: e.g. *Targum of the Writings*: 'You have ascended to heaven, that is Moses the prophet. You have taken captivity captive, you have learned the words of the Torah, you have given them as gifts to men', cited in Turner (1980: 122); see also Philo's writings and the Rabbinic writings cited in Lincoln (157). In this sense, Jesus is portrayed as the prophet-like-Moses through the Moses/Sinai allusions in Acts 2 (i.e. Jesus, as Moses ascended who received the gift of God, the Law, which was given to men at Sinai, is understood as 'new Moses', who ascended at the right hand of God, received the Holy Spirit as the gift of God, and poured out the Spirit to God's people at Pentecost; cf. Acts 2.22//7.36; 3.22-24//7.37; Lk. 24.19//Acts 7.22). Against this view, see Bock (1987: 181-83); Menzies (1991a: 235-44). Cf. Barrett's inconclusive view (1994: 149-50): 'How far the echoes of Ps. 68 (67) would have been picked up by Luke's readers, how far he intended them to be picked up, how far he was himself aware of them, are questions which it is difficult to answer. Overtones of a familiar passage of Scripture may have come out unconsciously'.

162. See Zwiep (1997: 184). In dealing with Pauline theology comprehensively in his recent work, Dunn observes (1998: 254 n. 105), 'In Paul, however, it is always God who is described as the one who gives the Spirit (1 Cor. 2.12; 2 Cor. 1.21-22; 5.5; Gal. 3.5; 4.6; 1 Thes. 4.8; Eph. 1.17; cf. the 'divine passive' of Rom. 5.5 and 1 Cor. 12.13), *in some contrast to Acts 2.33 and the original expectation of the Baptist (Mark 1.8 pars.)*' (emphasis added).

Yahweh's relationship to the Spirit in the Jewish Bible. In this respect, *the pentecostal Spirit is now understood to be dispensed or caused by the risen Jesus*;[163] this may explain why Jesus' disciples empowered/ inspired by the Spirit are to be characterized as *testifying about Jesus*. That is, the Spirit is to be presented as causing them to bear witness to the risen Jesus through their mighty words and deeds (see below). Both Jesus' words in Lk. 24.46-49; Acts 1.8 and Peter's speech in Acts 2.14-40 (inspired by the Spirit; see Acts 1.2; 2.4) prepare the reader to anticipate the forthcoming characterization of the Spirit in relation to the causal aspect of the plot. In Acts 4.8, 31, the Spirit is characterized as inspiring Peter and the apostles to proclaim God's word by bearing witness to the Messiah, Jesus (Acts 4.10-12, 20, 26-30). The Spirit is also said to give the disciples 'boldness' for their witness-mission (Acts 4.29, 31; see also 2.29 [Peter]; 4.13 [Peter]; 9.27 [Paul]; 13.46 [Paul and Barnabas]; 14.3 [Paul and Barnabas]; 18.26 [Apollos]; 19.8 [Paul]; 28.31 [Paul]; cf. Lk. 12.11-12).[164] Moreover, Acts 5.29-32 indicates that the Spirit not only inspires the apostles to witness about Jesus, but also testifies to the risen Jesus.[165]

We should also note that the implied author connects the characterization of the Spirit with a settled (Jewish-Christian) community. That is, the Spirit, in contrast to Satan,[166] is indirectly characterized as causing believers not to lie to God (Acts 5.4) for the nature of the Spirit is holy[167] (Acts 5.3, 9). In addition, Acts 5.1-11 implies that God's (eschatological) community after Pentecost is not just directed by the Spirit-filled apostles, like Peter, but by the Spirit directly.[168] Although the implied author highlights the references to the Spirit in relation to prophetic witnesses (i.e. Jesus and his disciples) who advance the 'way of witness', from time to time, he reports in passing the role of the

---

163. The Spirit from Acts 2 onwards, particularly in relation to Jesus' witnesses, can thus be envisaged as the power and presence of the exalted Jesus, i.e. the christological Spirit (e.g. 4.8-12; 7.55-60; 9.17-22; 10.44-48; 11.24-26; 16.7; cf. 14.3; 16.14).

164. The word παρρησία in Acts (not found in the Gospel) is thus employed in contexts in which the Spirit-filled characters (cf. Apollos in 18.26) preach the word of God or witness to Jesus. See Schlier (1967: 882).

165. See §5.1.1.4 in Chapter 4.

166. See §5.2.2.2 in Chapter 4.

167. See §5.1.1.1 in Chapter 4.

168. See §5.1.1.2 in Chapter 4.

Spirit in connection with settled communities (see also Acts 9.31; 15.22-29; 20.25-35; cf. 2.42-47; 3.32-37): the Spirit is presented as supervising God's eschatological community.

4.6.1.2. The Witness of Stephen. The internal conflict of the Jerusalem Church resulting from increasing numbers (Acts 6.1; cf. 2.41; 4.4; 5.14) introduces Stephen, Philip and the other five to resolve the dispute over food distribution among the Hebrew and the Hellenist widows. Thus, the seven are originally appointed to help the apostles, so that the apostles can devote themselves to prayer and preaching the word of God (Acts 6.2-3). These seven men are introduced as 'of good repute, full of the Spirit and of wisdom' (Acts 6.3)[169] and they are said to resolve the problem so that the Jerusalem Church continues to grow in numbers (Acts 6.7). So the Spirit, in this immediate context, is said to provide the seven with wisdom (cf. the LXX Exod. 28.3; Deut. 34.9; Wis. 7.7; 7.22-23), causing them wisely to serve the widows (i.e. the insiders of the Jerusalem Church) through their proper distribution of alms and care.

The narrative, however, singles out among the seven first Stephen (Acts 6.8–7.60)[170] and then Philip (Acts 8.4-40; see below) who both function as charismatic witnesses (i.e. in relation to outsiders of the Church). Stephen is thus described in terms like those applied to the apostles or Jesus: (1) Stephen is said to be a 'man of the Spirit' and a man 'full of faith and of the Holy Spirit' (6.5), and as fulfilling Jesus' promise (Lk. 21.12-15) by speaking boldly in 'wisdom and the Spirit' against his opponents (6.10). Hence, the Spirit appears to be characterized as making Stephen both faithful to the Lord (God and Jesus) and wise. However, his opponents are characterized in contrast with Stephen as those who, like their forefathers who falsely accused the Spirit-inspired Old Testament figures Joseph (7.9; cf. Gen. 41.38) and Moses (7.25-41; cf. Num. 11.17, 29), always resist the Holy Spirit (7.51, cf. 54, 57) and therefore put the Spirit-inspired Jesus (7.52; cf. 2.23) *and* Stephen (7.59-60) to death. In this sense, Stephen, like Jesus, is presented as caused to act as a witness by the Spirit, whereas his opponents are presented as resisting not only Stephen's witness, but also the

---

169. See §5.2.1.1 in Chapter 4.

170. For the detailed study of Stephen's speech in Acts, see Richard (1978: 243-352); Soards (1994: 57-70).

Spirit's.[171] (2) 'Full of grace and power'[172] (6.8; cf. references to Jesus' wisdom or power in Lk. 2.40, 52; 4.14; 5.17; 6.19; 7.35; 9.1; Acts 10.38), he is said to perform 'wonders and signs' (6.8), presumably caused by the Spirit, (although none are actually described) like Jesus (Acts 2.22) and the apostles (Acts 2.43; 5.12) have been doing. (3) He is depicted as seeing a vision (cf. Peter's in 10.17, 19; 11.5 and Paul's 16.9, 10; 18.9; 26.19) and giving inspired words caused by the Holy Spirit (7.55-56) in bearing direct witness to Jesus' standing at the right hand of God.[173]

So the Spirit is presented as causing/inspiring Stephen (1) to speak boldly and wisely, (2) to give prophetic utterance through a heavenly vision, (3) to witness to the risen Jesus and (4) to perform wonders and signs (although the last is indirectly indicated). In addition, Stephen's 'faith' and 'wisdom' (including 'grace and power') as charismatic gifts seem to be acquired through the inspiration of the Holy Spirit (cf. Acts 11.24).[174] All these features assure readers that Stephen is a reliable witness (in fact, he is named the 'Lord's [Jesus'] witness' by Paul in Acts 22.20) caused to act by the Holy Spirit, like both Jesus and the apostles,[175] and thus can be regarded as not simply a helper serving

171. In fact, the people who resist the Holy Spirit or oppose Spirit-filled figures are probably understood as those who are in the control of evil spirits and ultimately of Satan (Acts 5.3; cf. Lk. 4.1-14; 11.17-26; 13.11, 16; 22.3; Acts 13.6-11; 16.16-18; 19.11-20), i.e. those who are set against the 'way of witness' planned by God.

172. Some manuscripts have changed the phrase 'grace and power' by adding either 'faith' or 'Spirit' (Ψ) under the influence of Acts 6.5.

173. In addition, Stephen, like Jesus (Lk. 4.16-21; 24.44) and Peter (Acts 2.14-36), is shown to have authority to interpret the Old Testament, and, like Peter, to highlight the significance of the coming of Jesus (Acts 7.51-53); see Kilgallen (1989: 184). Also, Stephen's rejection by the religious and the temple authorities mirrors that of Jesus (Lk. 19.47; 20.1-2; 22.1, 66; 23.10), Peter and the other apostles (Acts 4.1, 5-6; 5.17, 24). Above all, a detailed account describing Stephen's death outside Jerusalem and the disposition of clothing in 7.58, his prayer for his spirit's acceptance in 7.59, his asking forgiveness for his murderers in 7.60 and his burial by pious Jews in 8.2, is reminiscent of Jesus' death (Lk. 23.32, 34, 46, 34, 50-55). In this episode, the narrator initially introduces the character Saul in passing as one who is on the side of Stephen's opponents (7.58; 8.1). However, Stephen's asking the Lord, Jesus (7.59-60), for forgiveness of his opponents is later dramatically answered in the case of Saul (9.5, 15-16; 22.15; 26.16).

174. See §5.2.1.1 in Chapter 4.

175. In the development of the plot, the risen Jesus is regarded as the core of the

tables as the apostles originally supposed, but a legitimate co-preacher or prophetic-witness like the apostles. The Spirit, thus, legitimates Stephen as Jesus' witness by empowering him in a manner similar to the apostles.

4.6.1.3. *Summary.* This subsection, 'Witness in Jerusalem' (Acts 2.14–7.60), therefore, shows that the Spirit, as foreshadowed in Lk. 24.46-49; Acts 1.8, is mostly presented *as empowering Peter and the other apostles, and Stephen at Jerusalem, to bear witness to the resurrected and ascended Jesus by causing them especially to speak prophetic words boldly and wisely and perform signs and wonders powerfully.* On one occasion, however, the Spirit is also characterized *as inspiring the lives of (true) believers* in a Christian community. The Spirit, from this stage onwards, is interpreted as sent or *caused not only by God* (5.32; 11.17; 15.8), *but also by the risen and exalted Jesus* (2.33; 9.17; 19.4-6; cf. 16.7). The risen Jesus is portrayed as another cause of the Spirit's endowment, particularly to his witnesses (i.e. his disciples in 2.33; Paul in 9.17; cf. Peter in 4.7, 13; Stephen in 6.10; Philip in 8.35, 39; Lk. 12.12; 21.15).[176] This relationship prepares the reader for the parallel

message and at the same time he is characterized in certain aspects as the ideal model of a witness for his disciples/witnesses. For the latter point, (1) Peter's (including the other apostles) preaching the word of God, especially the message of repentance (Acts 2.38; 3.19; 5.31), is reminiscent of that of Jesus (Acts 5.32; see also John the Baptist's in Lk. 3.3, 7-14; cf. 24.47). (2) Their performance of signs and wonders (Acts 2.43; 4.16, 22, 30; 5.12) also recalls Jesus' earthly healing ministry (esp. see Peter's healing of the lame man at the temple in Acts 3.1-10; cf. 5.15-16; 9.32-43). (3) The divided response of acceptance (mainly by the people: 2.41; 4.4, 21-22) and rejection (mainly by the leaders of the people: Acts 4.1, 5-6; 5.17, 21, 24) of the apostles is a literary pattern alluding to the case of Jesus. And above all, (4) they, like Jesus, are deliberately described by the narrator as 'people of the Spirit' and thus considered as reliable witnesses; cf. Johnson (1977: 58-59); Moessner (1986: 227-56). Hence, the implied reader may recognize that the true leadership over Israel is not assigned to the religious leaders among the Sanhedrin, but to the apostles. The narrator characterizes the former as 'false witnesses' against God and his messengers (Acts 6.13; cf. Lk. 23.14; Acts 21.20-24), *filled with jealousy* (Acts 5.17; see also Lk. 4.28; 6.11; Acts 13.45), whereas the latter as 'true witnesses' carrying on God's plan, *filled with the Holy Spirit* (Acts 2.4; 4.8, 31; 5.32), which is given to those who obey God, i.e. God's human agents (Acts 4.19; 5.29).

176. Cf. Zwiep (1997: 184), who comments, 'Jesus must be exalted to heaven because it is only as the Exalted One that he can pour out the Spirit upon the Church'.

roles or functions of the Spirit and the risen Jesus described in the later narrative.[177]

4.6.2. *Witness in Judea and Samaria (Acts 8.1–11.18)*. As a result of Spirit-filled Stephen's bold witness and his death, and the following persecution of the Jerusalem Church, Jesus' world-wide commission to his disciples as narrated in Acts 1.8 expands from the territory of Jerusalem to that of Judea and Samaria (8.1).

The Spirit-filled characters, Philip, Saul/Paul and Peter, are described as bearing witness to Jesus in Judea and Samaria.[178] The narrator's geographical references, however, picture the mission expansion towards the territory of Samaria and other areas. Hence, the narrator simply reports in passing the successful result of the witness-mission in Judea and Galilee through a brief summary (Acts 9.31; cf. 5.16).[179] The Holy Spirit in relation to Philip's ongoing mission is dynamically characterized as a 'mission-director', and this foreshadows the role of the Spirit in the future mission carried out by Peter, and Barnabas and Paul. The characters who advance the plot of the narrative thus continue to be portrayed as Jesus' witnesses empowered and directly guided by the Holy Spirit as promised by Jesus in Lk. 24.47-48 and Acts 1.8.

4.6.2.1. *The Witness of Philip*. Philip, previously introduced as the one of the seven men 'full of the Spirit and wisdom' (Acts 6.3), is now, like

177. See §5.1.1.3 in Chapter 4. The phrase 'Jesus' name' in Acts (see n. 90 in Chapter 4), which is often used as the source of healing power, is thus construed as the name of the exalted Jesus who sends the Spirit (cf. Lk. 9.49; 10.17). In this sense, 'Jesus' name' in Acts is another expression that signifies the power or activity of the Spirit conveyed by the risen Jesus upon his witnesses (e.g. 3.6, 16; 4.10, 30-31; 9.27, 29; 16.18; 19.5-6; cf. 8.16-17). Cf. Hill (1984: 24), who suggests, 'The Spirit is the power and presence of Jesus released from the constrictions of place and time to be with and among his followers everywhere and always'.

178. In Acts 8.1, the narrator indicates (1) 'Judea' (see also Acts 1.8; Lk. 6.17; cf. Acts 9.31; 26.20) and (2) 'Samaria' (the Samaritans are considered neither full Jews nor mere Gentiles). On the use of the term 'Judea' in Luke–Acts, see Hengel (1983: 99, 193 nn. 21-24); Barrett (1994: 402). Hengel (121) is right in saying that 'There [Samaria] the mission stands to some degree as a connecting link between the mission (to the Jews) in Jerusalem and Judaea on the one hand and the world-wide mission (to the Gentiles) on the other'.

179. So Conzelmann (1987: 7) outlined the book of Acts as follows: Jerusalem/ Judea (chs. 1–7), Samaria (chs. 8–9) and the ends of the earth (chs. 10–28) based on 1.8.

Stephen, singled out and given the role of witness to Jesus in new mission fields: the city of Samaria, the road from Jerusalem to Gaza, Azotus and Caesarea.

Though there is no explicit reference to the Spirit in relation to Philip's activity in Samaria (cf. 8.29, 39), three aspects in the episode of his successful mission imply that Philip's activity, like those of Jesus, the apostles and Stephen, is inspired/empowered by the Spirit. (1) Philip proclaims (κηρύσσω: 8.5; cf. Lk. 4.18, 19, 44; 8.1; 9.2) and preaches good news (εὐαγγελίζομαι: 8.12; cf. Lk. 4.18, 43; 9.6; Acts 5.42) to the Samaritans, focusing on (the name of) 'Jesus Christ' (8.5, 12; cf. 4.17, 18; 5.28, 40) and the 'Kingdom of God' (8.12; cf. Lk. 4.43; 8.1; 9.2). (2) He exercises power to cast out unclean spirits and heal the paralysed or the lame (8.7; cf. Lk. 4.33-36, 40-41; 7.21-22; 8.1-2; 9.37-42; 11.14-26; Acts 3.6-10) in performing 'signs' and 'great miracles' (8.6, 13; cf. 2.43; 4.16, 22; 5.12; 6.8). Finally (3) the Samaritans and Simon Magus[180] are said to be baptized by Philip (8.12, 13). This narrative suggests that the power of the Spirit causes Philip (cf. 6.3; 8.29, 39; later named 'evangelist' [Φιλίππου τοῦ εὐαγγελιστοῦ] by the narrator in 21.8) to perform these works at Samaria recalling those of the Spirit-inspired Jesus, the apostles and Stephen in Galilee and Jerusalem.

Philip's ministry in Samaria is, on the other hand, represented as incomplete until the coming of Peter and John as the 'emissaries' of the apostles in Jerusalem, who had already heard that 'Samaria had received the word of God' (8.14-15; cf. 11.1; 17.11). But the Samaritan believers, although already baptized in the name of Jesus, are described as not yet endowed with the Holy Spirit (8.16). This tension, however, is resolved through the narrator's further report that the Samaritan believers received the Spirit through the two apostles' praying (8.15) and laying their hands on them (8.17). The other occasions in which the bestowal of the Spirit is related to the 'laying on of hands' appear in Acts 9.17 and 19.6. However, the Spirit is not always given in conjunction with this rite (see Acts 2.38; 10.44); and the rite is not always

---

180. Simon Magus who is said to work by 'the power of God that is called Great' (ἡ δύναμις τοῦ θεοῦ ἡ καλουμένη μεγάλη) *by the Samaritans* (8.9-11) is, nevertheless, contrasted with Philip who performs 'signs and great miracles' (τε σημεῖα καὶ δυνάμεις μεγάλας: 8.13); the narrative presupposes Simon's magic is performed through the power of the devil (cf. 13.5-10) whereas Philip's signs are through the power of Jesus' name/the Spirit (cf. 3.6; 4.30-31; 10.38). For Simon Magus misconception of the Spirit in 8.18-24, see §5.1.1.1 in Chapter 4.

followed by the gift of the Spirit (see Acts 6.6; 13.3). In this light, the laying on of hands[181] is not viewed as a necessary means of receiving the Spirit; rather this episode indicates that God as the ultimate cause provides the Samaritans with the Spirit as his (sovereign) gift in response to the prayer of Peter and John (cf. Lk. 11.13). In other words, the bestowing of the Spirit is not considered a human prerogative[182] (see also the other references to the Spirit as God's gift in Acts 2.38; 10.45; 11.17; 15.8; cf. 5.32).

This account also suggests a gap between baptism and the coming of the Spirit (cf. Acts 9.18; 10.47), which has been interpreted in various ways.[183] This episode (along with Acts 10.44-48, i.e. the outpouring of the Spirit *before* baptism in Jesus' name) can be, so to speak, considered abnormal on the basis of Acts 2.38.[184] Readers may then ask why the Samaritans do not receive the Spirit when they are baptized in

181. There are three relevant contexts in which mention is made of the 'laying on of hands': (1) healing as the transfer of power (Lk. 4.40; 13.13; Acts 9.12, 17; 28.8), (2) commissioning for ministry as the formal transfer of authority (Acts 6.6; 9.17; 13.3; cf. Num. 27.20; Deut. 34.9) and (3) the bestowal of the Spirit with prayer (Acts 8.17; 19.6). Cf. Parratt (1968/69: 210-14); Johnson (1992: 107); Menzies (1991a: 259); Turner (1996b: 372-73). Against Menzies's view (1991a: 259-60), however, I cannot find a clue in the immediate contexts that the Samaritans in 8.17 are given the Spirit as empowering for mission.

182. Nor is the bestowal of the Spirit through the laying on of hands, according to the narrator/Luke, a privilege limited to the apostles or to representatives of Jerusalem: see Acts 9.17 (Ananias); 19.6 (Paul).

183. The following different explanations need to be mentioned (Turner [1996b: 360-75]): (1) source-critical explanations (e.g. by Haenchen [1971: 307-308]), (2) the Spirit suspended from baptism because of defective Samaritan faith (by Dunn [1970a: 63-68]), (3) the reception of the Spirit in 8.17 as a second gift of the Spirit, i.e. as spiritual gifts rather than as the Spirit himself (by Beasely-Murray [1994: 118-19]) and (4) the Spirit in 8.17 as *donum superadditum*, empowering for mission (by Pentecostal scholars, e.g. Stronstad [1984: 63-65]; Shelton [1991: 130]; Menzies [1991a: 258]); cf. Turner's (1980: 160-70; 1996a: 373-75) position: the Spirit in 8.17 is understood as technically subsequent to conversion; nevertheless not as a *donum superadditum*. The last three approaches have been shaped on the basis of two opposite dogmas, i.e. the gift of the Spirit as 'conversion-initiation' vs as 'second blessing'.

184. The Samaritan believers' lack of the Spirit after being baptized in Jesus' name (8.12) and receiving the word of God (8.14) seems to make Peter and John bewildered; this is the reason why they are said to pray for them to receive the Spirit (see γάρ in 8.16).

Jesus' name. This may also be related to the following question: Why is it not Philip, but the apostles, Peter and John, who are involved in the Samaritans' reception of the Spirit?[185] These two questions might be answered in relation to the (narrative) significance of the recipients, Samaritans who were hostile to the Jews (cf. Lk. 9.51-56; Ezra 4), yet are now dramatically incorporated into God's restored community.[186] In other words, the narrator neither reports Philip's ministry in Samaria as unsuccessful, nor intends to show that the Samaritans' faith or their baptism in Jesus' name is defective or useless; he rather confirms Philip's mission through the reliable characters' co-work (i.e. praying and laying on of hands) of the apostles[187] (sent from Jerusalem) and God's sending the Spirit. In this sense, the coming of the Spirit upon the Samaritan believers proves that Philip's ministry is an expression of God's plan (see also 8.26, 29, 39). In relation to the causal aspect of the plot, the Spirit here, caused by God himself (cf. the characterization of the Spirit as God's gift[188] in 8.20) in response to the apostles' prayer, can thus be *characterized as apologetically verifying the Samaritan believers as God's true people* regardless of their past ethnic or cultural hostility to Jews.[189]

A further account of Philip's mission in 8.26-40[190] provides an

185. Spencer (1992: 220-23) attempts to answer this question in suggesting that the Philip–Peter relationship is understood in terms of the model of 'forerunner–culminator', analogous to the role of John the Baptist in relation to Jesus; 'the mission to Samaria in Acts 8 reflects a similar collaborative effort between Philip the forerunner who baptizes with water and Peter/John the culminators who impart the Spirit, in no way stigmatizing the 'great' evangelistic achievements of the former' (1997: 88). Cf. Tannehill (1994: 102, 104).

186. Dunn (1996: 107) rightly comments, 'Presumably Luke understood that the exceptional course of events were God's way of dealing with exceptional circumstances—that is, of healing the generations-old hostility between Jew and Samaritan. It is only by the (Jewish) apostles (still) in Jerusalem validating (through Peter and John) the acceptance of the Samaritans that the Spirit comes upon them'.

187. On their way back to Jerusalem, Peter and John are said to 'proclaim the good news to many villages of the Samaritans' (8.25).

188. See §5.1.1.4 in Chapter 4.

189. Cf. Shepherd 1994: 181 n. 92, 182.

190. The references to the name of cities in association with Philip's mission in Acts 8.26-40 are also worthy of our attention: the regions of Gaza (26), Azotus (40) and Caesarea (40), among 'all the towns until Philip came to Caesarea' (8.40), are 'Hellenistic places' in Palestine, with a strong Gentile element in their population in comparison to the Jewish towns, Lydda and Joppa, where Peter visited before

explicit characterization of the Spirit: the Spirit (8.29, 39),[191] like an angel of the Lord (8.26; cf. 5.19; 10.3; 12.7; 27.23),[192] is presented as a mission-director who 'says to' and 'snatches away' Philip.[193] The narrator calls the 'good news of Jesus' (8.35; cf. 40) what the Spirit-impelled Philip tells the Ethiopian eunuch.[194] So *the Spirit here is characterized as a mission-director, causing Philip to testify about Jesus* in a place near Gaza, so, beyond Samaria.

Thus, in relation to the causal aspect of the plot, the Spirit is characterized (1) (indirectly) as empowering Philip to proclaim the gospel and to perform miracles in bearing witness to Jesus in Samaria, (2) as verifying the Samaritan believers as God's people and (3) as a responsible mission director who forces and guides Philip[195] to preach/teach about Jesus to the Ethiopian eunuch and Hellenistic people at Azotus.

4.6.2.2. Saul's Conversion/Call and his Witness. The account of Saul's conversion/call[196] (9.1-19a) is presented between the episode of Philip's

arriving at Cornelius's house in Caesarea (9.32-43). See Hengel (1983: 112-13).

191. See §5.1.1.2 in Chapter 4.
192. See §5.2.2.1 in Chapter 4.
193. See §§5.1.2.1 and 5.1.2.2 in Chapter 4.
194. The man that Philip encounters on the way to Gaza is introduced as a eunuch from Ethiopia (cf. LXX Ps. 67.32; Zeph. 3.10: it has been disputed whether the Ethiopian eunuch was a proselyte or a God-fearing Gentile; see Johnson [1992: 159]; Barrett [1994: I, 424-26]; Tannehill [1994: 108-109]; Hengel [1983: 111]; it is clear in the context, however, that the eunuch [cf. Deut. 23.1] must be regarded as an outcast to the Jews), possibly assumed to be one of the regions at the 'ends of the earth' (for the Ethiopians regarded as those living at the ends of the earth in ancient literature, Homer, *Odyssey* 1.23; Herodotus 3.25, 3.114; Strabo, *Geography* 1.1.6, 1.2.24, cited in Thornton [1978: 375]; see also Hengel [1983: 200 n. 85]; Gaventa [1986: 105, 124]). That the Ethiopian eunuch received the 'good news' and was baptized (8.35-38) indicates the double fulfilment of Old Testament prophecy for both a eunuch (Isa. 56.3-8) and an Ethiopian (Isa. 11.11). In this way, this episode concerning Philip's preaching the gospel to the Ethiopian eunuch can be seen as the partial fulfilment of the outreach of the gospel to the ends of the earth, which is confirmed by Peter and the Jerusalem Council (15.6-29) after the Cornelius incident, and then continued by Paul, under the sanction of the Holy Spirit.
195. Philip as a man of the Spirit can, thus, be regarded as a 'pioneering missionary' for non-Jewish people as well as a charismatic witness to Jesus. See Spencer (1992: 271-76).
196. Concerning the nature of and variations in Saul's experience on the Damascus Road found in Acts 9, 22 and 26, scholars disagree: (1) Saul's conversion, see Dunn (1970a: 73-78) or (2) Saul's call for particular commissioning, see Stendahl

encounter with the Ethiopian eunuch (9.26-40) and that of Peter's encounter with a Roman centurion Cornelius and his household (10.1-48) in contexts foreshadowing and launching the witness mission toward the 'ends of the earth'. Through this episode of Saul's encounter with the risen and exalted Jesus, the narrator, thus, begins to transform Saul *from* the man who persecuted Jesus[197] (cf. Saul's attitude to the 'Way' in 7.58; 8.1, 3; 9.1-2) *to* the man, called 'a chosen instrument' (σκεῦος ἐκλογῆς; cf. Acts 1.2, 24-25; 6.5) and 'servant and witness' (ὑπηρέτης καὶ μάρτυς; cf. Lk. 1.2), who is persecuted for the Way of Jesus (Acts 9.16; cf. 24.5, 14).

How is the Holy Spirit characterized in this section in relation to the causal aspect of the plot? The reference to the Spirit in relation to Saul's conversion/call is found in Ananias's words to Saul in Acts 9.17: 'He [Ananias] laid his hands[198] on Saul and said, "Brother Saul, the Lord Jesus, who appeared to you on your way here, has sent me so that you may regain your sight and be filled with the Holy Spirit (πλησθῇς πνεύματος ἁγίου)"'. Although there is no actual description of the coming of the Spirit on Saul, the narrative depicts through Ananias's speech that Saul, baptized and his sight restored, is filled with the Spirit and thus equipped as an inspired witness to Jesus. The narrative suggests that Saul's reception of the Spirit is caused by the risen Lord Jesus

(1976: 7-23); Lampe (1951: 72-75); Stronstad (1984: 66); Menzies (1991a: 260-63). My view is that Acts 9 describes Saul's conversion along with his special commissioning, whereas both Acts 22 and 26 focus on his commissioning. For a similar position, see Gaventa (1986: 66, 76, 90): 'Paul is not converted in order to savor the experience but always in order to witness' (92); Hedrick (1981: 415-32); Witherup (1992: 67-86); Marguerat (1995: 127-55); cf. Turner (1996b: 375-78). On the other hand, the variations found in three accounts of Saul's conversion/call have long been explained on the basis of source-analysis (see Hedrick). Recently, however, these accounts have been evaluated not only in each particular literary context (e.g. the audience [the Jewish people in Acts 22; the king, Agrippa in Acts 26]; the story-teller [Acts 9 by the narrator; Acts 22 and 26 by Paul himself]; see Gaventa), but also by means of 'functional redundancy' (which usually produces 'expansion', 'truncation', 'change of order', 'grammatical transformation' and 'substitution'; see Witherup and Marguerat). In so doing, it has been demonstrated afresh that the variations in these accounts do not indicate contradictions ignored by Luke, but represent a significant literary strategy designed by Luke.

197. Saul's persecution of the Jewish Christian believers is interpreted as persecution of Jesus himself in Acts 9.4-5; 22.7-8; 26.14-15 (see Lk. 10.16: 'whoever rejects you [Jesus' witnesses] rejects me [Jesus]').

198. See n. 181 in this chapter.

(9.17).[199] Saul is thus characterized as the man of the risen Jesus (Acts 13.47; 20.24; 26.16). Indeed, Saul's reception of the Spirit explains why he is called a chosen instrument/witness for Jesus (Acts 9.15-16; 22.15, 21; 26.16; cf. 1.8).[200] The Spirit is presented as not only validating Saul to become Jesus' witness (cf. Acts 1.8), but also causing/ empowering Saul to bear witness to Jesus. This understanding is supported by the subsequent account of Saul's activity in Damascus and Jerusalem. After being filled with the Spirit (9.17; cf. 13.2, 4, 9; 16.6, 7; 19.6, 21; 20.22, 23), Paul is characterized as a witness to Jesus who immediately (καὶ εὐθέως) began to proclaim (κηρύσσω) and to prove (συμβιβάζω) Jesus to be the Son of God and the Messiah in the Damascus synagogues (9.20, 22). In addition, Saul (9.26) is said to continue to speak boldly (παρρησιάζομαι; cf. 13.46; 28.31) in the name of Jesus (ἐν τῷ ὀνόματι Ἰησοῦ) in Jerusalem as in Damascus (9.27-28).[201]

One more matter for comment is the narrator's summary statement reviewing church growth in association with the Spirit in Acts 9.31: 'Meanwhile the church throughout Judea, Galilee, and Samaria had peace and was built up. Living in the fear of the Lord (cf. Acts 2.43; 5.5, 11) and in the comfort of the Holy Spirit (τῇ παρακλήσει τοῦ ἁγίου πνεύματος), it increased in numbers'. This shows that, in spite of persecution, the gospel/God's word (Acts 6.7) has reached beyond

---

199. In this sense, the risen Jesus' promise of the Spirit to his apostles in Lk. 24.46-49; Acts 1.8 is to be extended to Saul/Paul. In regard to the contexts in which the Spirit is said to be sent from Acts 2 onwards, the narrative suggests that God is described as the (final) cause who gives the Spirit to his people generally (Acts 2.38-39; 5.32) or apologetically (Acts 8.17; 11.17-18; 15.8)—occasionally in response to their prayer (cf. Lk. 11.13), whereas it is the risen Jesus who is presented as the cause who sends the Spirit upon *his witnesses* (Acts 2.33; 9.17; cf. Lk. 24.48; Acts 1.8) or encourages/empowers their witnessing through the Spirit (Acts 4.8-14; 6.10; 7.55; cf. Lk. 12.8-12; 21.12-15).

200. Cf. Tannehill (1994: 122), who comments, 'Saul has become not only a Christian but also a missionary through the preceding events'.

201. Saul's rejection by the Jews, who even plot to kill him, echoes that of both Jesus and his witnesses (Acts 9.23). The characterization of Saul/Paul as Jesus' witness to the ends of the earth is further clarified and reinforced by his two defence speeches telling of his own experience on the Damascus road in front of two different audiences, i.e. the Jews in Acts 22.1-21 and the king Agrippa in Acts 26.2-23; see Witherup (1992: 70).

Jerusalem to the territory of Judea, Galilee and Samaria.[202] Here the Spirit is depicted as 'comforter'[203] of the members of the Christian community (cf. Lk. 2.25): the Spirit is characterized as causing the church members to be encouraged or comforted (even in the face of persecution; cf. Acts 4.1-4; 5.17ff.; 8.1-3; 9.1-2) so that they might sustain their Christian life (cf. Acts 5.1-11; 6.3; 7.51; 11.24; 15.28; cf. the 'sustaining role of God's Spirit' in the DSS [see my excursus]; see also the summary passages in Acts 2.42-47; 4.32-37; 5.12-16, presumably influenced by the power and guidance of the Spirit) and thus the church increased (cf. Acts 6.1, 7).[204]

In terms of the development of the plot, therefore, the narrator now begins to focus on the character Saul and describes how he dramatically encounters the risen Jesus. Saul is then immediately introduced as being filled with the Spirit prior to being portrayed as the man of Jesus; the Spirit is thus (indirectly) characterized as empowering and inspiring Saul to bear bold witness to Jesus in Damascus and Jerusalem. At the same time, however, the Spirit is also characterized as comforting/encouraging God's people who already believe in Jesus in Judea, Galilee and Samaria, and thereby causing the church's expansion.

4.6.2.3. The Witness of Peter. The narrator, at the beginning of Acts 10, introduces a certain Gentile, named Cornelius, who is a Roman centurion in Caesarea.[205] In spite of Cornelius's ethnic background, the

202. Readers may be puzzled by the abrupt mention of the growth of Christians in Galilee, which is not previously reported. It seems that the narrator attempts to signify the spread and growth of God's Church (note the singular form ἐκκλησία in v. 31) throughout all Jewish areas. Cf. Barrett (1994: 472-73); Johnson (1992: 176).

203. The word παράκλησις (cf. the Spirit as παράκλητος in Jn 14.16, 26; 15.26; 16.7) can be understood as 'consolation' (Lk. 2.25; 6.24); 'exhortation' or 'encouragement' (Acts 13.15; 15.31?; cf. 4.36); 'comfort' (Acts 9.31; 15.31?; cf. 16.40; 20.12; LXX Isa. 40.1; 61.2). See Maddox 1982: 173; Barrett 1994: 474, 258. Bruce (1990a: 246), Haenchen (1971: 333), Johnson (1992: 177) and Dunn (1996: 128) interpret τῇ παρακλήσει τοῦ ἁγίου πνεύματος as a subjective genitive, 'the encouragement/comfort given by the Holy Spirit'. Shepherd (1994: 194 n. 132) understands this phrase as either 'the comfort or encouragement provided by the Holy Spirit' or 'the exhortation inspired by the Holy Spirit'.

204. Cf. Turner (1996b: 401-27). Contra Ervin (1984); Stronstad (1984: 12): 'for Luke, the Holy Spirit is not brought into relation to salvation or to sanctification, as is commonly asserted, but is *exclusively* brought into relation to a third dimension of Christian life—service' (emphasis added); Menzies (1991a: 278-79).

205. The city Caesarea in Acts seems to be regarded as not assigned to the

narrator's direct characterization of him is unusual, reminding the reader of that of pious Jews: 'a devout man who feared God'[206] (cf. Lk. 2.25; Acts 2.5; 8.2; 9.31; 22.12), 'giving alms' (cf. Lk. 7.5; Acts 9.36) and 'praying constantly to God' (cf. Lk. 11.1-13; Acts 1.12-14; 3.1; 10.9). In addition, Cornelius, like Peter and other reliable characters in Luke–Acts, is said to have a vision in which he receives an annunciation from an angel of God (9.3-6). It is not surprising, therefore, that Cornelius and his household, at the end of the episode, are said to receive the Holy Spirit while Peter is delivering the message about Jesus to them (9.44). The significance of this episode is to show that (God-fearing) *Gentiles* are also to receive the Holy Spirit as were the Jews on the day of Pentecost in Acts 2 (10.47; 11.16). In regard to the characterization of the Spirit in this episode,[207] three factors should be noted in association with Peter, Cornelius and his household, and Jesus respectively.

First, the Holy Spirit is said to appear in the context in which Peter thinks over the vision and the men sent by Cornelius are about to enter into the tanner Simon's house where Peter is staying (10.9-19). Peter first seems to suppose that by the vision God is testing his fidelity to food laws (10.14). But the subsequent heavenly voice, 'What God has made clean, you must not call profane' (10.15), puzzles him. At that very moment, the Holy Spirit is said to speak to Peter directly about

territory of Judea (12.19; 21.10; cf. 10.37; 11.1). In this respect, this episode, i.e. Peter's (as the representative of the Jerusalem Church) visit to the Gentile house of a *Roman* centurion, not only anticipates the mission to the ends of the earth as does that of the Ethiopian eunuch in Acts 8, but also partly actualizes it. See Gaventa (1986: 124).

206. Though it is still disputed whether there are people called by this technical term 'God-fearers' (οἱ φοβούμενοι τὸν θεόν: Acts 10.2, 22, 35; 13.16, 26) within both the narrative and the social worlds in Luke–Acts, there are devout God-worshippers (οἱ σεβόμενοι [τὸν θεόν]: Acts 16.14; 17.4; 18.7; cf. 13.43, 50; 17.17) who are neither Jews nor proselytes. See Cohen (1989: 13-33); Jervell (1988: 11-20); Wilcox (1981: 102-122); De Boer (1995: 50-71).

207. From the beginning to the end of this episode (Acts 10.1–11.18), the narrator utilizes the 'divine frame of reference' within direct discourse: a vision (to Cornelius in 10.3; to Peter in 10.10-12, 17; 11.5), an angel of God (to Cornelius in 10.3-4, 6, 22, 30; 11.13), a heavenly voice (to Peter in 10.11-13, 15; 11.7, 9) and particularly the Holy Spirit (to Cornelius, his household, and his friends in 10.44, 45, 47; 11.15; to Peter in 10.19; 11.12; cf. 10.38; 11.16). This signals and highlights that it is God's will/plan that even Gentiles are to be legitimately incorporated into the people of God.

what he should do without giving any explanation of the vision, which causes Peter first to show Cornelius's messengers hospitality[208] and then directs him to come to Caesarea to see their master, Cornelius.[209] At their meeting, Cornelius's retelling his vision helps Peter further to discern the will of God (10.34-35), which was conveyed through the vision, the divine voice and the Holy Spirit, and leads him to preach the gospel about Jesus (10.36-43).[210] The Spirit is, therefore, characterized not only as guiding Peter directly to what/where he should do/go, to Cornelius's house at Caesarea, but also as revealing God's will to him: to bear witness to Jesus (10.36-43) and to baptize Gentiles in the name of Jesus (10.44-48).

With respect to the descent of the Spirit upon the Gentiles in Cornelius's house, the narrator employs phrases or expressions reminiscent of the day of Pentecost: the 'gift' (Acts 10.45; 2.38; 11.17); the 'Holy Spirit had been poured out' (Acts 10.45; 2.17). In this immediate context, the Spirit is said to cause them to speak in tongues[211] and extol God (10.47), as seen in the case of Jews (Acts 2.4, 11). Thus, Peter declares, 'Can anyone withhold the water for baptizing these people (Gentiles) who have received the Holy Spirit just as we (Jews) have?' (10.47; see also Acts 11.15-17). In this sense, the coming of the Spirit upon Gentiles alongside notable manifestations is apologetically designed to verify *Gentiles*, like the Samaritan believers, as members of

208. For the importance of the theme of reciprocal hospitality (10.23, 48) in the episode, see Gaventa (1986: 109, 113, 116, 120).
209. This episode shows that those who are already portrayed as 'Spirit-filled characters' do not always (immediately) perceive God's will/plan, and need to be re-directed by the Holy Spirit. This implies thus that the Holy Spirit is presented as helping them break their own (cultural-religious) preoccupation, which sometimes turns out to be a stumbling block against God (cf. the case of Paul and his companions in Acts 16.6-10: see also n. 252 and §5 in this chapter). On the other hand, the further reference to the Holy Spirit here serves to highlight Peter's mission towards non-Jews as God's initiating plan.
210. In this episode (Acts 10.1–11.18), not only Cornelius, but also Peter, is said to discern the will of God gradually through the divine promptings within the 'repeated direct discourse' narrated by different characters. See Barthes (1979: 122-34). For the significance of the narrative function of the repetitions in the episode, see Witherup (1993: 45-66).
211. However, speaking in tongues in Acts 10.47 (and 19.6), unlike in Acts 2.4, 6, 8, does not seem to mean xenoglossy, i.e. 'speaking in a foreign tongue'. Rather it simply means glossolalia, i.e. 'ecstatic utterance'. See Haenchen (1971: 354); Menzies (1991a: 265 n. 3); Esler (1992: 136). Contra Shepherd (1994: 201 n. 150).

God's community. Hence, the Spirit here is presented as the decisive
and legitimate verifying cause of Cornelius and his household's (i.e.
Gentiles') acceptance by God.[212]

Another important reference to the Spirit is employed in Peter's
explanation of the nature of Jesus' earthly ministry in a 'mini-gospel'[213]
(10.34-43) to the Gentiles: 'That message spread throughout Judea,
beginning in Galilee after the baptism that John announced: how God'
anointed Jesus of Nazareth *with the Holy Spirit and with power*; how he
went about doing good and healing all who were oppressed by the
devil, for God was with him' (10.37-38). This confirms that the Holy
Spirit, given by God, according to Peter, empowers Jesus to accomplish
his earthly ministry powerfully and successfully, particularly in releasing devil-oppressed people (see the previous arguments in this chapter).
Jesus' mission empowered by the Spirit demonstrates that God is at
work through Jesus (cf. Lk. 4.43; 7.16; 8.39; 9.48; 10.16, 22; 11.20).
Moreover, Peter's witness to Jesus before the Gentiles (e.g. 'Jesus
Christ—he is Lord of all' in v. 36; Jesus as 'the one ordained by God as
judge of the living and the dead' in v. 42) may possibly be presented as
inspired by the Spirit who directly instructs him to go down to the
Cornelius house.[214]

212. See Tannehill (1994: 143); Esler (1992: 136, 142); Fowl (1995: 355). Cf.
the two theological opposite positions on Cornelius's (and his household's)
reception of the Spirit: (1) Dunn (1970a: 81) and Bruner (1970: 196) have argued
that the gift of the Spirit is the sign for the Gentiles' conversion-initiation, i.e.
God's gift of repentance unto life; (2) Stronstad (1984: 67) and Menzies (1991a:
267) have contended that the Spirit is the second blessing for the missionary enterprise. On the other hand, Turner (1996b: 387) and Shelton (1994) are more cautious
than the above scholars, but in the end Turner (387) is in line with the former,
Shelton (132, 133) with the latter. It is no wonder that the word πιστεύσασιν ('having believed') in 11.17 is interpreted, on the one hand, as 'when having believed'
by Dunn (86-87); on the other, as 'after having believed' by Shelton (150 n. 20).
Compare my view with that of Shepherd (1994: 204): 'the coming of the Spirit on
the Gentile believers...is a reliable sign that there are to be no distinctions between
Jew and Gentile'.
    213. See Witherup (1993: 56). In fact, Acts 10.34-43 summarizes the Gospel of
Luke in chronological order; it can be represented as follows: (1) the angel's and
John's witness to Jesus (vv. 36-37), (2) Jesus' charismatic witness empowered by
the Holy Spirit (vv. 38-41) and (3) the risen Jesus' commission to his witnesses (vv.
42-43). It is also noted that Peter, like Jesus (Lk. 24.25-27), regards Old Testament
prophets as witnesses to Jesus (v. 43).
    214. Witherup (1993: 60) comments, 'Ultimately, Peter is led to the point where

Hence, the following roles are played by the Spirit in relation to Peter's ministry in Acts 10.1–11.18: the Spirit is presented not only *as guiding Peter to visit Cornelius' house*, that is, *Gentiles, for the proclamation of the gospel (about Jesus)*, but also *as verifying them as God's people by causing them to speak in tongues and extol God*. In this way, the Spirit serves to initiate *and* validate the Gentile mission, which will be taken up by Barnabas and Saul.

4.6.2.4. *Summary.* The narrator, in this subsection of 'Witness in Judea and Samaria' (Acts 8.1–11.18), advances the plot by focusing on three leading characters: Philip, Saul and Peter. In relation to the causal aspect of the plot, the role/function of the Spirit is as follows: *the Spirit is (directly or indirectly) characterized as empowering and guiding Philip, Saul and Peter to bear witness to Jesus* in each context; at the same time, *the Spirit verifies the Samaritans and the Cornelius household as God's people, especially by causing the Gentiles, like Jews, to speak in tongues and praise God.*[215] As in the Jerusalem Church (Acts 5.1-11), the Spirit is also characterized *in relation to the daily life of early Christians in a settled community in Judea, Galilee and Samaria: as encouraging or comforting them so that the church continues to expand.* The narrative also confirms through Peter's preaching that the Spirit functions as empowering the earthly Jesus, from Galilee to Jerusalem, to accomplish his messianic mission in mighty words and deeds.

4.6.3. *Witness towards the Ends of the Earth (Acts 11.19–28.15).* In Acts 11.19-21, the narrator introduces a new geographical development of the mission (cf. the previous introduction to the gospel expansion in Acts 8.1-3): Phoenicia, Cyprus and Antioch. Within this geographical framework, Antioch is recurrently mentioned in subsequent verses (11.19, 20, 22, 26, 27), which foreshadows its future role as the 'Gentile mission centre' (Acts 13.1-3; 14.26-28; 15.22, 35; 18.22).[216] At the same time, the narrator begins to place both Barnabas and Saul centre stage (Acts 11.22-26, 30), whereas Peter is gradually moved off stage (Acts 12.17).[217] In so doing, leadership of the Gentile mission moves

he can eloquently defend the movement to the Gentiles as ordained by God and guided by the Holy Spirit'.

215. Cf. Stonehouse (1950: 10).

216. Cf. Alexander (1995: 42).

217. See Dupont (1979: 24). It is not incidental that the Gentile mission is launched by Peter (as one of the representatives of the Jerusalem Church) through

from Peter (Acts 12.17; cf. 15.7-11), *via* Barnabas and Saul/Paul (Acts 11.25-26; 13.2–14.28; 15.12, 35) *to* Paul and his companions (from Acts 16 onwards). References to the Spirit from Acts 11.19 onwards, therefore, are mostly related to Barnabas and especially to Saul/Paul: 11.24, 28; 13.2, 4, 9, 52; 15.8, 28; 16.6, 7; 19.2a, 2b, 6, 21; 20.22, 23, 28; 21.4, 11.

4.6.3.1. The Witness of Barnabas and Saul/Paul. Barnabas, introduced earlier as a 'son of encouragement' (Acts 4.36), is now depicted as a 'good man, full of the Holy Spirit and of faith' in Acts 11.24. It is likely that his goodness (cf. 'God's *good* Spirit' in Ps. 143.10; Neh. 9.20) and faith are understood to be caused by the Spirit (cf. Acts 6.3-5).[218] This description of Barnabas serves to make authoritative and trustworthy his following activities and/or functions: his seeking Saul in Tarsus, bringing him to Antioch and teaching with him many people and disciples, there first called 'Christians' (Acts 11.25-26); as intermediary[219] between the twelve apostles and Saul, and at the same time between the Jerusalem Church and the Antioch Church (Acts 11.22, 30; 12.25; 15.2, 12, 22, 35). When this narrative role of Barnabas is successfully complete, the narrator begins to focus sole attention on Saul/Paul's activity, particularly from Acts 16 onwards.[220]

In Acts 11.28, the Spirit is presented as inspiring Agabus, one of the prophets come from Jerusalem to Antioch, to predict (ἐσήμανεν διὰ

the Spirit, and is later taken over by Barnabas and especially by Paul, also impelled by the Spirit. See Johnson (1992: 179); Witherup (1993: 65). On the other hand, the narrator also links the Antioch Church to the Jerusalem Church by means of Barnabas (11.22) and Agabus (11.27-28), both characterized as 'men of the Spirit'. Note also the visit of Barnabas and Saul to Jerusalem and their returning to Antioch (Acts 11.30; 12.25).

218. See also §5.2.1.1 in Chapter 4.

219. To some extent, Ananias, presented in Acts 9.10-19a (characterized as a 'disciple' in v. 10) and in Acts 22.1-21 (as a 'devout man according to the law and well spoken of by all the Jews' in v. 12), is seen to function in a similar role of intermediary in support of Saul/Paul to Jewish Christians, Jews (there is no mention of Ananias when Paul appears before Agrippa in Acts 26) and the reader.

220. Until Acts 15.35 (see Paul's first initial suggestion to Barnabas in 15.36), Barnabas is said to be in charge of their co-ministry. It is interesting to note that the narrator usually presents them, if together, by the order 'Barnabas and Saul' (Acts 11.30; 13.2, 7; 14.14; cf. 9.27; 11.25). However, after Saul's other name Paul is given (13.9), the order is reversed and, 'Paul and Barnabas' is more often employed (13.43, 46, 50; 15.2 [×2], 12, 22, 25, 35).

τοῦ πνεύματος)[221] a severe famine in the regions governed by Rome including Palestine.[222] In other words, the Spirit is characterized as the prophetic Spirit (see Acts 1.16; 4.25; 21.11; 28.25; cf. Lk. 1.41, 67). As a result, the Gentile believers in the Antioch Church are said to send relief and dispatch Barnabas and Saul as their representatives in order to meet the needs of the Jewish Christians in the Jerusalem Church (Acts 11.29-30). Acts 11.27-30 thus serves to present the narrative significance of the Antioch Church as well as Barnabas and Saul, implying that the Church (cf. Acts 13.1-3) and the men (cf. Acts 9.17; 11.24; 13.4) are led indirectly by the Spirit to demonstrate partnership with the Jerusalem Church governed by the twelve apostles and elders.[223] In doing so, the implied author intimates the reliability of both the Antioch Church and Barnabas and Saul, in relation to the forthcoming Gentile mission in the subsequent plot development.

This reading is substantiated and further developed by additional indicators at the beginning of Acts 13: there are 'prophets and teachers' in the Antioch Church and, above all, when they are 'worshipping the Lord and fasting', they are informed directly by the Holy Spirit: '"Set apart[224] for me [Holy Spirit] Barnabas and Saul for the work to which I have called them"' (13.2). The Spirit here is characterized as a mission director (Acts 8.29, 39; 10.19; 11.12; 16.6-7; cf. 19.21; 20.22), causing the Antioch Church leaders to separate Barnabas and Saul for the

221. The verb σημαίνω is often used to mean 'indicate' or 'signify' (see Acts 25.27; LXX Exod. 18.20; Num. 10.9; Jn 12.33; 18.32; 21.19); it is also employed in connection with inspired oracle (Plutarch, *Sayings of the Spartans*, Callicratidas 6; Epictetus, *Discourses* 1, 17, 18; Josephus, *War* 7.214; 10.241; Dan. 2.23, 45; Rev. 1.1; cf. Thucydides 2.8.2; Josephus, *Ant.* 6.50; 8.409). See Johnson (1992: 205); Barrett (1994: 562-63).

222. For the interpretation of 'over all the world' (ἐφ' ὅλην τὴν οἰκουμένην; Acts 11.28; cf. Lk. 2.1; 4.5; Acts 17.6; 24.5), see Haenchen (1971: 376-77); Johnson (1992: 208).

223. Cf. Shepherd (1994: 208 n. 171). For the Lukan function of the collection delineated here in comparison with Paul's own version of it in Gal. 2.10; 1 Cor. 16.1-4; 2 Cor. 8-9; Rom. 15.25-32): see also Haenchen (1971: 377-79); Johnson (1992: 208-209, 6-7).

224. This verb ἀφορίζω, which is also translated as 'separate/make holy', is found in the LXX (Exod. 13.12; 29.26-27; Lev. 13.4; Num. 12.24; 2 Sam. 8.1; Isa. 52.11; more relevant are the Pauline epistles in which the verb is used for explaining his own understanding of his call by God [Rom. 1.1; Gal. 1.15]). See Johnson (1992: 221).

Gentile mission. The narrator continues to present the Spirit as a mission director in Acts 13.4: 'So, being sent out by the Holy Spirit (ἐκπεμφθέντες ὑπὸ τοῦ ἁγίου πνεύματος), they [Barnabas and Saul] went down to Seleucia; and from there they sailed to Cyprus'.[225] This means that the expansion of the gospel, through proclaiming the word of God or the Lord (Jesus),[226] into new territories beyond Jerusalem, Judea and Samaria, e.g. Salamis (13.5), Pisidian Antioch (13.14), Iconium (13.51), and Lystra and Derbe (Acts 14.6-7, 8-20a; 20b-21), is initiated and led by the Holy Spirit through Barnabas and Saul as God's human agents or Jesus' witnesses accomplishing the Lord's (both God's and the risen Jesus'; Acts 13.2; 14.3; cf. 16.6, 7, 10) desire/plan (cf. Lk. 24.48-49; Acts 1.6-8).

This mission-oriented role of the Spirit is further intensified through Acts 13.4–14.26, which echoes those of the preceding witnesses portrayed as 'men of the Spirit' (i.e. Jesus, Peter, Stephen and Philip).[227] (1) They are said to proclaim boldly the word of God (13.5, 7, 44, 46, 48, 49; esp. see 14.3) and the forgiveness of sins (13.38). (2) They are said to perform 'signs and wonders' (14.3; 15.12; cf. 13.11-12; 14.8-12). (3) Their preaching is centred on Jesus; they are characterized as witnesses to Jesus (13.23-39; cf. 14.3). And finally, (4) the double response

225. Dunn (1996: 173) comments on 'I' terms in Acts 13.2 as follows: 'Alternatively expressed, the "I" of the prophecy is understood not as God or as the exalted Jesus speaking, but the Spirit—that is, of course, the Spirit as the mouth piece of God and/or Jesus (cf. 16.7)'. Cf. Bruce (1990a: 294), who suggests in passing that these revelations in Acts 13.2, 4 are presumably discerned and reported 'through one of the prophets' at the Antioch Church. From the narrative criticism perspective, however, the Holy Spirit is used by the narrator to stress the divinely propelled origin of the witness mission (esp. for the Gentile mission), not just to be undertaken by the Antioch Church. For the speech and action of the Spirit in Luke–Acts, see §§5.1.2.1 and 5.1.2.2 in Chapter 4.

226. The two interchangeable terms, 'word of God' (Acts 13.4, 7, 44, 46, 48; 17.13; 18.5, 11; 20.32a; cf. 4.31; 6.7) and 'word of the Lord' (Acts 13.49; 15.18, 35, 36; 16.32; 19.10, 20), often appear from Acts 13 onwards, epitomizing the message that both Barnabas and/or Saul/Paul preach and signifying the expansion of the Kingdom of God (cf. Lk. 8.4-15). The 'word of the Lord' seems to be intentionally employed to refer to *both/either* God *and/or* the risen Jesus (cf. Acts 16.32). The content of the proclamation is also presented by two phrases, the 'word of this salvation' (Acts 13.26) and the 'word of [the Lord's/God's] grace' (Acts 14.3; 20.32b). Also note similar expressions, 'way of the Lord' (Acts 18.25): 'way of God' (Acts 18.26) and 'way of salvation' (Acts 16.17).

227. See Johnson (1977: 53-54).

among the people to their witness follows the same pattern of acceptance and rejection (13.42-50; 14.4, 19-21). Although there is no explicit
reference to the Spirit in these contexts (except in 13.9; see below), the
Spirit is implicitly characterized as causing Barnabas and Saul to proclaim the gospel and perform miracles in bearing bold witness to Jesus.

However, in the context (Acts 13.6-12) in which Paul (whose name
had previously been given as Saul)[228] is engaged in conflict with Elymas (or the force of Satan), the Spirit is explicitly presented in v. 9 as
inspiring Paul—'filled with the Holy Spirit' (πλησθεὶς πνεύματος
ἁγίου)[229]—to overcome the force of the evil or Satan (cf. Lk. 4.1, 14)
with mighty words (Acts 13.10) and deeds (Acts 13.11). The Spirit is
then characterized not only as directing Paul (and Barnabas) where to
go, but also as inspiring what he says and does. Hence, if somebody is
presented as interrupting the 'way of witness' of Barnabas and Saul,
they not only rejects their gospel message, but also thwart the 'way of
God/the Lord' (cf. Lk. 7.29-30; 10.16), propelled and/or directed by the
Spirit.[230]

On the other hand, the narrator connects the Holy Spirit in passing
with the Gentile believers at Antioch of Pisidia[231] while he reports their

228. It is supposed that Paul had three names as a Roman citizen—*praenomen,
nomen* and *cognomen*, or even four, if we include *signum* or *supernomen*. In Paul's
case, the *cognomen* is Paul; the *signum* Saul, although the others are unknown. See
Bruce (1990a: 298); Haenchen (1971: 399 n. 1).

229. See §5.2.1.2 in Chapter 4.

230. For instance, the magician Elymas is characterized as a 'Jewish false
prophet' (Acts 13.6), 'son of the devil', 'enemy of all righteousness' and 'full of all
deceit and villainy', 'who makes crooked the way of the Lord' (διαστρέφων τὰς
ὁδοὺς τοῦ κυρίου τὰς εὐθείας)' in 13.10, whereas Paul is contrasted with him,
portrayed as 'true prophet' (Acts 13.1), 'full of the Holy Spirit' (Acts 13.9; cf. 9.17;
11.24) and 'servant and witness' of Jesus (9.15; 22.15; 26.16), who makes straight
the way of the Lord; for conflict between the Holy Spirit and Satan, see §5.2.2.2 in
Chapter 4. Also both Barnabas and Saul are called 'apostles' (Acts 14.4, 14; see
Bruce [1990a: 319] and Barrett [1994: 671-72]), yet still distinguished from the
twelve apostles (Acts 9.27; 15.2, 4, 6, 22, 23; cf. 1.21-26). This implies that the
narrator characterizes Barnabas and (particularly) Paul as reliable and authoritative
in a similar way to the portrait of the Twelve (i.e. Paul is portrayed as a 'chosen
instrument' sent by the risen Jesus in Acts 9.15), because Barnabas and Paul are
said to be called and sent by the Jerusalem Church (Acts 15.22; 25) and the Antioch
Church (Acts 11.30; 13.1-4) as well.

231. The word μαθηταί here is understood as referring to Gentile Christians, seen
in Acts 14.21, 22; 15.10; cf. 6.1; 19.2; see Barrett (1994: 661); Dunn (1996: 185).

emotional and/or spiritual condition, even though Barnabas and Paul are said to be persecuted by Jews and so move to Iconium: 'And the disciples were filled with joy and with the Holy Spirit (οἱ τε μαθηταὶ ἐπληροῦντο χαρᾶς ⃞καὶ πνεύματος ἁγίου)' in Acts 13.52. So the Spirit seems here to be characterized as causing them to be full of joy (see also Lk. 1.44, 15; 10.21; Wis. 9.17-18; 1QH 9.32; cf. Acts 8.8; 11.23; 13.48; 15.3, 31) in spite of persecution (cf. Acts 5.41).[232]

In Acts 11–13, the narrator continues to characterize the Holy Spirit in relation to the expansion of the 'way of witness', although the centre of this divine enterprise begins to be shifted from the Jerusalem Church to the Antioch Church: the Spirit is presented as a mission director for the Gentile mission, by calling and sending Barnabas and Saul/Paul, as well as empowering/inspiring them (especially Paul) to proclaim the gospel (about Jesus and God's Kingdom) and perform miracles. The Spirit is also characterized in connection with the life of Christians, suggesting that the Spirit is the source of 'goodness', 'faith' (in relation to Barnabas) and 'joy' (in relation to the Antioch Christians).

4.6.3.2. The Decision of the Jerusalem Council and the Holy Spirit. Two references to the Holy Spirit (Acts 15.8, 28) are found at the beginning and end of the episode of the Jerusalem Council (Acts 15),[233] in which 'the apostles and the elders' (15.6) are said to discuss whether circumcision and keeping the law of Moses are to be required of Gentile believers. In dealing with this issue, the implied author makes the Spirit appear twice at a critical moment of the plot-development[234] in an attempt to show how the Gentile mission is *officially* (cf. Acts 8.29, 39; 10.19; 11.12, 17-18) accepted and encouraged by the Jerusalem Church through God's inspiration.

The report about the process and decision made by the Jerusalem Council in regard to the issue is presented in Acts 15.6-29.[235] This

232. Marshall (1991a: 231) comments, 'the group of new disciples experienced the *joy* that comes from the presence of *the Holy Spirit* with believers' (emphasis original). See also Bruce (1988: 269; 1990a: 316); Kistemaker (1990: 309).

233. For general discussion on the Jerusalem Council in Acts 15, see Lake (1933c: 195-212); Haenchen (1971: 455-72); Wilson (1973: 171-95).

234. Shepherd (1994: 215) rightly comments, 'Luke now draws the threads of his plot together and brings the first half of Acts to a close'. However, he neither provides the definition of a plot, nor suggests the plot of Luke–Acts.

235. On Lukan skill in achieving his narrative goal in Acts 15, see Dunn (1996: 195-96).

account shows that each testimony of Peter (vv. 7-11), and of Barnabas
and Paul (v. 12) plays a crucial part in preparing for the apostolic decision finally made by James's discerning leadership (vv. 13-21).[236]
Through his testimony, Peter states with conviction[237] that Gentile
Christians do not need to be circumcised to be saved because they have
already been accepted by God, not by means of circumcision, but
'through the grace of the Lord Jesus' (Acts 15.11). How does Peter,
then, perceive whether or not Gentile Christians have the Lord's grace?
According to Peter (and the implied author), those who, regardless
whether they are Jews or Gentiles, receive the gift of the Holy Spirit are
verified as God's people: 'God, who knows the human heart, testified to
them by giving them [the Gentiles] the Holy Spirit, just as he did to us
[the Jews]' (Acts 15.8).[238] So, the Spirit is characterized as being given
(or caused) by God to his people without any distinction between Jews
and Gentiles and is thus presented as God's verifier, signifying those
who receive the Spirit as God's people.[239]

As a result, the apostles, the elders and the whole church (Acts 15.6,
22) are said to consent that circumcision is not to be required of Gentile
Christians; but they advise them 'to abstain only from things polluted
by idols and from fornication and from whatever has been strangled and
from blood' (Acts 15.20).[240] This means that the testimonies of Peter,

236. Johnson (1992: 268) notes, 'Luke gathers his main characters together for
the first time only for the fashioning of this decision, and then disbands them'.
237. The Western text gives further emphasis to the role of the Holy Spirit in
order to enhance the authority of Peter's speech, by adding the phrase 'in the (Holy)
Spirit' (ἐν [ἁγίῳ] πνεύματι; D, 614, 1799, 2412) before or after Πέτρος (15.7).
238. See Menzies (1991a: 266-67).
239. Peter's testimony for Gentile Christians is further supported by that of
Barnabas and Paul, who witness to 'all the signs and wonders that God had done
through them among the Gentiles' (Acts 15.12) by the power of the Spirit (Acts
9.17; 11.24; 13.2-4, 9; 14.3; cf. 2.22, 43; 4.30; 5.12; 6.8; 10.38). Their experience
serves to discern God's affection/desire to accept Gentiles as his people. James,
after listening to the two testimonies of Peter, and of Barnabas and Paul, confirms
in Acts 15.15-18 that Gentile Christians, without (first) being circumcised, are to be
recognized as God's people on the basis of the additional evidence of the 'words of
the prophets', i.e. Scripture (LXX Amos 9.11-12; cf. Jer. 12.15; Isa. 45.21). Dunn
(1996: 203) notes that Amos 9.11 is also quoted by the Qumran community in CD
7.11; 4Q174 1.12 as a reference to the restoration of Israel.
240. For the issue of the slightly different versions (Acts 15.20, 29; 21.25) of the
'apostolic decree' along with their textual variants, see Metzger (1975: 429-34);
Haenchen (1971: 468-72, 449).

Barnabas and Paul, and the proposal of James[241] work effectively to convince the Church leaders of the irresistible plan of God. To put it another way, the apostles and the elders (and other Jewish Christians) are not to resist God (or his desire/plan toward Gentiles; note the word θεός in Acts 15.4, 7, 8, 10, 12, 14, 19; see also vv. 16-18), who works through his human agents empowered and guided/directed by the Holy Spirit (Acts 8.29, 39; 9.17; 10.19, 44-48; 11.12, 24; 13.2, 4, 9; see also 16.6-7; 19.21; 20.22).

Another reference to the Spirit is recorded in the Jerusalem Council's letter written by 'the brethren (ἀδελφοι), both the apostles and the elders, to the brethren (ἀδελφοῖς) who are of the Gentiles in Antioch and Syria and Cilicia' (Acts 15.23; RSV).[242] 'For it has seemed good to the Holy Spirit and to us to impose on you no further burden than these essentials' (Acts 15.28). The Holy Spirit is here characterized as God's reliable and authoritative decision-maker who not only resolves a conflict within the Jerusalem Church, but also encourages and secures (the mission project of) the Gentile Christian leaders at Antioch.

Hence, in reporting the *Jewish* Christians' council at Jerusalem, the narrator characterizes the Holy Spirit as given by God, as signifying God's will/plan, and thus (1) verifying that Gentiles are God's people and (2) as God's reliable and authoritative decision-maker in relation to the issue that God's church needs to settle. In the rest of Acts, the narrator advances the plot by focusing on Paul's[243] witness mission to Gentiles,[244] which is endorsed by the Jerusalem Church under the guidance of and appeal to the Holy Spirit, so, by God.

241. In comparison with Peter (who is previously depicted as the leader of the Church) as a witness for the Church, James is described as the leader/spokesperson of the Church (Acts 15.13; 21.18; cf. 12.17; see also 1 Cor. 15.7; Gal. 1.19; 2.9, 12). See Bruce (1990a: 339); Johnson (1992: 264).

242. Verse 23 confirms that the Jewish Christian leaders at Jerusalem obey God's council of salvation towards Gentiles through the dynamic activity of his Spirit, by calling them 'brothers'.

243. It is worth noting that Paul, along with Barnabas, is introduced in the Council's letter sent by the Jerusalem Church to the Antioch Church (which should know Paul better than does the Jerusalem Church!; cf. 11.26) as 'the beloved [one] who [has] risked [his] [life] for the sake of our Lord Jesus Christ' in Acts 15.25-26. This is the first (official) reference *by the Jerusalem Church* to Paul as a co-worker for God's enterprise.

244. Thus, Johnson (1992: 280) rightly comments, 'Acts 15 is a watershed within the narrative because it frees Luke finally to concentrate almost entirely on the

4.6.3.3. *The Witness of Paul*. Under the following three subheadings: (1) Paul and the Beginning of the European Mission, (2) Paul and the Ephesian Disciples and (3) Paul's Planning to Visit Rome via Jerusalem, I shall continue to examine the characterization of the Holy Spirit in relation to the causal aspect of the plot.

4.6.3.3.1. *Paul and the Beginning of the European Mission*. The narrative shows that after the breach between Paul and Barnabas,[245] due to their differences over Mark-John as their missionary co-worker (Acts 15.36-39; cf. 13.13), Paul chooses Silas[246] (and Timothy later; Acts 16.1-3) as his new missionary companion (Acts 15.40).[247] In relation to this mission, a double reference to the Spirit is provided.[248]

> They went through the region of Phrygia and Galatia, *having been forbidden by the Holy Spirit* (κωλυθέντες ὑπὸ τοῦ ἁγίου πνεύματος) to speak in Asia. When they had come opposite Mysia, they attempted to go into Bithynia, but *the Spirit of Jesus did not allow them* (καὶ οὐκ εἴασεν αὐτοὺς τὸ πνεῦμα Ἰησοῦ); so, passing by Mysia, they went down to Troas (Acts 16.6-8).

At first glance, the Spirit, in contrast with previous references, seems to be presented as preventing Paul and his companions from preaching the

mission of Paul, and the effective opening of 'the door of faith for the Gentiles' (14.27)'.

245. The record about the 'sharp dispute' (v. 39) between Paul and Barnabas is the first reference that indirectly implies that there could be disagreement even between Spirit-filled figures (cf. Acts 20.22-23; 21.4, 11: see §5 in this chapter). At this narrative juncture, the narrator does not comment on who is right or wrong (cf. Paul's own account in Gal. 2.11-14), but simply describes the incident, and then advances the narrative by giving attention to Paul and his companions' way of witness.

246. Like Barnabas, Silas is previously said to be commissioned by the Jerusalem Church (15.27) and is depicted by the narrator as a prophet (15.32). Cf. the Western text, which strengthens the reliability of Silas (including Judas) by adding πλήρεις πνεύματος ἁγίου after ὄντες in Acts 15.32. For the picture of Silas, see Kaye (1979: 13-26).

247. Hence, Paul's ongoing mission is certified as God's endorsed enterprise through the co-operation of the prophetic figure Silas authorized by the Jerusalem Church (15.27; cf. 16.4) and the unchanging support from members in the Antioch Church (15.40), and this is followed by the report of success in Derbe and Lystra: 'So the churches were strengthened in the faith and increased in numbers daily' (Acts 16.5). For the route and commentary on Paul's journeys in Asia Minor, see French (1994: 49-58).

248. See also §5.1.2.2 in Chapter 4.

gospel to Gentiles, but what the Spirit is said to forbid is not their mission itself, but their mission plan to go to Asia.[249] 'When he [Paul] had seen the vision, we immediately tried to cross over to Macedonia, being convinced that God had called us to proclaim the good news to them' (16.10). Hence, the Holy Spirit, also presented as the 'Spirit of Jesus' (τὸ πνεῦμα᾽Ιησοῦ),[250] is characterized as a mission director (see also Acts 8.26, 29; 10.19; 11.12; 13.2), who decisively guides Jesus' witnesses towards Europe by forbidding (κωλύω)[251] them to speak in Asia.[252] The narrator thus makes it obvious that Paul's witness mission to the new territory Europe is, from the beginning, divinely initiated by employing the Spirit twice (as well as a divine vision in 16.9, 10).

The subsequent accounts of Paul's witness in Philippi (16.12-40), Thessalonica (17.1-9), Beroea (17.10-15), Athens (17.16-34) and Corinth (18.1-17) imply that his ministry is empowered or caused by the Spirit by recounting features found in the ministry of the former Spirit-filled witnesses: (1) bearing witness to Jesus (16.18, 31; 17.3, 18, 31; 18.5), (2) proclaiming/teaching the word of the Lord/God (16.32; 17.13, cf. 17.11; 18.5, 11), (3) performing signs/wonders (16.18, cf. 16.25-26) and (4) giving rise to the divided response of acceptance and rejection (17.4-9, 12-13; 18.6-8).

The fact that the *Holy* Spirit (16.6) is identified with the Spirit *of Jesus* (16.7) suggests the presence or activity of the Spirit is caused not only by God (cf. Acts 15.8), but also by the risen Jesus (cf. Acts 2.33). And the Spirit continues to be characterized as a mission director to Europe by forbidding Paul and his companions to speak in Asia.

---

249. The word 'Asia' (Acts 2.9; 6.9; 16.6; 19.10, 22, 26, 27; 20.4, 16, 18; 21.27; 24.19; 27.2; cf. 20.4) may refer either to the western coastal cities and adjacent territory, or to the Roman province as seen in Acts 19.10, 26-7; 27.2. As for the general designation of 'Asia' in Acts, Trebilco (1994: 300-302) prefers the former view whereas Hemer (1990: 203-204) the latter.

250. See §5.1.1.3 in Chapter 4. The risen Jesus is, in fact, characterized as a direct 'mission commentator' (particularly to Paul) in Acts 18.9-10; 22.18, 21; 23.11; cf. 9.15-16; 22.7-10; 26.14-18.

251. For the use of κωλύω, as in Acts 16.6, as a circumstantial participle, see Lk. 9.49-50; 11.52; 23.2; Acts 8.36; 10.47; 11.17. See Johnson (1992: 285).

252. The narrative here betrays that those who are already presented as 'full of the Holy Spirit' nevertheless fail to recognize God's plan, and have to be corrected by the Holy Spirit. This reference to the Spirit thus functions as highlighting God's plan towards a new mission direction this time out of Asia (cf. Peter's case in Acts 10: see also n. 209 and §5 in this chapter).

4.6.3.3.2. *Paul and the Ephesian Disciples.* In Acts 19.1-7,[253] the narrator tells of Paul's encounter with the disciples[254] of John the Baptist in Ephesus. In their conversation and the narrator's description, reference to the Spirit is found three times:

> He [Paul] said to them [the Ephesian disciples], 'Did you receive *the Holy Spirit* when you became believers?' They replied, 'No, we have not even heard that there is a *Holy Spirit'*. Then he said, 'Into what then were you baptized?' They answered, 'Into John's baptism'. Paul said, 'John baptized with the baptism of repentance, telling the people to believe in the one who was to come after him, that is, in Jesus'. On hearing this, they were baptized in the name of the Lord Jesus. When Paul had laid his hands on them, *the Holy Spirit* came upon them, and they spoke in tongues and prophesied—altogether there were about twelve of them (Acts 19.2-7).[255]

253. The Western text adds the following: 'And although Paul wished, according to his own plan, to go to Jerusalem, the Spirit told him to return to Asia. And having passed through the upper country he comes to Ephesus...', while omitting the clause, 'while Apollos was in Corinth'. See Metzger (1975: 468).

254. Some German scholars who regard the Ephesian disciples as 'anomalous semi-Christians' have argued that this episode in Acts 19.1-7 (as seen in Acts 8.14-17) reflects Luke's early Catholicism, i.e. *Una sancta apostolica.* See Käsemann (1964: 136-48); Conzelmann (1987: 157-60); Haenchen (1971: 554-57). This position has, however, been criticized by others: for instance, Schweizer (1970: 71-79); Marshall (1991a: 303-304); Barrett (1984: 35-36).

255. The meaning of this dialogue concerning the reception of the Spirit has been interpreted in two opposite ways. For instance, (1) the disciples in Ephesus, understood as 'immature/deficient Christians', become ordinary Christians when they receive the Spirit, i.e. the Spirit as the crucial factor in conversion-initiation: e.g. Dunn (1970a: 96) insists, 'one cannot separate the act of faith from the gift of the Spirit' (see also 1970a: 88-89, 102; 1996: 255-56); (2) seen as already converted Christians, they receive the Spirit in order to be equipped for mission, i.e. the Spirit as a *donum superadditum*: e.g. Menzies (1991a: 275-76) avers, 'In short, Luke separates the conversion (forgiveness granted in response to faith) of the twelve Ephesians from their reception of the Spirit'. Undoubtedly, the first view translates the participle 'having believed' (πιστεύσαντες in Acts 19.2) as '*when* you believed', whereas the second view as '*after* you believed' (a similar case is made in Acts 11.17). Their arguments are also based on their own different understanding of the term τινες μαθηταί in Acts 19.1. According to Menzies (1991a: 271), the term refers to Jesus' (true) disciples; Dunn (1970a: 85) insists that it denotes 'disciples, but they do not belong to *the* disciples [Jesus' disciples]' (emphasis original). Cf. Turner (1996b: 391 n. 133), the term 'does not *necessarily* refer to Christians' (emphasis original); see also Barrett (1984: 36-38).

According to this dialogue, Paul, like Peter in Acts 2.38, seems to presuppose the intimate link between 'faith', 'baptism in the name of Jesus' and the 'Holy Spirit' (cf. Acts 8.14-17; 10.44-48). The Spirit, in this context, is then characterized in relation to the disciples' hearing of or belief in Jesus and their baptism in the name of Jesus through Paul's laying on of hands.[256] Earlier Jesus' witnesses (Lk. 24.49; Acts 1.5), unlike the Samaritan believers or Cornelius's household, are said to be endowed with the Spirit through the risen Jesus (see Acts 2.33; 9.15-17; cf. 4.8-13; 6.10; Lk. 21.15). Here, however, the twelve[257] disciples of John the Baptist, who were simply baptized into John's water-baptism, become those of Jesus after being baptized into Jesus' Spirit-baptism and Paul's laying on of hands (Acts 19.9, 30; 20.1).[258]

On the other hand, the Spirit, as in the Cornelius episode in Acts 10.46, is presented as causing the Ephesian disciples to speak in tongues and prophesy, but by means of Paul's laying on of his hands.[259] In relation to both the recipients, the Baptist's disciples at Ephesus and their associated human agent, Paul, the characterization of the Spirit can be elaborated. (1) The Spirit is apologetically employed to verify that the Ephesian Baptist's disciples are to be incorporated into the people of God,[260] as previously in relation to the Samaritans (Acts 8.14-17) and Cornelius's (Gentile's) household (Acts 10.44-48).[261] This verifying

256. For the use of the 'laying on of hands' in Luke–Acts, see n. 181 in this chapter.

257. This number reminds the reader of Jesus' twelve disciples/witnesses (see Lk. 6.13; 9.1-6; Acts 1.21-26). Cf. Johnson (1992: 338), who interprets this number as symbolically representing a realization of 'Israel'.

258. F. Pereira, *Ephesus: Climax of Universalism in Luke–Acts. A Redaction-Critical Study of Paul's Ephesian Ministry (Acts 18.23-21.1)* (JTF, 10.1; Anand, India: Gujarat Sahitya Prakash, 1983), p. 112, comments, 'It may be reasonably assumed that when Paul went to the synagogue in Ephesus, the twelve disciples, specially endowed with the "Pentecostal" gift of the Holy Spirit, accompanied him (cf. 19.9b...τοὺς μαθητάς)'; quoted in Menzies (1991a: 276 n. 3).

259. In relation to (the sequence of) baptism in the name of Jesus (Acts 2.38; 19.5-6 vs Acts 8.16; 9.17-18; 10.44-48), laying on of hands (Acts 8.17; 9.17; 19.6 vs Acts 2.4; 10.44) and speaking in tongues and/or prophesying (Acts 2.4; 10.46; 19.6 vs Acts 8.17; 9.17), the Spirit is not consistently described in Luke–Acts. See New (1933: 132-38); Stonehouse (1950: 4-5, 9, 14-15).

260. Cf. Shepherd (1994: 229-30).

261. Elsewhere, however, when the narrator describes people who are incorporated into God's people, he does not make any reference to the Spirit: Acts 18.8; 2.47; 4.4; 5.14; 6.7; 11.21; 13.48; 19.10, 20, including the contexts (Acts

function of the Spirit is part of the iterative theme of the coming of the Spirit upon *certain groups* since the day of Pentecost in Acts 2.1-4, when the witness-mission is about to cross some religio-ethnic boundary in reaching out to the ends of the earth.[262] Moreover, the coming of the Spirit upon them with the manifestations of tongues and prophecy (cf. Acts 2.4; 10.46) signals or confirms that God is at work (cf. Acts 18.21) in the Baptist's disciples[263] in Ephesus.[264] (2) It is not Peter and/ or John but Paul who takes the initiative in the incident of the outpouring of the Spirit at Ephesus; in other words, Paul is here portrayed as possessing the same authority as Peter and/or John in the previous episodes (Acts 8.14-17; 10.44-48; cf. 10.36-43).[265] Paul is also said to convey the gift of the Spirit by the same means of laying on of his hands upon the Ephesians, as Peter and John did upon the

2.41; 16.15, 33) in which people are said to be baptized.

262. Cf. Richard (1990: 133-49, esp. 148).

263. Shepherd (1994: 229) comments as to the reference to John the Baptist in this episode as follows: 'Luke gives closure to one of his major sub-plots: John the Baptist, one of the main figures of Luke's Gospel, looked forward to the coming of Messiah Jesus, and now the disciples taught by him have come into the community established by Jesus and his disciples through the Spirit'. Cf. Darr (1992: 83), who suggests that the image of Baptist Jews in Luke–Acts indicates 'a group of properly-prepared Jews...who grasp the true significance of the gospel message and embrace it'.

264. Ephesus seems to become the centre for the Gentile mission (cf. Acts 19.10, 20) in succession to Antioch. Cf. Johnson (1992: 344). For the importance of Ephesus to Paul, see Lampe (1951: 76); Dunn (1996: 258).

265. O'Toole (1980: 855-66, esp. 862), noting the Lukan structure, suggests that the functional relationship of Paul to Apollos in Ephesus mirrors that of Peter and John to Philip in Samaria. For a more elaborate discussion, see Spencer (1992: 233-40). Although Apollos and his work are generally described in positive terms, we should notice that, unlike Philip, there are at least two negative points that may indicate certain deficiencies in Apollos and his ministry: (1) Apollos knew only the baptism of John (18.25) and (2) he needed to be taught (by Priscilla and Aquila) the Word of God more accurately (18.26). In light of this presentation of Apollos, it is better to interpret the expression ζέων τῷ πνεύματι in Acts 18.25 (cf. Rom. 12.11) as 'being fervent in spirit' (RSV; cf. 'he spoke with burning enthusiasm' in NRSV); Louw and Nida (1989: I, 297-98) interpret the phrase as 'to show enthusiasm, to commit oneself completely to'. Johnson's (1992: 335) comment is helpful: 'Apollos is "ardent in the spirit" and "eloquent" but he is not "full of the Holy Spirit" nor does he speak "God's word", or perform "signs and wonders"'. See also Shepherd (1994: 226 n. 227). Contra Dunn (1970a: 88-89; 1996: 250); Menzies (1991a: 271); Turner (1996b: 389 n. 124); cf. Haenchen (1971: 550 nn. 7-8).

Samaritans.[266] The following manifestations of tongues and prophecy thus function to certify that not only the Ephesians' reception of the Spirit is authentic, but also that Paul's prophetic status and ministry is authoritative and reliable (cf. Acts 19.11, 15).[267] This is also strengthened by the narrator's report about the success of Paul's ministry: 'all the residents of Asia, both Jews and Greeks, heard the word of the Lord' (Acts 19.10); 'So the word of the Lord grew mightily and prevailed' (Acts 19.20; see also Paul's own testimony in Acts 20.18-21, 27, 31).

Thus, in Acts 19.1-7 the Spirit is characterized in relation to belief and baptism in the name of Jesus (cf. Acts 2.38) and as causing the Ephesian disciples to speak in tongues and prophesy (cf. Acts 2.4; 10.46). As a result, the Spirit further advances the way of witness not only by verifying that the Ephesian disciples become those of Jesus and the Baptist's community at Ephesus is incorporated into God's restored people, but also by confirming that Paul, who will play a crucial role as Spirit-impelled witness in the coming development of the plot, is on a par with Peter and John.

4.6.3.3.3. *Paul's Planning to Visit Rome via Jerusalem.* After reporting briefly the success of Paul's ministry in Ephesus, the narrator, then, appears to move his narrative into a new geographical direction by giving the following reference to the Spirit[268] in Acts 19.21:

> Now after these things had been accomplished, Paul resolved in the Spirit (ἔθετο ὁ Παῦλος ἐν τῷ πνεύματι) to go through Macedonia and Achaia, and then to go on to Jerusalem. He said, 'After I have gone there, I must (δεῖ) also see Rome'.

266. Marshall (1991a: 308) suggests that the laying on of hands here, like in the case of the Samaritan believers in Acts 8, 'should be understood as a special act of fellowship, incorporating the people concerned into the fellowship of the church'.

267. See Johnson (1992: 344); cf. Turner (1996b: 396-97). For a detailed discussion about the parallels between Peter and Paul in comparison with Jesus, see Praeder (1984: 23-49).

268. The phrase ἐν τῷ πνεύματι itself, as in Acts 20.22, may translate in either psychological terms or divine terms. But the immediate (i.e. 'divine δεῖ' in 19.21b) and remote (i.e. 20.22-23) favour God's Spirit. For the latter understanding, see Bruce (1988: 370-71 n. 43); Marshall (1991a: 312-13); Dunn (1996: 262); Haenchen (1971: 568). Tannehill (1994: 239) also notes rightly, 'A reference to the Holy Spirit in 19.21 would also attribute this new journey to the same divine initiative as Paul's first journey from Antioch (13.2, 4)'.

The Spirit is characterized as causing Paul to visit Rome via Jerusalem as similarly described in Acts 13.2, 4. In relating the Spirit to δεῖ, the reader can also understand that God (and/or the risen Jesus)[269] causes Paul to visit Rome via Jerusalem through the revelatory activity of the Spirit (cf. Acts 20.22-23). In this way, the narrator makes this verse function as a programmatic narrative index of the remainder of Acts: Paul's travelling to Macedonia (20.1), Achaia (20.2-3), Jerusalem[270] (cf. 20.16, 22-23; 21.4, 11-17) and then Rome[271] (cf. 23.11; 25.10-12, 21; 26.32; 27.1, 23-24; 28.14; cf. 28.30-31).[272]

Paul's planning to go to Jerusalem is again introduced in association with the Holy Spirit within his 'farewell address' in Acts 20.17-35 to the Ephesian elders in Miletus.[273]

269. In Luke–Acts, the divine δεῖ is used in relation to God's sovereign plan (e.g. Lk. 2.49; 4.43; Acts 1.16, 21; 3.21); yet on three occasions (9.6, 16; 23.11), the word rather reflects the will of the risen Jesus conveyed to Paul. For reference to δεῖ in Luke–Acts, see n. 12 in this chapter.

270. Both Paul's decision to proceed towards Jerusalem (Acts 19.21-21.17; cf. Lk. 9.51-19.28) and his four trial scenes (Acts 23.1-10; 24.1-23; 25.6-12; 25.23-26.32) remind the reader of those of Jesus in the Gospel (Lk. 22.56-71; 23.1-7; 23.8-12; 23.13-25). When Paul is said to arrive in Jerusalem (21.17), he is before long arrested and afflicted as predicted by the Spirit (20.22-23; 21.11). However, Paul is portrayed as a 'faithful witness' to Jesus standing before the 'sons of Israel' (22.1-22; 23.1-10), the 'Gentile (governors)' (24.1-25.12) and the 'Jewish king' (25.13-26.32) as foreseen by the risen Jesus in Acts 9.15 (cf. Lk. 21.12); see Rapske (1994: 398-411).

271. According to Paul's own letter, he even wanted to visit Spain by way of Rome (Rom. 15.24, 32). Along with this, the narrator's reticence about the reason for Paul's visit to Jerusalem in Acts is also provided in Paul's letters (1 Cor. 16.1-4; 2 Cor. 8-9; Rom. 15.25-32; cf. Acts 24.17), i.e. Paul's delivering his collection of money for the Jerusalem Church from his Gentile churches. See Johnson (1992: 346); Bruce (1988: 445). It seems that Luke, although knowing about the collection (cf. Acts 24.17), is more concerned with Paul's prophetic witness (e.g. Paul's defensive speeches in Acts 21.37-22.21; 24.10-21; 26.1-29) than his motivation to go to Jerusalem, drawing out the parallel with Jesus.

272. Paul's Roman citizenship helps in plotting Paul's (as a Roman prisoner) journey to Rome through his appeal to Caesar (Acts 16.37-38; 22.25-29; 23.27; 25.10-12, 16, 21, 25; 26.32). When Paul reaches Rome, however, the narrator portrays Paul not as just a prisoner, but as a bold witness, as the 'prisoner of Jesus' (see below). For Paul's triple identity, i.e. as a Tarsian, a Roman and a Jew and his social status, see Rapske (1994: 71-112).

273. On Paul's farewell address, see Barrett (1977: 107-121); Lambrecht (1979: 307-337); Soards (1994: 104-108).

And now, *as a captive to the Spirit* (δεδεμένος ἐγὼ τῷ πνεύματι),[274] I [Paul] am on my way to Jerusalem, not knowing what will happen to me there, except that *the Holy Spirit testifies to me* (τὸ πνεῦμα τὸ ἅγιον διαμαρτύρεταί μοι) in every city that imprisonment and persecutions are waiting for me (Acts 20.22-23).

Paul himself explains to them why he must visit Jerusalem by employing the verb δέω metaphorically[275] with the first reference to the Spirit. In the second reference to the Spirit, Paul suggests that the Spirit not only forces him to go on to Jerusalem, but also reveals to him the forthcoming trials and tribulation there.[276]

Readers, however, may be surprised at the subsequent statement in Acts 21.4: 'Through the Spirit (διὰ τοῦ πνεύματος) they [the disciples in Tyre] told Paul not to go on to Jerusalem'. This statement, unlike in the previous characterization of the Spirit in 19.21 (by the narrator) and 20.22-23 (by Paul), characterizes the Spirit as causing these disciples to instruct Paul *not* to visit Jerusalem. Notice that neither Paul nor the narrator is said to comment on the disciples' urging Paul not to go on to Jerusalem. Meanwhile, readers encounter an additional reference to the Spirit in relation to the prophetic words made by Agabus who predicts Paul's impending hardships at Jerusalem:

> While we were staying there [the house of Philip the evangelist at Caesarea] for several days, a prophet named Agabus came down from Judea (cf. 11.27-28). He came to us and took Paul's belt, bound his own feet and hands with it, and said, 'Thus says the Holy Spirit (τάδε λέγει τὸ πνεῦμα τὸ ἅγιον),[277] "This is the way the Jews in Jerusalem will bind the man who owns this belt and will hand him over to the Gentiles"'[278] (Acts 21.10-11).

274. For understanding τῷ πνεύματι as the divine Spirit, see Barrett (1977: 112); Haenchen (1971: 591); Dunn (1996: 272); Bruce (1988: 390); Marshall (1991a: 331); Tannehill (1994: 254); Johnson (1992: 361).

275. See n. 118 in Chapter 4.

276. Interestingly enough, the narrator portrays Paul, who was once eager for binding Christians (Acts 9.2, 14, 21; 22.5), not only as Jesus' witness metaphorically bound by the Spirit (Acts 20.22), but also as a Roman prisoner physically chained by Roman soldiers (cf. Acts 21.11, 13, 33; 22.29; 24.27; 26.29). The implied reader thus perceives that God's plan (Lk. 2.28-35; Acts 15.14-17; cf. 27.23-24) or Jesus' mission command (Lk. 24.46-49; Acts 1.8; 9.15-16; 23.11; 26.17-18, 23) would be advanced and fulfilled in this way as the plot moves to the end stage.

277. See §5.1.2.1 in Chapter 4.

278. Agabus's prophetic words, which are reminiscent of Jesus' own predictions

Readers are, thus, able to fill in the gaps more properly in the light of both previous (19.21; 20.22-23) and subsequent (21.11) references to the Holy Spirit, that is, through their reading process, concerning the relationship of the characterization of the Spirit to the issue of Paul's visit to Jerusalem: Acts 21.4 does not seem to intend to show the counter-characterization of the Spirit in relation to earlier ones in 19.21; 20.22-23; the verse rather implies that the Spirit is continually characterized as *revealing* Paul's impending hardships to the Tyrian disciples as to Paul himself (20.23) and Agabus (21.11). It is thus likely that the narrator[279] reports the Tyrian disciples' *interpretation* of Paul's approaching imprisonment and persecutions foreseen through the Spirit,[280] rather than the Spirit's direct speech (cf. Acts 8.29; 10.19-20; 11.12; 13.2; 21.11). This understanding may be supported by the narrator's description of a similar response of Paul's companions and other Christians at Caesarea when they are told by Agabus's Spirit-inspired words about Paul's hardships at Jerusalem, 'When we heard this, we and the people there urged him not to go up to Jerusalem' (Acts 21.12). However, their warning rather functions as preparing Paul to accept the forthcoming trials as part of God's will in recalling his previous visions (20.23; 9.15-16)[281] and making himself ready even for death (cf. 21.13-14). Hence, the Spirit is characterized as revealing Paul's personal future to the Tyrian disciples and Agabus (like to Paul himself),

of his passion in Jerusalem (Lk. 9.22, 44; 18.31-33), are loosely fulfilled after Paul arrives in Jerusalem (esp. see Acts 21.27 [the Jews from Asia], 30, 33 [the tribune as Gentile]; cf. Paul's own description of his arrest in Acts 26.21; 28.17; see also a Jewish spokeman's report before Felix in Acts 24.6).

279. Notice that Acts 21.1-18 is narrated by the first- (plural) person point of view. I do not mean that the 'we-section' narrative (Acts 16.10-17; 20.5-15; 21.1-18; 27.1–28.16) is unreliable; but it can be assumed that the first-person narrator (i.e. 'telling') is less authoritative than the third-person narrator (i.e. 'showing') in terms of its point of view. Cf. Shepherd 1994: 221 n. 214.

280. Tannehill (1994: 263) comments, 'This is an interesting case of conflict in understanding the Spirit's directions... Perhaps the Spirit's message is consistent, but the prophets in Tyre have mixed their own conclusion with the Spirit's message'; cf. Shepherd (1994: 237, 238; see also 247): 'These episodes raise the question of what it means for Spirit-filled, prophetic figures to disagree and be in conflict... The issue is finally resolved by appeal to the prophetic pattern Luke has set forth throughout his narrative. Paul appeals to the example of Jesus and all the prophets, who go to Jerusalem only to suffer and die (cf. Luke 11.49-51; 13.33-34)'. See also Conzelmann (1987: 178); Haenchen (1971: 602 n. 1); Bruce (1988: 398).

281. See Polhill (1992: 433).

although through the same revelation, Agabus is said to tell what the Spirit exactly says; on the other hand, the Tyrian disciples are said to interpret it (see also the response of Paul's companions and other Christians at Caesarea after listening to Agabus's prophetic words): to urge Paul not to visit Jerusalem.[282]

One more reference to the Spirit is mentioned in Paul's farewell address to the Ephesian elders in Miletus: 'Keep watch over yourselves and all the flock, of which the Holy Spirit has made you overseers (ὑμᾶς τὸ πνεῦμα τὸ ἅγιον ἔθετο ἐπισκόπους), to shepherd the church of the Lord that he purchased with his own blood' (Acts 20.28).[283] The Spirit here is characterized in relation to a settled Christian community (cf. Acts 5.3-11; 6.3-7; 9.31; 11.24; 13.52; 15.28) as creating a leadership of 'church-supervisors' (ἐπίσκοπος).[284]

4.6.3.4. Summary. The narrator, in this subsection of 'Witness towards the Ends of the Earth (Acts 11.19–28.15)', develops the plot by focusing on Paul as a witness of Jesus to Gentiles. And the characterization of the Spirit is mostly associated with Paul and his witness-mission for Gentiles: *the Spirit is characterized as a mission director*, causing the Antioch Church leaders to appoint Paul (and Barnabas) or causing Paul (and his other companions) directly to bear witness to Jesus to the people (Jews and Gentiles) in Asia Minor and Europe. In relation to this mission to Gentiles, the Spirit is also presented *as God's decision-maker*, causing the Jerusalem Church leaders to follow God's will/plan by encouraging and securing the mission project on the terms already undertaken through the Spirit-filled Paul and Barnabas sent by the Antioch Church. Furthermore, the Spirit is characterized as causing Paul to visit Rome via Jerusalem while revealing the sufferings he would encounter at Jerusalem. On the other hand, when the Spirit reveals Paul's impending hardships to the Tyrian disciples and Agabus, the disciples and Agabus's hearers are said to urge Paul not to go on to Jerusalem. The Spirit is also characterized as verifying that the Ephesian

---

282. See also §5 in this chapter, in which I discuss the tensions among the characterizations of the Spirit. Cf. Johnson (1983; 1992: 271-72).

283. For textual variants in this verse, see n. 113 in Chapter 4.

284. It is not clear whether the term ἐπίσκοπος is identified with πρεσβύτερος in Acts 20.17 (cf. Acts 14.23); it seems to mean 'supervisors' or 'guardians' (cf. Acts 1.20; Phil. 1.1; 1 Tim. 3.2; Tit. 1.7; cf. the verb ἐπισκέπτομαι in Jer. 23.2; Ezek. 34.11; Zech. 10.3; 11.16). See Johnson (1992: 362-63); Bruce (1990a: 433); Shepherd (1994: 234 n. 253).

disciples are God's people by causing them to speak in tongues and prophesy. Finally, the Spirit is sometimes characterized in passing in relation to (1) the life of Christians (Barnabas and the believers at Antioch of Pisidia) in causing them to be 'good', 'faithful' and 'joyful'; (2) the settled Ephesian Church as responsible for providing leaders for the Christian community.

4.7. *Open-Ended Finale (Acts 28.16-31): Paul's Witness in Rome*
4.7.1. *The Final Open-Ended Witness of Paul.* Rome is the final geographical setting for the last scene in the narrative of Luke–Acts: 'When we came into Rome' (῞Οτε δὲ εἰσήλθομεν εἰς Ῥώμην in Acts 28.16; see also καὶ οὕτως εἰςῦτὴν Ῥώμην ἤλθαμεν in Acts 28.14). Hence Jesus' mission command 'to the ends of the earth' (Lk. 24.47-49; Acts 1.8; 9.15-16; 22.21; 23.11; 26.15-18) and Simeon's prophetic oracle (Lk. 2.31-32) are accomplished by Paul, once a persecutor *binding* Jesus' followers (Acts 9.2), but now 'a servant and a witness' of Jesus (Acts 26.16) *bound in the Spirit* (Acts 20.22) as well as a Roman prisoner *bound* with chains (Acts 21.33; 28.17, 20). Then how does the narrator intend to show that Paul's arriving and witnessing in Rome is God's plan? He mentions and characterizes the Holy Spirit as causing Paul to see Rome for the witness-mission (Acts 19.21), which is also additionally encouraged by the risen Lord Jesus (Acts 23.11) and confirmed through the angel of God (Acts 27.23-24). In this way, Paul's witness-mission to Rome, caused by the Spirit, is a *narrative* omega-point, consummating the 'way of witness' initiated and undertaken by Jesus and his witnesses who are also inspired/empowered by the Spirit. The ending of the narrative thus indicates that God's plan/will would not fail, although God's human agents are said to encounter a series of conflicts or sufferings from the beginning to the end of the narrative.

The narrator's summary words about Paul's activity in Acts 28.23 suggest that the Spirit continues to inspire his ongoing witness in Rome in echoing a similar feature found in the preceding presentations of Spirit-filled witnesses. Paul is said to testify (διαματύρομαι) to the Kingdom of God (cf. Lk. 9.2; 10.9-11; Acts 8.12; 14.22; 19.8; 20.25) and to Jesus (see also Acts 28.31 below).[285] This report allows the reader to understand that the narrator is interested in Paul not as a

---

285. As already noted, the Kingdom of God and Jesus are interrelated in Luke–Acts. For this, see §3 of this chapter in dealing with the four main features of the plot of Luke–Acts.

prisoner, but as a bold and victorious witness (Acts 28.23; cf. Acts 19.21; 23.21). Thus, the Spirit is, in this final plot-stage, implicitly characterized as causing Paul to proclaim the gospel in Rome.[286] On the other hand, in Acts 28.25-27, the narrator mentions and characterizes the Spirit as inspiring Isaiah to speak God's word to his generation. Paul's use of Isa. 6.9-10 and his authoritative interpretation remind the reader of Jesus' (Lk. 4.18-19; cf. 24.27, 44) and Peter's (Acts 2.17-21; 4.11, 25-26) earlier use of Scripture, although this particular passage from Isaiah is not used by the Lukan Jesus as it is in Mk 4.12; 8.18 and Mt. 13.14-15. By way of this scriptural quotation, Paul thus attempts to legitimate and highlight the Gentile mission for salvation as the (original) plan of God (cf. Lk. 2.30-35; Acts 9.15; 15.14-18; 22.21; 26.17, 20). This also implies that as the Spirit inspired Isaiah to speak God's message to his contemporary Jews, so does the same Spirit inspire Paul (cf. Acts 13.46-47; 18.6; 24.14-15; 26.20; 28.20).[287]

As we can see, the last scene of this final plot-stage is open-ended,[288]

---

286. The response of the Roman Jews in regard to Paul's witness follows the same pattern of acceptance and rejection as delineated in relation to earlier witnesses: 'Some were convinced by what he [Paul] had said, while others refused to believe' (Acts 28.24), which also fulfils Simeon's inspired oracle in Lk. 2.34-35.

287. Readers encounter the final expression 'turning to the Gentiles' in Acts 28.28. Nevertheless, this announcement does not seem to exclude Jews as potential members of the restored people of God. This understanding can be supported by the following reasons: (1) the previous reports about Paul's continuing mission towards Jews (e.g. 17.1-2, 10, 17; 18.4, 8; 19.10, 17-18) even after his similar declaration of turning to the Gentiles (13.46-47; 18.6), (2) Paul is described as a man loyal to the 'hope of Israel' (28.17-20; cf. 26.6-7) and (3) the narrator's final description of Paul's activity implies this view, saying 'He...welcomed all (πάντας) who came to him' (28.30). Note that the Western text adds Ἰουδαίους τε καὶ Ἕλληνας in order to explain πάντας. Contra Tannehill (1994), 'the chief emphasis of the end of Acts is on the unsolved problem of Jewish rejection' (349); 'the close of Acts is not triumphant but tragic and anguished in tone' (348). However, he also later admits, 'Paul in Rome continues to preach the themes with which he had addressed the Jews, suggesting that Jews are at least included in his audience' (351).

288. For the closing of a novel, M. Torgovnick, Closure in the Novel (Princeton: Princeton University Press, 1981), employs four technical terms: (1) Circularity: 'the ending of a novel clearly recalls the beginning in language, in situation, in the grouping of characters, or in several of these ways', (2) Parallelism: 'when language, situation, or the grouping of characters refers not just to the beginning of the work but to a series of points in the text', (3) Linkage: when the closing 'links the novel not to its own beginning and middle, but to the body of another, often as yet

leaving the reader with some unresolved issues,[289] and so is the characterization of the Holy Spirit in relation to the causal aspect of the plot:
'The work of the narrative is over, but the work of the reader is unfin-
ished' (Parsons 1987: 113). Particularly in the light of the Lukan
narrator's final open-ended remarks in Acts 28.30-31, readers may
postulate that the 'way of witness' is still in process, and Rome is to be
considered part of the world-wide mission rather than the final mission
to 'the ends of the earth'.[290] And if the witness-mission as God's enterprise or the risen Jesus' command remains incomplete, the work of the
Holy Spirit would continue through bold witnesses.[291]

In summing up his last report about Paul, the narrator, without providing the outcome of the verdict as 'guilty' or 'not guilty',[292] shows
and implies the characterization of the Spirit, not only as the present
cause of Paul's activity to bear bold witness to Jesus to Jews and
Gentiles at Rome, but also as the ongoing divine cause of those who are
to continue to carry on the mission to other parts of the earth, by ending
with the following triumphant remarks: 'He lived there two whole years
at his own expense and welcomed all who came to him, proclaiming
(κηρύσσων) the kingdom of God and teaching (διδάσκων) about the
Lord Jesus Christ (τοῦ κυρίου Ἰησοῦ Χριστοῦ; cf. Acts 2.36) with all
boldness (παρρησίας) and without hindrance' (Acts 28.30-31).[293] In
this way, the narrator rounds off the last scene by suggesting that Paul's

unwritten, novel' and (4) Incompletion: when the closing 'omits one or more
crucial elements necessary for full circularity or parallelism', quoted in Parsons
(1986: 202-203). In this aspect, the ending of Acts (plus that of the Gospel) contains some indications of Circularity (e.g. the theme of witness), Parallelism (e.g.
Paul's witness) and Incompletion/Openness. See also Tannehill (1994: 354-57); cf.
Dunn (1996: 278-79).

289. For instance, (1) the report of Paul's trial before Caesar (cf. Acts 28.16-19);
(2) the relationship of Paul to the Roman Jews and/or the Roman Christians (Acts
28.21-22); (3) the result and effect of Paul's ongoing witness to Jesus in Rome (cf.
Acts 28.23-24, 30-31); (4) God's salvation plan for Jews in relation to Mary's and
Zechariah's prophetic oracle (Lk. 1.46-55, 67-79).

290. See also n. 129 in this chapter.

291. See Chapter 6.

292. In some sense, the narrator already shows the reader that Paul is innocent of
'any charge worthy of death' (Acts 23.29; 25.25; 26.31) through the vindication
given by divine warrant, rather than by the Roman Emperor (Acts 28.1-7). See
Dunn (1996: 344); Johnson (1992: 466).

293. For the Lukan use of κηρύσσω and διδάσκω, see n. 21; for παρρησία, see
n. 164 and the main text in this chapter.

mission is still inspired, empowered and directed by the Holy Spirit for accomplishing the will/plan of God (Acts 22.14; 26.22; 27.24) or the Lord Jesus (Acts 21.14; 9.15-16; 22.21; 23.11; 26.17).

4.7.2. *Summary.* Paul (and the narrator), in this final plot-stage, characterizes the Spirit as inspiring Isaiah to reproach his fellow-Jews for their spiritual ignorance and uses Isaiah's inspired words to vindicate his turning to Gentiles (cf. Acts 15.14-18, 28). This indicates that the Spirit is indirectly characterized as the divine cause of Paul's previous (e.g. Acts 13.2-4) and future (see the word πάντας [i.e. Jews and Gentiles] in Acts 28.30) Gentile mission. The narrator's summary of Paul's activity at Rome also indicates that the Spirit is implicitly characterized as God's causing Paul to arrive in Rome and as still inspiring Paul to effect God's plan by bearing witness to God's Kingdom and the risen Jesus.

5. *Conclusion*

Now I first want to mention four tensions among the characterizations of the Holy Spirit in relation to the causal aspect of the plot and attempt to explore their implications. Then, I shall highlight three narrative functions of the Holy Spirit by summarizing the elucidation of section 4 in this chapter. While presenting the tensions and functions of the characterization of the Spirit, I clarify my points by applying Greimas's *actantial* model[294] to them.[295]

(1) The narrative of Luke–Acts shows that the reception of the Spirit is closely associated with 'prayer' (Lk. 11.13), 'baptism in the name of Jesus' with repentance (Acts 2.38) or 'laying on of hands' (Acts 8.17; 19.6; cf. Deut. 34.9; Num. 27.18; 1 Sam. 16.13; 10.1-13; cf. speaking in tongues or prophecy/praise as an effect). In particular, the narrator tends to evince the importance of human prayers in relation to receiving the Spirit; nevertheless prayer is not the cause (cf. Acts 2.38).[296] Moreover, as noticed, there is no consistent relationship between the endowment of the Spirit and baptism or laying on of hands.[297] All the evidence indicates that the Spirit is *God's sovereign gift* and cannot be obtained

---

294. See n. 16 in this chapter.
295. I shall deal with the issue of the plot effect on the reader in my final chapter.
296. See n. 84 in this chapter.
297. See §4.6.2.1 and nn. 181, 259 in this chapter.

by human efforts (cf. Acts 8.18-24), but is granted by God as the ultimate cause:

Diagram 2

SENDER	→	OBJECT	→	RECEIVER
God		to receive the HS		God's people

		↑		
OPPONENT	→	SUBJECT	←	HELPER
Jewish believers'		God's will		God Himself
preoccupation and reluctance?				(in response to prayer)
(cf. Acts 8.14; 10.9-16, 34-35;				
15; 19.3)				

(2) As noted, Acts 21.4 seems to characterize the Spirit as causing the Tyrian disciples to tell Paul *not* to go to Jerusalem, in contrast to the characterization of the Spirit in Acts 19.21 and 20.22-23, according to which the Spirit inspires Paul to go to Jerusalem. So the Spirit might be understood as both 'opponent' and 'helper' to Paul's way of witness in Jerusalem:

Diagram 3

SENDER	→	OBJECT	→	RECEIVER
the Lord[298]		to visit to Jerusalem[299]		Paul

		↑		
OPPONENT	→	SUBJECT	←	HELPER
the Holy Spirit?		the Lord's Will		the Holy Spirit

This tension could be resolved *within the narrative* by another reference to the Spirit in regard to Paul's future found just a few verses later (v. 11): it suggests that the Spirit did *not directly say* (cf. Acts 8.29; 10.19; 11.12; 13.2; 21.11) to the Tyrian disciple*s* that they should urge Paul not to go to Jerusalem, but (just) revealed Paul's sufferings in Jerusalem as to Paul himself (20.23) and Agabus (20.11). That Paul's companions and people at Caesarea, after hearing the inspired words given by

298. The Lord (see n. 80 in Chapter 4) as 'sender' may signify both God (cf. Acts 23.1; 26.20) and the risen Jesus (cf. Acts 9.15-17; 23.11; 25.19); see also Acts 20.21; 22.14-15; 24.14-16; 26.15-18; 28.23, 31 and below.

299. In Jerusalem, Paul is depicted as 'faithful witness' to Jesus before the 'sons of Israel' (Acts 22.1-22; 23.1-10), the 'Gentile (governors)' (Acts 24.1–25.12) and the 'Jewish king' (Acts 25.13–26.32) as commissioned by the risen Jesus in 9.15.

Agabus, also ask Paul not to go to Jerusalem (i.e. the same reaction as that of the Tyrian disciples) suggests this reading. The tension is also resolved *within the narrative* by Paul's personal resolution (cf. Acts 9.16; 20.24) to live and die for (the name of) Jesus (21.13), following the example of Jesus (Lk. 9.51, 22; 22.47-23.49; cf. 6.22-23; 21.12, 17) and other prophetic witnesses (cf. Lk. 11.49-51; 13.33-34), like Stephen (Acts 7.54-60) or James (Acts 12.3).[300] However, the passages in Acts 20.22-23; 21.4, 11-14 imply that God's people, *in reality*, can be divided over what is the Lord's will in their own (different) responses or interpretations to the similar or even the same revelations caused by the (same) Holy Spirit. This suggests that, even with the inspiration of the Holy Spirit, defining the will of God is not straightforward (cf. Acts 11.18; 13.1-3; 21.14; cf. Stephen's and Philip's work not only as serving believers, as the Jerusalem Church appointed them to do, but also as witnesses to 'non-believers').

(3) In similar fashion, our narrative also suggests that those who are presented as 'full of (or filled with) the Holy Spirit' nevertheless may (at first) fail to perceive God's plan, although this difficulty or tension is later resolved *within the narrative* by the further revelation of the Holy Spirit and God's vision: Peter in Acts 10.9-43; Paul (and his companions) in Acts 16.6-10. These two cases are related in narrative contexts in which the new direction of God's mission (i.e. towards non-Jews or Europe) is highlighted for the characters (and to the reader). Moreover, the 'sharp dispute' between Paul and Barnabas (Acts 15.36-41) over John-Mark also suggests that there could be disagreement among Spirit-filled leaders (unlike in the previous episode of Acts 15.1-35). In this instance, their conflict is not said to be resolved but they separate (vv. 39-40). This split between Paul and Barnabas, who are represented as inspired by the Holy Spirit (cf. Acts 20.30), would thus be in tension not only with the characterization of the Spirit in Acts 13.1-3; 15.1-35 (the role of decision-making among Spirit-filled leaders in agreement), but also with those of the Spirit in Acts 9.31; 20.28 (the role of comforting or encouraging and supervising God's people; through Spirit-inspired leaders). Once again, this suggests that Spirit-filled people themselves could be in difficulty over discerning God's will/plan and be involved in conflict with one another.[301]

300. Cf. Shepherd (1994: 238).

301. Cf. Parker (1996: 199-203) who offers three Pentecostal guidelines ('holistic knowing', 'integrating needs of self and community' and 'ultimate versus finite

(4) The Lukan narrator, like those of the Jewish Bible, implicitly and explicitly presents God as the cause, who grants the Holy Spirit to his Messiah, Jesus (Lk. 3.21-22; 4.18; Acts 10.38) and his people (Lk. 11.13; Acts 2.16-21; 3.39; 4.24-31; 5.32; 8.14-17; 15.8). However, 'the risen Jesus' is also said to 'send his disciples the promise of the Father, that is, the Holy Spirit' (Lk. 24.49a). This seems to be inconsistent with what Jesus himself told his disciples, as in Lk. 11.13. This tension is resolved by Peter's christological interpretation of the (name of the) Lord in Joel 2.28-32 (Acts 2.16-36, 38; 4.12),[302] and particularly by Acts 2.33: '[Jesus] being therefore exalted...and having received from the Father the promise of the Holy Spirit, he has poured out this'. So God's promise to send the Holy Spirit, according to Peter (and the narrator), is accomplished on the day of Pentecost through the exalted Jesus. Jesus' sending of the Spirit is also interpreted by Jesus himself (Acts 1.5) and Peter (Acts 11.16) as the fulfilment of John the Baptist's inspired words: 'He [Jesus] will baptize you with the Holy Spirit and fire' (Lk. 3.16b). So the following *actantial* diagram can be delineated:

Diagram 4

SENDER[303]	→	OBJECT	→	RECEIVER
God (I)		to be saved/verified as God's people (I)		God's people (I)
(through) the risen Jesus (II)[304]		to seek God's people (II)		Jesus' witnesses (II)

↑

OPPONENT	→	SUBJECT	←	HELPER
(ultimately)		God's will (I)		the Holy Spirit (I; II)
Satan		Jesus' desire (II)		the Spirit of Jesus (II)
				the name of Jesus (II)

The narrator thus seems to show that *the risen Jesus is God's (unique) agent in sending the Spirit to his witnesses* (Lk. 24.49; Acts 2.33; 9.15-

concerns') for discerning 'Spirit leading', and emphasizes 'ambiguity', saying that 'Human behavior is extremely complex; there always remains a quality of ambiguity to claims of Spirit leading... Discerning the divine will always involve risk; there is no way to know for certain that one's choices or allegiances are ultimately the right ones' (202).

302. See §4.6.1.1 in this chapter; for the name Jesus, see n. 90 in Chapter 4.

303. The terms ἀποστέλλω and πέμπω are employed very frequently in Luke–Acts: ἀποστέλλω occurs 26 times in the Gospel and 24 times in Acts (Lk. 1.19, 26; 4.18 x 2, 43; 7.3, 20, 27; 9.2, 48, 52; 10.1, 3, 16; 11.49; 13.34; 14.17, 32; 19.14, 29,

17; 8.39; 16.7; 19.4-6 [?]; cf. Lk. 12.12; 21.15; Acts 4.8; 6.10), whereas, on one occasion, God is represented as giving the same Spirit to Gentiles that Jesus' disciples had received (cf. Acts 11.17).[305] It is thus not incidental that the word 'witness(es)' in Acts is frequently attributed to Jesus (rather than to God),[306] and most witness-characters are also said to perform miracles by means of Jesus' name (Acts 16.18; 19.13, 17; Lk. 9.1, 49; 10.17).[307] Hence, this tension in regard to the cause of sending the Spirit after Jesus' ascension appears to be resolved by the new status[308] of the exalted Jesus who is given authority or power by God and can be called not only the Messiah, but also the Lord. If we attempt to harmonize the above passages altogether, it might be said that *after Jesus' ascension, the Holy Spirit is sent by God, the final Cause through the risen Jesus.*

We have seen that the Lukan narrator, while developing the plot, presents the references to the Holy Spirit at every plot-stage without exception.[309] We have also observed that the Spirit is always presented in association with human characters who serve, in one sense or another, to advance the Lukan plot. Hence, the narrative function of the

---

32; 20.**10**, 20; 22.*8*, *35*; 24.*47*; cf. 5.32; 7.34; 9.56; 12.49; 18.8; 19.10; Acts 3.**20**, **26**; 5.21; 7.14, **34**, **35**; 8.14; 9.*17*, 38; 10.8, 17, <u>20</u>, **36**; 11.11, 13, 30; 13.15; 15.27, 33; 16.35, 36; 19.22; 26.*17*; 28.**28**; cf. Acts 8.<u>26</u>, <u>29</u>, <u>*39*</u>; 13.<u>2-3</u>, <u>4</u>; 16.<u>6-7</u>; 19.<u>21</u>; 20.<u>22</u>; 23.*11*; 27.23-24), whilst πέμπω occurs 10 in the Gospel and 11 in Acts (Lk. 4.**26**; 7.6, 10, 19; 15.15; 16.24, 27; 20.**11**, **12**, **13**; Acts 10.5, 32, 33; 11.29; 15.22, 25; 19.31; 20.17; 23.30; 25.25, 27): **bold** indicates *Sender* is God; *italic* Jesus; <u>underline</u> the Holy Spirit (see below). Cf. Hubbard 1977: 103; 1978: 187-98.

304. Jesus is also characterized as 'sender', twice in the Gospel (Lk. 9.1-6; 10.1-16), commissioning his 12 and 70/2 disciples to proclaim the Kingdom of God by giving them *his* 'power and authority' (Lk. 9.2; 10.19) or 'name' (Lk. 10.17; cf. 9.48-49), identified as 'helper' (cf. Acts 3.6, 16; 4.10, 12, 17-18; 5.28, 40-41; 8.12; 9.27, 29, 34; 10.43, 48). In this way, the disciples are depicted as not only Jesus', but also God's representatives: Lk. 10.16. The activities of Jesus' disciples in the Gospel are thus their 'rehearsal' for the future witness-mission described in Acts.

305. This observation is also related to the narrative functions (1 and 2) of the Holy Spirit (see below).

306. See n. 15 in this chapter.

307. The narrator only mentions God twice as the cause of giving (healing or miraculous) power to Jesus' witnesses in Acts 15.12; 19.11.

308. See §4.6.1 and n. 316 in this chapter.

309. 74 references to the Spirit are found as follows: 4 (1st plot-stage); 6 (2nd stage); 6 (3rd stage); 50 (4th stage); 1 (5th stage); cf. 7 in the 'prologue'.

Spirit can also be explored in relation to the causal aspect of the plot by focusing on the activities of human characters. Considering this, I conclude this chapter by outlining three narrative functions of the Holy Spirit in Luke–Acts.

(1) *The most discernible function of the Spirit is to empower and guide some individual (named) characters as leading witnesses, making them responsible, powerful and reliable human agents of God and Jesus in carrying out God's plan/will successfully.* From 'Beginning' (Lk. 3.1–4.13) to 'Central Point' (Lk. 19.45–Acts 2.13), the Spirit causes Jesus (Lk. 1.35; 3.16, 22; 4.1, 14, 18-19; Acts 10.38) to testify about the Kingdom of God and himself as the Messiah sent by God, *by inspiring his words and deeds,* after the Spirit had also *inspired* John the Baptist (1.15-17, 44; 3.15-17), like other characters in the 'prologue' (Elizabeth [1.41-43], Mary [1.35, 46-55], Zechariah [1.67-79] and Simeon [2.25-35]), *to bear witness to Jesus,* acting as 'forerunner-witnesses'. From 'Development towards the End' (Acts 2.14–28.15) to the last stage 'Open-Ended Finale' (Acts 28.16-31), the Spirit as 'helper' *and* 'sender'[310] *empowers* the following characters to take over Jesus' mission and sometimes (as a mission-director) *directly guides* them to extend it to the ends of the earth *by inspiring them to bear witness to the Kingdom of God and the risen Jesus* through their powerful words and deeds: Peter (3.14-41; 4.8-12; 10.19, 34-48; 11.12-18; 15.7-11;); Peter and other apostles (4.23-31, 33; 5.29-32, 41-42); Stephen (6.5, 10; 7.51-60); Philip (6.5; 8.5-13, 29-40); Barnabas and/or Saul (12.24-26; 13.2-4; 14.3); Paul (9.17-22; 13.9-12, 23, 33, 38-39; 16.6-10, 31; 17.3; 18.5; 19.21; 20.21-25; 24.14-16, 24; 26.19-23; 28.23, 31).[311] In this light, the key passages highlighting this function of the Spirit in relation to the causal aspect of the plot are Lk. 4.18-19 (cf. Acts 10.38); 24.46-49; Acts 1.8 (cf. 9.15-19; 13.1-4; 19.21). Hence, the *actantial* structure is schematized as follows:

---

310. In terms of *actant*, the Spirit is constantly characterized as 'helper' throughout Luke–Acts (see below); the Spirit is additionally introduced as the direct 'sender' (Acts 8.29; 10.19-20; 11.12; 13.2-3), which is anticipated in the Gospel (Lk. 2.26; 4.1, 14).

311. Cf. the Tyrian disciples (Acts 21.4) and Agabus (Acts 11.28; 21.11), who act as minor characters supplementing the plot.

Diagram 5

SENDER	→	OBJECT	→	RECEIVER
God (I)		to witness to the Kingdom of God and Jesus		**Jesus** (I)

the risen Jesus (II) by preaching good news and performing miracles   **Jesus' witnesses**
the Holy Spirit (III)   (II; III)

↑

OPPONENT	→	SUBJECT	←	HELPER
Satan and his earthly agents		God's will (I)		**the Holy Spirit** (I; II; III)
		the risen Jesus' desire (II)		by empowering/inspiring

and guiding them to bear
witness to God and Jesus
through powerful words
(preaching) and deeds (miracles)

(2) As the plot develops from the day of Pentecost onwards, *the Spirit also begins to function as verifying certain group-characters (unnamed) as incorporated into God's (eschatological) community*: the Samaritan believers evangelized by Philip, Peter and John (Acts 8.4-25); Cornelius's household by Peter (Acts 10.1-48; 11.4-18; 15.7-11); the Ephesian Baptist's believers by Paul (Acts 19.1-7). In relation to these group-characters' reception of the Spirit, the Spirit is sometimes said to cause them to speak in tongues and prophesy/praise, reminding (the reader of) similar divine manifestations given to Jesus' Jewish group at Pentecost.[312] As a result, these phenomena serve to signify (to reliable characters [i.e. Peter and John; Peter; Paul] and readers) that they receive the Spirit and are thus accepted by God (see Acts 10.44-45; 11.15; 19.5-6). Hence, the narrator's accounts legitimate not only the recipients of the Spirit as God's people, but also the trustworthy witnesses as God's agents led by the Spirit. In so doing, the way of witness to God's Kingdom and Jesus turns out to be the way of salvation, not only for Jews, but also for the people who have been ethnically or religiously ignored or isolated by Jewish (Christian) believers. The governing passage in relation to this verifying function of the Spirit is Acts 2.38-39. And the *actantial* structure is delineated as follows:

---

312. Acts 8.17 presumably implies the similar effect upon the Samaritans when we think of the magician Simon's response: 'Now when Simon *saw* (the effect?) *that the Spirit was given* through the laying on of the apostles' hands, he offered them money, saying, "Give me also *this power* so that anyone on whom I lay my hands may receive the Holy Spirit" ' (8.18-19).

Diagram 6

SENDER	→	OBJECT	→	RECEIVER
God		to be incorporated into God's people		**Samaritans; Gentiles**
		(cf. the Holy Spirit as God's gift/promise)		**Ephesian Baptist's Groups**

↑

OPPONENT	→	SUBJECT	←	HELPER
Jewish believers'		God's will		**the Holy Spirit**
preoccupation and reluctance?				by verifying them as God's people, sometimes with accompanying divine manifestations

(3) As the way of witness is successfully advanced in spite of persecutions and conflicts, the narrator sometimes presents in passing (usually by summary statements) the function of the Spirit in relation to the life-situations of believers in settled (eschatological) communities (cf. the Qumran community; see my excursus). In relation to these accounts,[313] the Spirit functions as granting both individuals (Stephen in Acts 6.3, 5, 10 and Barnabas in Acts 11.24; cf. the unborn John in Lk. 1.44; Jesus in Lk. 10.21) and groups (the seven men in Acts 6.5; the Pisidian Antioch believers in Acts 13.52) some spiritual gifts: 'faith', 'wisdom' and 'joy', or as comforting/encouraging them in Judea, Galilee and Samaria (Acts 9.31). In addition, the Spirit also functions as supervising the believing community, the Jerusalem Church (Acts 5.1-11) or as acting to provide community leaders who supervise members of the Ephesian Church (Acts 19.28). Similarly, the Spirit is presented as a decision-maker for significant church expansions (e.g. Gentile mission) in the Jerusalem and Antioch Churches (Acts 15.28; cf. 13.1-3).[314] Hence, the actantial structure can be diagrammed as follows:

313. In this category, we may include the Old Testament figures, David (Acts 1.16) and Isaiah (Acts 28.25), who are said to be inspired by the Spirit to prophesy for New Testament people.

314. These minor functions of the Spirit in Luke–Acts are reminiscent of Paul's teaching about the Spirit in his epistles (e.g. see Gal. 5.16-25; Rom. 8.9-17; 14.17-19; 1 Cor. 2.10-16; 3.16-23; 12.13-26). In a general comparison between Luke and Paul, it can be noted that Lukan pneumatology, in his narrative form of 'story', is more concerned with the (somewhat extraordinary) activities of Jesus' original witnesses acting in live mission-fields, whereas Pauline pneumatology, in his narrative form of 'letters', is mostly concerned with the religio-ethical life of Christian members in settled communities.

Diagram 7

SENDER	→	OBJECT	→	RECEIVER
God		to be sustained as God's people		**people who are already Christians**

↑

OPPONENT	→	SUBJECT	←	HELPER
believers inside the church?		God's will		**the Holy Spirit**
(Acts 5.1-11; cf. 15.1, 5);				(cf. the Lord's or God's Word)[315]
non-believers outside the church				by granting God's gifts;
(Acts 20.28-29)				encouraging and supervising them;
				acting to provide church leaders
				and decide church matters

All these observations indicate that as the Lukan plot develops, so do the characterizations of the Holy Spirit.[316] Nevertheless, *the major function of the Spirit* in terms of the causal aspect of the plot is (as 'helper' and sometimes as 'sender'): empowering and guiding *main characters* to bear witness to God's Kingdom and the risen Jesus by inspiring them to speak and perform mighty deeds in accordance with the plan of God.

---

315. See Acts 6.7; 13.44, 48-49; 15.18; 18.11; 19.10, 20; 20.32; see also n. 226. Cf. the wisdom literature, in which the law or the study of the law is understood as the means of obtaining 'wisdom' or 'God's Spirit'; see §4.1.2 in Chapter 2.

316. Similarly, it might also be claimed that as the characterization of Jesus develops (e.g. after his resurrection and ascension), so does that of the Holy Spirit. For instance, it is of interest and value to take account of the picture of Jesus in association with his relationship to the Holy Spirit: Jesus as the Spirit-conceived Davidic Son of God; Jesus as the Spirit-anointed regal (cf. Isa. 11.2; *Pss. Sol.* 17.37, 42) and prophetic (cf. 1 Chron. 16.22; Ps. 105.15; 2 Chron. 15.1; 20.14; Neh. 9.30) servant (Isa. 42.1)-Messiah; Jesus as the Spirit-sender/baptizer after his ascension, i.e. the Lord of the Spirit (cf. Acts 2.33; 16.7).

Chapter 6

CONCLUDING REMARKS ON 'A DYNAMIC READING OF
THE HOLY SPIRIT IN LUKE–ACTS'

The aim of this study has been to examine the Holy Spirit in Luke–Acts through a new perspective: 'dynamic biblical narrative criticism'. By means of this methodology, I read the text of Luke–Acts as a final and unified form of ancient and canonical narrative in which the Holy Spirit is rhetorically presented as part of the 'divine frame of reference' and a 'divine character' in relation to the narrator, human characters and the plot of Luke–Acts. This has involved the extratext of Luke–Acts, the Jewish Bible, as the literary repertoire of Lukan references to the Holy Spirit. And in the process of this study, I have also considered the dynamic interaction among the implied author/narrator, the text and the implied reader.

Now in this final chapter, I summarize the conclusions that I offered at the end of each chapter[1] and briefly draw out implications of the results of this study as a whole: (1) the theological significance of the Lukan presentation of the Holy Spirit and (2) the relationship of the Holy Spirit to (a) the narrator or implied author, (b) the text and (c) the implied reader of Luke–Acts, with final remarks about the legitimacy of Lukan ideology, the power of modern readers and my reading.

1. *Summary*

Chapter 1 briefly surveyed the past and present issues in the study of the Holy Spirit in Luke and Acts by focusing on three representative scholars: J.D.G. Dunn; R.P. Menzies; M.M.B. Turner, classifying the main issues debated into four tables. I noted here that their research (including that of other influential scholars) was almost always undertaken by 'historical critical methods', especially 'redaction criticism'. I

---

1. See the conclusion section of each chapter.

explained my use of 'dynamic biblical narrative criticism' as an attempt
to provide a new and holistic portrait of the Holy Spirit in Luke–Acts,
which I compared with the study of W.H. Shepherd (1994).

Towards this end, Chapter 2 provided the literary repertoire of the
Lukan Holy Spirit by examining the use of *rûaḥ* or *pneuma* in the Jewish Bible. I concluded that the divine Spirit in the extratext is characterized as God's own Spirit, revealing his will/purpose by representing his
power, activity and presence through his human agents (see also the
usage of *rûaḥ* in the DSS in my excursus). In the literary repertoire, the
roles played by the Spirit are as follows: giving prophecy or revelatory
speeches, miracles, wisdom, craftsmanship and the interpretation of
visions-dreams to members of the Israelite communities, and inspiring
fidelity to God and social justice among the Israelites. And endowment
with God's Spirit is also connected with future expectations of both the
coming Davidic figure and the restoration of the people of God.

Chapters 3, 4 and 5 explored the Holy Spirit in Luke–Acts as dynamic biblical narrative. Chapter 3 discussed the relationship between the
narrator's point of view and the Spirit and noted especially that this
point of view focuses not only on God and Jesus, but also on the Holy
Spirit. References to the Holy Spirit are used to suggest narrative reliability: both the narrator and the characters are positively associated with
the divine frame of reference through references to the Holy Spirit.

Chapters 4 and 5 elucidated the Holy Spirit as a literary character
through narrative theories of 'character' and 'characterization'. So
Chapter 4 showed that the Holy Spirit in Luke–Acts is portrayed as an
enigmatic divine character, through two dialectic (i.e. 'person-likeness'
and 'person-unlikeness') paradigms. The Holy Spirit, in terms of character-presentation (i.e. 'direct definition', 'indirect presentation' and
'analogy'), is characterized as God's promised holy Spirit giving God's
power and insight for his ongoing plan to God's human agents and his
people in general as anticipated in the literary repertoire. At the same
time, however, I noted that the Holy Spirit is also characterized in close
relation to Jesus the Messiah and Lord and is once directly depicted as
the 'Spirit of (the risen) Jesus'. It was not surprising, therefore, that the
Holy Spirit, after Jesus' ascension, is almost always presented in contexts in which Jesus' witnesses are said to bear witness to the risen
Jesus, not only to Jews, but also to Gentiles. This witness-mission,
according to the Lukan narrator, expresses God's counsel/will (Acts
15.14-18; cf. Lk. 2.30-32; Acts 22.14-15) as well as that of the risen

Jesus (Lk. 24.46-48; Acts 1.8; 9.15; 26.17-18, 23).

Chapter 5 further explored the characterization of the Holy Spirit in terms of the narrative function of the Spirit in relation to the causal aspect of the plot. I argued that the major narrative function of the Holy Spirit (as 'helper' and 'sender') is to empower and guide individual characters as God's human agents and Jesus' witnesses to seek and save God's people in accordance with the plan of God. We also saw, on the one hand, that references to the Spirit function to verify group characters as incorporated into God's people; and on the other, the Spirit is employed in relation to the life-situations of believers in settled communities by granting them charismatic gifts, or comforting and encouraging them or initiating forms of patriarchal leadership. Hence, as the plot of Luke–Acts develops, so do the functions of the Holy Spirit.

2. *Implications*

2.1. *The Theological Significance of the Lukan Holy Spirit*
The Lukan narrator or implied author presents the 'Holy Spirit' in terms of the arrival of the 'Spirit of the Lord/God' as promised in the Jewish Bible. It can thus be said that the Holy Spirit in Luke–Acts is characterized as Yahweh's holy Spirit. At the same time, however, the characterization of the Holy Spirit in Luke–Acts is developed in ways which are distinctive in relation to the Jewish Bible's presentation of God's Spirit.[2] I shall highlight two distinctive features:[3] (1) the Holy Spirit in relation to Jesus and (2) the Holy Spirit in relation to non-Jews.

(1) In Luke–Acts, the Holy Spirit is characterized in relation to the risen Jesus as well as to God. According to the risen Jesus (Lk. 24.49; Acts 1.5) and Peter (Acts 2.33; 11.16), the Holy Spirit is said to be given to the resurrected Jesus by God and to *be sent* or *caused by him* (cf. Acts 9.17; 19.4-6). This is also suggested by the direct definition 'Spirit *of Jesus*' in Acts 16.7. It should also be noted that the Holy Spirit, after Jesus' ascension, is portrayed as playing a role in Acts which is *parallel* to that of the risen Jesus (Acts 9.11-12, 15-16; 18.9-

---

2.   For comparison between the several immediate effects of the 'Spirit of God' in the Jewish Bible and those of the 'Holy Spirit' in Luke–Acts, see §5.2.1.1 in Chapter 4; for other comparisons in terms of 'speech', 'action', 'external appearance', 'environment' and the relationship with 'evil spirit(s)', see Chapter 4 and Appendices I and II.

3.   For my definition 'theological significance', see n. 63 in Chapter 1.

10; 22.18, 21; 23.11; cf. Lk. 12.12; 21.15). The Spirit in the Jewish Bible and the Gospel is God's holy Spirit revealing God's will to his people through his human agents, *but in Acts God's Spirit is given through Jesus, and God's will is defined in terms of the effects of Jesus' life, death and resurrection* (cf. Acts 2.22-23, 36; 3.13-15; 10.40; 13.33-39). Several features of the religious activities of God's people, particularly Jesus' witnesses, in Acts in relation to the risen Jesus may be explained in connection with this theological significance of the Lukan Holy Spirit:[4] (a) baptizing in the name of Jesus (Acts 2.38; 8.16; 10.48; 19.5; 22.16); (b) witnessing primarily to the risen Jesus, rather than directly to God;[5] (c) using the name of Jesus in teaching/preaching or performing miracles (Acts 3.6, 16; 4.7, 10, 12, 17, 18, 30; 5.28, 40; 9.27, 28; cf. 19.13, 17-20); (d) reinterpretation of the Jewish Bible (about God) as reference to Jesus;[6] (e) religious experiences of the risen Jesus through visions (Acts 7.55-56; 9.4-6, 10-16; 18.9-10; 22.7-10, 18, 21; 23.11; 26.14-18); (f) prayer to the exalted Jesus (Acts 7.59-60; 1.24; cf. Lk. 24.52; Acts 19.17);[7] (g) following and instructing for the 'Way' (Acts 9.2; 19.9, 23; 22.4; 24.14, 22; cf. 5.14; 9.35, 42; 11.17, 21b, 24; 16.15, 31; 18.8) of the sect of the Nazarenes (Acts 24.5, 14). In this way, Jesus is represented not only as God's Messiah (God's agent), but also as Lord (God's co-regent): 'Repentance toward God' is linked with 'faith in Jesus as Lord and Christ' (Acts 20.21).[8]

---

4. Cf. Hurtado (1988: 100-124), who claims that 'the early Christian mutation in Jewish monotheism was a religious devotion with a certain binitarian shape' (124) by noting six features of the religious devotion of early Christianity: (1) hymnic practices, (2) prayer and related practices, (3) use of the name of Christ, (4) the Lord's Supper, (5) confession of faith in Jesus and (6) prophetic pronouncements of the risen Christ.

5. See n. 15 in Chapter 5.

6. For instance, 'calling upon the name' (Joel 2.32) of Jesus as the Lord (Acts 2.21, 38; 4.12; 9.14, 21; 22.16; cf. 1 Cor. 1.2; Rom. 10.13). See also §3.3.1.4 in Chapter 3.

7. Cf. 2 Cor. 12.2-10; 1 Cor. 16.22; prayer to God through Christ: Rom. 1.8; 7.25; 2 Cor. 1.20; Col. 3.17.

8. Cf. 1 Cor. 8.5-6; 2.16//Isa. 40.13; Phil. 2.10-11//Isa. 45.23; Rom. 9.5. Dunn (1991: 191) concludes, '*To call Jesus "Lord"...was evidently not understood in earliest Christianity as identifying him with God.* What Paul and the first Christians seem to have done was to claim that *the one God had shared his lordship with the exalted Christ*' (emphasis original); cf. Hurtado (1988: 94-99; 123-24).

(2) On the day of Pentecost, the Holy Spirit is said to be poured out upon 'all flesh' (i.e. Jewish men and women including slaves) as promised in Joel 2.28-32 (cf. Num. 11.29). So the coming of the Holy Spirit in Acts 2 is interpreted by Peter (and the narrator) as the eschatological outpouring of God's Spirit. However, as the story of Acts continues, this eschatological community embraces not only Jews, *but also non-Jews on the grounds that they are also, like Jews, said to receive God's same gift, the Holy Spirit* (Acts 10.47; 11.17-18; 15.8). Hence, as demonstrated in Chapter 4, *the Spirit's direct speeches and actions are noticeably highlighted in relation to the witness-mission to non-Jews* (Acts 10.19; 11.12; 13.2-4; 15.28; 16.6-7; 19.21; cf. 8.29, 39).[9] In short, the Holy Spirit in Acts is presented as the Spirit who incorporates non-Jews into God's eschatological people, whereas the Spirit of the Lord/ God in the Jewish Bible is consistently characterized as the Spirit who inspires God's faithful Jews past, present and future.[10] Hence, the Lukan Holy Spirit is presented as the missiological Spirit empowering God's human agents to witness to the risen Jesus not only to Jews, but also to non-Jews.

These two points reflect the religious ideology of the implied author or community of Luke–Acts, which can be compared with that of the implied authors of the Jewish Bible as a whole,[11] and this ideology affects the implied reader (see below).[12]

---

9. Also noted is that the 'divine frame of reference' is employed as verifying the mission to non-Jews as God's will: an angel of the Lord (Acts 8.26; 10.3; 27.23); heavenly voices (Acts 10.13, 15; 11.7, 9); visions (Acts 10.3, 17, 19; 11.5; 16.9, 10; cf. 22.21; 23.11); scriptural citations (Acts 13.47; 15.16-17; 28.28; cf. Lk. 2.32).

10. The only exception is found in Num. 24.2 and the LXX Num. 23.7 in which God's Spirit inspires Balaam the pagan diviner to give prophetic oracles blessing God's people, Israel.

11. In this sense, the implied author of Luke–Acts shares a 'religious ideology' of the Holy Spirit similar to that of other New Testament writers, like Paul and John. Cf. Isaacs (1976), who after examining the concept of the Spirit both in Hellenistic Judaism of the intertestamental period and in the New Testament, claims, 'For all N.T. writers the power and presence of God, signified by πνεῦμα, is grounded exclusively in Jesus, the Christ. Therefore, pneumatology and christology are inextricably bound up with each other, since the church's concept of the Spirit of God has become conditioned by its beliefs about Jesus, Πνεῦμα Θεοῦ has become Πνεῦμα Χριστοῦ' (124; see also 142).

12. To post-biblical Christian readers, the 'theological significance' of the Holy Spirit in Luke–Acts (and other books in the New Testament) seems to have

2.2. The Narrator/Implied Author, the Text and the Implied Reader in Relation to the Holy Spirit

I want to highlight here the results of the studies in Chapters 3 and 5.[13] (1) As has been argued earlier,[14] reliable characters (e.g. Jesus, Peter and Paul) are said to be filled with the Holy Spirit. In the literary framework, however, such characters' speeches and actions are all controlled by the implied author or the narrator with a view to making his whole narrative reliable and authoritative. In this sense, the narrator is characterized *as an off-stage character full of the Holy Spirit*, who perceives the inside views of other inspired characters.[15] In so doing, the narrator who tries to persuade his readers to adopt his own ideology is implicitly characterized *as the most powerful witness to the Kingdom of God, Jesus and the Holy Spirit* through his narrative as a whole.

(2) If the narrator/implied author is implicitly characterized as an off-stage Spirit-filled character, then the text of Luke–Acts, organized and/ or narrated by him, is presented as *a Spirit-inspired narrative and is thus claimed to be reliable and authoritative* (cf. Lk. 1.4), like that of the Spirit-filled Lukan characters' speeches, including those of Old Testament figures, David (Acts 1.16; 4.25) and Isaiah (Acts 28.25).[16]

(3) What is the possible impact of the portrait of the Holy Spirit on the reader? I want to limit this question to the possible effect of the plot on the 'implied reader' in relation to the narrative functions of the Holy Spirit. The implied reader who is a faithful believer may be led to expect that the Holy Spirit would grant them charismatic gifts or comfort and encourage them in times of trouble or initiate patriarchal leadership to sustain the life of 'saints' in a settled community. Readers may also be led to recognize that they are saved or verified as God's people through their personal experience of 'baptism in the Holy Spirit' in some extraordinary ways, e.g. speaking in tongues or prophesying.

---

exercised various influences: e.g. '*filioque*', 'christocentric' approach to the Spirit, the 'missiological' Spirit, 'doctrine of Trinity' and so on, departing to a certain extent from the Jewish understanding of God's Spirit. See Burgess (1984; 1989); Colle (1993: 91-112); McIntyre (1997); Badcock (1997).

13. See also Hur (1997: 21-22).

14. §3.3.2 in Chapter 3.

15. It is interesting to see that some old Latin manuscripts (b, q) of Lk. 1.3a ('it seemed good to me also') add the phrase *et spiritui sancto* ('and to the Holy Spirit'). Cf. Acts 15.28.

16. In this way, the text of Luke–Acts is presented as biblical narrative like that of the Jewish Bible.

Moreover, this implied reader may be encouraged to become a witness to Jesus, expecting to be inspired to preach in powerful words and/or to perform miraculous deeds, and to be met with acceptance and rejection. Implied readers are encouraged to believe that the Holy Spirit would empower and guide them to fulfil the will of God or the desire of Jesus, in spite of difficulties and hardships ultimately caused by Satan. In this way, the implied reader might identify either with the charismatic witnesses of Jesus or with the ordinary members of local communities, confessing Jesus as the Lord and God's Messiah. In either case, the reader as faithful believer is led to recognize that their religious life before God cannot be sustained without the power and/or encouragement of the Holy Spirit.

If the reader does not accept Jesus as 'Lord and Messiah', the narrative implies that such a reader resists the Holy Spirit (cf. Lk. 12.8-12; Acts 5.32; 7.51-53) and the will/plan of God (cf. Lk. 9.48; 10.16; Acts 3.13-26; 10.34-43). After reading the narrative, the reader is thus left with only two options (cf. Lk. 2.34-35; Acts 14.4; 17.4-5; 28.24; see also 2.37; 16.30; 26.28). In terms of the plot, the narrative of Luke–Acts can thus be read as a challenging story for Jesus' charismatic witnesses and/or ordinary yet faithful believing members led by the Holy Spirit (cf. Lk. 9.23-27; 57-62; 12.8-10; 24.46-49; Acts 1.7-8).[17]

On the other hand, however, the implied reader as Spirit-inspired believer notes that they may misinterpret the will/plan of God and thus need continuously to be guided by the Holy Spirit (Acts 10.9-35; 16.6-10; cf. Gal. 5.16; Eph. 5.17-18; 1 Thess. 5.19). The reader also recognizes that revelatory words or prophecy claimed to be inspired by the Holy Spirit could sometimes be differently interpreted among believers (Paul in Acts 20.22-23; the Tyrian's disciples in 21.4; Agabus and his hearers in 21.11-14; cf. 1 Cor. 14.29-33). Moreover, believing group/community leaders acknowledged as inspired by the Holy Spirit could be in conflict (e.g. Paul and Barnabas in Acts 15.36-41; cf. 1 Cor. 3). This is another implied aspect that may challenge faithful readers: 'If

---

17. According to the narrator's point of view, however, to 'be a witness' or 'to be saved' is determined by the will of God/Jesus (cf. Lk. 5.8-11; 6.13; 9.1; 10.1; Acts 9.15; 10.41; 13.48; 18.10; 22.14; 26.17). Cf. Lincoln (1990), who, highlighting the implied readers' identification with the disciples in Matthew, points out, 'Matthew's gospel should be read as a story for would-be teachers. The implied author is in effect saying to the implied reader, "So, you want to be teacher? Let me tell you a story"' (125).

you know or are convinced that you are inspired and led by the Holy Spirit, be humble and cautious, and respect your brothers who have different opinions'.

2.3. *The Legitimacy of Lukan Ideology, the Power of Modern Readers and my Reading*

How are these influences that I have mentioned above relevant to the modern 'flesh and blood reader'? To put it differently, is this Lukan ideology in regard to the portrait of the Holy Spirit adequate or acceptable to the twentieth-century modern and secular reader? More specifically, how does the modern reader respond to the following four issues?:[18]

(1) How does the reader know that what they experience is the effect caused by the Holy Spirit and not by an evil spirit or by personal illusion? What counts as evidence of inspiration by God rather than, say, self-interest? Similarly, how does the reader know that they are baptized in or inspired by the Holy Spirit?

(2) In the Lukan characterization of the Holy Spirit, what roles or effects resonate still and what should or may be excluded?

(3) To what extent is the 'theological significance' of the Lukan Holy Spirit helpful or meaningful?

(4) How and on what basis does the reader decide what the will of God is in a context in which two different people or groups inside a believing community are claiming that their different perceptions of the will of God are revealed/caused by the Holy Spirit?

Though all these questions are practical and important, particularly in the churches today, I have to acknowledge that it is very difficult to answer them. Responses are variously and differently made depending on the identity of the reader and his or her communities.[19] It has been

18. Cf. Parker's (1996: 208-209) 23 interview questions about 'Spirit Leading Experiences' to the congregation belonging to the International Holiness Pentecostal Church: e.g. 'Have you ever had occasion for "second thoughts" about decisions you made based on the conviction that it was the Spirit's leading? How have you resolved this?' (209).

19. Lukan readers are, for instance, categorized as two groups: 'believing' and 'non-believing'. Among contemporary believing readers, there are other groups: 'conservative', 'liberal' and 'radical'. They are also divided among different denominations (e.g. the Roman Catholic, the Church of England, Methodist, Presbyterian, Baptist, Pentecostal, Reformed and so forth). In addition, these are groups that can be distinguished in terms of gender, ethnicity, age and the like. Each reader

claimed that interpretative meaning or significance is engendered through a diverse 'fusion of horizons' between the text (the past) *and* the reader (the present).[20] As seen in Chapter 1, critical readers (e.g. Dunn; Menzies; Turner) produce different views of the meaning of the reception of the Spirit in spite of using the same methodology.

For instance, in regard to the relevance of the apostolic miracles or gifts (e.g. healings, prophecies, verbal revelations and the like) to our times today, four different views have been suggested even in evangelical circles' appeals to the New Testament:[21] (1) the 'cessationist' position—there are no miraculous gifts of the Holy Spirit today as there were in the apostolic New Testament period (Gaffin 1979: 89-116; 1996: 25-64); (2) the 'Pentecostal/charismatic' position—standing in clear opposition to the cessationist's interpretation, people in this position encourage practices that are depicted in Acts as evidence of inspiration by the Holy Spirit (Oss 1996: 239-83); (3) the 'third wave' position—[22] encouraging such gifts in a manner similar to the 'pentecostal/charismatic' position yet teaching that every Christian receives the Holy Spirit at conversion and distinguishing this from subsequent experiences of the Spirit (Storms 1996: 175-223); (4) the 'open but cautious' position—open to the possibility of charismatic gifts to believers, including that of miraculous healings today, but not making this central to Christian practice (Saucy 1996: 97-148). As a more specific example, most Pentecostal theologians regard 'speaking in tongues' as the 'initial evidence' of baptism in the Holy Spirit,

---

cannot but give their own response to the text, which is, consciously or unconsciously, bound up with the reader's and/or one's community's self-existence or ideology. Cf. Schweizer (1996: 12) who professes, '*how* we experience the Spirit is also influenced by where and in what tradition we are growing up and living' (emphasis original).

20. Cf. Gadamer (1993: 305-307); Thiselton (1980: 15-16; 307-310).

21. See Grudem (1996); cf. Ruthven (1993); Turner (1996a: 286-359).

22. C.P. Wagner, the mission professor at Fuller Theological Seminary, classified charismatic renewal movements into three 'waves' (Grudem 1996: 11-12): the Pentecostal renewal (e.g. the Assemblies of God; the Church of God in Christ) as the first wave since 1901; the charismatic renewal movement as the second wave since the 1960s (not forming its own denomination); the 'empowered evangelicals' as the third wave since the 1980s (e.g. the Association of Vineyard Churches). All these groups could be defined within 'Pentecostalism'; see Parker (1996: 206).

whereas non-Pentecostals do not.[23] Then whose (i.e. which readers' or interpretative communities') interpretation of the Holy Spirit and whose responses to other related issues are legitimate and normative?[24] And which criteria can we establish to evaluate them correctly? It appears that decisions on the legitimacy of one's interpretation depend on *other* (internal or external) readers' or communities' acceptance.[25] That is to say, each biblical or theological reader or community (academics and churches) interprets their 'own Bible/bible' in terms of their own interested goals or ideologies.[26]

23. See the twelve articles edited by McGee (1991). For the former position, see McGee 96-118; 119-30; for the latter, see Hurtado 189-201; Michaels 202-218; cf. Lederle 131-41.

24. Cf. Fee (1991) who, as one of the most prominent Pentecostal scholars yet rejecting the *traditional* Pentecostal position, questions the normative value of some narrative-units in the book of Acts (esp. the episodes of the Samaritans [8.14-17], Paul and the Ephesians [19.1-7] as a normative theology for the Pentecostal 'doctrine of subsequence', i.e. receiving the Holy Spirit as a second blessing after conversion) in our times in asserting that '[the book of] Acts which may be regarded as normative for Christians is related primarily to what any given narrative was *intended* to teach... Historical precedent, to have normative value, must be related to *intent*' (91-92; emphasis original). By contrast, Menzies (1994a: 232-43), another leading Pentecostal scholar, supporting Stronstad's view (1984: 8; i.e. 'since Luke has a theological interest, his narratives, although they are historical, are always more than simply descriptions or the record of "brute" facts'), argues that the narrative of Acts (esp. Lukan pneumatology) provides an important and relevant model for Pentecostal theology today. Most Pentecostal scholars' positions seem to be grounded in their own 'spiritual and physical experience' of baptism in the Holy Spirit. Stronstad (1992: 16-20) elsewhere thus claims the 'validity of charismatic experiential presuppositions' as the first of five components in a Pentecostal hermeneutics. Recently, Pentecostals have attempted to develop their hermeneutics in the light of post-modernism: see Cargal (1993: 136-87); Johns (1995: 73-95).

25. Cf. Fish (1980: 338-55). Clines (1993: 79) states, 'What the academic community today decides counts as a reasonable interpretation of a text *is* a reasonable interpretation, and until my community decides that my interpretation is acceptable, it *isn't* acceptable' (emphasis original).

26. Cf. P. Davies (1995: 17-55). It has generally been acknowledged that no critical reading or interpretation can be neutral; rather the readers/interpreters, whether critical or otherwise, inevitably express their own ideology or world view. For instance, see Bultmann (1961: 342-51); Stanton (1977: 60-71); Thiselton (1980: 103-114); Morgan and Barton (1988: 29, 291-93). Cf. Poythress (1987: 69-91). Patte (1995), self-defined as a once 'androcentric and Eurocentric exegete',

This study offers *a* reading of the Lukan Holy Spirit by means of *a* new perspective. This means that I, as a would-be implied reader and critical scholar, have attempted to seek and provide (explicit and implicit) *evidence in the text* (including the extratext and other cited literature) in order to make the study logical and cogent. At the same time, however, as a Korean male reader at Sheffield University,[27] I have to acknowledge that this present work of 'dynamic reading' has been *my interested reading* of the Holy Spirit in Luke–Acts *through my interested hermeneutic tools.* Whether my reading of the Lukan Holy Spirit is relevant and cogent either to biblical academic communities or to theological confessional communities today is a question I have to leave to each reader/community to decide.

acknowledges his limitation in exegetical practices and suggests an ethically responsible reading by rejecting one-dimensional exegesis, allowing multi-dimensional insights.

27. Born in 1963, converted from Buddhism to Christianity (Presbyterian/Reformed) in 1980 and educated (BA) in Seoul, South Korea, I read my first degree in theology (Mdiv, 1993) at Westminster Theological Seminary, Philadelphia, USA and have researched the present topic at Sheffield since October 1993.

THE PRESENTATION OF THE SPIRIT OF THE LORD/GOD IN THE JEWISH BIBLE

1. *Character-Presentation I*

1.1. *Direct Definition*

Direct Definition	Text
Spirit of God [רוח אלהים; πνεῦμα θεοῦ] (13 times)	Gen. 1.2; 41.38; Exod. 31.3; 35.31; Num. 24.2; 1 Sam. 10.10; 11.6; 19.20, 23; Ezek. 11.24; Job. 33.4; 1 Chron. 15.1; 24.20; cf. 1 Sam. 16.15, 16, 23; 18.10
Spirit of the Lord [רוח־יהוה; πνεῦμα κυρίου] (24 + 1 [Old Testament Apocrypha])	Judg. 3.10; 6.34; 11.29; 13.25; 14.6, 19; 15.14; 1 Sam. 10.6; 16.13, 14a; 2 Sam. 23.2; 1 Kgs 18.12; 22.24; 2 Kgs 2.16; Isa. 11.2; 40.13; 61.1; 63.14; Ezek. 11.5; 37.1; Mic. 2.7; 3.8; 1 Chron. 18.23; 20.14; Wis. 1.7
My (God's) Spirit [רוחי; τὸ πνεῦμα μου] (14)	Gen. 6.3; Isa. 30.1; 42.1; 44.3; 59.21; Ezek. 36.27; 37.14; 39.29; Joel 3.1, 2; Hag. 2.5; Zech. 4.6; 6.8; Prov. 1.23
His (God's) Spirit [רוחו; τὸ πνεῦμα αὐτοῦ] (5 + 1)	Num. 11.29; Isa. 34.16; 48.16; Zech. 7.12; Ps. 106.33; Bel 1.36
Your (God's) Spirit [רוחך; τὸ πνεῦμα σου] (2 + 1)	Ps. 139.7; Neh. 9.30; Jdt. 16.14
His (God's) holy Spirit [רוח קדשו; τὸ πνεῦμα τὸ ἅγιον αὐτοῦ] (2)	Isa. 63.10, 11
Your (God's) holy Spirit [רוח קדשך; τὸ πνεῦμα τὸ ἅγιον σου] (1 + 1)	Ps. 51.13; Wis. 9.17
Your (God's) good Spirit [רוחך טובה; τὸ πνεῦμα σου τὸ ἀγαθον] (2)	Ps. 143.10; Neh. 9.20
Your (God's) immortal Spirit [τὸ ἄφθαρτόν σου πνεῦμα] (1)	Wis. 12.1

Direct Definition	Text
Spirit of the holy gods/God [רוּחַ־אֱלָהִין קַדִּישִׁין; πνεῦμα θεοῦ ἅγιον] (4)	Dan. 4.5, 6, 15; 5.11 (LXX 4.8, 9, 18)
Spirit of gods/God [רוּחַ אֱלָהִין; πνεῦμα θεοῦ] (1)	Dan. 5.14 (LXX 5.11)
holy Spirit [τὸ πνεῦμα τὸ ἅγιον] (1)	Sus. 1.45
holy and disciplined Spirit [ἅγιον πνεῦμα παιδείας] (1)	Wis. 1.5
Spirit of wisdom [רוּחַ חָכְמָה; πνεῦμα σοφίας] (2 + 1)	Exod. 28.3; Deut. 34.9 (cf. LXX); Wis. 7.7; cf. Wis. 7.22-23
Spirit of wisdom, understanding, counsel, might, knowledge, the fear of the Lord/fidelity [רוּחַ חָכְמָה וּבִינָה רוּחַ עֵצָה וּגְבוּרָה רוּחַ דַּעַת וְיִרְאַת יְהוָה; πνεῦμα σοφίας καὶ συνέσεως πνεῦμα βουλῆς καὶ ἰισχύος πνεῦμα γνώσεως καὶ εὐσεβείας] (1)	Isa. 11.2; cf. Dan. 5.14; Sir. 39.6
Spirit of justice [רוּחַ מִשְׁפָּט; πνεῦμα κρίσεως] (1)	Isa. 28.6
Spirit of compassion and supplication [רוּחַ חֵן וְתַחֲנוּנִים; πνεῦμα χάριτος καὶ οἰκτιρμοῦ] (1)	Zech. 12.10
kindly Spirit [φιλάνθρωπον πνεῦμα] (1)	Wis. 1.6

1.2. Indirect Presentation
1.2.1. Speech

Speech	Text
to speak	2 Sam. 23.2 (cf. 1 Kgs 22.21//2 Chron. 18.20; 1 Kgs 22.24// 2 Chron. 18.23

1.2.2. Action

Action Verbs in MT (39 cases)	Text
נשׂא [Qal: to lift/raise] (9 times)	Ezek. 3.14b; 1 Kgs 18.12; 2 Kgs 2.16a; Ezek. 3.12, 14; 8.3a; 11.1a, 24a; 43.5a
בוא [Qal: to go\ Hiphil: to bring/carry] (6)	Ezek. 2.2a; 3.24\ Ezek. 8.3b; 11.1b, 24b; 43.5b
צלח [Qal: to fall on/be powerful] (6)	Judg. 14.6, 19; 1 Sam. 10.6, 10; 11.16; 16.13

Action Verbs in MT (39 cases)	Text
עמד [Hiphil: to set\ Qal: to stay] (3)	Ezek. 2.2b; 3.24b\ Hag. 2.5
לבש [Qal: to clothe] (3)	Judg. 6.34; 1 Chron. 12.19; 2 Chron. 24.20
נוח [Qal: to rest] (3)	Num. 11.25b, 26; Isa. 11.2
לקח [Qal: to take] (1)	Ezek. 3.14b
שלך [Hiphil: to throw away] (1)	2 Kgs 2.16b
עוד [Hiphil: to warn/ admonish; witness] (1)	Neh. 9.30
סור [Qal: to leave] (1)	1 Sam. 16.14a
פעם [Qal: to impel/push] (1)	Judg. 13.25
נפל [Qal: to fall upon] (1)	Ezek. 11.5
קבץ [Piel: to gather together] (1)	Isa. 34.16
רחף [Piel: to hover] (1)	Gen. 1.2
נחה [Hiphil: to lead] (1)	Ps. 143.10

Action Verbs in LXX (55 cases)	Text
γίνομαι [to come upon] (9 times)	LXX Num. 23.7; 24.2; Judg. 3.10; 11.29; 1 Sam. 19.20, 23; 2 Kgs 2.9; 2 Chron. 15.1; 20.14
ἀναλαμβάνω [to take up] (6)	Ezek. 3.12, 14; 8.3a; 11.1a, 24a; 43.5a
(ἐφ)ἄλλομαι [to come/leap upon] (6)	Judg. 14.6, 19; 1 Sam. 10.6, 10; 11.6; 16.13
(συν)άγω [to lead] (5)	Ezek. 8.3b; 11.1b, 24b; 43.5b; Isa. 34.16
ἐπαναπαύω [to rest upon] (4)	Num. 11.25b, 26; 2 Kgs 2.15; 1 Sam. 11.2
πορεύομαι [to go] (3)	Ezek. 1.12, 20; 3.14b
(ἐπ)ἔρχομαι [to come upon] (3)	Isa. 32.15; Ezek. 2.2a; 3.24a
ἐνδύω [to clothe] (3)	Judg. 6.34; 1 Chron. 12.19; 2 Chron. 24.20
ἐξαιρω [to lift up] (2)	Ezek. 2.2b; 3.14a
αἴρω [to raise] (2)	1 Kgs 18.12; 2 Kgs 2.16a
ἵστημι [to stand] (2)	Ezek. 3.24b; Hag. 2.5
ῥίπτω [to cast/throw down] (1)	2 Kgs 2.16b
ἐπιμαρτυρέω [to bear witness] (1)	Neh. 9.30
ἀφίστημι [to depart] (1)	1 Sam. 16.14a
συνεκπορεύομαι [to go out with] (1)	Judg. 13.25
πίπτω [to fall upon] (1)	Ezek. 11.5
(ἐπι)φέρω [to move] (1)	Gen. 1.2
ὁδηγέω [to lead/guide] (1)	Ps. 142.10 (ET: 143.10)

1.2.3. *External Appearance*
Cf. the contexts in which *rûaḥ* or *pneuma* is referring to mighty wind (see nn. 6, 38, 52 in Chapter 2).

1.2.4. *Environment*

Environment	Text
from on high	Isa. 32.15; Wis. 9.17; cf. Ezek. 1.12-20

2. *Character-Presentation II*

2.1. *Repetition and Similarity*
2.1.1. *Repeated Effects of Spirit-Endowment*

Repeated Effects	Text
Prophecy and/or revelatory words including unintelligible prophecy	Num. 11.25, 26; 24.2; 1 Sam. 10.6, 10; 19.10, 23; 1 Chron. 12.19; 2 Chron. 15.1; 20.14; 24.20; Joel. 3.1-2; Sus. 1.45
Wisdom	Gen. 41.38; Exod. 28.3; 31.3; 35.31; Deut. 34.9; Isa. 11.2; Dan. 4.5, 6, 15; 5.11, 14; Sir. 39.6; Wis. 1.6; 7.7, 22; 9.17
Charismatic power with miracles and guidance	Judg. 14.6, 9; 15.14; 2 Kgs 2.16; Isa. 11.2; Ezek. 3.12, 14; 8.3; 11.1, 24; 43.5; Mic. 3.8; Sir. 48.12; Bel 1.36
Source for the religious or ethical commitment of individuals/ groups	Isa. 11.2; 28.6; 32.15; 42.1; Ezek. 36.27; Zech. 12.10; Ps. 51.13; 139.7; 143.10; Wis. 1.5

2.1.2. *Similar Expressions for Spirit-Endowment*[1]

Similar Expressions in MT	Text
צלח [Qal: to fall/be powerful] (7 times)	Judg. 14.6, 19; 15.14; 1 Sam. 10.6, 10; 11.6; 16.13
מלא [Qal: to be full of] (6)	Deut. 34.9; Exod. 28.3; 31.3; 35.31; Mic. 3.8
נתן [Qal: to give/offer] (4)	Num. 11.29; Neh. 9.20; Isa. 42.1; Ezek. 37.14
ב היה [to remain in] (4)	Gen. 41.38; Num. 27.18; 2 Kgs 2.9; Dan. 4.5
לבש [Qal: to clothe] (3)	Judg. 6.34; 1 Chron. 12.19 (ET: 12.18); 2 Chron. 24.20
שפך [Qal: to pour out] (3)	Joel 3.1, 2 (ET: 2.28, 29); Zech. 12.10
נוח [Qal: to rest] (3)	Num. 11.25b, 26; Isa. 11.2

---

1. The verbs that are used more than three times are listed. For the less used verbs, see tables IV and V in Chapter 2.

Similar Expressions in LXX	Text
γίνομαι [to come upon] (9 times)	Num. 23.7 (LXX addition; ET: 23.6); 24.2; Judg. 3.10; 11.29; 1 Sam. 19.20, 23; 2 Kgs 2.9; 2 Chron. 15.1; 20.14
(ἐμ/ἐν)πίμπλημι [to fill/be filled with] (8)	Deut. 34.9; Exod. 28.3; 31.3; 35.31; LXX Isa. 11.3; Mic. 3.8; Sir. 39.6; 48.12
(ἐφ)άλλομαι [to rush on] (7)	Judg. 14.6, 19; 15.14; 1 Sam. 10.6, 10; 11.6; 16.13
(εἰμί) ἐν [to be in/on] (5)	Dan. 4.8, 9, 18; 5.11, 14
δίδωμι [to put/give] (4)	Num. 11.29; Neh. 9.20; Isa. 42.1; Ezek. 37.14
ἐπαναπαύω [to rest on] (4)	Num. 11.25b, 26; 2 Kgs 2.15; Isa. 11.2
ἐνδύω [to clothe/take possession of] (3)	Judg. 6.34; 1 Chron. 12.19; 2 Chron. 24.20
(ἐπ)έρχομαι [to enter into] (3)	Isa. 32.15; Ezek. 2.2a; 3.24
ἐπιτίθημι [to put] (3)	Num. 11.17, 25a; Isa. 44.3
ἐκχέω [to pour out] (3)	Joel 3.1, 2; Zech. 12.10
ἔχω [to have] (3)	Gen. 41.38; Num. 27.18; Dan. 4.8 (MT: 4.5)

2.2. Comparison and Contrast

Comparison	Contrast
an angel of the Lord/God; see n. 21 in Chapter 2	an evil spirit (Judg. 9.23; 1 Sam. 16.14b, 15, 16, 23a, 23b; 18.10; 19.9;); a lying spirit (1 Kgs. 22.22, 23//2 Chron. 18. 21, 22); a spirit of confusion (2 Kgs 19.7; Isa. 19.14); a spirit of deep sleep (Isa. 29.10); a spirit of whoredom (Hos. 4.12; 5.4); an unclean spirit (Zech. 13.2); an evil spirit/demon (Tob. 6.8): see §§2.1.1; 3.1.1 in Chapter 2 and 4 in Excursus.
supernatural beings/spirits (LXX Num. 16.22; 27.16; Wis. 7.20; 2 Macc. 3.24)	

APPENDIX II

THE PRESENTATION OF THE HOLY SPIRIT IN LUKE–ACTS

1. Character-Presentation I

1.1. Direct Definition

Direct Definition	Text
Holy Spirit 54 times (τὸ ἅγιον πνεῦμα) [τὸ πνεῦμα τὸ ἅγιον] { πνεῦμα ἅγιον}	(Lk 12.10, 12; Acts 1.8; 2.38; 4.31; 9.31; 10.45; 13.4; 16.6); [Lk. 2.26; 3.22; 10.21; Acts 1.16; 2.33; 5.3, 32; 7.51; 10.44, 47; 11.15; 13.2; 15.8, 28; 19.6; 20.23, 28; 21.11; 28.25]; {Lk. 1.15, 35, 41, 67; 2.25; 3.16; 4.1a; 11.13; Acts 1.2, 5; 2.4a; 4.8, 25; 6.5; 7.55; 8.15, 17, 19; 9.17; 10.38; 11.16, 24; 13.9, 52; 19.2 ×2}
my [God's] Spirit	Acts 2.17, 18
Spirit of the Lord (τὸ πνεῦμα κυρίου)	Lk. 4.18; Acts 5.9; 8.39
Spirit of Jesus (τὸ πνεῦμα Ἰησοῦ)	Acts 16.7
promise of my [Jesus']/the Father (τὴν ἐπαγγελίαν τοῦ πατρός μου)	Acts 1.4
power from on high (ἐξ ὕψους δύναμιν)	Lk. 24.49
witness (μαρτύριον)	Acts 5.32
gift (δωρεά)	Acts 11.16-17; cf. 2.38; 8.20

1.2. Indirect Presentation
1.2.1. Speech

Speech	Text
to say	Acts 8.29; 10.19; 11.12; 13.2; cf. Acts 1.16; 28.25

1.2.2. *Action*

Action	Text
to reveal (χρηματίζω)	Lk. 2.26
to descend upon (καταβαίνω ἐπί)	Lk. 3.22
to teach (διδάσκω)	Lk. 12.12
to give somebody the ability to speak out (δίδωμι; ἀποφθέγγομαι)	Acts 2.4
to snatch away (ἁρπάζω)	Acts 8.39
to send (ἀποστέλλω; ἐκπέμπω)	Acts 10.20; 13.4
to forbid (κωλύω)	Acts 16.6
to allow (ἐάω)	Acts 16.7
to compel (δέω)	Acts 20.22
to testify (διαμαρτύρομαι)	Acts 20.23
to make somebody on overseer (τίθημι ἐπίσκοπος)	Acts 20.28

1.2.3. *External Appearance*

External Appearance	Text
like a dove	Lk. 3.22
like the rush of a violent wind	Acts 2.2
as of fire	Acts 2.3

1.2.4. *Environment*

Environment	Text
heaven	Acts 3.21
from on high	Lk. 24.49

2. Character-Presentation II

2.1. *Repetition and Similarity*
2.1.1. *Repeated Effects of Spirit-Endowment*

Repeated Effects	Text
prophetic/revelatory inspired oracle and/ or speech	Lk. 1.41-45, 67-79; Acts 4.8; 7.55-60; 11.28; 13.9-11; 21.4, 11
revelation or revelatory guidance through visions or dreams	Lk. 2.26-27; 4.1, 14; Acts 10.19; 13.2; 16.6-10; 20.23
speaking in tongues	Acts 2.4; 10.44-46; 19.6
miracle	Lk. 4.18-41; Acts 10.38; cf. Lk. 1.17, 35; 4.14; 24.49; Acts 1.8
wisdom; faith; joy	Acts 6.3, 5, 10; 11.24; Lk. 10.21; Acts 13.52
source of religious and ethical life for individual believers/believing groups	Acts 2.42-47; 4.31-37; 5.1-11; 6.3; 11.24

2.1.2. *Similar Expressions for Spirit-Endowment*[1]

Similar Expressions	Text
to be filled with (πίμπλημι; πληρόω)	Lk. 1.15, 41, 67; Acts 2.4; 4.8, 31; 9.17; 13.9, 52
to be full of (πλήρης)	Lk. 4.1; Acts 6.3, 5; 7.55; 11.24
to receive (λαμβάνω)	Acts 2.33, 38; 8.15, 17, 19; 10.47; 19.2
to give (δίδωμι)	Lk. 11.13; Acts 5.32; 8.18; 11.17; 15.8
to pour out upon (ἐκχέω ἐπί)	Acts 2.17, 18, 33; 10.45
to come upon (ἐπερχομαι; γίνομαι ἐπί; ἔρχομαι ἐπί)	Lk. 1.35; Acts 1.8; Lk. 3.22; Acts 19.6
to baptize (βαπτίζω)	Lk. 3.16; Acts 1.5; 11.16
to fall upon (ἐπιπίπτω)	Acts 8.16; 10.44; 11.15
to anoint (χρίω)	Lk. 4.18; Acts 10.38

2.2. *Comparison and Contrast*

2.2.1. *Comparison*

Comparison	Text
an angel of the Lord/God	Lk. 1.11; 2.9; Acts 5.19; 8.26; 10.3; 12.7, 23; 27.23
an angel	Lk. 1.13, 18, 19, 26, 30, 34, 35, 38; 2.10, 13, 21; 22.43; Acts 7.30, 35, 38; 10.7; 11.13; 12.8, 9, 10; 6.15; 23.8, 9
angels	Lk. 2.15; 4.10; 12.8, 9; 15.10; 16.22; 20.36; 24.23; Acts 7.53
holy angel(s)	Lk. 9.26; Acts 10.22
his [Lord's] angel	Acts 12.11

2.2.2. *Contrast*

Contrast	Text
evil/unclean spirit(s) (ἀκάθαρτος; πονηρός; ἀσθένεια; πύθων)	singular: Lk. 4.33; 8.29; 9.39, 42; 11.24; 13.11; Acts 16.16, 18; 19.15, 16; plural: Lk. 4.36; 6.18; 7.21; 8.2; 10.20; 11.26; Acts 5.16; 8.7; 19.12, 13
demon(s) (δαιμόνιον; δαίμων)	singular: Lk. 4.33, 35; 7.33; 9.42; 11.14 ×2; plural: Lk. 4.41; 8.2, 27, 30, 33, 35, 36, 38; 9.1, 49; 10.17; 11.15 ×2, 18, 19, 20; 13.32
devil (διάβολος)	Lk. 4.2, 3, 5, 13; 8.12; Acts 10.38; 13.10
Beelzebul (Βεεζεβούλ) or Satan (σατάν)	Lk. 11.15, 18; 10.18; 11.18; 13.16; 22.3, 31; Acts 5.3; 26.18

1.   For other infrequent verbs used in referring to Spirit-endowment, see n. 159 in Chapter 4.

APPENDIX III

THE HOLY SPIRIT AND ITS RELATED CHARACTERS
IN LUKE–ACTS[1]

Characters	Text	Characters	Text
John the Baptist	Lk. 1.15	Mary	Lk. 1.35
Elizabeth	Lk. 1.41	Zechariah	Lk. 1.67
Simeon	Lk. 2.25, 26, 27	Jesus	Lk. 1.35; 3.22; 4.1, 14, 18; 10.21; Acts 1.2; 2.33; 10.38
Peter	Acts 4.8; 8.17; 10.19; 11.12	Stephen	Acts 6.3, 5; 7.55
Philip	Acts 6.3 (5), 8.29, 39	Prochorus, Nicanor, Timon, Parmenas and Nicolaus: the prophets and teachers at Antioch	Acts 6.3 (5) [including Barnabas and Paul]
Paul	9.17; 13.2, 4, 9; 16.6-7; 19.6, 21; 20.21-22	Barnabas	Acts 11.24; 13.2, 4
Agabus	Acts 11.28; 21.11	Simeon, Lucius of Cyrene, Manaen	Acts 13.2
Jesus' apostles and/or disciples	Acts 2.4; 4.31; 11.15, 17; 15.8; cf. Lk. 12.12; 24.49; Acts 1.8	the apostles and elders in the Jerusalem Church	Acts 15.28
Cornelius and his household	Acts 10.44-48	the Samaritan believers	Acts 8.17
the Pisidia Antioch believers	Acts 13.52	the Baptist's disciples in Ephesus	19.1-7
the elders in the church at Ephesus	Acts 20.28	the disciples at Tyre	Acts 21.4

1.   Cf. p. 66 Table 2 in Chapter 2.

the church (members) throughout Judea, Galilee and Samaria	Acts 9.31	every one whom the Lord God calls'	Acts 2.38-39; cf. Lk. 11.13
those who obey God	Acts 5.32	David; Isaiah	Acts 1.16; 4.25; 28.25

APPENDIX IV

THE COMPARISON OF THE PHRASE 'HOLY SPIRIT' NARRATED IN THE SYNOPTIC GOSPELS

The following tables are designed to compare the Lukan use of the Holy Spirit with that of Matthew and Mark (13 times in Luke; 5 in Matthew; 4 in Mark; cf. 41 in Acts). Some observations based on these tables have been discussed in Chapter 5.

Table 1. *The Synoptic Parallels or Similar Passages*

Passage	Naming the Spirit	Context	Speaker
Mt. 3.11	Holy Spirit [+ fire]	John the Baptist's	John the Baptist
Mk 1.8	Holy Spirit	prophecy about the	John the Baptist
Lk. 3.16	Holy Spirit [+ fire]	coming Messiah	John the Baptist
Mt. 3.16	Spirit of God	The Baptism of Jesus	narrator
Mk 1.10	Spirit		narrator
Lk. 3.22	Holy Spirit		narrator
Mt. 4.1	Spirit	Before the temptation	narrator
Mk 1.12	Spirit	of Jesus	narrator
Lk. 4.1a, 1b	Holy Spirit, Spirit		narrator
Mt. 12.31, 32	Spirit, Holy Spirit	The Blasphemy against	Jesus
Mk 3.29	Holy Spirit	the Spirit	Jesus
Lk. 12.10	Holy Spirit		Jesus
Mt. 10.20	Spirit of your Father	The Holy Spirit will	Jesus
Mk 13.11	Holy Spirit	teach what Jesus'	Jesus
Lk. 12.12	Holy Spirit	disciples should say	Jesus

Table 2. *The Similar Contexts of Matthew and Luke*

Passage	Naming the Spirit	Context	Speaker
Mt. 1.18	Holy Spirit	The conception of Jesus	narrator
Mt. 1.20	Holy Spirit	by Mary	an angel of the Lord
Lk. 1.35	Holy Spirit		an angel of the Lord

Table 3. *Lukan Omissions?*

Passage	Naming the Spirit	Context	Speaker
Mt. 22.43	Spirit	David's words	Jesus
Mk 12.36	Holy Spirit	inspired by the Spirit	Jesus
cf. Acts 1.16; 4.25; 28.25			
Mt. 12.28	Spirit of God	the Beelzebul	Jesus
cf. Lk. 11.20; see also Acts	cf. the finger of	controversy	Jesus
7.25; 13.11 (19.11)	God		
Mt. 28.19	Holy Spirit	the Great	Jesus
cf. Lk. 24.46-49; Acts 1.4-8	cf. power from	Commission	Jesus
	on high	cf. witness to all	
		nations	

Table 4. *Lukan Additions?*

Passage	Naming the Spirit	Context	Speaker
1.15	Holy Spirit	the birth of John	an angel of the Lord
1.41	Holy Spirit	Elizabeth's fullness	narrator
1.67	Holy Spirit	Zechariah's fullness	narrator
2.25	Holy Spirit	Simeon	narrator
2.26	Holy Spirit	Simeon	narrator
2.27	Spirit	Simeon	narrator
4.14	Spirit	after Jesus' temptation	narrator
4.18	Spirit of the Lord	Jesus' sermon	Jesus
10.21	Holy Spirit	Jesus' joy	narrator
11.13	Holy Spirit	Jesus' teaching about	Jesus
cf. Mt. 7.11	cf. good things	prayer: God will give the Spirit to those who ask him	Jesus

BIBLIOGRAPHY

Abrams, M.H.

1993   *A Glossary of Literary Terms* (New York: Harcourt Brace College Publishers, 6th edn).

Alexander, L.C.A.

1986   'Luke's Preface in the Context of Greek Preface-Writing', *NovT* 28.1: 48-74.

1993   *The Preface to Luke's Gospel: Literary Convention and Social Context in Luke 1.1-4 and Acts 1.1* (SNTSMS, 78; Cambridge: Cambridge University Press).

1995   '"In Journeyings Often": Voyaging in the Acts of the Apostles and in Greek Romance', in Tuckett 1995: 17-50.

Allison Jr, D.C.

1992   'The Baptism of Jesus and a New Dead Sea Scroll', *BARev* 18.2: 58-60.

1993   *The New Moses: A Matthean Typology* (Edinburgh: T. & T. Clark).

Alter, R.

1981   *The Art of Biblical Narrative* (New York: Basic Books).

Anderson, A.A.

1962   'The Use of "Ruah" in 1QS, 1QH and 1QM', *JSS* 7: 293-303.

1972   *The Book of Psalms: 1-72* (NCB; London: Marshall, Morgan & Scott).

Arnold, B.T.

1996   'Luke's Characterizing Use of the Old Testament in the Book of Acts', in B. Witherington, III (ed.), *History, Literature, and Society in the Book of Acts* (Cambridge: Cambridge University Press): 300-23.

Atkinson, W.

1995   'Pentecostal Response to Dunn's Baptism in the Holy Spirit: Luke–Acts', *JPT* 6: 87-131.

Aune, D.E.

1983   *Prophecy in Early Christianity and the Ancient Mediterranean World* (Grand Rapids: Eerdmans).

Bach, A.

1993   'Signs of the Flesh: Observations on Characterization in the Bible', in Malbon and Berlin 1993: 61-80.

Badcock, G.D.

1997   *Light of Truth and Fire of Love: A Theology of the Holy Spirit* (Grand Rapids: Eerdmans).

Baer, H. von

1926   *Der Heilige Geist in den Lukasschriften* (Stuttgart: Kohlhammer).

Bar-Efrat, S.
1992 *Narrative Art in the Bible* (JSOTSup, 70; Sheffield: Almond Press).

Barrett, C.K.
1947 *The Holy Spirit and the Gospel Tradition* (London: SPCK).
1961 *Luke the Historian in Recent Study* (London: Epworth Press).
1977 'Paul's Address to the Ephesian Elders', in J. Jervell and W.A. Meeks (eds.), *God's Christ and his People* (Oslo: Universitetsforlaget): 107-121.
1984 'Apollos and the Twelve Disciples of Ephesus', in W.C. Weinrich (ed.), *The New Testament Age* (Festschrift B. Reicke; Macon, GA: Mercer University Press): 29-39.
1988 'Luke/Acts', in D.A. Carson and H.G.M. Williamson (eds.), *It Is Written: Scripture Citing Scripture* (Festschrift B. Lindars; Cambridge: Cambridge University Press): 231-44.
1994 *The Acts of the Apostles* (vol. 1; ICC; Edinburgh: T. & T. Clark).

Barthes, R.
1977 'The Struggle with the Angel: Textual Analysis of Genesis 32:22-32', in *idem, Image-Music-Text* (trans. S. Heath; London: Fontana/Collins): 125-41.
1979 'The Structural Analysis of a Narrative from Acts X–XI', in A.M. Johnson Jr (ed. and trans.), *Structuralism and Biblical Hermeneutics: A Collection of Essays* (PTMS, 22; Pittsbrugh, PA: The Pickwick Press): 109-143.
1990 *S/Z* (trans. R. Miller; Oxford: Blackwell; orig. pub. in French, 1973).

Bauer, D.R.
1988 *The Structure of Matthew's Gospel: A Study in Literary Design* (JSNTSup, 31; Sheffield: Almond Press).

Baumgärtel, F.
1968 'πνεῦμα', in *TDNT*, VI, 359-67.

Beal, T.K.
1992 'Glossary', in Fewell 1992: 21-24.

Beasley-Murray, G.R.
1986 *Jesus and the Kingdom of God* (Grand Rapids: Eerdmans).
1994 *Baptism in the New Testament* (repr.; Grand Rapids: Eerdmans).

Betz, O.
1967 'The Eschatological Interpretation of the Sinai-Tradition in Qumran and in the New Testament', *RevQ* 6: 89-107.

Bieder, W.
1968 'πνεῦμα', in *TDNT*, VI, 367-75.

Black, M.
1981 'The Holy Spirit in the Western Text of Acts', in E.J. Epp and G.D. Fee (eds.), *New Testament Textual Criticism: Its Significance to Exegesis* (Festschrift B.M. Metzger; Oxford: Clarendon Press): 160-78.

Bock, D.L.
1987 *Proclamation from Prophecy and Pattern: Lucan Old Testament Christology* (JSNTSup, 12; Sheffield: JSOT Press).
1994a 'Proclamation from Prophecy and Pattern: Luke's Use of the Old Testament for Christology and Mission', in C.A. Evans and J.A. Sanders (eds.),

The Gospels and the Scriptures of Israel (JSNTSup, 104; SSEJC, 3; Sheffield: Sheffield Academic Press): 280-307.

1994b, 1996   *Luke* (2 vols.; BECNT; Grand Rapids: Baker Books).

Booth, W.C.

1991   *The Rhetoric of Fiction* (New York: Penguin Books, 2nd edn; orig. pub. in 1961).

Bovon, F.

1987   *Luke the Theologian: Thirty-Three Years of Research (1950–1983)* (trans. K. McKinney; Allison Park: Pickwick Publications).

1989   *Das Evangelium nach Lukas (Lk 1,1–9,50)* (Zürich: Benziger/Neukirchen–Vluyn: Neukirchener Verlag).

Bratcher, R.G.

1987   *Old Testament Quotations in the New Testament* (London: UBS, 3rd edn).

Brawley, R.L.

1990   *Centering on God: Method and Message in Luke–Acts* (LCBI; Louisville: Westminster/John Knox Press).

Briggs, C.A.

1900   'The Use of רוח in the Old Testament', *JBL* 19: 132-45.

Brook, P.

1984   *Reading for the Plot: Design and Intention in Narrative* (Cambridge, MA: Harvard University Press).

Brooke, G.J.

1995   'Luke–Acts and the Qumran Scrolls: The Case of MMT', in Tuckett 1995: 72-90.

Brown, C. (ed.)

1975   *The New International Dictionary of New Testament Theology* (3 vols.; Exeter: Paternoster Press).

Brown, R.E.

1993   *The Birth of the Messiah: A Commentary on the Infancy Narratives in the Gospel of Matthew and Luke* (New York: Doubleday, rev. edn).

1994   *The Death of the Messiah: A Commentary on the Passion Narratives in the Four Gospels* (2 vols.; New York: Doubleday).

Bruce, F.F.

1973   'The Holy Spirit in the Acts of the Apostles', *Int* 27: 166-83.

1974   'The Speeches in Acts: Thirty Years After', in R. Banks (ed.), *Reconciliation and Hope* (Grand Rapids: Eerdmans): 53-68.

1988   *The Book of the Acts* (NICNT; Grand Rapids: Eerdmans, rev. edn).

1990a   *The Acts of the Apostles: Greek Text with Introduction and Commentary* (Grand Rapids: Eerdmans, 3rd edn).

1990b   'Luke's Presentation of the Spirit in Acts', *CTR* 5.1: 15-29.

Brueggemann, W.

1990   *First and Second Samuel* (Louisville: John Knox Press).

Bruner, F.D.

1970   *A Theology of the Holy Spirit: The Pentecostal Experience and the New Testament Witness* (Grand Rapids: Eerdmans).

Büchsel, F.

1926   *Der Geist Gottes im Neuen Testament* (Gütersloh: C. Bertelsmann).

Buckwalter, H.D.
1996   *The Character and Purpose of Luke's Christology* (SNTSMS, 89; Cambridge: Cambridge University Press).
Bullinger, E.W.
1979   *Word Studies on the Holy Spirit* (Grand Rapids: Kregel Publications) (orig. pub. 1905 as *The Giver and His Gifts* [London: Eyre & Spottiswoode]).
Bultmann, R.
1951, 1955 *Theology of the New Testament* (trans. K. Grobel; 2 vols.; New York: Charles Scribner's Sons).
1961   'Is Exegesis without Presuppositions Possible?', in S.M. Ogden (ed. and trans.), *Existence and Faith* (London: Hodder and Stoughton): 342-51.
Burgess, S.M.
1984   *The Holy Spirit: Ancient Christian Traditions* (Peabody: Hendrickson).
1989   *The Holy Spirit: Eastern Christian Traditions* (Peabody: Hendrickson).
Burnett, F.W.
1993   'Characterization and Reader Construction of Characters in the Gospels', in Malbon and Berlin 1993: 3-28.
Burridge, R.A.
1992   *What Are the Gospels? A Comparison with Graeco-Roman Biography* (SNTSMS, 70; Cambridge: Cambridge University Press).
Burrows, M.
1955   *More Light on the Dead Sea Scrolls* (New York: Viking).
Butcher, S.H. (ed. and trans.)
1943   *Aristotle: On Man in the Universe* (New York: Walter J. Black).
Cadbury, H.J.
1917   'A Possible Case of Lukan Authorship (John 7:53–8:11)', *HTR* 10: 237-44.
1922   'Appendix C: Commentary on the Preface of Luke', in Foakes-Jackson and Lake 1922: II, 489-510.
1927   *The Making of Luke–Acts* (New York: Macmillan).
Cargal, T.B.
1993   'Beyond the Fundamentalist–Modernist Controversy: Pentecostals and Hermeneutics in a Postmodern Age', *Pneuma* 15: 163-87.
Charles, R.H. (ed.)
1913   *The Apocrypha and Pseudepigrapha of the Old Testament* (2 vols.; Oxford: Clarendon Press).
Chatman, S.
1972   'On the Formalist–Structuralist Theory of Character', *JLS* 1: 57-79.
1978   *Story and Discourse: Narrative Structure in Fiction and Film* (Ithaca, NY: Cornell University Press).
Clarke, W.K.L.
1922   'The Use of the Septuagint in Acts', in Foakes-Jackson and Lake 1922: II, 66-105.
Clines, D.J.A.
1993   'Possibilities and Priorities of Biblical Interpretation in an International Perspective', *BibInt* 1.1: 67-87.
1995   *Interested Parties: The Ideology of Writers and Readers of the Hebrew Bible* (JSOTSup, 205; Sheffield: Sheffield Academic Press).

1997   *The Sheffield Manual for Authors and Editors in Biblical Studies* (Manuals, 12; Sheffield: Sheffield Academic Press).

Clines, D.J.A., S.E. Fowl and S.E. Porter (eds.)
1990   *The Bible in Three Dimensions: Essays in Celebration of Forty Years of Biblical Studies in the University of Sheffield* (JSOTSup, 87; Sheffield: JSOT Press).

Cohen, S.
1989   'Crossing the Boundary and Becoming a Jew', *HTR* 82: 13-33.

Coleridge, M.
1993   *The Birth of the Lukan Narrative: Narrative as Christology in Luke 1–2* (JSNTSup, 88; Sheffield: JSOT Press).

Colle, R.D.
1993   'Spirit-Christology: Dogmatic Foundations for Pentecostal–Charismatic Spirituality', *JPT* 3: 91-112.

Combrink, H.J.B.
1973   'The Structure and Significance of Luke 4:16-30', in *Essays on the Gospels of Luke and Acts: Annual Publication of Die Nuwe-Testamentiese Werkgemeenskap van Suid-Afrika* (Neotestamentica, 7; Pretoria: University of Pretoria): 27-48.

Conzelmann, H.
1960   *The Theology of St. Luke* (trans. G. Buswell; London: Faber; Tübingen: J.C.B. Mohr, 1953).

1987   *Acts of the Apostles* (Philadelphia: Fortress Press).

Cope, L., D.L. Dungan, W.R. Farmer, A.J. McNicol, D.B. Peabody and P.L. Shuler
1992   'Narrative Outline of the Composition of Luke according to the Two Gospel Hypothesis', in E.H. Lovering (ed.), *SBLSP 1992* (Atlanta: Scholars Press): 98-120.

1993   'Narrative Outline of the Composition of Luke according to the Two Gospel Hypothesis', in E.H. Lovering (ed.), *SBLSP 1993* (Atlanta: Scholars Press): 303-33.

1994   'Narrative Outline of the Composition of Luke according to the Two Gospel Hypothesis', in E.H. Lovering (ed.), *SBLSP 1994* (Atlanta: Scholars Press): 516-73.

1995   'Narrative Outline of the Composition of Luke according to the Two Gospel Hypothesis', in E.H. Lovering (ed.), *SBLSP 1995* (Atlanta: Scholars Press): 636-88.

Cosgrove, C.H.
1984   'The Divine ΔΕΙ in Luke–Acts: Investigation into the Lukan Understanding of God's Providence', *NovT* 26.2: 168-90.

Crespy, G.
1974   'The Parable of the Good Samaritan: An Essay in Structural Research', in Crossan 1974: 27-50.

Crossan, J.D. (ed.)
1974   *The Good Samaritan* (Semeia, 2; Missoula, MT: Scholars Press).

Crump, D.M.
1992   *Jesus the Intercessor: Prayer and Christology in Luke–Acts* (WUNT, 2.49; Tübingen: J.C.B. Mohr).

Culler, J.
1975 *Structuralist Poetics: Structuralism, Linguistics, and the Study of Literature* (Ithaca, NY: Cornell University Press).

Culpepper, R.A.
1983 *Anatomy of the Fourth Gospel: A Study in Literary Design* (Philadelphia: Fortress Press).
1984 'Story and History in the Gospels', *RevExp* 81: 467-78.

Danker, F.W.
1988 *Jesus and the New Age: A Commentary on St. Luke's Gospel* (Philadelphia: Fortress Press).

Darr, J.A.
1992 *On Character Building: The Reader and the Rhetoric of Characterization in Luke–Acts* (Louisville: Westminster/John Knox Press).
1993 'Narrator as Character: Mapping a Reader-Oriented Approach to Narration in Luke–Acts', in Malbon and Berlin 1993: 43-60.

Davidson, M.J.
1992a *Angels at Qumran: A Comparative Study of 1 Enoch 1–36, 72–108 and Sectarian Writings from Qumran* (JSPSup, 11; Sheffield: JSOT Press).
1992b 'Angels', in Green *et al.* 1992: 8-11.

Davies, E.W.
1995 *Numbers* (NCB; London: Marshall Pickering).

Davies, M.
1992 *Rhetoric and Reference in the Fourth Gospel* (JSNTSup, 69; Sheffield: JSOT Press).
1993 *Matthew* (Readings; Sheffield: JSOT Press).

Davies, P.R.
1995 *Whose Bible Is It Anyway?* (JSOTSup, 204; Sheffield: Sheffield Academic Press).

Davies, W.D.
1958 'Paul and the Dead Sea Scrolls: Flesh and Spirit', in K. Stendahl (ed.), *The Scrolls and the New Testament* (London: SCM): 157-82.

Davis, C.J.
1996 *The Name and Way of the Lord: Old Testament Themes, New Testament Christology* (JSNTSup, 129; Sheffield: Sheffield Academic Press).

Davis, J.A.
1984 *Wisdom and Spirit: An Investigation of 1 Corinthians 1.18–3.20 against the Background of Jewish Sapiential Traditions in the Graeco–Roman Period* (Lanham, MD: University Press of America).

Dawsey, J.M.
1986 *The Lukan Voice: Confusion and Irony in the Gospel of Luke* (Macon: Mercer University Press).
1989 'The Literary Unity of Luke–Acts: Questions of Style—A Task for Literary Critics', *NTS* 35: 48-66.

De Boer, M.C.
1995 'God-Fearers in Luke–Acts', in Tuckett 1995: 50-71.

de Jonge, M.
1960 'Christian Influence in the Testaments of the Twelve Patriarchs', *NovT* 4: 182-235.

1988   *Christology in Context: The Earliest Christian Response to Jesus* (Philadelphia: Westminster Press).
Denova, R.I.
1997   *The Things Accomplished among Us: Prophetic Tradition in the Structural Pattern of Luke–Acts* (JSNTSup, 141; SSEJC, 4; Sheffield: Sheffield Academic Press).
Dibelius, M.
1936   *A Fresh Approach to the New Testament and Early Christian Literature* (Hertford: Stephen Austin & Sons).
Dillon, R.J.
1978   *From Eye-Witnesses to Ministers of the Word: Tradition and Composition in Luke 24* (AB, 82; Rome; Pontifical Biblical Institute Press).
1981   'Previewing Luke's Project from his Prologue (Luke 1:1-4)', *CBQ* 43: 205-27.
Doble, P.
1996   *The Paradox of Salvation: Luke's Theology of the Cross* (SNTSMS, 87; Cambridge: Cambridge University Press).
Drumwright Jr, H.L.
1974   'The Holy Spirit in the Book of Acts', *SWJT* 17: 3-17.
du Plessis, I.I.
1974   'Once More: The Purpose of Luke's Prologue (Lk 1,1-4)', *NovT* 16: 259-71.
Dunn, J.D.G.
1970a   *Baptism in the Holy Spirit: A Re-examination of the New Testament Teaching on the Gift of the Spirit in Relation to Pentecostalism Today* (Philadelphia: Westminster Press).
1970b   'Spirit and Kingdom', *ExpTim* 82: 36-40.
1970c   'Spirit-Baptism and Pentecostalism', *SJT* 23: 397-407.
1972   'Spirit-and-Fire Baptism', *NovT* 14: 81-92.
1975   *Jesus and the Spirit: A Study of the Religious and Charismatic Experience of Jesus and the First Christians as Reflected in the New Testament* (London: SCM Press).
1977   'The Birth of a Metaphor: Baptized in the Spirit', *ExpTim* 89: 134-38, 173-75.
1979   '"They Believed Philip Preaching (Acts 8.12)": A Reply', *IBS* 1: 177-83.
1980   *Christology in the Making: A New Testament Inquiry into the Origin of the Doctrine of Incarnation* (London: SCM Press).
1990   *Unity and Diversity in the New Testament: An Inquiry into the Character of Earliest Christianity* (London: SCM Press, 2nd edn).
1991   *The Partings of the Ways: Between Christianity and Judaism and their Significance for the Character of Christianity* (London: SCM Press; Philadelphia: Trinity Press International).
1993   'Baptism in the Spirit: A Response to Pentecostal Scholarship on Luke–Acts', *JPT* 3: 3-27.
1996   *The Acts of the Apostles* (EC; Peterborough: Epworth Press).
1998   *The Theology of Paul the Apostle* (Edinburgh: T. & T. Clark).

Dupont, J.
1973   '*Ascension du Christ et don de l'Espirt d'après Actes 2:33*', in Lindars and Smalley 1973: 219-28.
1979   *The Salvation of the Gentiles: Studies in the Acts of the Apostles* (New York: Paulist Press).

Dupont-Sommer, A.
1961   *The Essence Writings from Qumran* (trans. G. Vermes; Oxford: Blackwell).

Durken, D. (ed.)
1979   *Sin, Salvation and the Spirit* (Collegeville: Liturgical Press).

Eco, U.
1979   *The Role of the Reader: Explorations in the Semiotics of Texts* (Bloomington: Indiana University Press).

Egan, K.
1978   'What Is a Plot?', *NLH* 9: 455-73.

Ehrhardt, A.
1958   'The Construction and Purpose of the Acts of the Apostles', *ST* 12: 45-79.

Eichrodt, W.
1961, 1967 *Theology of the Old Testament* (trans. J. Baker; 2 vols.; London: SCM Press).

Ellis, E.E.
1974   *The Gospel of Luke* (NCB; London: Oliphants/Marshall, Morgan & Scott).

Ervin, H.M.
1968   *These Are Not Drunken, as ye Suppose* (Plainfield, NJ: Logos).
1984   *Conversion–Initiation and the Baptism in the Holy Spirit: An Engaging Critique of James D.G. Dunn's Baptism in the Holy Spirit* (Peabody: Hendrickson).

Esler, P.F.
1992   'Glossolalia and the Admission of Gentiles into the Early Christian Community', *BTB* 22: 136-42.

Evans, C.F.
1990   *Saint Luke* (London: SCM Press).

Evans, C.A.
1983   'The Prophetic Setting of the Pentecost Sermon', *ZNW* 74: 148-50.

Evans, C.A., and J.A. Sanders
1993   *Luke and Scripture: The Function of Sacred Tradition in Luke–Acts* (Minneapolis: Fortress Press).

Farmer, W.R.
1988   'Source Criticism: Some Comments on the Present Situation', *USQR* 42: 49-57.
1994   *The Gospel of Jesus: The Pastoral Relevance of the Synoptic Problem* (Louisville: Westminster/John Knox Press).

Farmer, W.R. (ed.)
1983   *New Synoptic Studies: The Cambridge Gospel Conference and Beyond* (Macon, GA: Mercer University Press).

Farris, S.
1985   *The Hymns of Luke's Infancy Narratives: Their Origin, Meaning and Significance* (JSNTSup, 9; Sheffield: JSOT Press).

Fee, G.D.
  1991   *Gospel and Spirit: Issues in New Testament Hermeneutics* (Peabody: Hendrickson).
  1994   *God's Empowering Presence: The Holy Spirit in the Letters of Paul* (Peabody: Hendrickson).
Fewell, D.N.
  1992   'Introduction: Writing, Reading, and Relating', in Fewell 1992: 11-20.
Fewell, D.N. (ed.)
  1992   *Reading between Texts: Intertextuality and the Hebrew Bible* (Louisville: Westminster/John Knox Press).
Fish, S.
  1980   *Is There a Text in This Class? The Authority of Interpretive Communities* (Cambridge, MA: Harvard University Press).
Fitzmyer, J.A.
  1966   'Jewish Christianity in Acts in Light of the Qumran Scrolls', in Keck and Martyn 1966: 233-57.
  1981, 1985 *The Gospel according to Luke* (2 vols.; AB, 28; New York: Doubleday).
  1989   *Luke the Theologian: Aspects of his Teaching* (London: Geoffrey Chapman).
Flanagan, N.
  1979   'The What and How of Salvation in Luke–Acts', in Durken 1979: 203-13.
Fletcher-Louis, C.H.T.
  1997   *Luke–Acts: Angels, Christology and Soteriology* (WUNT, 2.94; Tübingen: J.C.B. Mohr).
Foakes-Jackson, F.J., and K. Lake
  1920   'The Development of Thought on the Spirit, The Church, and Baptism', in Foakes-Jackson and Lake 1920: I, 321-44.
Foakes-Jackson, F.J., and K. Lake (eds.)
  1920–33   *The Beginnings of Christianity* (5 vols.; London: Macmillan): *The Jewish, Gentile and Christian Backgrounds* (1920: I); *Criticism* (1922: II); *The Text of Acts* (1926: III); *English Translation and Commentary* (1933: IV); *Additional Notes to the Commentary* (1933: V).
Foerster, W.
  1961/1962 'Der Heilige Geist im Spätjudentum', *NTS* 8: 117-34.
Forbes, C.
  1995   *Prophecy and Inspired Speech in Early Christianity and its Hellenistic Environment* (WUNT, 75; Tübingen: J.C.B. Mohr).
Forster, E.M.
  1927   *Aspects of the Novel* (New York: Harcourt, Brace & World).
Fowler, R.M.
  1993   'Characterizing Character in Biblical Narrative', in Malbon and Berlin 1993: 97-104.
Fowl, S.
  1995   'How the Spirit Reads and How to Read the Spirit', in J.W. Rogerson, Davies and M.D. Carroll (eds.), *The Bible in Ethics: The Second Sheffield Colloquium* (JSOTSup, 207; Sheffield: Sheffield Academic Press, 1995): 348-63.

Franklin, E.
1975   *Christ the Lord: A Study in the Purpose and Theology of Luke–Acts* (London: SPCK).

French, D.
1994   'Acts and the Roman Roads of Asia Minor', in Gill and Gempf 1994: II, 49-58.

Gadamer, H.-G.
1993   *Truth and Method* (trans. J. Weinsheimer and D.G. Marshall; London: Sheed & Ward, 2nd rev. edn).

Gaffin Jr, R.B.
1979   *Perspectives on Pentecost: New Testament Teaching on the Gifts of the Holy Spirit* (Phillipsburg: Presbyterian and Reformed Publishing Company).
1996   'A Cessationist View', in Grudem 1996: 25-64.

Garrett, S.R.
1989   *The Demise of the Devil: Magic and the Demonic in Luke's Writings* (Minneapolis: Fortress Press).

Gasque, W.W.
1974   'The Speeches of Acts: Dibelius Reconsidered', in R.N. Longenecker and M.C. Tenney (eds.), *New Dimensions in New Testament Study* (Grand Rapids: Zondervan): 232-50.
1989a   'A Fruitful Field: Recent Study of the Acts of the Apostles', *A History of the Interpretation of the Acts of the Apostles* (Peabody: Hendrickson, 2nd edn): 345-59; orig. pub., *Int* 42 (1988): 117-31.
1989b   *A History of the Interpretation of the Acts of the Apostles* (Peabody: Hendrickson, 2nd edn).

Gaventa, B.R.
1986   *From Darkness to Light: Aspects of Conversion in the New Testament* (OBT, 20; Philadelphia: Fortress Press).
1988   'Toward a Theology of Acts: Reading and Rereading', *Int* 42: 146-57.
1992   'Bibliography of Henry Joel Cadbury', in Parsons and Tyson 1992: 45-51.

Gero, S.
1976   'The Spirit as a Dove at the Baptism of Jesus', *NovT* 18: 17-35.

Gilbert, M.
1984   'Wisdom Literature', in M.E. Stone (ed.), *Jewish Writings of the Second Temple Period* (Philadelphia; Fortress Press): 283-324.

Gill, D.W.J., and C. Gempf (eds.)
1994   *The Book of Acts in its First Century Setting. II. The Book of Acts in its Graeco-Roman Setting* (Grand Rapids: Eerdmans; Carlisle: Paternoster Press).

Given, M.D.
1995   'Not Either/Or but Both/And in Paul's Areopagus Speech', *BibInt* 3.3: 356-72.

Goldingay, J.E.
1989   *Daniel* (WBC, 30; Dallas: Word Books).

Gooding, D.
1987   *According to Luke: A New Exposition of the Third Gospel* (Grand Rapids: Eerdmans).

1990   *True to the Faith: A Fresh Approach to the Acts of the Apostles* (London: Hodder & Stoughton).

Goulder, M.D.
1994   *Luke: A New Paradigm* (2 vols.; JSNTSup, 24; repr.; Sheffield: Sheffield Academic Press).

Gowler, D.B.
1989   'Characterization in Luke: A Socio-Narratological Approach', *BTB* 19: 54-62.
1990   *Host, Guest, Enemy and Friend: Portraits of the Pharisees in Luke and Acts* (ESEC, 2; New York: Peter Lang).
1994   'Hospitality and Characterisation in Luke 11.37-54: A Socio-Narratological Approach', in V.K. Robbins (ed.) *The Rhetoric of Pronouncement* (Semeia, 64; Atlanta: Scholars Press): 213-51.

Green, J.B., S. McKnight and I.H. Marshall (eds.)
1992   *Dictionary of Jesus and the Gospels* (Downers Grove and Leicester: IVP).

Green, J.B., and M. Turner (eds.)
1994   *Jesus of Nazareth: Lord and Christ. Essays on the Historical Jesus and New Testament Christology* (Festschrift I.H. Marshall; Grand Rapids: Eerdmans).

Greeven, A.
1968   'περιστερά', in *TDNT*, VI, 63-72.

Greimas, A.J.
1983   *Structural Semantics: An Attempt at a Method* (trans. D. McDowell *et al.*; Lincoln: University of Nebraska Press); orig. pub., *Semantique structurale: recherche de méthode* (Paris: Larousse, 1966).

Grudem, W.A. (ed.)
1996   *Are Miraculous Gifts for Today? Four Views* (Leicester: IVP; Grand Rapids: Zondervan).

Guelich, R.A.
1989   *Mark 1–8.26* (WBC, 34a; Dallas: Word Books).

Gunkel, H.
1979   *The Influence of the Holy Spirit: The Popular View of the Apostolic Age and the Teaching of the Apostle Paul* (trans. R.A. Harrisville and P.A. Quanbeck Jr; Philadelphia: Fortress Press); orig. pub. as *Die Wirkungen des Heiligen Geistes nach der Populären Anschauung der Apostolischen Zeit und nach der Lehre des Apostels Paulus* (Göttingen: Vandenhoeck & Ruprecht, 1888).

Gunn, D.M.
1990   'Reading Right: Reliable and Omniscient Narrator, Omniscient God, and Foolproof Composition in the Hebrew Bible', in Clines *et al.* 1990: 53-64.

Haenchen, E.
1966   'The Book of Acts as Source Material for the History of Early Christianity', in Keck and Martyn 1966: 258-78.
1971   *The Acts of the Apostles: A Commentary* (trans. B. Noble and G. Shinn; Oxford: Blackwell).

Hamm, D.
1986   'Sight to the Blind: Vision as Metaphor in Luke', *Bib* 67: 457-77.

Hanson, R.P.C.
1967   *The Acts* (Oxford: Oxford University Press).
Harvey, W.J.
1965   *Character and the Novel* (Ithaca: Cornell University Press).
1978   'Characterisation in Narrative', *Poetics* 7: 63-78.
Hatch, E., and H.A. Redpath
1954   *A Concordance to the Septuagint and the Other Greek Versions of the Old Testament* (2 vols.; Graz–Austria: Akademische Druck–U. Verlagsanstalt).
Haya-Prats, G.
1975   *L'Esprit force de l'église: Sa nature et son activité d'après les Actes des Apôtres* (trans. J. Romero; LD, 81; Paris: Cerf).
Head, P.
1993   'Acts and the Problem of Its Text', in Winter and Clarke 1993: I, 415-44.
Hedrick, C.W.
1981   'Paul's Conversion/Call: A Comparative Analysis of the Three Reports in Acts', *JBL* 100.3: 415-32.
Hemer, C.J.
1990   *The Book of Acts in the Setting of Hellenistic History* (ed. Conrad H. Gempf; Winona Lake: Eisenbrauns).
Hengel, M.
1981   *The Charismatic Leader and his Followers* (trans. J.C.G. Greig; Edinburgh: T. & T. Clark).
1983   *Between Jesus and Paul: Studies in the Earliest History of Christianity* (London: SCM Press).
Hesse, F.
1974   'χρίω', in *TDNT*, IX, 496-509.
Hill, D.
1967   *Greek Words and Hebrew Meanings: Studies in the Semantics of Soteriological Terms* (SNTSMS, 5; Cambridge: Cambridge University Press).
1971   'The Rejection of Jesus at Nazareth (Lk. 4.16-30)', *NovT* 13: 161-70.
1984   'The Spirit and the Church's Witness: Observations on Acts 1:6-8', *IBS* 6: 16-26.
Hitchcock, F.R.M.
1923   'Is the Fourth Gospel a Drama?', *Theology* 7: 307-317.
Hochman, B.
1985   *Character in Literature* (Ithaca: Cornell University Press).
Horn, F.W.
1992   'Holy Spirit', in *ABD*, III, 260-80.
Howell, D.B.
1990   *Matthew's Inclusive Story: A Study in the Narrative Rhetoric of the First Gospel* (JSNTSup, 42; Sheffield: JSOT Press).
Hubbard, B.J.
1977   'Commissioning Stories in Luke–Acts: A Study of their Antecedents, Form and Content', in R.W. Funk (ed.), *Literary Critical Studies of Biblical Texts* (Semeia, 8; Missoula, MT: Scholars Press): 103-126.
1978   'The Role of Commissioning Accounts in Acts', in Talbert 1978: 187-98.

Hull, J.H.E.
1967   *The Holy Spirit in the Acts of the Apostles* (London: Lutterworth).
Hultgren, A.J.
1981   'Interpreting the Gospel of Luke', in Mays 1981: 183-96.
Hur, J.
1997   'The Literary Traits of the Lukan Narrator with Special Reference to the
              'Divine Frame of Reference' in Luke–Acts', unpublished paper presented
              at the Synoptic Evangelists seminar of the 1997 British New Testament
              Conference: 1-22.
2000   'The Unity, Genre and Purpose of Luke–Acts Revisited', *KTJ* 3: 227-58.
Hurtado, L.W.
1988   *One God, One Lord: Early Christian Devotion and Ancient Jewish Mono-
              theism* (London: SCM Press).
1991   'Normal, but Not a Norm: Initial Evidence and the New Testament', in
              McGee 1991: 189-201.
1992   'Christ', in Green *et al.* 1992: 106-117.
Isaacs, M.
1976   *The Concept of Spirit: A Study of Pneuma in Hellenistic Judaism and its
              Bearing on the New Testament* (HM, 1; London: Heythrop College).
Iser, W.
1971   'Indeterminacy and the Reader's Response to Prose Fiction', in J.H.
              Miller (ed.), *Aspects of Narrative* (New York: Columbia University
              Press): 1-45.
1974   *The Implied Reader: Patterns of Communication in Prose Fiction from
              Bunyan to Beckett* (Baltimore: Johns Hopkins University Press).
1978   *The Act of Reading: A Theory of Aesthetic Response* (Baltimore: Johns
              Hopkins University Press).
James, H.
1948   *The Art of Fiction* (New York: Oxford University Press).
Jeremias, J.
1971   *New Testament Theology* (New York: Charles Scribner's Sons).
Jervell, J.
1988   'The Church of Jews and Godfearers', in Tyson 1988: 11-20.
Johns, J.D.
1995   'Pentecostalism and the Postmodern Worldview', *JPT* 7: 73-95.
Johnson, L.T.
1977   *The Literary Function of Possessions in Luke–Acts* (SBLDS, 39;
              Missoula, MT: Scholars Press).
1983   *Decision Making in the Church: A Biblical Model* (Philadelphia: Fortress
              Press).
1991   *The Gospel of Luke* (SPS, 3; Collegeville: Liturgical Press).
1992   *The Acts of the Apostles* (SPS, 5; Collegeville: Liturgical Press).
1993   'The Social Dimensions of *Soteria* in Luke–Acts and Paul', in E.H.
              Lovering (ed.), *SBLSP 1993* (Atlanta: Scholars Press): 520-36.
Johnston, G.
1960   '"Spirit" and "Holy Spirit" in the Qumran Literature', in H.K. McArthur
              (ed.), *New Testament Sidelights* (Festschrift A.C. Purdy; Hartford: Hart-
              ford Seminary Foundation Press): 27-42.

Jones, D.L.
1974   'The Title KURIOS in Luke–Acts', in G.W. McRae (ed.), SBLSP, II
           (Cambridge, MA: SBL): 85-101.
Kamlah, E.
1975   'Spirit, Holy Spirit', in Brown 1975: III, 689-93.
Karris, R.J.
1985   *Luke: Artist and Theologian—Luke's Passion Account as Literature* (New
           York: Paulist Press).
1996   Review of *The Narrative Function of the Holy Spirit as a Character in
           Luke–Acts* (SBLDS, 147; Atlanta, GA: Scholars Press, 1994), by W.H.
           Shepherd Jr, in *JBL* 115: 744-45.
Käsemann, E.
1964   *Essays on New Testament Themes* (SBT, 41; London: SCM Press).
Kaye, B.N.
1979   'Acts' Portrait of Silas', *NovT* 21: 13-26.
Keck, L.E.
1970   'The Spirit and the Dove', *NTS* 17: 41-68.
Keck, L.E., and J.L. Martyn (eds.)
1966   *Studies in Luke–Acts* (Festschrift P. Schubert; Nashville: Abingdon;
           London: SPCK, 1968).
Keegan, T.
1985   *Interpreting the Bible: A Popular Introduction to Biblical Hermeneutics*
           (New York: Paulist Press).
Keener, C.S.
1997   *The Spirit in the Gospels and Acts: Divine Purity and Power* (Peabody:
           Hendrickson).
Kelber, W.H.
1987   'Narrative As Interpretation and Interpretation of Narrative: Herme-
           neutical Reflections on the Gospels', in L.H. Silberman (ed.), *Orality,
           Aurality and Biblical Narrative* (Semeia, 39; Decatur, GA: Scholars
           Press): 107-34.
Kilgallen, J.J.
1989   'The Function of Stephen's Speech (Acts 7, 2-53)', *Bib* 70: 173-93.
Kim, H.S.
1993   *Die Geisttaufe des Messias: Eine kompositionsgeschichtliche Unter-
           suchung zu einem Leitmotiv des lukanischen Doppelwerks* (Bern: Peter
           Lang).
Kimball, C.A.
1994   *Jesus' Exposition of the Old Testament in Luke's Gospel* (JSNTSup, 94;
           Sheffield: JSOT Press).
Kingsbury, J.D.
1989a   *Conflict in Mark: Jesus, Authorities, Disciples* (Minneapolis: Fortress
           Press).
1989b   *Matthew as Story* (Philadelphia: Fortress Press, 2nd edn).
1991   *Conflict in Luke: Jesus, Authorities, Disciples* (Minneapolis: Fortress
           Press).
1994   'The Plot of Luke's Story of Jesus', *Int* 48: 369-78.

Kissling, P.J.
1996   *Reliable Characters in the Primary History: Profiles of Moses, Joshua, Elijah and Elisha* (JSOTSup, 224; Sheffield: Sheffield Academic Press).
Kistemaker, S.J.
1990   *Exposition of the Acts of the Apostles* (NTC; Grand Rapids: Baker Book House).
Klein, R.W.
1983   *1 Samuel* (WBC, 10; Waco, TX: Word Books).
Koch, R.
1970   'Spirit', in J.B. Bauer (ed.), *Encyclopedia of Biblical Theology* (3 vols.; London: Sheed and Ward): III, 869-89.
Kremur, J. (ed.)
1979   *Les Actes des Apôtres: Traditions, rédaction, théologie* (Leuven: Leuven University Press).
Krodel, G.
1978   'The Functions of the Spirit in the Old Testament, the Synoptic Tradition, and the Book of Acts', in P.D. Opsahl (ed.), *The Holy Spirit in the Life of the Church from Biblical Times to the Present* (Minneapolis: Augsburg): 10-46.
Kuhn, K.G.
1960   *Konkordanz zu den Qumrantexten* (Göttingen: Vandenhoeck & Ruprecht).
Kurz, W.S.
1987   'Narrative Approaches to Luke–Acts', *Bib* 68: 195-220.
1993   *Reading Luke–Acts: Dynamics of Biblical Narrative* (Louisville: Westminster/John Knox Press).
Lake, K.
1933a   'Note IX: The Holy Spirit', in Foakes-Jackson and Lake 1933: V, 96-111.
1933b   'Note X: The Gift of the Spirit on the Day of Pentecost', in Foakes-Jackson and Lake 1933: V, 111-21.
1933c   'The Apostolic Council in Jerusalem', in Foakes-Jackson and Lake 1933: V, 195-212.
Lambrecht, J.
1979   'Paul's Farewell-Address at Miletus (Acts 20:17-38)', in Kremur 1979: 307-337.
Lampe, G.W.H.
1951   *The Seal of the Spirit* (London: Longmans).
1957   'The Holy Spirit in the Writings of St. Luke', in Nineham 1957: 159-200.

1977   *God as Spirit: The Bampton Lectures, 1976* (Oxford: Clarendon Press).
Le Déaut, R.
1970   'Pentecost and Jewish Tradition', *DL* 20: 250-67.
Lederle, H.I.
1991   'Initial Evidence and the Charismatic Movement: An Ecumenical Appraisal', in McGee 1991: 131-41.
Leisegang, H.
1922   *Pneuma Hagion: Der Ursprung des Geistesbegriffs der synoptischen Evangelien aus der griechischen Mystik* (Leipzig: J.C. Hinrichs).

Levison, J.R.
1995   'The Angelic Spirit in Early Judaism', in E.H. Lovering (ed.), *SBLSP 1995* (Atlanta: Scholars Press): 464-93.
Licht, J.
1958   'An Analysis of the Treatise on the Two Spirits in DSD', in C. Rabin and Y. Yadin (eds.), *Aspects of the Dead Sea Scrolls* (Jerusalem: Manges Press): 88-100.
Lincoln, A.T.
1981   *Paradise Now and Not Yet: Studies in the Role of the Heavenly Dimension in Paul's Thought with Special Reference to his Eschatology* (Grand Rapids: Baker Book House).
1984/85   'Theology and History in the Interpretation of Luke's Pentecost', *ExpTim* 96: 204-209.
1990   'Matthew—A Story for Teachers?', in Clines *et al.* 1990: 103-125.
Lindars, B.
1961   *New Testament Apologetic: The Doctrinal Significance of the Old Testament Quotations* (London: SCM Press).
Lindars, B., and S.S. Smalley (eds.)
1973   *Christ and Sprit in the New Testament* (Festschrift C.F.D. Moule; Cambridge: Cambridge University Press).
Lohfink, G.
1975   *Die Sammlung Israels: Eine Untersuchung zur lukanischen Ekklesiologie* (München: Kösel).
Lohse, E.
1968   'πεντηκοστή', in *TDNT*, VI, 44-53.
1974   'χείρ', *TDNT*, IX, 429-37.
Lohse, E. (ed.)
1971   *Die Texte aus Qumran: hebräisch und deutsch* (München: Kösel).
Longenecker, R.N.
1975   *Biblical Exegesis in the Apostolic Period* (Grand Rapids: Eerdmans).
Longman, III, Tremper
1987   *Literary Approaches to Biblical Interpretation* (FCI, 3; Grand Rapids: Zondervan).
Louw, J.P., and E.A. Nida
1989   *Greek-English Lexicon of the New Testament Based on Semantic Domains* (2 vols.; New York: UBS, 2nd edn).
MacRae, G.W.
1973   '"Whom Heaven Must Receive until the Time"', *Int* 27: 151-65.
Maddox, R.
1982   *The Purpose of Luke–Acts* (FRLANT, 126; Gottingen: Vandenhoeck & Ruprecht).
Malbon, E.S.
1986   *Narrative Space and Mythic Meaning in Mark* (San Francisco: Harper and Row).
Malbon, E.S., and A. Berlin (eds.)
1993   *Characterization in Biblical Literature* (Semeia, 63; Atlanta: Scholars Press).

Marguerat, D.
1995   'Saul's Conversion (Acts 9, 22, 26) and the Multiplication of Narrative in
            Acts', in Tuckett 1995: 127-55.
Marshall, I.H.
1970   *Luke: Historian and Theologian* (Grand Rapids: Zondervan).
1973   'The Meaning of the Verb "to Baptize"', *EvQ* 45: 130-40.
1976   *The Origins of New Testament Christology* (Downers Grove: IVP).
1977   'Significance of Pentecost', *SJT* 30: 347-69.
1977/78   'Preaching the Kingdom of God', *ExpTim* 89: 13-16.
1978   *The Gospel of Luke: A Commentary on the Greek Text* (NIGTC; Grand
            Rapids: Eerdmans).
1991a   *The Acts of the Apostles* (TNTC, 5; Leicester: IVP, 2nd printed).
1991b   'Luke and his "Gospel"', in P. Stuhlmacher (ed.), *The Gospel and the
            Gospels* (Grand Rapids: Eerdmans): 273-92.
1992   *The Acts of the Apostles* (NTG; Sheffield: Sheffield Academic Press).
1993   'Acts and the "Former Treatise"', in Winter and Clarke 1993: I, 163-82.
Martin, W.
1986   *Recent Theories of Narrative* (Ithaca: Cornell University Press).
Matera, F.J.
1987   'The Plot of Matthew's Gospel', *CBQ* 49: 233-53.
Mattill Jr, A.J.
1975   'The Jesus–Paul Parallels and the Purpose of Luke–Acts: H.H. Evans
            Reconsidered', *NovT* 17: 15-46.
May, H.
1963   'Cosmological Reference in the Qumran Doctrine of the Two Spirits and
            in Old Testament Imagery', *JBL* 82: 1-14.
Mays, J.L. (ed.)
1981   *Interpreting the Gospels* (Philadelphia: Fortress Press).
McCasland, S.V.
1944   'The Demonic 'Confessions' of Jesus', *JR* 24: 33-36.
McCracken, D.
1993   'Character in the Boundary: Bakhtin's Interdividuality in Biblical Narra-
            tives', in Malbon and Berlin 1993: 29-42.
McGee, G.B.
1991a   'Early Pentecostal Hermeneutics: Tongues as Evidence in the Book of
            Acts', in McGee 1991: 96-118.
1991b   'Popular Expositions of Initial Evidence in Pentecostalism', in McGee
            1991: 119-30.
McGee, G.B. (ed.)
1991   *Initial Evidence: Historical and Biblical Perspectives on the Pentecostal
            Doctrine of Spirit Baptism* (Peabody: Hendrickson).
McIntyre, J.
1997   *The Shape of Pneumatology: Studies in the Doctrine of the Holy Spirit*
            (Edinburgh: T. & T. Clark).
Mckenzies, J.L.
1968   *The Second Isaiah* (AB; New York: Doubleday).

McQueen, L.R.
1995   *Joel and the Spirit: The Cry of a Prophetic Hermeneutic* (JPTSup, 8; Sheffield: Sheffield Academic Press).

Menzies, R.P.
1991a   *The Development of Early Christian Pneumatology with Special Reference to Luke–Acts* (JSNTSup, 54; Sheffield: JSOT Press).
1991b   'The Distinctive Character of Luke's Pneumatology', *Paraclete* 25: 17-30.
1993a   'James Shelton's *Mighty in Word and Deed*: A Review Article', *JPT* 2: 105-115.
1993b   'Spirit and Power in Luke–Acts: A Response to Max Turner', *JSNT* 49: 11-20
1994a   *Empowered for Witness: The Spirit in Luke–Acts* (JPTSup, 6; Sheffield: Sheffield Academic Press).
1994b   'Luke and the Spirit: A Reply to James Dunn', *JPT* 4: 115-38.

Metzger, B.M.
1975   *A Textual Commentary on the Greek New Testament* (London: UBS, 2nd edn).

Michaels, J.R.
1991   'Evidence of the Spirit, or the Spirit as Evidence? Some Non-Pentecostal Reflections', in McGee 1991: 202-218.

Minear, P.S.
1973   'Dear Theo: The Kerygmatic Intention and Claim of the Book of Acts', *Int* 27: 131-150.

Moessner, D.P.
1986   'The Christ Must Suffer: New Light on the Jesus–Peter, Stephen–Paul Parallels in Luke–Acts', *NovT* 28: 227-56.
1988   'The Ironic Fulfillment of Israel's Glory', in Tyson 1988: 35-50.
1992   'The Meaning of ΚΑΘΕΞΗΣ in the Lukan Prologue as a Key to the Distinctive Contribution of Luke's Narrative among the "Many"', in F.V. Segbroeck *et al.* (eds.), *The Four Gospels* (Festschrift F. Neirynck; Leuven: Leuven University Press), II: 1513-28.

Montague, G.T.
1994   *The Holy Spirit: Growth of a Biblical Tradition* (Peabody: Hendrickson).

Moore, S.D.
1987   'Are the Gospels Unified Narratives?', in *SBLSP 1987* (Atlanta: Scholars Press): 443-58.
1989a   *Literary Criticism and the Gospels: The Theoretical Challenge* (New Haven: Yale University Press).
1989b   'Doing Gospel Criticism as/with a "Reader"', *BTB* 19: 85-93.

Morgan, R., and J. Barton
1988   *Biblical Interpretation* (OBS; Oxford: Oxford University Press).

Moule, C.F.D.
1966   'The Christology of Acts', in Keck and Martyn 1966: 159-185.
1978   *The Holy Spirit* (MLT; Oxford: Mowbrays).

Mowery, R.L.
1986   'The Articular References to the Holy Spirit in the Synoptic Gospels and Acts', *BR* 36: 26-45.

Mowinckel, S.

1934   ' "The Spirit" and the 'Word' in the Pre-exilic Reforming Prophets', *JBL*
         53: 199-227.

Mudrick, M.

1960/61 'Character and Event in Fiction', *YR* 50: 202-218.

Müller, M.

1996   *The First Bible of the Church: A Plea for the Septuagint* (JSOTSup, 206;
         CIS, 1; Sheffield: Sheffield Academic Press).

New, S.

1933   'Note XI: The Name, Baptism, and the Laying on of Hands', in Foakes-
         Jackson and Lake 1933: V, 121-40.

Nineham, D.E. (ed.)

1957   *Studies in the Gospels* (Festschrift R.H. Lightfoot; Oxford: Blackwell).

Noack, B.

1962   'The Day of Pentecost in Jubilees, Qumran, and Acts', *ASTI* 1: 73-95.

Nolland, J.

1989, 1993   *Luke 1–9:20; 9:21–18:34; 18:35–24:53* (3 vols.; WBC, 35A, B and C;
             Dallas: Word Books).

O'Brien, P.T.

1973   'Prayer in Luke–Acts', *TynBul* 24: 111-27.

O'Neill, J.C.

1955   'The Use of *KYRIOS* in the Book of Acts', *SJT* 8: 155-74.

O'Reilly, L.

1987   *Word and Sign in the Acts of the Apostles: A Study in Lukan Theology*
         (AnGreg, 243; Rome: Editrice Pontificia Università Gregoriana).

Oss, D.A.

1996   'A Pentecostal/Charismatic View', in Grudem 1996: 239-83.

O'Toole, R.F.

1980   'Christian Baptism in Luke', *RevRel* 39: 855-66.

1981   'Activity of the Risen Jesus in Luke–Acts', *Bib* 62: 471-98.

1997   'Εἰρήνη, an Underlying Theme in Acts 10,34-43', *Bib* 77: 461-76.

Opsahl, P.D. (ed.)

1978   *The Holy Spirit in the Life of the Church from Biblical Times to the
         Present* (Minneapolis: Augsburg).

Page, S.H.T.

1995   *Powers of Evil: A Biblical Study of Satan & Demons* (Grand Rapids:
         Baker Book House).

Paige, T.P.

1993   'Spirit at Corinth: The Corinthian Concept of Spirit and Paul's Response
         as Seen in 1 Corinthians' (unpublished PhD dissertation; University of
         Sheffield).

Parker, S.E.

1996   *Led by the Spirit: Toward a Practical Theology of Pentecostal Discern-
         ment and Decision Making* (JPTSup, 7; Sheffield: Sheffield Academic
         Press).

Parratt, J.K.

1968/69 'The Laying on of Hands in the New Testament', *ExpTim* 80: 210-14.

Parsons, M.C.

1986 'Narrative Closure and Openness in the Plot of the Third Gospel: The Sense of an Ending in Luke 24:50-53', in K.H. Richards (ed.), *SBLSP 1986* (Atlanta: Scholars Press): 201-223.

1987 *The Departure of Jesus in Luke–Acts: The Ascension Narratives in Context* (JSNTSup, 21; Sheffield: JSOT Press).

1993 'The Narrative Unity of Luke–Acts', in Parsons and Pervo, 1993: 45-83.

Parsons, M.C., and R.I. Pervo

1993 *Rethinking the Unity of Luke and Acts* (Minneapolis: Fortress Press).

Parsons, M.C., and J.B. Tyson (eds.)

1992 *Cadbury, Knox, and Talbert: American Contributions to the Study of Acts* (Atlanta: Scholars Press).

Patte, D.

1974 'An Analysis of Narrative Structure and the Good Samaritan', in Crossan 1974: 1-26.

1990 *The Religious Dimensions of Biblical Texts: Greimas's Structural Semiotics and Biblical Exegesis* (Atlanta: Scholars Press).

1995 *Ethics of Biblical Interpretation: A Reevaluation* (Louisville: Westminster/John Knox Press).

Penney, J.M.

1997a *The Missionary Emphasis of Lukan Pneumatology* (JPTSup, 12; Sheffield: Sheffield Academic Press).

1997b 'The Testing of New Testament Prophecy', *JPT* 10: 35-84.

Pervo, R.I.

1987 *Profit with Delight: The Literary Genre of the Acts of the Apostles* (Philadelphia: Fortress Press).

Petersen, N.R.

1978 *Literary Criticism for New Testament Critics* (Philadelphia: Fortress Press).

Pinnock, C.H.

1963 'The Concept of the Spirit in the Epistles of Paul' (unpublished PhD dissertation; University of Manchester).

Plummer, A.

1900 *The Gospel according to S. Luke* (ICC; Edinburgh: T. & T. Clark).

Polhill, J.B.

1992 *Acts* (NAC, 26; Nashville: Broadman Press).

Polzin, R.

1993 'Response: Divine and Anonymous Characterization in Biblical Narrative', in Malbon and Berlin 1993: 205-213.

Powell, M.A.

1989 *What Are They Saying about Luke?* (New York: Paulist Press).

1991 *What Are They Saying about Acts?* (New York: Paulist Press).

1993 *What Is Narrative Criticism? A New Approach to the Bible* (London: SPCK; Minneapolis: Augsburg Fortress, 1990).

1994 'Toward a Narrative-Critical Understanding of Luke', *Int* 48: 341-46.

Poythress, V.S.

1987 *Symphonic Theology: The Validity of Multiple Perspectives in Theology* (Grand Rapids: Zondervan).

Praeder, S.M.
    1984   'Jesus–Paul, Peter–Paul, and Jesus–Peter Parallelisms in Luke–Acts:
                  A History of Reader-Response', in H.K. Richards (ed.), *SBLSP 1984*
                  (Chicago: Scholars Press): 23-39.
Prior, M.
    1995   *Jesus the Liberator: Nazareth Liberation Theology (Luke 4.16-30)* (TBS,
                  26; Sheffield: Sheffield Academic Press).
Procksch, O.
    1964   'ἅγιος', in *TDNT*, I, 100-115.
Pryke, J.
    1965   '"Spirit" and "Flesh" in the Qumran Documents and Some New
                  Testament Texts', *RevQ* 5: 345-60.
Rabin C., and Y. Yadin (eds.)
    1958   *Aspects of the Dead Sea Scrolls* (Jerusalem: Manges Press).
Rahlfs, A.
    1979   *Septuaginta* (Stuttgart: Deutsche Bibelgesellschaft, 2nd edn).
Rapske, B.
    1994   *The Book of Acts in its First Century Setting. III. Paul in Roman Custody*
                  (Grand Rapids: Eerdmans; Carlisle: Paternoster Press).
Reese, R.A.
    1995   'Writing Jude: The Reader, the Text, and the Author' (unpublished PhD
                  dissertation; University of Sheffield).
Rese, M.
    1969   *Alttestamentliche Motive in der Christologie des Lukas* (NovTSup, 1;
                  Gütersloh: Gütersloher Verlagshaus).
Resseguie, J.L.
    1975   'Interpretation of Luke's Central Section (Luke 9:51–19:44) since 1856',
                  StBT 6: 3-36.
Rhoads, D., and D. Michie
    1982   *Mark as Story: An Introduction to the Narrative of a Gospel* (Phila-
                  delphia: Fortress Press).
Richard, E.
    1978   *Acts 6:1–8:4: The Author's Method of Composition* (SBLDS, 41;
                  Missoula: Scholars Press).
    1983   'Luke—Writer, Theologian, Historian: Research and Orientation of the
                  1970's', *BTB* 13: 3-16.
    1990   '"Pentecost as a Recurrent Theme in Luke–Acts"', in Richard 1990:
                  133-49.
Richard, E. (ed.)
    1990   *New Views on Luke and Acts* (Collegeville: Liturgical Press).
Rimmon-Kenan, S.
    1983   *Narrative Fiction: Contemporary Poetics* (London: Routledge).
Ringgren, H.
    1963   *The Faith of Qumran* (Philadelphia: Fortress Press).
    1986   'Luke's Use of the Old Testament', *HTR* 79: 227-35.
Robbins, V.K.
    1995   'Social-Scientific Criticism and Literary Studies: Prospects for Cooper-
                  ation in Biblical Interpretation', in P.F. Esler (ed.), *Modelling Early*

Christianity: Social-Scientific Studies of the New Testament in its Context (London: Routledge): 274-89.

Rosner, B.S.
1993   'Acts and Biblical History', in Winter and Clarke 1993: I, 65-82.
Roth, S.J.
1997   *The Blind, the Lame, and the Poor: Character Types in Luke–Acts* (JSNTSup, 144; Sheffield: Sheffield Academic Press).
Rowdon, H.H. (ed.)
1982   *Christ the Lord* (Leicester: IVP).
Ruthven, J.
1993   *On the Cessation of the Charismata: The Protestant Polemic on Post-biblical Miracles* (JPTSup, 3; Sheffield: Sheffield Academic Press).
Sanders, J.A.
1993   'Isaiah in Luke', in Evans and Sanders 1993: 14-25.
Saucy, R.L.
1996   'An Open but Cautious View', in Grudem 1996: 97-148.
Schäfer, J.P.
1970   'Die Termini 'Heiliger Geist' und 'Geist der Prophetie' in den Targumim und das Verhältnis der Targumim Zueinander', *VT* 20: 304-314.
1972   *Die Vorstellung vom heiligen Geist in der rabbinischen Literatur* (München: Kösel-Verlag).
Schlier, H.
1967   'παρρησία', in *TDNT*, V, 871-86.
Schneider, G.
1977   *Das Evangelium nach Lukas* (2 vols.; ÖTKNT, 3; Gerd Mohn: Gütersloher).
1980, 1982 *Die Apostelgeschichte* (2 vols.; HTKNT, 5; Freiburg: Herder).
Schoemaker, W.R.
1904   'The Use of *Ruach* in the Old Testament, and of πνεῦμα in the New Testament', *JBL* 23: 13-67.
Scholes, R.
1974   *Structuralism in Literature: An Introduction* (New Heaven: Yale University Press).
Schreck, C.J.
1989   'The Nazareth Pericope: Luke 4,16-30 in Recent Study', in F. Neirynck (ed.), *L'Evangile de Luc—The Gospel of Luke* (Leuven: Leuven University Press): 399-471.
Schürmann, H.
1984   *Das Lukasevangelium* (vol. 1; HTKNT, 3; Freiburg: Herder, 3rd edn).
Schweizer, E.
1952   'The Spirit of Power: The Uniformity and Diversity of the Concept of the Holy Spirit in the New Testament' (trans. J. Bright and E. Debor), *Int* 6: 259-78.
1968   'πνεῦμα', in *TDNT*, VI, 389-455.
1970   'Die Bekehrung des Apollos, Apg 18,24-26', *Beiträge zur Theologie des Neuen Testaments: Neutestamentliche Aufsätze (1955–70)* (Zürich: Zwingli Verlag): 71-79.
1981   *The Holy Spirit* (trans. H. Reginald and I. Fuller; London: SCM Press).

| 1984 | *The Good News according to Luke* (trans. D.E. Green; Atlanta: John Knox Press). |

1996   'A Very Helpful Challenge: Gordon Fee's *God's Empowering Presence*', *JPT* 8: 7-21.

Scott, E.F.

1923   *The Spirit in the New Testament* (New York: George H. Doran).

Scott, J.M.

1994   'Luke's Geographical Horizon', in Gill and Gempf 1994: II, 483-544.

Scroggs, R.

1967   'Paul: ΣΟΦΟΣ and ΠΝΕΥΜΑΤΙΚΟΣ', *NTS* 14: 33-55.

Sekki, A.

1989   *The Meaning of Ruaḥ at Qumran* (SBLDS, 100; Atlanta: Scholars Press).

Sheeley, S.M.

1992   *Narrative Asides in Luke–Acts* (JSNTSup, 72; Sheffield: JSOT Press).

Shelton, J.B.

1988   ' "Filled with the Holy Spirit" and 'Full of the Holy Spirit': Lucan Redactional Phrases', in P. Elbert (ed.), *Faces of Renewal* (Festschrift S.M. Horton; Peabody: Hendrickson): 80-107.

1991   *Mighty in Word and Deed: The Role of the Holy Spirit in Luke–Acts* (Peabody: Hendrickson).

1994   'A Reply to James D.G. Dunn's "Baptism in the Spirit: A Response to Pentecostal Scholarship on Luke–Acts" ', *JPT* 4: 139-43.

Shepherd Jr, W.H.

1994   *The Narrative Function of the Holy Spirit as a Character in Luke–Acts* (SBLDS, 147; Atlanta: Scholar Press).

Siker, J.S.

1992   ' "First to the Gentiles": A Literary Analysis of Luke 4:16-30', *JBL* 111.1: 73-90.

Sloan, R.B.

1977   *The Favorable Year of the Lord: A Study of Jubilary Theology in the Gospel of Luke* (Austin: Scholars Press).

Smalley, S.S.

1973   'Spirit, Kingdom and Prayer in Luke–Acts', *NovT* 15: 59-71.

Smith, S.H.

1996   *A Lion with Wings: A Narrative-Critical Approach to Mark's Gospel* (TBS, 38; Sheffield: Sheffield Academic Press).

Soards, M.L.

1994   *The Speeches in Acts: Their Content, Context, and Concerns* (Louisville: Westminster/John Knox Press).

Soggin, J.A.

1981   *Judges* (trans. J. Bowden; OTL; London: SCM Press).

Spencer, F.S.

1992   *The Portrait of Philip in Acts: A Study of Roles and Relations* (JSNTSup, 67; Sheffield: JSOT Press).

1993   'Acts and Modern Literary Approaches', in Winter and Clarke 1993: I, 381-414.

1997   *Acts* (Readings; Sheffield: Sheffield Academic Press).

Squires, J.T.
1993   *The Plan of God in Luke–Acts* (SNTSMS, 76; Cambridge: Cambridge
            University Press).
Staley, J.L.
1988   *The Print's First Kiss: A Rhetorical Investigation of the Implied Reader
            in the Fourth Gospel* (Atlanta: Scholars Press).
Stanton, G.N.
1977   'Presuppositions in New Testament Criticism', in I.H. Marshall (ed.),
            New Testament Interpretation: Essays on Principles and Methods (Grand
            Rapids: Eerdmans): 60-71.
Stählin, G.
1973   'Το πνεῦμα' Ιησοῦ (*Apostelgeschichte* 16:7)', in Lindars and Smalley
            1973: 229-52.
Stendahl, K.
1976   *Paul among Jews and Gentiles and Other Essays* (Philadelphia: Fortress
            Press).
Sterling, G.E.
1992   *Historiography and Self-Definition: Josephus, Luke–Acts and Apologetic
            Historiography* (SNT, 64; Leiden: E.J. Brill).
Sternberg, M.
1985   *The Poetics of Biblical Narrative: Ideological Literature and the Drama
            of Reading* (Bloomington: Indiana University Press).
Stibbe, M.W.G.
1992   *John As Storyteller: Narrative Criticism and the Fourth Gospel*
            (SNTSMS, 73; Cambridge: Cambridge University Press).
1993a   *John* (Readings; Sheffield: JSOT Press).
1993b   '"Return to Sender": A Structuralist Approach to John's Gospel', *BibInt*
            1.2: 189-206.
1994   *John's Gospel* (London: Routledge).
Stone, M.E.
1984   *Jewish Writings of the Second Temple Period* (Philadelphia; Fortress
            Press).
Stonehouse, N.B.
1950   'Repentance, Baptism and the Gift of the Holy Spirit', *WTJ* 13: 1-18.
1979   *The Witness of the Synoptic Gospels to Christ* (repr.; Grand Rapids: Baker
            Book House); orig. pub. in 2 vols. 1944 and 1951, *The Witness of Matthew
            and Mark to Christ* and *The Witness of Luke to Christ*.
Storms, C.S.
1996   'A Third Wave View', in Grudem 1996: 175-223.
Strauss, M.L.
1995   *The Davidic Messiah in Luke–Acts: The Promise and its Fulfillment in
            Lukan Christology* (JSNTSup, 110; Sheffield: Sheffield Academic Press).
Stronstad, R.
1980   'The Influence of the Old Testament on the Charismatic Theology of St.
            Luke', *Pneuma* 2: 32-50.
1984   *The Charismatic Theology of St. Luke* (Peabody: Hendrickson).
1992   'Pentecostal Experience and Hermeneutics', *Paraclete* 26.1: 14-30.

Swete, H.B.
   1921   *The Holy Spirit in the New Testament: A Study of Primitive Christian Teaching* (London: Macmillan).
Talbert, C.H.
   1974   *Literary Patterns, Theological Themes, and the Genre of Luke–Acts* (SBLMS, 20; Missoula: Scholars Press).
   1981   'Shifting Sands: The Recent Study of the Gospel of Luke', in Mays 1981: 197-213; orig. pub., *Int* 30 (1976): 381-95.
Talbert, C.H. (ed.)
   1978   *Perspectives on Luke–Acts* (Edinburgh: T. & T. Clark).
   1984   *New Perspectives from the SBLS* (New York: Crossroad).
Tannehill, R.C.
   1972   'The Mission of Jesus according to Luke 4.16-30', in W. Eltester (ed.), *Jesus in Nazareth* (Berlin: de Gruyter): 51-75.
   1986, 1990 *The Narrative Unity of Luke–Acts: A Literary Interpretation* (2 vols.; Philadelphia: Fortress Press).
   1996   *Luke* (ANTC; Nashville: Abingdon).
Tate, M.E.
   1990   *Psalms 51–100* (WBC, 20; Dallas: Word Books).
Tate, W.R.
   1991   *Biblical Interpretation: An Integrated Approach* (Peabody: Hendrickson).
Taylor, V.
   1926   *Behind the Third Gospel: A Study of the Proto-Luke Hypothesis* (Oxford: Clarendon Press).
Thibeaux, E.R.
   1993   'Reading Readers Reading Characters', in Malbon and Berlin 1993: 215-25.
Thiselton, A.C.
   1980   *The Two Horizons: New Testamental Hermeneutics and Philosophical Description with Special Reference to Heidegger, Bultmann, Gadamer, and Wittgestein* (Grand Rapids: Eerdmans).
   1992   *New Horizons in Hermeneutics* (Grand Rapids: Zondervan).
Thompson, M.M.
   1993   '"God's Voice You Have Never Heard, God's Form You Have Never Seen": The Characterization of God in the Gospel of John', in Malbon and Berlin 1993: 177-204.
Thornton, T.C.G.
   1978   'To the End of the Earth: Acts 1:8', *ExpTim* 89: 374-75.
Tiede, D.L.
   1988   '"Glory to thy People Israel": Luke–Acts and the Jews', in Tyson 1988: 21-34.
   1992   'The Future of the Study of the Lukan Writings in North American Scholarship', in Parsons and Tyson 1992: 255-64.
Tinsley, E.J.
   1965   *The Gospel according to Luke* (Cambridge: Cambridge University Press).
Tolbert, M.A.
   1989   *Sowing the Gospel: Mark's World in Literary-Historical Perspective* (Minneapolis: Fortress Press).

Tompkins, J.P.
    1980   'An Introduction to Reader-Response Criticism', *idem* (ed.), *Reader-
                Response Criticism: From Formalism to Post-Structuralism* (Baltimore,
                MD: Johns Hopkins University Press): ix-xxvi.
Trebilco, P.R.
    1994   'Asia', in Gill and Gempf 1994: II, 291-362.
Treves, M.
    1962   'The Two Spirits of the Rule of the Community', *RevQ* 3: 449-52.
Trites, A.A.
    1977   *The New Testament Concept of Witness* (SNTSMS, 31; Cambridge: Cam-
                bridge University Press).
    1978   'The Prayer Motif in Luke–Acts', in Talbert 1978: 168-86.
    1992   'Witness', in Green *et al.* 1992: 877-80.
Tuckett, C.M. (ed.)
    1995   *Luke's Literary Achievement: Collected Essays* (JSNTSup, 116; Sheffield:
                Sheffield Academic Press).
Turner, M.M.B.
    1980   'Luke and the Spirit: Studies in the Significance of Receiving the Spirit in
                Luke–Acts' (unpublished PhD dissertation; University of Cambridge).
    1981a   'Jesus and the Spirit in Lucan Perspective', *TynBul* 32: 3-42.
    1981b   'The Significance of Receiving the Spirit in Luke–Acts: A Survey of
                Modern Scholarship', *TJ* 2: 131-58.
    1981c   'Spirit Endowment in Luke–Acts: Some Linguistic Considerations', *VE*
                12: 45-63.
    1982   'The Spirit of Christ and Christology', in H.H. Rowdon (ed.), *Christ the
                Lord* (Leicester: IVP): 168-90.
    1985   'Spiritual Gifts Then and Now', *VE* 15: 7-64.
    1991   'The Spirit and the Power of Jesus' Miracles in the Lucan Conception',
                NovT 33.2: 124-52.
    1992a   'Holy Spirit', in Green *et al.* 1992: 341-51.
    1992b   'The Spirit of Prophecy and the Power of Authoritative Preaching in
                Luke–Acts: A Question of Origins', *NTS* 38: 66-88.
    1994a   'Empowerment for Mission? The Pneumatology of Luke–Acts: An
                Appreciation and Critique of James B. Shelton's *Mighty in Word and
                Deed*', *VE* 24: 103-122.
    1994b   'The Spirit of Christ and "Divine" Christology' in Green and Turner
                1994: 413-36.
    1994c   'The Spirit of Prophecy and the Ethical/Religious Life of the Christian
                Community', in M.W. Wilson (ed.), *Spirit and Renewal* (Festschrift J.R.
                Williams; Sheffield: Sheffield Academic Press): 166-90.
    1996a   *The Holy Spirit and Spiritual Gifts Then and Now* (Carlisle: Paternoster
                Press).
    1996b   *Power from on High: The Spirit in Israel's Restoration and Witness in
                Luke–Acts* (JPTSup, 9; Sheffield: Sheffield Academic Press).
Turner, N.
    1955/56   'The Relation of Luke I and II to Hebraic Sources and to the Rest of
                Luke–Acts', *NTS* 2: 100-109.

Twelftree, G.H.
  1992   'Demon, Devil, Satan', in Green *et al.* 1992: 163-72.
Tyson, J.B.
  1978   'Source Criticism of the Gospel of Luke', in Talbert 1978: 24-39
  1983   'Conflict as a Literary Theme in the Gospel of Luke', in W.R. Farmer
             (ed.) *New Synoptic Studies* (Macon, GA: Mercer University Press, 1983):
             303-27.
  1986   *The Death of Jesus in Luke–Acts* (Columbia: University of South Carolina
             Press).
  1991   'The Birth Narratives and the Beginning of Luke's Gospel', in D.E. Smith
             (ed.), *How Gospels Begin* (Semeia, 52; Atlanta: Scholars Press): 121-44.
Tyson, J.B. (ed.)
  1988   *Luke–Acts and the Jewish People: Eight Critical Perspectives* (Min-
             neapolis: Augsburg).
Uspensky, B.
  1973   *A Poetics of Composition* (Berkeley: University of California Press).
van Roon, A.
  1974   'The Relation between Christ and the Wisdom of God according to Paul',
             NovT 16: 207-39.
van Unnik, W.C.
  1966   'Luke–Acts, A Storm Center in Contemporary Scholarship', in Keck and
             Martyn 1966: 15-32.
  1973   'Once More St. Luke's Prologue', in *Essays on the Gospels of Luke and
             Acts* (Neotestamentica, 7; Pretoria: University of Pretoria): 7-26.
VanGemeren, W.A.
  1988   'The Spirit of Restoration', *WTJ* 50: 81-102.
Vermes, G.
  1990   *The Dead Sea Scrolls in English* (New York: Penguin Books, 3rd edn).
Via Jr, D.O.
  1975   *Kerygma and Comedy in the New Testament* (Philadelphia: Fortress
             Press).
von Rad, G.
  1964   'ἄγγελος', in *TDNT*, I, 76-80.
Weaver, D.J.
  1990   *Matthew's Missionary Discourse: A Literary Critical Analysis* (JSNTSup,
             38; Sheffield: JSOT Press).
Weber, K.
  1996   'Plot and Matthew', in *SBLSP 1996* (Atlanta: Scholars Press): 400-31.
Weinsheimer, J.
  1979   'Theory of Character: Emma', *PT* 1: 185-211.
Wernberg-Møller, P.
  1961   'A Reconsideration of the Two Spirits in the Rule of the Community',
             RevQ 3: 413-41.
Wilcox, M.
  1981   'The God-Fearers in Acts: A Reconsideration', *JSNT* 13: 102-122.
Williams, J.F.
  1994   *Other Followers of Jesus: Minor Characters as Major Figures in Mark's
             Gospel* (JSNTSup, 102; Sheffield: Sheffield Academic Press).

Wilson, R.
    1979   'The Bright Chimera: Character as a Literary Term', *CI* 5: 725-49.
Wilson, S.G.
    1973   *The Gentiles and the Gentile Mission in Luke–Acts* (SNTSMS, 23; Cambridge: Cambridge University Press).
Winter, B.W., and A.D. Clarke (eds.)
    1993   *The Book of Acts in its First Century Setting*. I. *Ancient Literary Setting* (Grand Rapids: Eerdmans; Carlisle: Paternoster Press).
Witherup, R.D.
    1992   'Functional Redundancy in the Acts of the Apostles: A Case Study', *JSNT* 48: 67-86.
    1993   'Cornelius Over and Over and Over Again: 'Functional Redundancy' in the Acts of the Apostles', *JSNT* 49: 45-66.
Zehnle, R.F.
    1971   *Peter's Pentecost Discourse: Tradition and Lukan Reinterpretation in Peter's Speeches of Acts 2 and 3* (SBLMS, 15; New York: Abingdon Press).
Zwiep, A.W.
    1997   *The Ascension of the Messiah in Lukan Christology* (NovTSup, 87; Leiden: E.J. Brill).

INDEXES

INDEX OF BIBLICAL REFERENCES

OLD TESTAMENT

NEW TESTAMENT

INDEX OF AUTHORS

JOURNAL FOR THE STUDY OF THE NEW TESTAMENT
SUPPLEMENT SERIES